THE COMPLETE GUIDE TO
PREGNANCY
BABYCARE
& BABY FOOD

THE COMPLETE GUIDE TO
PREGNANCY BABYCARE & BABY FOOD

AN EXPERT VISUAL SOURCEBOOK ON ALL ASPECTS OF PREGNANCY AND CARING FOR YOUR NEW BABY

Alison Mackonochie & Sara Lewis

HH
HERMES HOUSE

A very special thank you to Robin for his unfailing support, to Lucy and Kate, without whom we would not have had Christmas, and to Dominic for just being himself. (AM)

This edition is published by Hermes House, an imprint of Anness Publishing Ltd, Hermes House, 88–89 Blackfriars Road, London SE1 8HA; tel. 020 7401 2077; fax 020 7633 9499

www.hermeshouse.com; www.annesspublishing.com

If you like the images in this book and would like to investigate using them for publishing, promotions or advertising, please visit our website www.practicalpictures.com for more information.

Publisher: Joanna Lorenz
Project Editors: Casey Horton, Nicky Thompson, Judith Simons, Emma Wish, Molly Perham
Editor: Elizabeth Longley
Designers: Bobbie Colgate Stone, Sue Storey
Special Photography: Alistair Hughes, John Freeman
Additional Photography: Carin Simon
Illustrations: Ian Sidaway
Home Economists: Sara Lewis, Jacqueline Clarke, Petra Jackson
Stylist: Judy Williams
Hair and Make-up: Bettina Graham

ETHICAL TRADING POLICY
Because of our ongoing ecological investment programme, you, as our customer, can have the pleasure and reassurance of knowing that a tree is being cultivated or your behalf to naturally replace the materials used to make the book you are holding. For further information about this scheme, go to www.annesspublishing.com/trees

Previously published as *The Practical Encyclopedia of Pregnancy, Babycare & Nutrition for Babies & Toddlers* (updated for this edition)

NOTES
Bracketed terms are intended for American readers.
For all recipes, quantities are given in both metric and imperial measures and, where appropriate, in standard cups and spoons. Follow one set of measures, but not a mixture, because they are not interchangeable. Standard spoon and cup measures are level.
1 tsp = 5ml, 1 tbsp = 15ml, 1 cup = 250ml/8fl oz.
Australian standard tablespoons are 20ml. Australian readers should use 3 tsp in place of 1 tbsp for measuring small quantities.
American pints are 16fl oz/2 cups. American readers should use 20fl oz/2.5 cups in place of 1 pint when measuring liquids.
Electric oven temperatures in this book are for conventional ovens. When using a fan oven, the temperature will probably need to be reduced by about 10–20°C/20–40°F. Since ovens vary, you should check with your manufacturer's instruction book for guidance.
Medium (US large) eggs are used unless otherwise stated.

PUBLISHER'S NOTE
Although the advice and information in this book are believed to be accurate and true at the time of going to press, neither the authors nor the publisher can accept any legal responsibility or liability for any errors or omissions that may have been made nor for any inaccuracies nor for any loss, harm or injury that comes about from following instructions or advice in this book.

CONTENTS

INTRODUCTION

BEING A PARENT is the most important and responsible role you will ever have. And it begins long before the birth of your child. By making sure that you and your partner are both healthy before conception, you will be giving your baby the best possible start in life. Once you have conceived, and your pregnancy is confirmed, you will want to do everything you can to ensure that you are doing the best for your developing baby.

Understanding what happens during your pregnancy and how your baby is developing will help you to cope with both the physical and the emotional changes that you are likely to experience. Part One of this book guides you through your pregnancy. To keep things simple, a new topic is discussed for each week of your pregnancy. Do remember, though, that every pregnancy is different, and many of the topics that are mentioned will be relevant throughout the baby's development and not just for the week in question.

Thankfully the days when you had to give birth lying in bed, on your back, are gone. Today, you and your partner can usually choose where and how you give birth. Although this is good news, you may find it difficult to know what would be best for you. Once you know about the available options, you can then make informed decisions.

As the end of the nine months draws near, it is natural to be concerned about the approaching birth. Sometimes fear about how you will cope can overshadow what is the most miraculous event you are likely ever to encounter. By preparing yourself for labour and understanding what will happen, both you and your partner will be able to make the most of this unique experience.

Once your baby is born, your role as a parent begins in earnest. You are responsible for the care and well-being of this person. This can seem rather daunting at first as your baby will expect you to be on call whenever he wakes. Coping with tiredness, a completely new routine and the demands of a new baby can be overwhelming, so it is most important that you look after yourself.

As time goes by, you will develop a routine that suits you both, but at first you may need some help. Part Two guides you through the necessary daily babycare routines. So, whether you are concerned about feeding, bathing or nappy changing, you'll find help and practical advice in this section. Having a baby isn't all hard work and, if you use the time you spend each day on babycare to play with and get to know your baby, you'll find that even the chores will be a pleasure!

Your baby's health and development are very important, and as a parent you will be concerned about what to do if your child is ill or injured in any way. The chapters on first aid and illnesses are designed to be a quick and easy reference guide to help you to cope with emergencies and know when you should call the doctor.

When your baby celebrates his first birthday, you will look back and marvel at how much he has learned in this first year. Part Three explains, month by month, how your baby will progress during the first twelve months. Each month he will grow stronger, learn to control his

A toddler should still have about a pint of milk a day, but he is now grown up enough to drink from his own cup rather than a bottle.

movements and start to understand the world around him. Do remember that this is only a guide and that every child develops at his own rate.

So that you will be able to help and encourage your child, the final chapters of this section look in more detail at the development of your child's senses and explain how he learns to talk and walk. Play and social behaviour are also an integral part of your child's development.

The right food is, of course, the basis of good health, and providing a balanced diet can be one of the most challenging aspects of babycare. Nutritional needs change dramatically over the first couple

of years, and you need to be aware of your baby's requirements – at every meal. Children eat four or five times a day, so Part Four takes a slightly different approach, focusing on the practical aspects of food.

It provides sound nutritional advice on what foods you should introduce at each stage of development, and which are best avoided. Time-saving tips are included, along with guidance on common food problems: hygiene, fussy eating and going vegetarian.

This section also provides over 200 recipes, each fully illustrated and set out in a step-by-step style. From first purées for a baby to fun meals for a fussy two-year-old, the recipes are easy to follow and perfectly designed to meet the nutritional needs of your

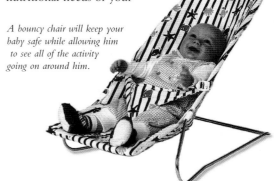

A bouncy chair will keep your baby safe while allowing him to see all of the activity going on around him.

child. There is also a special section on cooking for all the family, helping you to adapt a single recipe so that it can feed a baby, a toddler and their parents.

Tips such as these help make life easier, taking the stress out of deciding what to eat, showing the simple steps required to prepare a meal and perhaps preventing food fads from becoming an overwhelming problem. They help you to concentrate

Even when she is accepting solid foods, your baby still needs her bottle; settle down and enjoy this quiet time with her.

on the important things in life: sharing a pleasant meal with your family and enjoying their company.

This book has been written by two experienced mothers, drawing on their own first-hand knowledge. The aim is to give you a comprehensive source of information and, most important of all, the reassurance that you are doing everything "right." We hope you find it a helpful companion during your pregnancy and your baby's first year.

Left: As you eat together, don't forget to praise your child for good behaviour. This forms the basis for good table manners later.

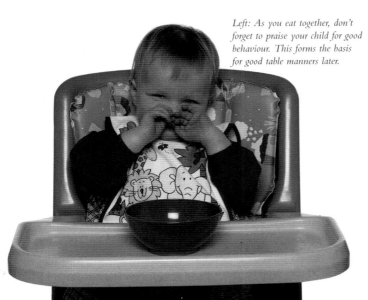

Above: Toddlers learn how to interact with others of their own age and build the basic skills for friendship.

PART ONE

PREGNANCY

PREGNANCY IS A VERY SPECIAL TIME for both you and your partner.
Knowing what is happening to you and your growing baby during
the weeks ahead will help you both to enjoy this exciting period in
your lives. Starting with pre-conceptual care, this section explains
how conception takes place and then looks at pregnancy and your
baby's development week by week. Many of the issues raised will
be relevant throughout your pregnancy and not just during the
week in which they are first mentioned, so do read it all.

It is normal to experience some minor discomforts during
pregnancy and you will want to know how to cope with them.
More serious problems can occasionally occur, and it is important to
recognize the symptoms so that you will know when immediate
medical treatment is required. The birth is something you may feel
anxious about and it will help if you understand the choices available
in both ante-natal care and childbirth. By being informed you will
be able to choose the type of care and birth that is right for you.

As your body adapts to the changes that pregnancy brings, you
will begin to prepare yourself physically, emotionally and practically
for parenthood. A well-balanced, healthy diet is essential for both
your well-being and that of your baby. Exercise has an important
part to play too, not just in keeping you fit but also in preparing
your body for the birth. Looking good will help you to feel good,
so you should take care of your physical appearance throughout
your pregnancy. Knowing how to select the right clothes to suit
your changing shape and how to use make-up to emphasize your
best features will help you to feel confident and make your
pregnancy an even more enjoyable experience.

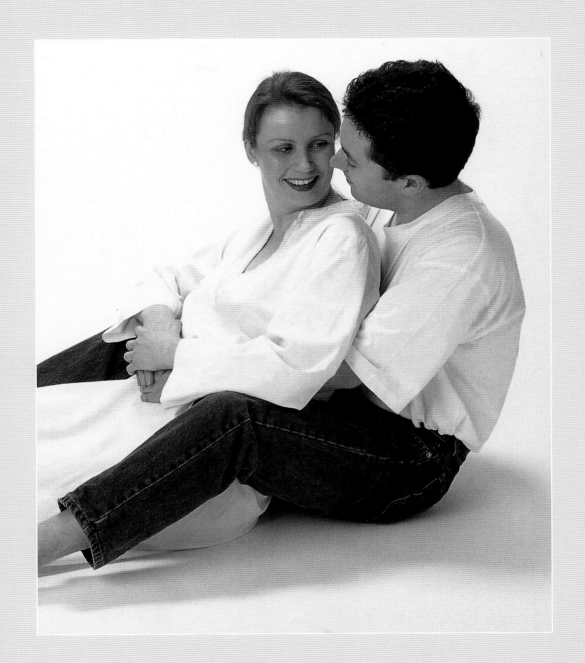

PREPARING FOR PREGNANCY

Once you have decided that you want to have a baby, you and your partner should concentrate on getting yourselves fit and healthy before you try to conceive. Ideally, you should begin preparing for pregnancy at least three months before conception so that you can be sure that your child will get the best possible start in life. If your pregnancy is unplanned, then start taking extra care of yourself as soon as you suspect that you might be pregnant. This may involve some basic changes in your lifestyle.

There is evidence that suggests that smoking by either partner can delay conception, so if you or your partner smoke you should stop now. In addition, smoking during pregnancy will put the baby at risk and can also affect your well-being; giving up before conception will benefit you and your child.

Alcohol can inhibit fertility, so both you and your partner should keep alcohol consumption to a minimum or avoid drinking altogether while trying to conceive. Once you are pregnant, alcohol, if taken in excess, can restrict fetal development and can even cause malformation. It is advisable to drink no more than one unit of alcohol a week during pregnancy.

MEDICATION
Fertilization and early development of a baby are controlled by delicately balanced chemical processes in the body. Additional chemicals entering your body as medication can upset this development, so if possible you should avoid taking any medicines before conception and during pregnancy. If you are on long-term medication, you will need to talk to your doctor about your options. Medicines that are available over the counter, natural remedies and vitamin supplements should also be avoided, unless they have been recommended by your doctor.

Oral contraceptives rely on chemically-produced hormones to control fertility. If you are taking the pill, change to a barrier method, such as the condom or diaphragm, for three months before trying to conceive. This allows your body to clear itself of synthetic hormones and to re-establish its own cycle.

IMMUNIZATIONS
An unborn baby exposed to rubella (German measles) during its early development can be born severely handicapped. Don't assume that because you were vaccinated in your teens, or you have had the infection,

Before trying for a baby, both partners should get fit by walking and doing other exercise.

By doing regular stretching exercises at home, or at an organized class, you will strengthen yourself for pregnancy.

Salmon is ideal as part of a balanced diet, because it is low in fat but full of vitamins.

that you are automatically immune. Ask your doctor to give you a blood test to check. If you are not immune you can be vaccinated, but you should not get pregnant until the vaccine virus has cleared from your blood, which takes about three months. If you have been given vaccines for tropical diseases, you should also wait for three months before getting pregnant.

NUTRITION AND EXERCISE

A well-balanced and healthy diet is essential for both your well-being and that of your baby. Everything that you eat and drink will also become your unborn child's nourishment, and what you store before pregnancy is important for early fetal development when all the major organs are formed.

One of the B vitamins, folic acid, helps prevent neural tube defects (NTD), such as spina bifida, in unborn babies. It is recommended that all women planning a pregnancy should increase their average daily intake to 0.6 mg by taking a 0.4 mg supplement before attempting conception, and during the first 12 weeks of pregnancy. This is the time when your baby's organs and body systems are forming. If you are epileptic and take drugs to control your epilepsy you should consult your doctor before taking folic acid.

Regular exercise is important as it will help you get fit before conception and it will strengthen muscles in your lower back, stomach, and legs, which will help your body cope better with the demands of pregnancy.

As your legs have to carry more weight during pregnancy, try to do regular daily exercises such as running on the spot to build them up.

THE   FIRST   TRIMESTER

WEEKS 1–4: CONCEPTION

You and your body

You won't be aware of the changes that are happening inside your body during these early weeks, although it is possible that you may experience very slight bleeding at the time when your next period would have been due. Usually the first indication that you are pregnant will be a missed period.

During the first half of the menstrual cycle two chemical substances called hormones are released from special glands into the bloodstream. One hormone stimulates the process that results in the production of an ovum, or ripe egg. The other hormone stimulates the endometrium, or lining of the uterus (womb), to thicken in readiness to receive a fertilized ovum. Midway through the menstrual cycle the work of the first hormone is completed and you ovulate; that is, a ripe ovum is released from one of your ovaries. Conception occurs if your partner's sperm fertilizes this ovum. This usually takes place in the Fallopian tube that connects the ovary to the uterus. The fertilized ovum completes its journey to the uterus, where it implants into the thickened uterine lining. Once this process occurs the cervix increases slightly in width and becomes softer, and a thick mucous plug seals off the uterus to protect it from infection. After two weeks, if there has been no conception, the thickened uterine lining is shed and menstruation takes place.

AFTER FERTILIZATION

The fertilized single-cell egg multiplies into two, then four cells, and it carries on multiplying so that by about day seven, when it reaches the uterus, it has grown into a ball of over 100 cells with a fluid-filled cavity. This ball, called a blastocyst, has two layers: the outer one becomes the placenta, while the inner one forms the embryo, which develops into your baby. The embryo is made up of three layers of tissue, each of which forms separately. The outer layer develops into the nerves and skin; the middle layer forms the bones, cartilage, muscles, circulatory system, kidneys, and sex organs; and the inner layer becomes the respira-

tory and digestive systems. The placenta is the unborn baby's life-support system. It is attached to the lining of the uterus and separates the developing baby's circulation from its mother's. It allows oxygen

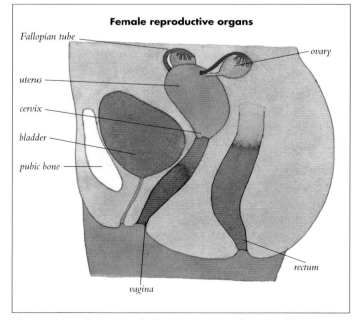

Female reproductive organs

Fallopian tube

ovary

uterus

cervix

bladder

pubic bone

rectum

vagina

If an egg in the Fallopian tube is fertilized by a sperm, it will embed itself into the lining of the uterus. If not, it is shed down through the cervix and out through the vagina.

This fertilized egg now has two cells called blastomeres and is the primitive embryo. It will multiply to over 100 cells.

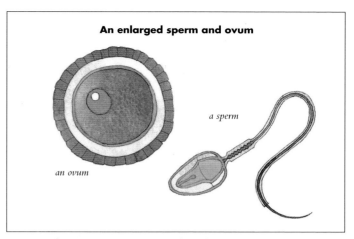

An enlarged sperm and ovum

a sperm

an ovum

A sperm and an ovum are tiny. A man ejaculates about 500 million sperm, while a woman usually produces one ovum halfway through her menstrual cycle.

and food, as well as protective antibodies, to pass from the mother along the umbilical cord to the baby.

The placenta is fully formed at the end of the 12th week of pregnancy, and then it is able to take over the production of the pregnancy hormones, oestrogen and progesterone, from the ovaries. Within the uterus, the embryo is contained in the amniotic sac. This is filled with fluid in which the developing child will float until the actual birth. The amniotic fluid offers the embryo protection from external pressures.

THE BABY'S SEX

A child's sex is determined by the father's sperm at the time of conception. Sperm carry either an X or Y chromosome while the egg has only an X chromosome. If a Y-chromosome sperm fertilizes the egg, the baby will be a boy. If the sperm carries an X chromosome, the baby will be a girl.

Male reproductive organs

bladder

seminal vesicle

vas deferens

penis

rectum

foreskin

glans

scrotum   testis

Sperm mature in both testes. When a man is sexually aroused, the penis becomes erect and the outlet from the bladder into the ejaculatory duct is closed leaving it free for sperm.

Trimesters

Pregnancy lasts approximately 40 weeks and is calculated from the first day of your last period, although conception will probably not have taken place until around two weeks after this. Pregnancy is divided into three parts known as trimesters. The first covers weeks 1–13, the second trimester weeks 14–26, and the third trimester week 27 until birth.

WEEK 5: CONFIRMING PREGNANCY

Pregnancy can be confirmed by means of a simple test that measures the levels of the pregnancy hormone, human chorionic gonadotrophin (HCG), that are present in your urine. The test can be carried out as soon as you reach the day that your next period should have started. Your doctor or Family Planning clinic may do the test free, or you can carry out a home test yourself using one of the pregnancy testing kits available from the pharmacist. Ensure that you choose one that will give an accurate result this early. Although many modern home-testing kits state that you can test your urine at any time, you may wish to use an early morning sample because this urine will contain the highest concentration of HCG.

If the result is positive, you must make an appointment to see your doctor so that he or she can make

Your growing baby

Although the embryo is only just visible to the naked eye, the spinal column and brain have already begun to grow and a blood vessel has developed which will become the heart. The embryo is 4mm/⅛in long.

arrangements for your ante-natal care and the birth.

EARLY SYMPTOMS
Some women experience all the early symptoms of pregnancy, while others sail through the first weeks without any feelings of discomfort.
• Your body is having to work hard to adapt to the demands of pregnancy, so you may feel very tired. Try to get as much rest as possible. You will find that sitting with your feet up for even half an hour will help.
• Your breasts may tingle or feel tender, rather as they do before a period; your nipples will appear darker and more prominent and the veins will be more noticeable. You should wear a good support bra from now until after your baby is born.
• You may experience a strange metallic taste in the mouth, which

You and your body

If you haven't been taking a folic acid supplement you should start now.

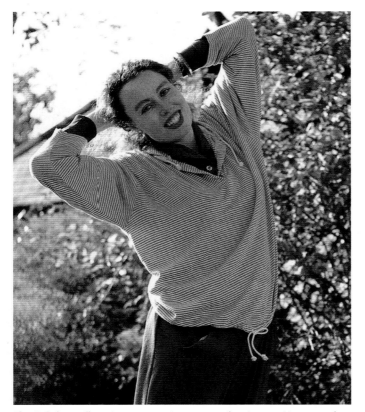

If you're lucky, you'll experience no nausea in pregnancy and continue exercising as normal.

get up in the morning. Try eating six small high-carbohydrate meals, during the day, such as pasta, potato, and bread. Avoid rich or fatty foods.
• Finally, as the enlarging uterus presses on your bladder you may need to urinate more frequently.

DATING THE BIRTH

Once your pregnancy is confirmed, you will want to know your baby's likely date of birth. You can calculate an estimated date of delivery (EDD) by counting 40 weeks from the first day of your last period. But you should remember that as you don't know the exact date of ovulation this EDD is approximate. At between 10 and 12 weeks you may be offered a scan to confirm your EDD.

To confirm a pregnancy, you can do a test with a kit from a pharmacist, but ensure you choose one that is suitable to use for a test at five weeks.

can be accompanied by going off certain foods and tea and coffee.
• A feeling of nausea, or even actual physical sickness in the morning or at any time during the day, is quite usual. It is often worse when your stomach is empty, so have a plain biscuit and a cup of tea when you

Estimated date of delivery

JANUARY	1	2	3	4	5	6	7	8	9	10	11	12	13	14	15	16	17	18	19	20	21	22	23	24	25	26	27	28	29	30	31	JANUARY
OCTOBER	8	9	10	11	12	13	14	15	16	17	18	19	20	21	22	23	24	25	26	27	28	29	30	31	1	2	3	4	5	6	7	NOVEMBER
FEBRUARY	1	2	3	4	5	6	7	8	9	10	11	12	13	14	15	16	17	18	19	20	21	22	23	24	25	26	27	28				FEBRUARY
NOVEMBER	8	9	10	11	12	13	14	15	16	17	18	19	20	21	22	23	24	25	26	27	28	29	30	1	2	3	4	5				DECEMBER
MARCH	1	2	3	4	5	6	7	8	9	10	11	12	13	14	15	16	17	18	19	20	21	22	23	24	25	26	27	28	29	30	31	MARCH
DECEMBER	6	7	8	9	10	11	12	13	14	15	16	17	18	19	20	21	22	23	24	25	26	27	28	29	30	31	1	2	3	4	5	JANUARY
APRIL	1	2	3	4	5	6	7	8	9	10	11	12	13	14	15	16	17	18	19	20	21	22	23	24	25	26	27	28	29	30		APRIL
JANUARY	6	7	8	9	10	11	12	13	14	15	16	17	18	19	20	21	22	23	24	25	26	27	28	29	30	31	1	2	3	4		FEBRUARY
MAY	1	2	3	4	5	6	7	8	9	10	11	12	13	14	15	16	17	18	19	20	21	22	23	24	25	26	27	28	29	30	31	MAY
FEBRUARY	5	6	7	8	9	10	11	12	13	14	15	16	17	18	19	20	21	22	23	24	25	26	27	28	1	2	3	4	5	6	7	MARCH
JUNE	1	2	3	4	5	6	7	8	9	10	11	12	13	14	15	16	17	18	19	20	21	22	23	24	25	26	27	28	29	30		JUNE
MARCH	8	9	10	11	12	13	14	15	16	17	18	19	20	21	22	23	24	25	26	27	28	29	30	31	1	2	3	4	5	6		APRIL
JULY	1	2	3	4	5	6	7	8	9	10	11	12	13	14	15	16	17	18	19	20	21	22	23	24	25	26	27	28	29	30	31	JULY
APRIL	7	8	9	10	11	12	13	14	15	16	17	18	19	20	21	22	23	24	25	26	27	28	29	30	1	2	3	4	5	6	7	MAY
AUGUST	1	2	3	4	5	6	7	8	9	10	11	12	13	14	15	16	17	18	19	20	21	22	23	24	25	26	27	28	29	30	31	AUGUST
MAY	8	9	10	11	12	13	14	15	16	17	18	19	20	21	22	23	24	25	26	27	28	29	30	31	1	2	3	4	5	6	7	JUNE
SEPTEMBER	1	2	3	4	5	6	7	8	9	10	11	12	13	14	15	16	17	18	19	20	21	22	23	24	25	26	27	28	29	30		SEPTEMBER
JUNE	8	9	10	11	12	13	14	15	16	17	18	19	20	21	22	23	24	25	26	27	28	29	30	1	2	3	4	5	6	7		JULY
OCTOBER	1	2	3	4	5	6	7	8	9	10	11	12	13	14	15	16	17	18	19	20	21	22	23	24	25	26	27	28	29	30	31	OCTOBER
JULY	8	9	10	11	12	13	14	15	16	17	18	19	20	21	22	23	24	25	26	27	28	29	30	31	1	2	3	4	5	6	7	AUGUST
NOVEMBER	1	2	3	4	5	6	7	8	9	10	11	12	13	14	15	16	17	18	19	20	21	22	23	24	25	26	27	28	29	30		NOVEMBER
AUGUST	8	9	10	11	12	13	14	15	16	17	18	19	20	21	22	23	24	25	26	27	28	29	30	31	1	2	3	4	5	6		SEPTEMBER
DECEMBER	1	2	3	4	5	6	7	8	9	10	11	12	13	14	15	16	17	18	19	20	21	22	23	24	25	26	27	28	29	30	31	DECEMBER
SEPTEMBER	7	8	9	10	11	12	13	14	15	16	17	18	19	20	21	22	23	24	25	26	27	28	29	30	1	2	3	4	5	6	7	OCTOBER

Find the first day of your last period on the white bands; the date on the tint band below is your EDD.

WEEK 6: ANTE-NATAL CHOICES

Who looks after you, and where your ante-natal care takes place, will depend a lot on the type of birth you want to have. If you decide on a home birth, the care will be carried out at home by a midwife and at your doctor's surgery. If you want a hospital birth your care will probably be shared between a midwife, your doctor and the hospital.

If you are not registered with a doctor, or you want a home birth but your particular doctor doesn't want to assist in the delivery, or you would rather be seen by a woman doctor and your doctor is a man,

you can go to see a different doctor just for your maternity care. The actual care you get will be similar wherever you receive it, because all ante-natal care is designed to ensure that you and your unborn baby remain healthy during pregnancy.

The best pattern of ante-natal care for a healthy first time mother is considered to be no more than 10 ante-natal appointments, and for subsequent pregnancies this is likely to be reduced to seven. If you have any concerns between these appointments, you can telephone your midwife or doctor for advice.

HOME BIRTH

A home birth means you give birth in the familiar surroundings of your home under the supervision of a midwife. If you want to deliver your baby in this way, you will need to talk to your doctor to see whether there are any medical reasons why this isn't advisable. It is also a good idea to contact the director of

You and your body

If you are suffering from morning sickness, you may find that the smell of certain things, such as tobacco smoke or frying food, brings on the sickness or makes it worse. Your skin may become dry and flaky, or you may get spots. Now is the time to start thinking about your ante-natal care, and the type of birth you want.

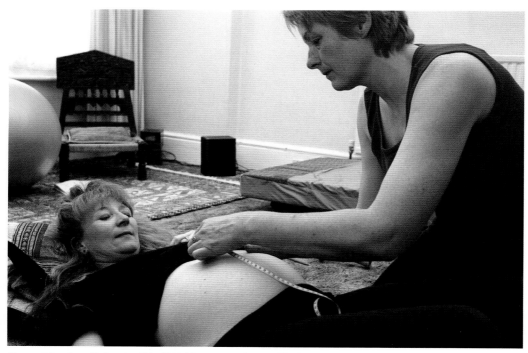

If you opt for a home birth, care will be divided between your home and local surgery.

maternity services (or supervisor of midwives) at your hospital in order to arrange for a midwife to visit you and discuss a home delivery in detail.

HOSPITAL BIRTH

Some women prefer a hospital birth because they feel safer knowing that there will be experts on hand to help if there are any complications. Also, if the baby needs special care this will be available almost immediately. Although hospitals try to cater for parents' wishes, not all of them are able to offer every type of birth. You will need to find out what facilities your local hospital offers. Before making your final decision talk to other mothers who have had their babies there recently. If you have any worries, discuss these with your doctor or community midwife.

There are a number of hospital birth schemes that involve your doctor and midwife to varying degrees:

Midwife unit This is usually based at the hospital and is run entirely by midwives who undertake ante-natal care, delivery and post-natal care for women having normal births. These units are not widely available throughout the country, so this may not be an option that is open to you.

Domino scheme The Domino scheme (Domiciliary In and Out) means that you are looked after by a team of community midwives throughout your pregnancy. Once you are in labour one of these midwives will come to your home and stay with you until you are ready to go into hospital. She then accompanies you to the hospital, where she delivers the baby. You can usually return home around six hours after the birth. The midwife then continues to look after you at

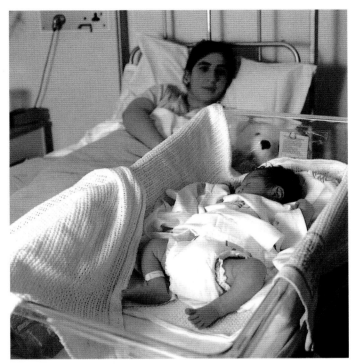

You can spend from between six hours to three days in hospital when you give birth, depending on your delivery. After the birth you may keep your baby beside you.

your home. Many women like the continuity this scheme gives them, but unfortunately it is only available in a few areas.

Shared care Your ante-natal care will be shared between your doctor and the community midwife and you may also see the obstetric consultant at the hospital where your baby is going to be born. The birth will take place in the maternity unit of the hospital.

PRIVATE CARE

If you can afford it, you may like to consider having a home birth with a private, or independent, midwife taking care of you. She will provide all your ante-natal and post-natal care and will also deliver your baby.

Alternatively, you can decide to have your baby in a private hospital or maternity home.

Your growing baby

The heart has now formed in the chest cavity and is beginning to beat. By the end of this week the stalk connecting the embryo to the placenta will have begun to grow into the umbilical cord and blood vessels will have started to form. The embryo is now about the size of your little fingernail and its movements can be picked up by ultrasound scan. The head has the beginning of the eyes, ears, and mouth and there are tiny buds which will become arms and legs.

WEEK 7: POSSIBLE PROBLEMS

Although most pregnancies go without a hitch, sometimes serious problems do occur and special care is needed. Complications can usually be resolved with monitoring, but occasionally the pregnancy comes to an end. Although the following conditions are not likely to affect you, you should be aware of their symptoms:

Bleeding in early pregnancy
Bleeding or spotting from the vagina is known as a threatened miscarriage. It is possible to bleed quite heavily and not miscarry or do any harm to the baby. All bleeding in pregnancy must be taken seriously, however, and you should report it to your doctor or midwife immediately. Your doctor is likely to carry out an internal pelvic examination and you may have an ultrasound scan to see whether the baby is developing normally, or a blood test to measure the levels of the pregnancy hormone human chorionic gondotropin (HGC). Providing everything is all right you will probably be told not to exert yourself until the bleeding has stopped.

Ectopic pregnancy This occurs when the fertilized egg implants itself in one of the Fallopian tubes rather than in the uterus. If it is undetected, the growing baby eventually ruptures the tube, which causes severe pain. Immediate surgery is required to terminate the pregnancy, and this often means losing the Fallopian tube as well. In extreme cases the ovary may also have to be removed. If the other ovary and Fallopian tube are healthy, there is no reason why another pregnancy should not take

You and your body
You may feel dizzy or even faint if you stand for too long or you are in a crowd. Overwhelming tiredness can also be a problem now, so make sure you get plenty of rest. If you don't feel like making love at the moment don't worry; this is quite normal and you may find that your sex life is better then ever in the second trimester.

place. If the ectopic pregnancy is discovered early enough, a drug can be given that causes the embryo to be reabsorbed by the body; this prevents the Fallopian tube from bursting. Symptoms of an ectopic pregnancy include pain in the side of the abdomen, vaginal bleeding, and fainting.

Miscarriage The most common time for miscarriage is during the first three months of pregnancy, although losing a baby at any time before the 24th week is described as a miscarriage. Some miscarriages

Regular blood pressure checks are essential at ante-natal clinics to detect pre-eclampsia.

occur for no known reason. Known causes of miscarriage include hormonal problems, disease or infection, abnormalities of the uterus, or an incompetent cervix. This last condition can be dealt with by a simple surgical suture that will be removed shortly before the EDD.

Although it is unlikely that sexual intercourse will cause miscarriage, women who have experienced bleeding early in their pregnancy or who are known to have a tendency to miscarry are usually advised by doctors not to have intercourse for the first 12 weeks, until their pregnancy is well established.

Pre-eclampsia This is a high blood pressure condition that rarely occurs before 20 weeks. It is the most common complication of pregnancy with around one in 10 pregnancies affected. If left untreated it causes the blood vessels of the placenta to spasm, which reduces the oxygen flow to the baby and puts it at risk; the fetal growth rate may also be affected. Symptoms include high blood pressure, oedema causing swelling of the hands, feet, and

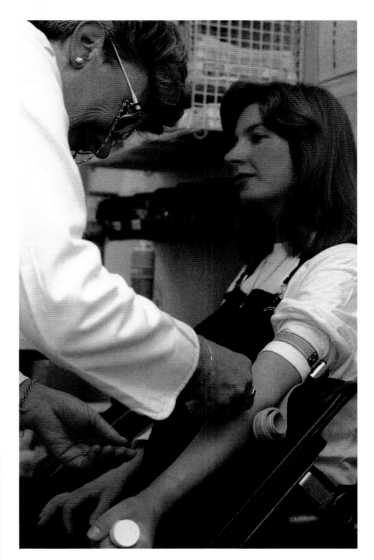

At your first ante-natal check-up, a blood sample will be taken to find out your blood group and type, and to make sure you're not anaemic or carrying a virus such as hepatitis B. You will have blood tests regularly through your pregnancy.

Your growing baby

The unborn baby is now known as a fetus and is about 1.3cm/½in long. The nostrils, lips, tongue, and teeth are beginning to form and the arms and legs are growing. Lungs are beginning to develop and the intestines, spine, and brain are almost fully developed.

ankles, protein in the urine and a sudden increase in weight. In severe cases flashing lights, blurred vision or spots before the eyes may occur. You will be routinely tested for signs of pre-eclampsia at each ante-natal check. If you develop pre-eclampsia you and your baby will be closely monitored and you may need to go into hospital. If the condition becomes severe immediate delivery of the baby may be necessary.

WEEK 8: BOOKING-IN/ROUTINE TESTS

Your first ante-natal check-up will take place between eight and 12 weeks, either at your doctor's surgery or at the hospital where you plan to give birth. This first visit is usually referred to as the booking clinic. You will be asked about your physical and mental health, family medical history and if there are areas where you need special support, such as domestic violence and sexual abuse. All this information is required to build up a picture of you and your pregnancy so that any potential risks can be spotted and help can be offered where needed.

If you have any questions or worries, this is a good time to discuss them. It's easy to forget to ask something important when there is so much to take in at one time, so it may help to write down things that you want to know about before you attend the clinic.

ROUTINE TESTS

Certain tests are carried out during pregnancy to ensure that both you and the baby are progressing well. Some of these will be repeated at each ante-natal visit; others are only carried out at the booking-in clinic.

Blood pressure This will be taken at each visit. Increased blood pressure could be a symptom of pre-eclampsia, which could endanger both you and the baby.

Urine You will be asked to bring a sample of urine with you to each ante-natal visit. This will be tested for bacteria, which could be a sign of a urinary tract infection which will require treatment, as well as for sugar and protein. Sugar in the urine could be a sign of gestational diabetes, a form of diabetes that only occurs in pregnancy which will need to be controlled, while protein may indicate the onset of pre-eclampsia.

You and your body

The changes to your body are becoming more noticeable as your breasts and nipples enlarge and become sensitive. Your vagina changes from light to dark pink, and you may notice an increased vaginal discharge. It is time for regular monitoring of your pregnancy.

Weight gain during pregnancy

Baby 39%

Blood 22%

Amniotic fluid 11%

Uterus 11%

Placenta 9%

Breasts 8%

Your weight increases by about ½–1 kg/1–2 lb weekly during months four to eight, with very little in the last month. As your breasts get larger, the uterus, placenta and baby develop, and the amniotic fluid increases, until they reach the percentages shown here.

The amount of weight that you will gain during pregnancy varies, depending on your height and size, but can be as much as 20 kg/44 lb.

Height and weight Your height and weight will be measured so that your body mass index (BMI) can be calculated (this is a medical classification system for your body weight). You are classed as underweight, normal weight and overweight or obese. If you are in the normal range your weight will probably not be checked again during pregnancy unless there are complications. If you are under- or

Your weight and height will be measured at your first ante-natal check-up, so that your body mass index can be calculated.

if you think you could be at risk, you can ask for a blood test. Other blood tests may also be carried out to detect any serious conditions that could affect your baby. If you are of Afro-Caribbean descent, they will test your blood for sickle-cell disease; if you are of a Mediterranean ethnic group you will be offered a test for thalassaemia.

Wrists and ankles These will be checked at each visit for swelling, or oedema, caused by fluid retention, since these signs could possibly indicate pre-eclampsia.

Palpation Your abdomen will be palpated (pressed), to feel the top of the uterus (fundus). The doctor or midwife will then feel down towards the pelvis to check the size of the fetus and the way it is lying. This will be done at every check up.

Dating scan You may be offered an appointment for a "dating" scan at between 10 and 12 weeks. This literally dates the pregnancy and confirms how many babies you are carrying.

Your growing baby

The fetus is now about 2.5cm/1in long, which is 10,000 times bigger than at conception. All the major organs are present, although still developing. The ears and eyes have formed and the skin covering the eyes will eventually split to form the eyelids. The middle ear, which controls balance as well as hearing, is also developing. The heart is now pumping with a regular beat, and blood vessels can be seen. As the arms and legs grow longer, the fetus begins to move around and starts to kick, although it is still too small at this stage for you to be able to feel it.

overweight you may need specialist care. You can expect to gain anything from 10 kg to 20 kg/22 lb to 44 lb during your pregnancy, with most of this extra weight going on after the 20th week. A sudden increase in weight could be an indication of pre-eclampsia.

Blood tests You will be asked at your first appointment to give a blood sample to confirm your blood group and to find out if you are rhesus negative or positive.

Your blood will also be checked to see if you are anaemic and if you are immune to rubella (German measles). You may be offered HIV, hepatitis B and syphilis screening tests. Although you will not be routinely screened for toxoplasmosis,

WEEK 9: SPECIAL TESTS

Your blood will be tested at your booking appointment to determine your blood group and to establish its rhesus (Rh) status. The rhesus status of your blood depends on whether or not it possesses the rhesus factor. If the factor is present, your blood is Rh-positive, and if it's absent, your blood is Rh-negative. Most people's blood is Rh-positive.

If both you and the baby's father are Rh-negative there is no problem. Complications will only occur when the father's blood is Rh-positive and yours is Rh-negative. The unborn baby may acquire the rhesus factor from its father, which can result in its blood being incompatible with yours. This can lead to a serious or even fatal illness for the baby before, or after its birth. Fortunately, this rarely affects a first pregnancy and it can be prevented in subsequent pregnancies by injections of Rh immunoglobulin (anti-D), an antibody given during pregnancy and again within 72 hours of a baby being delivered.

SCREENING TESTS

These are given to assess the risk of the baby having a birth defect such as Down's syndrome or spina bifida. In the UK it is recommended that pregnant women should be offered one of three types of test: the nuchal translucency scan and blood test in weeks 11 to 14, the triple or quadruple tests in the 14 to 20 week period, or the serum integrated test which combines nuchal fold measurements taken in the first trimester with a blood test in the

In an amniocentesis test the fetus's position is checked by ultrasound, before amniotic fluid is taken by a needle from the uterus.

second trimester. Most areas offer the triple test, although more centres now offer the nuchal translucency scan and blood test. The serum integrated test is not widely available and tends only to be offered in teaching hospitals or private clinics.

You and your body

You will start putting on weight now so it is a good idea to keep a record of any weight gain yourself if your ante-natal care doesn't include regular weight checks. Your gums are becoming softer and thicker because of hormone changes so you will need to pay special attention to oral hygiene.

You should now familiarize yourself with some of the other ante-natal procedures and tests.

Your growing baby

The face is now developing and the mouth and nose are clearly visible. The limbs continue to grow rapidly and the fetus now measures about 3cm/1¼in.

Nuchal translucency screening

This is an ultrasound scan that measurers the clear (translucent) space in the tissue at the back of the baby's neck, known as the nuchal fold. Fluid retention in the nuchal fold during the 11 to 14 week widow may be a marker for Down's syndrome. When combined with blood tests this test has been shown to be 95 per cent accurate. If your hospital doesn't offer nuchal translucency screening you can arrange to have it done privately.

Triple and quadruple tests

These are blood tests that measure the level of chemicals produced by the baby which are present in your blood stream. An usually high or low result could indicate that the baby has a birth defect. The triple test measurers three markers, while the quadruple test measurers four. Neither test can confirm that the

Brush your teeth and gums regularly.

baby is affected but it does indicate whether further diagnostic tests, such as amniocentesis, are required.

DIAGNOSTIC TESTS

These are used to further investigate a positive screening test. Diagnostic tests will give a definitive answer because they involve analysing DNA taken from your baby's cells.

Amniocentesis If you have a family history of genetic abnormalities or your blood shows an exceptionally low or high AFP level, you will be offered an amniocentesis. This test is also offered to all women over 35 years as they have a higher risk of having a Down's syndrome baby. Guided by an ultrasound scan, a long hollow needle is inserted through the wall of the abdomen and the uterus to draw out a sample of amniotic fluid which is tested for abnormalities. The test is done between 16 and 20 weeks and carries a small risk of miscarriage.

Chorionic villus sampling (CVS) This is done at 11 weeks to test for Down's syndrome or other genetic or chromosomal abnormalities. A fine tube is passed into the uterus to remove some cells from the tissue that surrounds the baby. The cells are then tested and the results known within a couple of weeks. There is a slightly higher risk of miscarriage with CVS than with amniocentesis.

GENETIC COUNSELLING

If you are worried about your baby inheriting a disease or handicap, a genetic counsellor will be able to explain the likelihood of a child being affected by the disorder and also about any tests that can be carried out. It is a good idea to have this discussion before attempting to get pregnant.

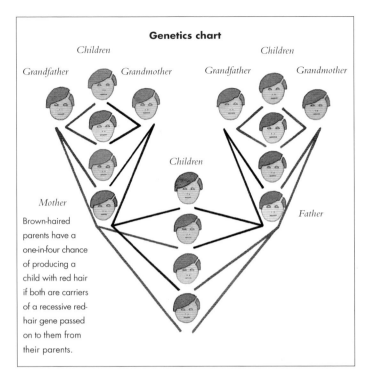

Genetics chart

Children   Children

Grandfather   Grandmother   Grandfather   Grandmother

Children

Mother

Brown-haired parents have a one-in-four chance of producing a child with red hair if both are carriers of a recessive red-hair gene passed on to them from their parents.

Father

This genetics chart shows how red hair that is inherited through a recessive gene can miss a generation, but has a high chance of re-appearing in the third generation. This can also apply to some inherited diseases.

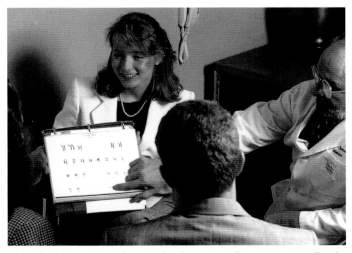

If your family has a history of a genetic disorder, you can talk to a genetic counsellor who will discuss with you and your partner the likelihood of your baby having a problem.

WEEK 10: HORMONES/ MATERNITY RECORD

Hormones play an important part during pregnancy and labour. The prime source of the hormones related to pregnancy are the ovaries during the early stages, and then the placenta once it is established at around 12 weeks. These hormones dictate how fast the baby grows and are responsible for the changes in your breasts and body. They also ensure that your labour occurs at the right time.

High levels of the hormone called human chorionic gonadotrophin (HCG) circulate in your body during the first 12 weeks of pregnancy. They are responsible for any emotional changes, feeling tired, nausea, and vomiting.

HORMONES AND YOUR EMOTIONS
Pregnancy can produce a number of conflicting emotions, ranging from feelings of pure joy to bouts of black depression. It is quite natural to feel like this as you adjust to your changing role and come to terms with the fact that your life will never be quite the same again. You may

find that you start worrying about if you are ready for motherhood, or the effect that a new baby may have on your established relationship with your partner.

You may also find that mood swings, often brought on by the hormonal changes going on in your body, cause petty arguments between you. So it is most important

You and your body

There is an increase in the amount of blood that is circulating in your body, which may cause you to feel warmer than usual. Your uterus is now the size of a large orange and your changing shape may mean that you are more comfortable in loose-fitting clothes that do not restrict you.

Other changes are also taking place in your body. Although these are not always physically obvious, they are in fact the result of shifts in your body's chemistry.

As you experience hormonal changes in your body you may find you become irritable and anxious. Discuss any of your worries with your partner who can talk things through with you and reassure you.

Your growing baby
The external ears are now visible on the head, which is growing fast to make room for the brain. The fetal body is elongating and its fingers and toes are clearly defined but are still joined with webs of skin. At this stage of your pregnancy the fetus is now about 4.5cm/1¾in long and weighs around 5g/¼oz.

As your emotions are probably mixed up at the moment, don't brood over rows with your partner, but apologize and make up.

If you find you're getting very tense, try practising relaxation techniques on your own, or some deep breathing exercises.

Terms and abbreviations

The following terms and abbreviations may appear on your maternity record.

AFP: Alpha-fetoprotein.

BP: Blood pressure.

Cephalic: Fetal head is nearest the cervix.

Cx: Cervix.

EDD: Estimated date of delivery.

FHH: Fetal heart heard.

FMF: Fetal movement felt.

Height Fundus: The distance from the pelvis to the top of the uterus is known as the fundus.

LMP: Last menstrual period. This is the date of the first day of your last period before pregnancy.

NAD: No abnormality detected.

Oedema: Swelling of hands and feet.

Relation of PP to Brim: The position of the baby's presenting part (PP), that is the part ready to be born first, in relation to the brim of the pelvis.

Transverse lie. The baby is lying across the uterus.

Urine P G O: Indicates whether your urine contains protein, glucose or anything else – other.

to make time to talk to each other so that you can both voice your feelings and share any worries or anxieties.

MATERNITY RECORD

You will be given your maternity record card at your booking–in clinic. It is used to record the results of the tests and examinations that are carried out during your pregnancy. You should keep it with you at all times, so that if you ever need medical attention when you are away from home all the information about your pregnancy is readily available to the medical staff.

WEEK 11: COMMON DISCOMFORTS

As your body prepares itself for birth, you may experience some physical discomfort. This is perfectly normal, can usually be dealt with easily, and should not leave any long-lasting effects. Knowing the reason for a complaint can often help you cope better with it.

Backache This can occur at any time, but usually happens when you try to compensate for your baby's weight by leaning backwards which puts a strain on the lower back's muscles and joints. Try to avoid lifting heavy objects, when you bend down keep your knees bent, wear

Your back is more vulnerable, so support it with a cushion when you sit down.

low-heeled shoes, and sit with your back well supported.

Bleeding gums Hormonal changes can cause a build-up of plaque on your teeth, which can lead to bleeding gums. It is important to pay special attention to oral hygiene and to avoid snacking on sweets and sugary drinks. Dental treatment is free while you are pregnant so have at least two check-ups during this time.

Cramp You may experience a sudden sharp pain in your legs and feet, often at night. Try pulling your toes upwards towards your ankles and rub the affected muscles. Regular gentle exercise will help to prevent cramp.

Constipation Some of the extra hormones produced in pregnancy can cause the intestines to relax and become less efficient. Eating plenty of fruit, vegetables and fibre, and drinking water will help.

You and your body

Any sickness should start to fade and you will begin to feel less tired. You should start to think seriously about ante-natal classes because private ones can get booked up quickly. Contact your hospital or the National Childbirth Trust, or ask at your doctor's surgery about local classes.

Fainting You may feel faint if you stand for too long or get up too quickly. This happens because not enough blood is getting to your brain. You can help prevent this by always rising slowly from either sitting or lying positions. If you feel faint sit down and lower your head towards your knees.

Piles Technically known as haemorrhoids, these are a form of varicose vein that appear around the back passage (anus). They can be very uncomfortable as they are itchy

Eating a high-fibre diet can help prevent painful constipation in pregnancy.

Your growing baby

Most of the major organs are formed, so the most vulnerable time will be over by the end of this week. The baby is now relatively safe from any congenital abnormalities and infections, excepting rubella.

The external genitals have formed, along with either ovaries or testicles. The heart is now pumping blood to all the major organs of the body. The baby weighs around 10g/½oz and is now about 5.5cm/2⅛in long.

Although you may now be feeling less tired than in the early weeks, you should still rest as much as you can.

and may even bleed. If left untreated they can become prolapsed, which means they protrude through the anus, causing a good deal of pain. Eating high-fibre foods will keep your stools soft so that you don't have to strain, which puts pressure on piles. An ice pack wrapped in a soft cloth, or a witch hazel compress, will bring relief, or you can buy a specially formulated haemorrhoid preparation from the pharmacist. Piles usually disappear within a couple of weeks of the birth.

Vaginal discharge An increase in vaginal discharge during pregnancy is quite normal as long as the discharge is clear and white. If it becomes coloured, smells, or makes you itchy, you may have developed an infection, such as thrush, which will need treatment.

Take some gentle, regular exercise with your partner as this will help to prevent cramps and keep you feeling fit.

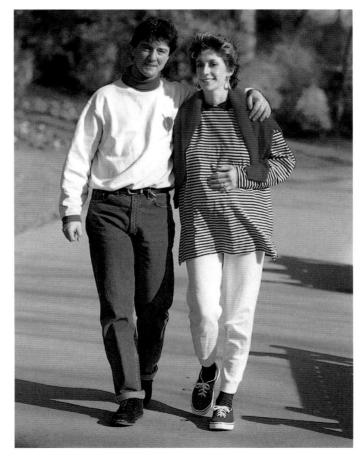

WEEK 12: HEALTHY EATING

Your baby gets all the nourishment he needs to grow from what you eat, so it is important to maintain a good diet throughout pregnancy. To achieve a healthy balanced diet you need to eat foods containing reasonable amounts of starchy carbohydrate, protein, fat, minerals, and vitamins each day. Starchy carbohydrates are found in bread, cereals, pasta, rice, and potatoes; they provide energy, vitamins, minerals, and fibre. Meat, fish, eggs, nuts, beans, peas, and lentils supply protein and minerals. Milk and dairy products such as hard cheese and yogurt will give you protein,

vitamins, and calcium. Fresh fruit and vegetables and washed salads are good sources of minerals and vitamins. Folic acid can be found, with other vitamins, in green leafy vegetables, fruit, nuts, bread, and rice.

If you are a vegetarian, you will need to increase your milk intake to at least 600 ml/1 pint a day of either pasteurized milk or fortified soya milk, or the equivalent in cheese, yogurt, and dairy products.

Vegans will need to discuss their diet with a qualified dietitian as they could be deficient in calcium, iron, and vitamin B_{12}, which is found in foods of animal origin. Try to avoid

You and your body

You can expect to put on about one-quarter of your pregnancy weight between now and week 20. You may be beginning to feel more energetic and generally better than during the past few weeks. You should consider telling your employer at this time that you are pregnant.

Meanwhile, look at your lifestyle and be sure that your diet includes a sensible range of foods – for you and the unborn baby.

eating sugary snacks and fizzy drinks and keep "junk" foods down to a minimum. Cut down on your caffeine intake from drinks like tea, coffee, chocolate and cola; try drinking bottled water and diluted fruit juices as alternatives.

Cut down on your caffeine levels and drink more diluted fruit juices.

Eat plenty of fruit when pregnant as it is a good source of minerals and vitamins.

A grain salad will give you plenty of fibre.

Vegetables are important in your pregnancy diet as they are low in fat and contain minerals, vitamins and folic acid in leafy varieties.

Use olive and sunflower oils for cooking.

YOUR WEIGHT

Although you need extra energy during pregnancy to meet the needs of the developing fetus, and to store fat ready for breast-feeding later, you are not likely to need special energy foods. If you were an acceptable weight for your build before pregnancy, the only extra calories you should need are during the last three months when you eat around 200 extra calories a day. However, if you were overweight or underweight your weight gain will need monitoring, and a special diet may be necessary. Ask a professional for advice.

Your growing baby

The baby's heart is beating at between 110 and 160 times a minute and its chest is beginning to rise and fall as it practises future breathing movements. Features are becoming more clearly defined and fingers and toes are now fully formed, with tiny nails beginning to grow. The baby can suck its thumb and it swallows amniotic fluid and passes it back as urine. The amniotic fluid is completely replaced every 24 hours. The baby is now about 6.5 cm/2½ in long and weighs 20 g/¾ oz.

WEEK 13: THE HEALTH PROFESSIONALS

Now that you have reached the end of the first trimester and your pregnancy is a visible state, you need to familiarize yourself with some of the professionals with whom you will regularly be interacting.

During pregnancy, and after the birth, a number of different people will be involved in your care. How many you see will depend on where you are having your baby and the kind of ante-natal care that is being offered. The type of professionals involved in your ante-natal and post-natal care will be the same wherever you are having your baby.

Midwife Your midwife has been trained to be an expert in pregnancy. A midwife will care for you from the time your pregnancy is confirmed until after the birth of your baby. She will be able to give you physical and psychological support and to help with any medical problems that arise during this time.

Building up a relationship with you and your family is an essential part of the midwife's job, so it is important to establish contact with her as soon after your pregnancy is confirmed as possible. In the UK the midwife will usually be found at your local health centre or your doctor's surgery, although it may also be possible to contact her direct through the Supervisor of Midwives at your local maternity unit. Your midwife will be able to help you make an informed choice about your right to have your baby where and how you wish. She will advise you on the most appropriate care for

your needs and, if specialist help is required, she will know the right person to contact.

In the UK the midwife will continue to look after you and your family until she hands over your care to a health visitor at between 10 and 28 days after the birth.

General practitioner This is your family doctor, who will probably have confirmed your pregnancy and who, along with the midwife, will help you plan your ante-natal care. He or she may be responsible for all or part of your ante-natal care and will work closely with your midwife. Some, but not all doctors are prepared to attend a home birth. If you think you would like to have your baby at home you will need to discuss this with your doctor.

You and your body
Your uterus is enlarging at a noticeable rate and you will be able to see the first signs of a visible bump. Your nipples have become darker and the blue veins in your breasts are a lot more obvious.

Your family doctor will provide medical care for both you and your baby during and after pregnancy. You will need to register your baby with your doctor as soon after the birth as possible. You can contact your doctor at any time if either you or your baby are ill. Your doctor may have an arrangement where young babies are seen without making an appointment, possibly at the beginning or end of the surgery, or it may be possible to obtain some advice over the phone surgery.

Obstetrician This is a doctor who specializes in the care of women throughout their pregnancy and

As your pregnancy progresses you may be examined by an obstetrician who specializes in birth and child care. She will advise on your baby's development and discuss any problems.

Your growing baby

The baby is now 7.5 cm/3 in long and weighs 30 g/1½ oz. The bone marrow, liver, and spleen have now taken over production of blood cells. The bones are developing and the teeth are in place. The baby may already be practising lip movements to develop the muscles needed for the sucking reflex after the birth.

The pediatrician will perform several checks on your baby after birth. Here he is checking that the newborn's foot reflex works correctly.

subsequent childbirth. If you are having a delivery in a hospital, the consultant you are under will be an obstetrician who is part of a special medical team.

Anaesthetist This is a specialist doctor responsible for providing pain relief. The anaesthetist can provide an epidural or spinal block during labour. If complications arise and a Caesarean becomes necessary the anaesthetist may need to administer a general anaesthetic.

Pediatrician This is a doctor who specializes in caring for babies and children. Your baby will be checked by a pediatrician after the birth.

Health visitor Your health visitor is a qualified nurse who has had extra training in caring for people in the community. Her role is to help families, especially those with young children. She will take over your care from the midwife and will visit you at home sometime after your baby is 10 days old. She can offer advice and give support if you have any worries about your baby or if you yourself have problems.

Your health visitor will visit you after your baby's birth and check that the navel is healing.

THE SECOND TRIMESTER

WEEK 14: SEX DURING PREGNANCY

For you to be able to enjoy sex it is important to know that making love cannot harm the developing baby. It is well protected in the uterus by the amniotic fluid and membranes, and the uterus itself is sealed with a plug of mucus, which stays in place until just before the birth. Even deep penetration is safe, but it should of course be gentle so that it doesn't cause discomfort.

Many women find that the middle months of pregnancy are a sensual and even erotic time. Physical changes, such as the increase in the size of your breasts, can actually serve to heighten your interest in sex, which in turn leads to an increase in sexual pleasure. Your genitals may also appear bigger and the pressure from the growing baby can actually make them more responsive. Some women find that they experience orgasm for the first time during pregnancy, while others come to orgasm much more quickly.

Experiencing orgasm is perfectly safe, in fact it can be considered to be beneficial since the uterus often remains hard and firm for several minutes afterwards. This is similar in effect to the Braxton Hicks, or practice contractions you experience towards the end of your pregnancy that prepare the uterus for the birth of your baby.

You may of course find that you feel a lessening of desire during pregnancy, or even a complete loss of interest in sex. These feelings are not uncommon, but they can cause unnecessary stress between you and your partner if they are not brought out into the open and discussed.

You and your body

You are now beginning the second trimester when you should start experiencing what is known as mid-pregnancy bloom. You will be feeling better about everything; if your sex drive has diminished over the last few months it will probably return and sex may be better than ever.

If you don't feel much like making love in early pregnancy, still cuddle your partner and show him lots of affection.

Your partner may feel that he is being rejected, so it is important to find alternative ways of giving each other love and reassurance.

DIFFERENT WAYS TO MAKE LOVE

It is important that you and your partner show each other physical affection during pregnancy, but this does not always have to involve sexual intercourse. You may find as your pregnancy progresses that you want lots of cuddles and other signs of affection from your partner without actually having sex. Men often find this hard to understand as they tend to link such physical contact with intercourse. Explain to your partner how you feel so that together you can find other ways of expressing your love for each other.

Try experimenting with forms of sex play that don't necessarily end in penetration, so that you can still make love even if you don't feel like intercourse. Take time to find out

Often during the middle months of pregnancy, you can start to feel more sensual and show renewed interest in sex.

Your growing baby

The baby is beginning to look human as the chin, forehead, and nose become more clearly defined. It can now turn its head and even wrinkle its brow. The baby may even respond to external stimulus by actually moving away when the doctor or midwife feels your abdomen. The baby is now 9cm/3½in long and weighs about 60g/2oz.

what you both enjoy and don't be afraid to tell your partner what you do and don't like. Stroking, massage, mutual masturbation, and oral sex are some alternative ways of making love which you can both enjoy and which may at times be more appropriate than full intercourse.

As you grow larger you'll find some positions for lovemaking more comfortable than others. Experiment with positions which keep your partner's weight off you.

USING SEX TO INDUCE LABOUR

Sex can sometimes be a way of inducing labour. Your partner's

semen contains a hormone called prostaglandin, which will help to soften the cervix in preparation for birth. Lovemaking will also stimulate the cells in the cervix to secrete their own prostaglandins; this too may help bring labour on.

Breast stimulation in late pregnancy sometimes produces quite strong contractions which are thought to help prepare the way for labour by softening and drawing up the cervix. It has been discovered that stimulating the nipples can reactivate a labour that has halted – something that your partner might like to remember.

WEEK 15: HEALTH AND SAFETY

You may hear about risks during pregnancy. Some are valid, others are based on misinformation. If you work with dangerous substances such as chemicals, or in a job that requires you to do heavy lifting, you could be risking your health and that of your child, and your employer must offer you an alternative job. If you are concerned about risks at work talk to your doctor, your employer, or union representative.

One common concern is that sitting all day in front of a computer screen will harm the developing baby, but extensive research shows no evidence of this.

A more cautionary approach is suggested towards the use of mobile phones. Although there is no evidence that they can harm the baby, it is recommended that calls should be kept to a minimum during your pregnancy.

You and your body

Your heart has enlarged to cope with the increased amount of blood circulating in your body and the baby's need for oxygen, and has increased its output by 20 per cent. You will be feeling more energetic than before and now is a good time to have a holiday before the birth.

HEALTH HAZARDS

While you are pregnant you should avoid eating unpasteurized milk and products made with unpasteurized milk; pâté made from meat, fish, or vegetables; soft and blue vein

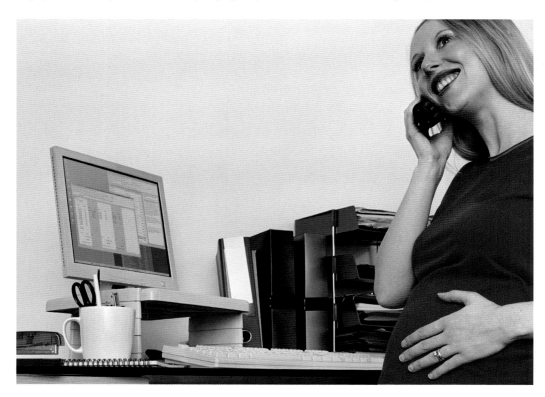

There is no evidence to show that there is any risk to the growing baby for women who regularly use computers, but use of a mobile phone should be kept to a minimum.

Left: Make sure you only eat hard-boiled eggs and drink pasteurized milk to avoid Listeria monocytogenes.

cheeses; soft-whip ice cream; pre-cooked poultry and cook-chill meals; and prepared salads (unless washed thoroughly) because of the risk of listeria.

Listeria monocytogenes is the bacterium which causes listeriosis in humans and animals. Animals that carry the bacterium are likely to infect the milk they produce and the meat that is produced from them. The bacterium is usually destroyed during the pasteurization of milk and milk products. However, if food is contaminated and then refrigerated the bacteria will continue to multiply. Listeriosis can also be spread through direct contact with animals that are infected.

Toxoplasmosis is a disease that occurs in both humans and animals. It can be extremely dangerous if it is contracted during pregnancy because it may cause miscarriage or severe fetal abnormality. The disease is spread to humans by eating undercooked or raw meat and through coming into contact with cat faeces. The infection can also be caught from sheep at lambing time. It is possible to have the disease without knowing it, so you should have a blood test to find out whether or not you have immunity. If you are immune, you definitely cannot infect your baby.

If you find that you are not immune, you should take a number of precautions during pregnancy. Avoid meat that has not been cooked thoroughly and wash your hands, cooking utensils, and surfaces after preparing raw meat. Wash fruit and vegetables to remove all traces of soil. Avoid unpasteurized goat's milk and goat's milk products. Finally, wear rubber gloves when gardening and wash your hands afterwards. Cover your children's sand boxes in the garden to prevent cats from using them as litter trays.

Food safety

Avoid putting yourself at risk during pregnancy by taking the following precautions with food.

● Wash all fruit, vegetables, and salads, including any pre-packed salads, thoroughly.

● Don't eat raw or undercooked meat.

● Eggs must be well cooked and all dairy products should be pasteurized.

● Don't eat liver and liver products, such as pâté and liver sausage. They contain high levels of vitamin A, which is toxic in excess amounts.

● Avoid eating any soft, imported cheeses such as Brie and Camembert, blue-vein cheeses, and those that are made from goat's and sheep's milk because of the risk of listeria.

● Avoid cook-chill meals and shellfish.

● Keep your fridge below 5°C/41°F and don't refreeze any previously frozen foods.

● Pay special attention to hygiene in the kitchen.

● Don't eat food that is past its "sell by" or "best before" date.

WEEK 16:
SCANS/TWINS

A scan can be carried out at any stage of pregnancy (a dating scan may be offered as early as 10 weeks) to check on your baby's progress. The anomaly scan, which is a detailed check to see if your baby is developing normally, is usually offered between 16 and 20 weeks.

The procedure is completely painless. High-density sound waves are used to create a picture of your baby in the uterus, and you will be able to see this on a screen. The best pictures are obtained when you have a full bladder so you will be asked to drink a lot of fluid beforehand. You lie on a couch and your stomach is lubricated so that the person doing the scan can pull the scanner smoothly across it. The picture that appears on the screen may not be clear, so ask the radiographer to explain the images to you, if you are unsure of what you are seeing.

The baby's age can be determined from a scan; it also shows up most abnormalities of the head and spine that may have occurred and will detect the presence of twins. The exact position of the placenta and the baby can be seen, so if there are any problems, for example when the placenta is situated very low down, extra care will be taken throughout your pregnancy. You may also be given the opportunity to find out your baby's sex.

TWINS

There is about a one in 80 chance that you and your partner will conceive twins. However, you are more likely to give birth to twins if you have a history of them in your, or your partner's, family. Identical twins come from one egg which, once fertilized, then splits into two separate cells. Each of the cells then grows into a separate baby, but they usually share the same placenta. Because identical twins originally came from the same cells they are always the same sex and look like each other. Non-identical twins, or fraternal twins, are the result of two

You and your body

You may feel your baby's first movements around this time. These early movements are like a fluttering, bubbling sensation. You may notice the beginning of *Linea nigra*, a dark line which appears down the centre of your abdomen. This will disappear after the birth.

eggs being fertilized by two different sperm at the same time. Each baby has its own placenta and the sex of the babies may differ. Fraternal twins usually don't look any more alike than other brothers and sisters.

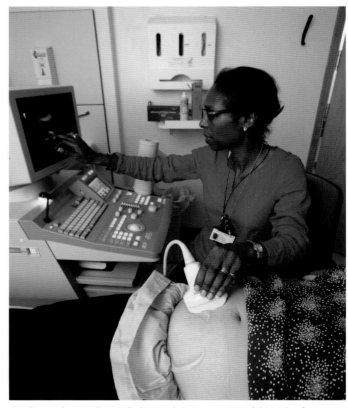

An ultrasound scan will normally be carried out between 16 and 20 weeks of pregnancy. It will show up any abnormalities in your baby and also indicate the presence of twins.

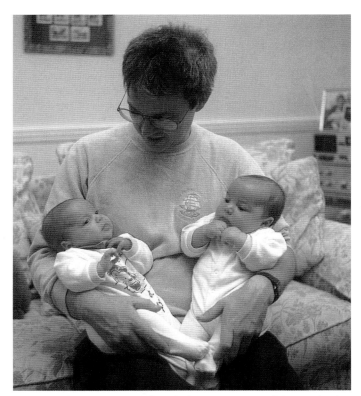

Your growing baby

The baby will be moving around frequently now, although you may have only just started to feel this. The body will become covered in a fine downy hair called lanugo, which is thought to maintain the right body temperature. It is possible to tell a baby's sex now through an ultrasound scan. The baby is 16cm/6¼in long and weighs 135g/5oz.

The arrival of twins can come as rather a shock. Get your partner to help as much as he can and you will soon find that you both start bonding with them.

The joy of having twins is that as they grow up they will learn to play with each other.

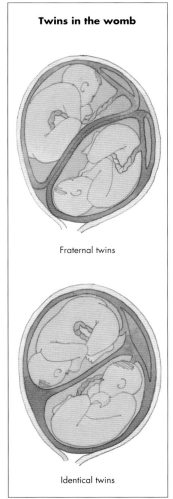

Twins in the womb

Fraternal twins

Identical twins

WEEK 17: YOUR PREGNANCY WARDROBE

You will find that ordinary clothes, in a bigger size if necessary, will see you through most of your pregnancy. A few basic garments that are interchangeable will help you achieve a variety of looks. Buy skirts and trousers with elasticated waists, and stretchy tops and T-shirts in natural fibres. Choose underwear with some cotton content for softness and absorbency and maternity tights or stockings to give your legs support. As your breasts are likely to increase in size rapidly during pregnancy, it makes sense to buy a well-fitting support bra as soon as your present bra feels tight. It is worth getting professionally measured so that you can be sure you are getting the correct size bra.

You and your body

Your waistline will have completely disappeared and you may have begun to develop stretch marks. Bleeding gums may be a problem, so if you haven't had a dental check-up now is the time to go. If you work, you should start thinking about when you intend to leave and whether you will want to return.

Your growing baby

Your baby's limbs are fully formed, as well as the skin and muscle. Its taste buds are beginning to develop so that it will be able to distinguish sweet from non-sweetened fluid. The baby is now about 18cm/7in long and weighs around 185g/6½oz.

Maternity rights and benefits

Once your pregnancy is confirmed, you should make enquiries about your maternity rights and benefits. You will probably be entitled to some financial and/or medical benefits from the government. If you work you are entitled to maternity leave and you may qualify for statutory maternity pay or maternity allowance from your employer. You are entitled to take time off work to attend ante-natal clinics and parentcraft classes, so you may want to let your employer know that you are pregnant before booking your visit. You can get more information from your employer, trade union, local Jobcentre Plus or Social Security office.

Look smart in the office in skirts with elasticated waists and flattering tops.

You can stay trendy in denim by wearing under-the-bump drawstring waist jeans or skirt.

Above: For formal occasions a little black dress with ruched sides, made from fabric that has plenty of stretch, will be perfect to wear throughout your pregnancy.

Far left: In summer stay cool by wearing cotton. A tiered dress will accommodate even the largest bump.

Left: There's no reason why you shouldn't wear shorts, matched with a pretty top.

WEEK 18: LOOKING YOUR BEST

You may find that your hair behaves in a rather unpredictable way while you are pregnant. Hormone changes mean that your hair may appear thicker than usual, or in some women the opposite happens and the hair loss increases so that the hair looks thinner. Dry hair may become even drier and oily hair more greasy. Whichever condition applies to you, just wash your hair using a mild shampoo. If your hair tends to be very dry, use a good conditioner after every wash and, if possible, allow it to dry naturally rather than using a hair dryer.

Dry hair will need extra conditioning during your pregnancy because it becomes drier as your hormones change.

Pregnancy hormones can affect the colour and texture of your skin. Uneven patches may appear and dark-skinned people sometimes

Try using hypoallergenic skin-cleansing products on your skin as it will be particularly sensitive at this time.

get a butterfly-shaped patch of pigmentation across the face that is known as "the mask of pregnancy". Concealing foundation will help hide these marks and a UVA sun screen will prevent any further increase in pigmentation. Pregnancy "bloom", which is caused by an increase in the tiny blood vessels under the surface of the skin, can be toned down with green cream or powder. It is a good idea to use hypoallergenic skin-care products as your skin may be particularly sensitive at this time.

FLUID RETENTION

Your body retains more water than usual during pregnancy, so your hands and feet may become slightly swollen and you may find that your

You and your body

You should be able to feel the fetal movements quite clearly now. Your nose may become blocked as pregnancy causes the membranes inside the nasal passages to swell. You may also notice an increase in vaginal discharge. You will find that there are several physical changes besides the predictable weight gain.

eyes get puffy and your face looks fuller. The best solution is to get as much rest as possible, sitting with your feet higher than your heart, as this will help reduce the swelling in your feet and ankles. While you are resting, place some cottonwool pads soaked in witch hazel, or slices of cucumber, on your eyes. This will soothe them and reduce any puffiness. You can disguise a fuller face by applying blusher below the cheekbones and blending a darker shade of foundation along your jawline. Alternatively, you can draw attention away from your face by wearing a colourful scarf or a chunky necklace round your neck.

Try not to be too critical of your looks; many other people will consider that this new, softer look to your appearance makes you seem younger and healthier.

Your growing baby

The skin is still wrinkled because the baby hasn't started to gain body fat and is very active. It is becoming aware of sounds outside the uterus and you may be able to feel it jumping at unexpected noises. The baby is now around 21cm/8½in long and weighs about 235g/8oz.

With extra care you can transform your face from looking tired and pale in pregnancy (left) to attractive and striking (right). A concealing foundation masks pigmentation marks, mascara and soft eye shadows can highlight your eyes, and a stunning lipstick can emphasize your mouth.

WEEK 19: EXERCISE

Regular, gentle exercise has an important part to play in keeping you fit during pregnancy and will help you get back into shape after the birth. Remember, if you ever feel faint, light-headed or breathless while you are exercising you must stop immediately. If you haven't been taking regular exercise, start swimming, or take up yoga or walking, as they can all be done at a gentle, rhythmical pace that can be adapted to suit each stage of your pregnancy. If you find it easier to follow an exercise routine you can do at home, never include sit-ups or exercises that involve raising the legs when you are lying down as these could damage the abdominal muscles. It is important to stop and relax

You and your body

You have started to put weight on your bottom, hips, and thighs as well as your abdomen. Tiny veins may start appearing on your face. These are very small broken blood vessels which are caused by circulation changes. They will disappear after the birth.

between exercises and to make sure that your breathing always remains at a controlled rate.

Toning your chest

1 *Hold arms at breast level with hands loosely clasping opposite arm. Tighten grip and hold briefly, then relax.*

2 *Still keeping your hands clasped, raise them to eye level and tighten your grip and hold, then relax.*

3 *Lower your arms down to your waist, tighten and hold, then relax. Repeat this sequence several times.*

Feet exercises

1 *To loosen ankles, sit down with feet flat on the ground. Lift one foot at a time and circle ankle five times in both directions.*

2 *To relax the feet, place your feet flat on the floor. Now lift your toes up as far as you can and hold briefly, then relax.*

3 *Now clench your toes hard, hold for a few seconds, then relax again. Repeat this technique, and Step 2, 10 times.*

Taylor sitting and squatting exercises

1 *To loosen the groin and hips and stretch the inner thighs, sit with the soles of your feet together. Holding ankles, bring your pelvis and feet together by moving your hips towards your feet.*

2 *This is a good position for labour. Squat down keeping a straight back; try to put your heels down keeping your weight even. Press your elbows against your thighs stretching the inner groin and thighs.*

Tummy toning exercises

1 *Put a folded towel or pillow under your head and lie with your knees bent and your feet flat on the floor. Tighten your tummy muscles so that your back is flat on the floor.*

2 *Keeping your back pressed well down onto the floor, slowly extend both your legs in front of you until they are both completely straight.*

3 *Draw one knee up and then the other, without lifting your back off the floor, then relax; repeat five times.*

Your growing baby

The baby is starting to put on weight and its rapid rate of growth has begun to slow down. The milk teeth have developed in the gums and the buds for the permanent teeth are beginning to form. The baby is around 23cm/9in long and weighs about 285g/10oz.

WEEK 20: SKIN CARE/CRAVINGS

Your breasts are likely to increase by as much as two bra sizes during pregnancy, so you will need to make sure that they are well supported so that they do not sag and become uncomfortable. Small bumps may appear in the skin around your nipples. These are sebaceous glands, which secrete sebum, a fatty lubricant. As your pregnancy progresses, your nipples grow softer and gentle massage will help make them supple and ready for breast-feeding. Your breasts may leak a yellow fluid called colostrum, which will form a crust on the nipples. You will need to wash and dry them gently and thoroughly at least twice a day.

Your nails are made of protein and are affected by the hormonal changes taking place in your body. Usually they grow longer and stronger during pregnancy, but occasionally pregnancy will cause them to split and break. If this happens, keep them short and protect them by wearing gloves when you are doing rough jobs or when you immerse your hands in water.

If the elasticity of your skin becomes overstretched as you put on

Your nails may be brittle during pregnancy so keep them short to stop them splitting.

Paint on a nail strengthener to keep your nails strong at this time.

Check your bra size by measuring around your ribcage. For the cup size measure around your bust at its fullest.

You and your body

Your uterus is enlarging quite rapidly now so that you look pregnant. Your navel may be flattened or pushed out and it will stay this way until after the birth. Heartburn may start to become a problem because the uterus is starting to push against your stomach.

weight, you may develop stretch marks. These usually appear on the breasts, stomach, and the tops of the thighs as thin, reddish lines. There is little you can do to avoid them, but keeping your skin well moisturized, and being careful not to put on too much extra weight, will help minimize them. Stretch marks fade to thin silvery lines after the birth.

Varicose veins can be caused by pregnancy hormones or, later in pregnancy, by the uterus pressing down and obstructing the flow of blood from the legs to the heart. Although not serious, they can lead to aching or sore legs. Try to avoid standing for long periods and put your feet up whenever possible to ease any discomfort. Walking will help the blood flow; put on support tights or stockings when you get out of bed in the morning to give your legs more support. Varicose veins usually disappear soon after the birth.

CRAVINGS

No one is sure why some pregnant women have cravings while others don't. Doctors disagree about them; some are sympathetic, while others doubt that they actually exist. If you desire a certain food there is no reason why you shouldn't indulge yourself within reason, but make sure that you don't exclude other more nourishing foods as a result.

Above: Your legs may ache more with the increased weight you're carrying, so try massaging them with a body lotion.
Right: You can't prevent stretch marks appearing on your stomach, but rubbing in moisturizing lotion may help.

Your growing baby

Vernix, a white greasy substance, is starting to form over the baby's skin to protect it from the amniotic fluid. This usually wears off before the birth, but sometimes traces of it can be seen. At this stage in your pregnancy the baby weighs around 340g/12oz and measures about 25.5cm/10in.

WEEK 21: MINOR COMPLAINTS

By now you may be experiencing some of the minor problems that occur later in pregnancy. These include:

Heartburn This is a strong burning feeling in your chest that often happens during the last few months of pregnancy. It is usually worse when lying down. Hormones cause the valve at the top of your stomach to relax, which allows stomach acid to pass back into the gullet (oesophagus), causing a burning sensation. Avoid eating spicy and fatty foods. Eating small, but frequent meals will help reduce heartburn. Sleeping propped up at night and drinking a glass of milk before you go to bed will also help ease the discomfort.

If you are suffering from heartburn, try drinking a glass of milk before you go to sleep at night.

Your doctor may prescribe an antacid if the problem frequently keeps you awake at night. If you buy an over-the-counter remedy always tell the pharmacist that you are pregnant because some of the remedies that are available are not suitable for use during pregnancy or breast-feeding.

You and your body

You should be able to see your abdomen ripple as the baby moves. You may be feeling slightly breathless as your expanding ribcage pushes upwards, giving your lungs less room. You will probably be feeling energetic so now is the time to tackle things such as planning the nursery.

Insomnia can be a problem in later pregnancy. If you can't sleep, try supporting your tummy on pillows to make yourself more comfortable.

Insomnia Sleeplessness is often a problem as your pregnancy progresses because you will find it difficult to get comfortable, and you have to make frequent trips to the toilet. Vivid dreams can also be a problem at this time. A bath followed by a warm drink at bedtime will help you relax. It is important to find restful sleeping positions, so use lots of pillows to support your abdomen when you lie on your side. You could also try practising some relaxation techniques.

Itching This often occurs on the areas of skin around the bump and is sometimes accompanied by a rash. Calamine lotion should help relieve the itching and since it is usually caused by sweating, wearing loose clothes made of natural fibres can help prevent it. Severe itching that occurs during the last three months of pregnancy could be a warning of pregnancy cholestasis – a rare but potentially dangerous liver disorder – and you should consult your doctor.

It's important to get plenty of rest so take the opportunity to sit down and relax whenever you can.

Your growing baby

The baby is very active now and you will probably be able to feel it kicking quite easily. If this disturbs you at night, stroke your tummy and talk to the baby because it will be soothed by the sound of your voice. The baby is now around 28cm/11in long and weighs about 390g/14oz.

Oedema (swelling) This occurs in the feet and ankles, and sometimes the hands, because your body is holding more fluid than normal. By the end of the day this fluid tends to gather in your feet, especially if the weather has been hot or you have been doing a lot of standing. Try to sit with your feet up whenever you can, as this will help reduce the swelling. Wear support tights and comfortable shoes during the day and avoid standing for long periods. You should always tell your midwife or doctor about any swelling that you experience as it could be a sign of pre-eclampsia.

Tiredness The extra weight you carry during late pregnancy can make you feel more tired than usual. It is important to have regular rest periods when you can sit down with your feet up. If the tiredness you are experiencing feels excessive, you may be suffering from anaemia. Make sure you are getting plenty of iron in your diet by eating lean red meat, whole grains, dark green leafy vegetables, nuts, and pulses. If the feeling still persists consult your midwife or doctor.

Swimming is an ideal exercise as the water supports the extra weight.

WEEK 22: RELAXATION AND MASSAGE

It is important to be able to relax, both mentally and physically, during pregnancy because this will help you to rest. Knowing how to make your body relax during labour will allow you to work with the contractions rather than against them.

Physical relaxation
Start by getting comfortable and make sure that every part of your body is supported.

Concentrate on tensing and relaxing individual parts of your body. Start at your toes and work gradually upwards to your head and then back down to your toes again. By the time you have finished this exercise you should be feeling nice and floppy.

Mental relaxation This requires deep concentration, so you need to be comfortable and in a quiet place where no one will disturb you. Empty your mind and concentrate on your breathing. Breathe in and hold your breath for a few seconds before letting it out slowly.

You and your body

Your lower ribs are starting to cause you pain as they get pushed outwards by your growing baby and your expanding uterus. Your ribcage rises by a small amount as it is pushed upward. To minimize the discomfort, try sitting up as straight as you can or lifting your arms above your head. This is an ideal time to investigate the different methods that you can use to ease discomfort now and during labour and birth.

Once you have established a steady pattern of breathing, make sure all your muscles are relaxed, then allow your mind to float away. One way to do this is to imagine that you are

OTHER TECHNIQUES

Massage is an excellent way of relieving tension. It is best done on bare skin, but if you find your skin is particularly sensitive, it can be carried out through a thin cotton nightdress. Massage strokes should be firm, smooth, and rhythmical.

Aromatherapy massage uses essential oils that are added to a carrier oil before being applied to your skin. Certain essential oils can be dangerous during pregnancy because they may trigger uterine contractions, so you must always get qualified professional advice. Many aromatherapists will not treat a pregnant woman at all. Most of those who will treat expectant mothers will do so only after the sixth month of pregnancy. One effective blend is mandarin oil well diluted (i.e. a maximum solution of one per cent: no more than 10 drops of oil to 50 ml carrier oil) in a sweet almond carrier oil. A well-diluted solution of true lavender, jasmine, and rose in sweet almond oil is also thought to be beneficial during labour and birth.

In acupuncture tiny needles are used to stimulate meridian points on the body's energy lines with the aim of rebalancing the energy flow. The treatment can help backache, but some points on the body are thought to stimulate uterine contractions, so it is important to let the practitioner know that you are pregnant.

Above: If you are suffering regularly from backache, having a soothing massage from a qualified practitioner can help. With an aromatherapy massage, make sure she chooses oils that will not affect the baby.
Below: Regular massage on your legs will help to relieve any aches and pains that you are experiencing.

WEEK 23: PREPARING THE NURSERY

This is a good time to think of practical things like planning the baby's nursery. Whether you have a spare room which you are going to turn into a nursery, or you intend to make a nursery corner in your own bedroom, you should start getting it ready now while you have the energy.

Before you begin you will need to take into consideration the shape and size of the area so you can work out how much furniture and baby equipment will comfortably fit into it. You should also check whether there are enough electrical sockets; that there is sufficient heating; and that the ceiling or wall lights are where you want them. Major changes such as rewiring or putting in another radiator are better done before you start to decorate or carpet the nursery.

Babies enjoy looking at bright, primary colours and big, bold patterns, so choose a colourful paint and paper; washable materials will make it easier to keep the walls looking bright and fresh. Transfers, borders, pictures and mobiles can be used effectively to brighten up a plain background if you are reluctant to commit yourself to a colour scheme until you know your baby's sex.

Rugs and polished floors look nice but are unsuitable because of the risk of you slipping on them

You and your body

The baby can be felt through your abdominal wall and the midwife or doctor will palpate your abdomen to see how the baby is lying. You may occasionally feel a pain rather like a stitch down the side of your stomach. This is the uterine muscle stretching and it will go away after you have had a rest.

while holding the baby. Any flooring needs to be warm underfoot and non-slip. Sealed cork tiles are ideal because they are warm and any spills can be wiped up without damage to the floor. Fitted carpets and carpet tiles are suitable alternatives, but don't buy expensive carpet because it will probably need replacing after a relatively short time.

An overhead light with a dimmer switch or a specially designed nursery light is very useful for night feeds as it gives out a soft comforting glow that won't startle either of you too much in the middle of the night. A plug or cot light will provide enough illumination for you to check on your sleeping baby, but you will need a brighter light for nappy changing and general care. Avoid any lamps with trailing flexes that you could trip over, and fit all unused electrical sockets with a safety cover.

FINISHING TOUCHES
The room where the baby sleeps must be draught-proof, so cover any windows with thick, lined curtains. These will not only keep out any draughts, but will also keep the morning light from waking your baby during the summer. Windows need to be fitted with childproof

Planning the nursery for your baby can be enjoyable. You can start to buy some outfits in advance, but remember that you will often be given baby clothes when your baby is born.

A cot will be necessary by the time your baby is three moths old. If you choose a secondhand one, it's a good idea to buy a new mattress. Make sure that the mattress is firm and fits snugly into the base of the cot.

locks and the curtains should be out of reach of the cot. Never place the cot or crib under a window or near radiators. Young babies cannot regulate their temperature, so they need to be kept in a comfortably warm environment at around 18ºC/ 65ºF. A special nursery thermometer or a thermostat fitted to the radiator will help ensure that you maintain the correct room temperature.

Babies actually require very little in the way of furniture. Somewhere to sleep, a cupboard or chest to keep clothes in, and somewhere for changing and storing toiletries and nappies, as well as a chair for you to sit in while you are feeding or rocking the baby, is all that you really need for the first few months. All nursery furniture should be sturdy enough that it can't be pulled over when babies are older and using it for support as they begin to pull

themselves up on to their feet. If you buy secondhand furniture, make sure that any paint or varnish is non-toxic and lead-free. If you are in any doubt, get someone to rub it down for you so you can repaint with safe materials. Also check that there are no broken bits that could harm your baby.

Your growing baby
The baby is beginning to look as it will at birth, with the head more in proportion to the body. In a boy, the scrotum is now well developed and in a girl the ovaries already contain several million eggs. (These will reduce to around two million at birth and will carry on decreasing until puberty.) The baby is around 31cm/ 12¼in long and weighs approximately 440g/15½oz.

A dresser is useful for organizing all your baby's essentials in one place, and includes a changing mat on top.

A Moses basket can by kept by or near your bed, and your baby can sleep in it for up to three months.

WEEK 24: BABY CLOTHES AND EQUIPMENT

Start planning what you need to buy for your baby so that by the time you give birth you will at least have purchased the major items. If you leave everything until the end of the pregnancy, you may be too tired to enjoy shopping for your baby.

Only buy a few basic first size or newborn garments as your baby will probably rapidly outgrow these. Also, most baby clothes are sized by the approximate age and height of

the child and you won't know the size of your child until she is born. Choose well-designed baby clothes, which will make your life easier and allow you to dress and undress your baby with the minimum of time and fuss. Clothes with envelope necks or a shoulder fastening will let you slip clothes over the baby's head easily, and poppers up the inside of legs of rompers or all-in-one suits will help with regular nappy changing.

You and your body

You will noticeably be putting on weight, perhaps as much as 0.5kg/1lb per week. Your feet and legs may start to feel the strain of carrying this extra weight, so make sure that you wear comfortable shoes and that you get plenty of rest.

Your new baby will probably get through as many as three changes of clothes a day, so it is a good idea to check the washing instructions on any garment before you buy. These instructions will tell you how best to care for each garment so that you can see whether it is easy-care, or if it will require a lot of attention.

Baby transport

A pram that converts to a pushchair is suitable from birth to the toddler years.

A traditional pram is sturdy with plenty of space for shopping, and it will take a toddler seat. It is probably the best option if you are planning to have another child fairly quickly.

A fold-flat buggy with a parcel tray is useful for shopping. Choose one that is light enough to carry on public transport.

Generally, prams are unsuitable for cars unless they have a detachable body. A 3-in-1 combination converts from pram to pushchair and has a separate baby carrier or carry cot.

A car seat carrier is easily transported and can be bought in different sizes to suit the age of your baby.

BABY'S TRANSPORT

Before you decide on a pram, buggy, or combination, you need to consider your lifestyle and the various methods of transport you will be using regularly. You also need to think about where it will be stored when not in use. Once you have selected the type most suitable to your needs, ask the shop you order it from to keep it for you until after the baby is born.

Your baby should always be in a car seat when travelling in the car. The seat must be suitable for your child's weight rather than age. Always buy new and make sure it complies with the relevant safety standard. Before placing your child's car seat in the front of the car make sure that the airbag has been disabled.

EQUIPMENT

Whether you buy a cot, Moses basket, or carrycot will probably depend on where your baby is going

Your growing baby

Vigorous movements followed by periods of quiet will start to occur as the baby develops its own waking and resting periods. The pattern that develops now may well continue after the birth so it's a good idea to monitor it for a few days to see how it compares with the sleep pattern once the baby is born. The heartbeat can be heard with an ordinary stethoscope and the baby can hear you clearly when you speak. It is now around 33cm/13in long and weighs about 0.5kg/1lb.

to sleep and how much space you have. If the baby is going to sleep in your room at first and you haven't much space, think about buying a cot later.

You need to have at least six sheets and several lightweight cot blankets for the cot and another six sheets and at least three more pram blankets for your chosen pram.

A twin stroller with adjustable backrests is desgined to last from birth through to the toddler years. It is also suitable for two children of different ages.

A two-level high-chair can be used in the higher position when your baby is young and in the lower position when he is older.

WEEK 25: FEEDING CHOICES

Now is the time to start thinking about how you are going to feed your baby. Whether to breast- or bottle-feed is a personal and emotional decision and one that you need to feel completely happy about. Before you make up your mind talk it over with your partner and your midwife, and get some first-hand experiences from other mothers.

BREAST-FEEDING

Breast milk is the best food for your baby because it contains everything he or she needs in the right proportions, and it changes as the baby grows. It contains antibodies, which will help protect the baby, and it is easily digestible so less likely to cause stomach upsets. Breast-fed babies are also less likely to develop conditions such as eczema and asthma and are less prone to some infections, such as glue ear.

Breast-feeding has advantages for you as well. Not only is breast milk free and always on "tap", at the correct temperature, breast-feeding releases hormones that encourage the uterus to shrink back to its original size more quickly. Breastfeeding for at least six months significantly reduces the risk of pre-menopausal cancer and can protect against osteoporosis and ovarian cancer.

During pregnancy the skin around your nipples will appear darker and raised sebaceous glands will appear as little bumps in the areola, the dark area surrounding the nipple. As your pregnancy progresses the nipples will grow softer. You can make them more supple by gently massaging them. Take extra care washing and drying your breasts towards the end of pregnancy, when they may leak a little, and avoid using soaps that have a drying effect on the skin. You may

You and your body

You should be looking rosy-cheeked and healthy because of the increase in blood circulation under the skin. Pressure from the growing uterus on the bladder means that you need to make frequent trips to the lavatory. Cramp, heartburn and backache are often problems now.

find that you need to use breast pads to prevent your clothes from becoming stained.

Breast milk is free, so the only additional cost involved at first is for nursing bras and breast pads. Choose cotton, front-opening nursing bras, with adjustable straps and fastenings because the size of your breasts will change. Wait until after your 30th week of pregnancy before buying a

Breast-feeding is the best way to nourish your baby, but if you decide to bottle feed make it a relaxing and enjoyable experience for you both.

nursing bra – one that fits you then should fit you after the baby is born. If you want to be able to express milk, you will also need a couple of bottles and teats, sterilizing equipment, and possibly a breast pump.

BOTTLE-FEEDING

Formula milk has been specially produced for bottle-fed babies. It contains the right balance of vitamins and minerals that a baby needs to thrive. Formula milk has more protein than breast milk, which means that it takes longer to digest. There are a number of brands to choose from and most are based on cow's milk, although alternatives are available for children who need special diets for medical reasons.

It is very important to follow the instructions when making up formula milk because too much or too little can be harmful. The baby will gradually settle into a routine but until then you will need to respond to his or her hunger just as you would if you were breast-feeding.

One of the main advantages of bottle-feeding is that you and your partner can share the feeds between you, so that you can both use the time when you are feeding to get to know your baby.

Hygiene is very important when you bottle-feed because your baby is not getting protection from the antibodies that he or she would have from breast milk. You will need to take particular care over washing and sterilizing bottles and teats until your baby is at least six months old.

As well as formula milk you will need at least six bottles and teats, with caps, a sterilizing unit or container, a bottle brush, and you may also find a bottle warmer is useful for the night feeds.

Breast-feeding can help you bond with your baby, and the milk will give her everything she needs, including protection against infection.

Massaging your nipples in pregnancy will make them more supple for breast-feeding.

Your growing baby

Fetal brain cells continue to develop and become more sophisticated and the bone centres are beginning to harden. The baby actively practises breathing, inhaling and exhaling amniotic fluid, as more air sacs develop in the lungs. When too much amniotic fluid is swallowed, you may feel a hiccup. The baby is about 34cm/13½in long and weighs around 0.6kg/1¼lb.

WEEK 26: PARENTCRAFT CLASSES

You should now be about to start parentcraft classes. You may choose one or more of these. Parentcraft classes show you practical techniques such as relaxation, breathing, and postures for labour and birth. The teacher can answer any questions you may have during the last few months of your pregnancy and will be able to give you information on the birth. Your partner will be welcome at some classes and you will find that they are a good way of meeting other pregnant women and sharing mutual anxieties.

The hospital and locally run classes are free, but classes such as National Childbirth Trust and Active Birth charge a fee.

HOSPITAL CLASSES

These are run by the hospital where you plan to give birth and usually take place over six to eight weeks, starting around the 28th week. You need to attend the course that is nearest to your expected date of delivery. Some hospitals have a parentcraft teacher who co-ordinates ante-natal education. You will be

You and your body

If you are working you need to decide when you are going to stop. Remember that you should notify your employer in writing by the end of the 15th week before your baby is due. Your partner must also tell his employer if he intends to take Paternity Leave. If you haven't started taking regular exercise you should now, because this will help prepare your body for the rigours of labour.

taken on a hospital tour so that you can see the labour ward, post-natal ward, and the special care baby unit.

LOCAL CLASSES

These are usually run by a midwife or a health visitor attached to your doctor's surgery or health centre.

Active birth classes

NATIONAL CHILDBIRTH TRUST (NCT)
NCT classes are privately run, usually by mothers who have been trained by the NCT. They need to be booked early because they are deliberately kept small and become fully booked very quickly. Although everything covered on the hospital and local parentcraft courses is included on the NCT course, the classes are more discussion-based and there are no rigid relaxation and breathing techniques. You are taught a variety of skills for dealing with labour and the birth, from which you can choose when the time comes.

ACTIVE BIRTH CLASSES
These privately run weekly classes concentrate on the physical preparation for labour and birth. You are taught a range of yoga-based stretching exercises as well as breathing and relaxation techniques. These classes are mainly for women, with a special session for fathers, and you can join them at any time.

BREATHING TECHNIQUES
Controlled breathing is important during labour and you need to practise the exercises you will be taught at your classes. Breathing needs to be slow and smooth with deep breaths, inhaled through your nose and exhaled through your mouth. A long slow breath at the beginning of each contraction will help oxygenate your blood and this may help relieve any pain caused by lack of oxygen to the muscles of your uterus. Oxygen is also carried in the blood flowing through the placenta into the umbilical cord, so if you do not get enough, your baby will suffer a shortage too.

During contractions you will be concentrating on each outward breath, as this will help you to relax your muscles. It will be important not to over-breathe during the second stage of labour, because this may make you feel dizzy and light-headed. If you do find yourself needing to breathe more quickly then you should concentrate on making each breath as light as you possibly can.

Your growing baby
Although still appearing rather scrawny, the baby is beginning to lay down fat under the skin. This fat will help regulate body temperature now and after the birth. The baby is around 35cm/13¾in long and weighs approximately 0.7kg/1½lb.

Gentle yoga-based exercises are ideal preparation for labour and help you to get ready physically and emotionally, so that you are in tune with the demands on your body. They should always be done under qualified supervision. Exercises include going down into a squatting position (far left and left) in anticipation of labour; massage, which particularly helps if you've got sciatica (below left), and stretching to ease pressure at the base of the spine (below right).

THE THIRD TRIMESTER

WEEK 27: CHOICES IN CHILDBIRTH

Now that you have entered the third trimester you should start planning the kind of birth that you want. If you are having a hospital birth, you will need to discover what facilities are on offer and then try to plan the birth around them. Although hospitals do try to accommodate a mother's wishes, not all are able to offer every type of birth.

For example, if you want a water birth, you will have to find out whether it is possible at your hospital. If you are having a home birth then having a water birth in a hired pool is easier to arrange. However, you need to remember that if complications occur during labour any decisions you make now may have to be changed.

If you opt for a water birth, you can have your baby in the water or outside the pool. Whichever you choose, the warm water will help ease the contractions.

You and your body

You will be getting noticeably larger and will have put on weight around your chest as well as your breasts. Make sure that you are wearing the correct size of maternity bra. Avoid lying on your back too much because this may make you feel faint, as the enlarged uterus presses directly against blood vessels.

NATURAL BIRTH

This is when you go through labour and birth without any of the medical procedures that often alter the natural rhythm of labour. Natural childbirth involves the use of breathing and relaxation techniques and sometimes homeopathic remedies.

WATER BIRTH

You spend part of your time in a birth pool, which is filled with warm water, and give birth either outside the pool or in the water. The warm water eases the pain of contractions, and helps you to relax. Although there is no evidence to prove that there is an increased risk of complications if you actually have your baby in the water, you should still talk to your midwife or doctor before planning to do this.

ACTIVE BIRTH

This means that you are free to move about during labour. Keeping mobile allows the contractions to be more effective. Being in an upright position helps the baby's circulation and encourages the baby to rotate into the best position for delivery.

In a natural birth you go through labour without painkillers, using only relaxation methods and maybe homeopathic treatments.

Gravity aids the baby's descent, and giving birth in a squatting or kneeling position increases the size of the pelvic outlet.

HIGH-TECH BIRTH

Labour is controlled by medical methods such as induction, where labour is started artificially using chemical substances, or the waters are broken manually.

Painkilling drugs are used and an episiotomy (a surgical incision in the perineum to allow passage of the baby's head when there is some fear that the perineum will otherwise be torn) may be done to enlarge the birth canal.

CAESAREAN BIRTH

This is when the baby is delivered through an incision that is made through the wall of the abdomen into the uterus. It is done under a general anaesthetic, or sometimes with a spinal block or an epidural. If a spinal block or an epidural is used you will be awake during the delivery, although a screen is placed across your body so that you don't actually see what is happening. You will be given your baby to hold as soon as it is born. After the birth, the incisions are stitched and you will be kept in hospital for about five days. A Caesarean may be chosen if the reasons that make it necessary are evident before labour begins. This is known as an elective Caesarean. If it is decided on after labour has started, it is known as an emergency Caesarean. Reasons for a Caesarean include abnormal presentation of the baby (that is, not head-first towards the cervix), fetal distress where the baby suffers from lack of oxygen, and high blood pressure in the mother.

When you hold your newborn baby in your arms all the hard work of labour will seem worthwhile.

Your growing baby

The baby's eyes are open and it will be able to see light through the skin of your abdomen. It will have started to practise sucking and may even be able to suck its thumb or fist. The baby is now about 36cm/14¼in long and weighs about 0.8kg/1¾lb.

An active birth involves moving around in labour and adopting different positions that will help your baby's descent.

WEEK 28: THE BIRTHPLAN

Some hospitals include a special form with your notes, on which you can make a written plan of the way you would like your labour and birth to be managed. If you haven't received one of these, talk to your midwife about drawing up your own plan.

Even if there are still some things concerning labour or the actual birth about which you are undecided, writing out a plan will help you focus on the type of birth that you want. It will also give you the opportunity to discuss the birth in detail with your partner.

When drawing up your birthplan it is important to remember that there is no right or wrong way to give birth. Your plan should reflect what you feel is right for you, while taking into account your medical history as well as the facilities available at the place where you are going to have your baby.

A birthplan is a guide to how you would like things to be, but in the event of a problem this ideal may become totally impractical so you will need to be flexible. Once you have finalized your birthplan ask for a copy to be kept with your notes so

You and your body

Your breasts are producing colostrum, the fluid which precedes breast milk. If your breasts are leaking put breast pads or folded tissues inside your bra. If you have an ante-natal appointment you will probably have a second blood test to check for anaemia. If you are anaemic, iron supplements may be offered.

that the doctor and midwife who attend you during labour have it to hand. Keep a copy for yourself so that your birth partner can refer to it if necessary.

BIRTH PARTNER
Although your partner will be encouraged to be with you during labour, you may prefer to have

Write a birthplan with your choices.

Birthplan checklist

The following questions will help you prepare your own birthplan.

- Whom do you wish to have with you during labour – your partner, your mother, a friend? You can choose more than one birth partner.
- Can your birth partner remain with you if you have to have a Caesarean or forceps delivery?
- Are there special facilities such as a birthing pool or bean bags available?
- Do you want to be free to move around during labour, or would you rather be constantly monitored while staying in bed?
- Is there any special position you want to use for the birth?
- Do you wish to wear your own clothes during labour and the birth?
- Would you like music, soft lighting, massage or other therapies to help you cope with getting through labour?

- How do you feel about pain relief? If you want to manage without any, you will need to make sure that everyone knows. If you want pain relief which sort do you want?
- Are you prepared to have an episiotomy if it is required, or would you rather tear naturally?
- Do you want your baby placed straight onto your abdomen after birth or do you want him or her cleaned up first?
- Are you going to breast-feed? If so, do you want to put your baby to the breast immediately?
- Do you want an injection to help deliver the placenta or would you prefer to wait for it to be delivered naturally after the birth?
- How soon after the birth would you like to go home, assuming that there are no complications?

If your partner is worried about being with you during labour, talk it through with him and make your feelings known if you're counting on his support.

another woman as your actual birth partner, especially if your partner is worried that he may not be able to cope with seeing you in pain. Whatever you decide, make sure you talk about it together so that there are no misunderstandings and you don't get upset about the final choice.

Your growing baby

Now fully formed, the baby would be viable if it were born at 28 weeks, although the body systems are still very immature. The heart is beating at a rate of around 150 beats a minute. The baby weighs around 0.9kg/2lb.

Once you've made your birthplan and put your feelings on your baby's birth in writing, you will feel happier.

WEEK 29: SPECIAL CARE

If you suffer from a medical condition or blood disorder your pregnancy will require careful managing. Your doctor will need to monitor your progress and you may have to have special ante-natal checks. If there is a possible problem, you will be offered another scan during the last trimester, which will clearly show the baby's breathing movements, how it is lying, and the position of the placenta.

Anaemia is caused by an abnormally low level of red corpuscles in the blood and is treated with iron supplements. You can build up your body's store of iron by eating a diet which includes red meat, whole grains, dark green leafy vegetables, nuts and pulses. Liver is not recommended during pregnancy because of the high levels of vitamin A, which could be toxic. A second blood test is done in late pregnancy to check for anaemia.

Kidney infection is usually caused by bacterial infection and you should contact your doctor if you think you have a kidney infection. Symptoms are pain, frequent urination accompanied by a burning sensation, and occasionally some blood in the urine. Other symptoms that you may experience include back pain, high fever, chills, nausea, and vomiting.

Placenta praevia is a rare condition which usually occurs when a woman has had more than one child. The placenta is situated low in the uterus so that it blocks, or partially blocks, the cervix. The pressure of the baby on the placenta may cause painless bleeding any time after 28 weeks.

You and your body

You will probably be able to feel the baby's bottom and feet as it moves around. The baby will be putting pressure on your stomach and diaphragm now and you will need to sit down and rest more often.

As your baby starts to put pressure on your stomach, you'll need to lie down more often to rest.

If this happens, you may have to stay in hospital until after your baby is born. If the obstruction is particularly severe, your baby may need to be delivered by Caesarean.

Abruptio placentae is when part of the placenta comes away from the wall of the uterus causing some abdominal pain and bleeding. You should call the doctor immediately. The baby could be at risk if a large part of the placenta has come away, because it will be deprived of necessary oxygen and nutrients. Sometimes a blood transfusion is necessary and in late pregnancy the baby may be delivered by Caesarean. If only a small part of the placenta has come away, you will need to have complete bedrest until the bleeding stops.

Placental insufficiency occurs when the placenta doesn't function efficiently and the baby grows more slowly than normal because of lack of nourishment. If this happens, you will be told to rest so that the blood flow from the placenta to the baby can improve. A urine test will also be taken to see whether the health of the baby is being affected and whether induction is going to be necessary for the birth.

Above: If the weather is pleasant, you might well prefer to take your regular rests in the garden, but remember to support your legs. Below: Resting on your side may be more comfortable than lying on your back.

Your growing baby

The baby is filling almost all the space in your uterus and its head is now more or less in proportion with the rest of the body. The eyebrows and eyelashes are fully grown and the baby has quite a lot of hair which is still growing. The eyes, which can now open and close, are beginning to focus. The baby weighs around 1kg/2¼lb and is about 38cm/15in long.

WEEK 30: TRAVEL/BACKACHE

There is no reason why you shouldn't travel during pregnancy, but during the later stages you should check with your doctor if you are going abroad. Airlines may not be willing to take you once you are past 28 weeks because of the risk of a premature labour occurring.

If you want to fly you will need to check with the airline before you book a ticket; the airline may insist on a medical certificate stating that it is safe for you to travel. If you wish to visit a country where immunization is required, you will have to get medical advice because some vaccines should be avoided completely in pregnancy.

You will probably want to avoid long car journeys towards the end of pregnancy because you may find them uncomfortable. When travelling by car it is important to wear your seat belt so that it fits neatly across your thighs and above your abdomen, but not across the middle. If the belt was worn across your body it could possibly cause damage to your baby if you were involved in a car accident.

Backache

This can be particularly troublesome during the last months of pregnancy. Hormones have softened your ligaments and the additional weight you are carrying inevitably puts a strain on your stomach muscles, which in turn puts strain on your back muscles. If the backache you are suffering is particularly severe, always check it out with your doctor because it can indicate the presence of a kidney infection.

You and your body

You will feel larger and clumsier now and your movements will be slower. It is important to try to maintain good posture to prevent backache. You may have problems sleeping and become a bit breathless if you walk too fast or climb stairs.

Ease upper backache by lying on a firm surface with pillows under your head and knees. Lower backache can be helped by kneeling on all fours, with your back straight and your hands and knees well apart, then dropping your head and arching your back. Repeat this exercise several times.

You can help to avoid backache by wearing low-heeled shoes and trying not to hollow your back when you are standing. When you sit down, put a cushion in the small of your back; when you get out of a chair, push yourself right to the edge before attempting to stand up.

A firm mattress will help when you are lying down; when you get up from the lying position, roll onto your side and then push yourself slowly up. If you have to bend down, always bend your body from the knees and then squat down to pick up anything from the floor.

Your growing baby

The baby is beginning to move about less vigorously now because it has less space to move around in the uterus. To get comfortable it is likely to adopt a curled-up position with arms and legs crossed. The baby is now about 39cm/15½in long and weighs around 1.1kg/2⅓lb.

Don't fasten your seat belt over your bump as your baby could be damaged in a accident.

Fasten your seat belt under your bump and across your thighs to protect your baby.

Bending in pregnancy

1 *In later pregnancy particularly, bend your knees, not from the waist, and pick up the object when you are squatting.*

2 *As you get up from the squatting position, keep your back straight and lift up the object at arm's length.*

3 *As you gradually become upright, straighten your bent knees without making any jerky movements.*

How to relieve backache

1 *To relieve painful aches in your lower back in pregnancy, try this exercise. Kneel down on the floor on all fours with your back straight, your head facing down, and your hands and knees spaced well apart.*

2 *Drop your head right down and arch your back to stretch out the painful muscles, hold for several seconds, then release, raising your head up again. Repeat the exercise several times for the best relief.*

WEEK 31: DEALING WITH DISCOMFORT

You and your body

Breathlessness may be more of a problem now, especially if you overdo things. Try to get as much rest as possible and slow down any exercise regime to a pace that suits you. If your breasts feel uncomfortable when you go to bed, wear a maternity or specially designed sleep bra at night.

The baby is getting quite big and will be putting pressure on your diaphragm, which may mean that you are now finding it more difficult to breathe. This breathlessness should pass once the baby's head drops into the pelvis and becomes engaged in a few weeks' time. Try sitting and standing as straight as possible, and put some extra pillows behind your shoulders when you are in bed.

You are likely to need a larger size of bra towards the end of pregnancy and the one that you buy now should fit you after the baby is born. If you are intending to breast-feed, buy a front-opening nursing bra that will be suitable now and after the birth.

Choose a bra with wide adjustable straps and fastenings and which has a broad supportive band under the cups. Make sure that the cups fit comfortably and do not gape under the arms. Buy one made from cotton or a cotton mixture that will be more comfortable to wear, and allow your skin to breathe properly, particularly in hot weather.

BRAXTON HICKS CONTRACTIONS
During pregnancy you will experience contractions which may be uncomfortable but are not usually painful. These are known as Braxton Hicks contractions, which tighten the muscles of the uterus about every 20 minutes throughout pregnancy, although you have probably not been aware of them during the early months. In the last weeks of pregnancy these contractions become more noticeable as they begin to prepare the uterus for labour by drawing up the cervix and making it thinner. When you have these contractions, practise your breathing techniques for labour.

Exercise like swimming, where you are supported in the water, will keep you fit in late pregnancy. It may also relieve backache as the motion will stretch the back muscles.

Above: Keep a kick count of your baby's movements on a chart.
Below: Try sitting in a yoga position with your back straight to alleviate the pressure your baby is putting on your diaphragm.

KICK COUNTS

You can check on your baby's well-being by keeping a count of the fetal movements. If there is any concern about the baby's development you may be asked to keep a kick chart recording the first 10 movements each day. For your own peace of mind you should be aware of these movements so that if for any reason they become less frequent, or even stop altogether, you will notice at once. If you are ever concerned about lack of movement, seek some medical advice from your doctor immediately because it could indicate some trouble with the baby.

As your pregnancy progresses and the baby gets bigger it has less room to manoeuvre, so movements will be more noticeable, but less frequent. By the end of your pregnancy the baby will probably move between 10 and 12 times in a 12-hour period.

Your growing baby

The organs are almost completely developed, apart from the lungs which are still not fully mature. The brain is still growing and the nerve cells and connections are now working. A protective sheath is developing around the nerve fibres so that messages travel faster, enabling the baby to learn more. It can feel pain, will move if prodded and you can feel it jump at loud noises. The baby is around 40cm/15¾in long and weighs about 1.4kg/3lb.

WEEK 32: POSITIONS FOR LABOUR

It is a good idea to practise some of the positions that will help you through the different stages of labour. During the first stage you should try to stay upright and keep active. Being upright will make your contractions stronger and more efficient. It will also allow gravity to keep the baby's head pressed down, which will help your cervix to dilate faster so that labour is speeded up. Remaining active will give you more control over labour so that you should feel less pain. If you are lying down, your uterus presses on the large blood vessels running down your back and this can reduce the blood flow through the placenta to and from the baby. If you feel you want to lie down during labour, try to position yourself on your side rather than on your back.

COPING WITH CONTRACTIONS

You should aim to give the baby as much room as possible in your pelvis and the best way to achieve this is by keeping your knees well apart and leaning forward so that the uterus tilts away from your spine. During the first-stage contractions it may help to lean against your partner, or if you prefer you can kneel down resting your arms and head on a cushion on the seat of a chair. If you find being upright tiring, try kneeling on all fours. This allows you to keep the weight of the baby off your lower back.

By the time your contractions are coming every few minutes you may want to adopt a squatting position, or you could try kneeling forward onto a pile of cushions or a bean bag with your legs wide apart. It may

You and your body

If you work, you may have left by now or will have a date when you are going to leave. Enjoy the last weeks of your pregnancy and spend time singing and talking to your baby. You may find your baby's movements uncomfortable now that it is so much bigger. Occasionally, you may feel its feet getting stuck under your ribs.

help if your partner massages your back while you are in this position.

When you reach the second stage you'll want to find a comfortable position for the birth. If you lie on your back you will literally have to push the baby uphill. If you remain upright your abdominal muscles will work more efficiently as you bear down, and gravity will help the baby out. Try squatting, supported on both sides, or with your partner supporting you from behind, so that your pelvis is at its widest and you have control over the pelvic floor

Labour positions

1 *Relax on all fours by flopping forward onto a pile of cushions or a bean bag to give the baby as much room as possible in the pelvis. Your partner can help by massaging your back.*

2 *Take the weight of the baby off your spine by kneeling on the floor on all fours with your arms and legs wide apart. Keep the small of your back flat and not hollowed.*

Your growing baby

The baby is now very energetic and it will have periods of extreme activity, and you will feel it twisting and turning. As it continues to grow it will have less and less room to move in, so it will soon settle, probably in the head-down position, ready for birth. The baby is about 40.5cm/16in long and weighs about 1.6kg/3½lb.

which you will need to relax. Kneeling with your legs wide apart and supported on both sides is another good position for pushing.

Once you have tried these positions, experiment with others which you feel may be right for you during labour. Try them on the floor, on the bed, leaning on or against furniture, or using your partner for support. This way, when you are in labour, you will already know how to get into positions that are comfortable for you and that will help you cope with contractions.

Partner support

1 *Practise using your partner for support during labour by leaning back against him, allowing him to take your weight.*

2 *Stand with feet well apart and lean on your partner, putting your head on your arms to ease pressure on your uterus.*

3 *Kneel on all fours with your forearms on the floor and your knees spread wide so that your abdomen is hanging between them. It can help to rock backwards and forwards in this position.*

4 *In this squatting position, your pelvis is wide open and the baby's head is pressed down. You may find that it helps to place your hands on the floor to give yourself some support.*

WEEK 33: EMOTIONS IN LATE PREGNANCY

It is not just your body that is going through great changes while you are pregnant. Your whole way of life is changing and this can lead to conflicting emotions, especially during the last few months. You may wonder how you are going to cope with all the new responsibilities and be concerned about your baby – whether it will be born perfect in every way. Vivid dreams are common at this time and can be worrying, especially if they are about the birth or babies. You may even feel occasionally that the whole thing has been a ghastly mistake and that you want to go back to the way things were before you became pregnant. Don't worry, all these feelings are quite normal.

It helps to talk about your fears and concerns, either to your partner or to a close friend who has had similar feelings. Parentcraft classes are also a good place to discuss these worries, especially as you will be with other women who are experiencing the same emotions. If you find that talking about it doesn't help and that anxiety is taking over your life, discuss how you feel with your midwife or doctor.

YOUR PARTNER

It is easy to forget that an expectant father is also going through some emotional changes as he comes to terms with impending parenthood. He doesn't have any outward sign of the change that is about to occur in his life, but that doesn't mean he isn't feeling the same concerns as you. He also has additional worries about you and how you will cope during labour; he may even secretly fear for your safety during the birth. If he is now solely responsible for providing financially for you and the baby he

You and your body

Your weight gain should have slowed down. If it hasn't and you are still gaining more than 1kg/2¼lb a week, you should check with your doctor that everything is all right.

may be feeling considerable stress. Make time to talk to each other about your feelings and try to ensure that these last weeks before the birth are special for you both. Share the preparation for the birth so that each of you is involved in what is going to happen. Plan some treats where you can be alone together, such as dinner at a favourite restaurant, a trip to the theatre, or a weekend away at a hotel. By making time for yourselves you are less likely to have misunderstandings which could lead to hurt and disappointment.

At ante-natal classes you learn what to expect in labour and the different positions you can adopt. Your partner is usually welcome to come with you and find out how he can help.

Your growing baby

The fingernails are fully formed although the toenails are not quite so advanced. The vernix covering the skin has become thicker. The lungs are almost fully developed and the baby will be practising breathing in preparation for the birth. It measures around 41.5cm/16½in and weighs about 1.8kg/4lb.

OTHER CHILDREN

If you have other children you may have told them about the new baby early on in your pregnancy. Very young children will need to have it explained to them over and over again, because the concept of a new baby is hard for them to grasp. Older children will probably be very excited and will enjoy being involved in any preparations you are making for their brother or sister.

How children react once the baby has arrived depends a lot on their age and personality, as well as their relationship with you. A pre-school child may react by being naughty for a period in an attempt to get your attention. A toddler who has recently been potty- trained, may start wetting or dirtying him- or herself again. Both age groups may start waking at night. Use common sense and tact to minimize any problems. Talk to your children about the new baby, encourage their help and involvement when he or she is born, but always make sure that they have special time with you on their own.

Right: Let an older child feel your bump, and talk to him or her about their new brother or sister, so they can get used to the idea of a new family member.
Below: When you are spending time with your other children, talk to them about the new baby.

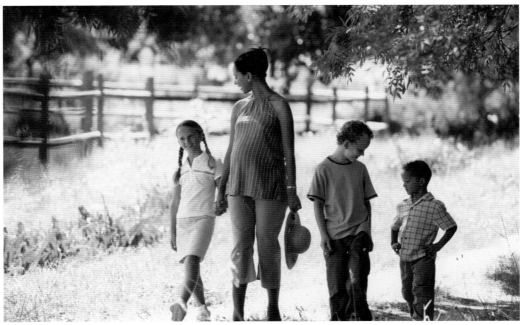

WEEK 34: OLDER FIRST-TIME MOTHERS

If you are 35 or over, you will have been offered an amniocentesis because of the higher risk of fetal abnormality. The amniotic fluid will have been screened for a number of chromosomal disorders, which include Down's syndrome and spina bifida. Of course, you don't have to have this test, but many mothers find it reassuring.

It is important that you attend all your ante-natal clinics so that a close check can be kept on you and the unborn baby all through pregnancy. Many older expectant mothers prefer to have the ante-natal care at a hospital where expert medical help

is on hand. The risk to the baby during labour and birth increases with rising maternal age, but many factors affect labour, including the general health of the mother during pregnancy.

Although nearly 70 per cent of women over 30 have normal deliveries, there is a slightly greater risk of complications during labour for women who are over 35. This is usually because the baby is in distress through lack of oxygen because of placental deterioration. As a result of these complications older women are more likely to have medical intervention such as forceps.

You and your body

Your blood pressure may be slightly raised and you will probably be told to take things easy. Swelling of the hands and feet could also be a problem so try to get as much rest as possible, preferably with your feet up.

BIRTH AND THE OLDER MOTHER

Most older women go full term, and if you are between 30 and 34 there is no reason why you shouldn't have a natural birth. If you are 35 or over, or if there is a suggestion that your baby may be small, you may be offered continuous monitoring. This may also be necessary if there is a some sign of staining. This means

Seeing your baby on an ultrasound scan can be very reassuring.

that you will be unable to move around freely. But this is a small price to pay for a healthy baby.

Babies born to older mothers are more likely to be born preterm, often because of the failure of the placenta, so that the baby is no longer getting sufficient nourishment and oxygen. If this happens you will have a forceps or ventouse delivery, or you may be offered a Caesarean.

Below: The doctor will talk about your baby and give you a printout of your scan.

Your growing baby

The weight gain continues to increase. The eyes respond to bright lights and the baby will practise blinking; eyebrows and eyelashes are fully developed. A boy's testicles will have descended into the groin. The baby is 43cm/17in long and weighs about 2kg/4½lb.

Right: Regular ante-natal checks are particularly important for older mothers.

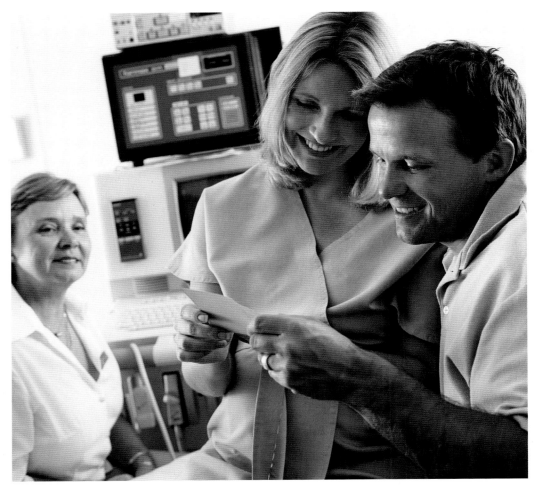

WEEK 35: FINAL PREPARATIONS

Even though your baby is not due for some weeks, you should be ready in case he or she decides to put in an early appearance. Check the nursery and make sure all the baby's sheets and blankets have been washed and aired. Sort out all the baby clothes and put the ones you will want immediately after the birth in your hospital case. It's a good idea to stock up on non-perishable goods and to fill the freezer. This will save you from having to do a lot of shopping over the next few weeks and will allow you more time with the baby when you first come home.

Make sure you know where your partner is going to be over the next few weeks; if he is out and about it may be a good idea for you both to have mobile phones. Keep your car filled with petrol and make sure that you both know the quickest route to the hospital. Have a list of emergency numbers, including a local taxi firm, beside the telephone.

You and your body

Discuss any worries you may have about labour and birth with your doctor or midwife. You will be feeling tired and even a little fed up, so try to get as much rest as you can. Pay special attention to your diet: you will be needing another 200 calories a day during these last weeks. Some practical planning now can save time and forestall anxiety at the time of labour and delivery.

THE HOSPITAL

Pack what you want to take to hospital several weeks before the delivery date; keep the bag where you can easily get it when the time comes. Remember that there are three separate aspects to consider: labour, your hospital stay, and going-home clothes for you and the baby.

You should bring any personal items that will make life more comfortable for you during labour. Include anything from an MP3 player and your favourite music to a face cloth and massage oils. You may even want to take along a bean bag if you are planning an active labour and your hospital doesn't provide these. Leave some room for last-minute items such as an ice pack for backache and even a snack and drink for your partner. Don't forget to put your birthplan and maternity record right at the top so that you can give these to the midwife when you arrive at the hospital. It is sensible

It is sensible to pack a small bag for your brief stay in hospital well in advance in case you have to leave in a rush. Don't forget some clothes for your new baby.

You might need to get to the hospital quickly, so have your bag packed and keep a local taxi number close to hand.

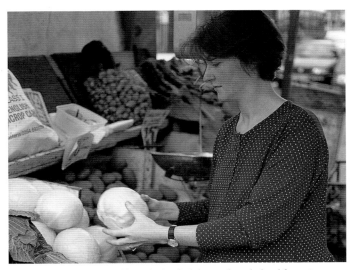

It is a good idea to buy vegetables and other food that can be cooked and frozen in preparation for when you return from the hospital.

to pack things for labour separately, since you will want to be able to get to them quickly.

How much you pack for the hospital depends on your planned length of stay after the birth. The hospital may issue a list of the items that you will need to bring with you. But if it doesn't, ask your midwife whether you need to take in baby clothes and nappies, or contact the maternity unit direct.

If you are staying in for a few days and aren't too tired, you might want to write cards to your friends and relatives announcing your baby's arrival, so remember to include birth announcement cards, your address book, and stamps. You should also bring a supply of small change in case you need to use hospital pay phones.

You will need clothes for you and the baby when it's time for you to return home. It is sensible to pack a small bag now with all the items you think you'll want for your return journey; you can either bring it with you or your partner can bring it later. Remember that although you will feel considerably slimmer than you were before the birth, it takes a while before you get your figure back, so your going-home outfit will still need to be loose.

Your growing baby

The baby is putting on weight each day and now fills most of the uterus, so you may find it uncomfortable when it moves around. The baby now does body rolls rather than the more energetic movements it made when it was smaller. It is now about 445cm/17½in long and weighs around 2.3kg/5lb.

WEEK 36: DISCOMFORTS IN LATE PREGNANCY

You and your body

You will be able to feel the top of your uterus just below your breastbone. This can make breathing uncomfortable and you may suffer from pain in your ribcage. Your ante-natal checks will be weekly from now on.

As you find getting around more difficult and everything generally more of an effort, you may become irritable over the smallest things. You will be impatient for your baby to arrive, and concern about the impending birth and worries about how you will cope with being a parent can make you short-tempered, especially with your partner. Tell him how you are feeling so that he understands why you are being so irritable and perhaps not paying him as much attention as usual.

Aches or pains around your pubic area, in your groin, or down the inside of your legs can be caused by your baby's head pressing on the nerves, or by your pelvic joints beginning to soften in preparation for labour. Pain under your ribs is caused by the expanding uterus pushing the ribs up. These aches and pains are not serious, but they can be quite uncomfortable. Sitting or standing as straight as you can, or stretching upwards, will help ease most of these discomforts, although

you may find lying down better for relief of pelvic pain. If you get severe pain in your abdomen, or if you suffer any abdominal pain that is also accompanied by vaginal bleeding, you must get in touch with your doctor at once.

It is quite common to suffer from heartburn and nausea towards the end of pregnancy. This is caused by the enlarged uterus pressing on your stomach. It often helps to eat

Soaking in a warm bath can help to relieve any aches and pains you are suffering.

small meals at more frequent intervals, rather than two or three big meals a day.

ANTE-NATAL CHECK

If there is any concern about the size of your pelvis in relation to your baby's size, or there is some other reason for the baby's delivery not being straightforward, you will be offered a scan and a Caesarean may be discussed. If this is thought to be necessary, the doctor at the hospital will explain the medical procedures that will be used.

As your baby increases in size, you may begin to find breathing uncomfortable and get some pain in your ribcage.

Your growing baby

The nervous system is maturing and the baby is getting ready for birth by starting to practise breathing movements, sucking, and swallowing. It is now about 46cm/18¼in long and weighs around 2.5kg/5½lb.

In this late stage of pregnancy you will probably be able to feel the top of your uterus which is now positioned just below your breastbone.

WEEK 37: AS BIRTH APPROACHES

Between weeks 36 and 38 the baby's head may "engage". This is when it settles downwards, deep in your pelvis ready for the birth. You should feel some relief from the pressure in your abdomen when this happens which is why it is sometimes referred to as "lightening". You will start to feel less breathless now because the baby is no longer putting any pressure on your diaphragm and your lungs. If this is not your first baby, the head may not engage until you actually go into labour.

Your growing baby

The lanugo, the fine hair that covers the baby's body, is beginning to wear off. The baby has started to produce a hormone called cortisone, which will help the lungs to become fully matured so that they are ready to cope with breathing once the baby is born. The baby will be practising breathing although there is no air in its lungs. The baby is now about 47cm/18½ in long and weighs around 2.7kg/6lb.

PREMATURE AND TWIN BIRTHS
If the baby is born before 37 weeks it will be described as being preterm or premature. Most premature babies are nursed in a special care baby unit (SCBU) or, if very sick or small, an intensive care baby unit (ICBU). Babies are given expert care and attention in these facilities, so even those who are born as young as 24 weeks have a chance of survival.

This is probably the last time for a while that you will have time to yourself, so make the most of it and rest often.

With modern technology even babies as young as 24 weeks normally survive in the special baby units.

If you are giving birth to twins, the labour doesn't usually take any longer than if you are giving birth to a single baby (singleton). Because twins tend to be smaller babies, the labour and birth can often be easier and less painful. Once the birth canal has been stretched to allow one baby to be born, the second baby will usually be born quite quickly. If twins share the placenta, they will both be born before it is delivered. Even if they are fraternal twins and each have their own placenta, they will usually be born first, although occasionally one baby is born, followed by its placenta, before the second baby arrives.

You and your body

Your baby could arrive at any time from now until the end of week 42, so check that you have everything organized. You will probably be given the chance to visit the hospital and see where you are going to give birth. Don't be afraid to ask questions if there is anything you don't understand about hospital procedures.

Sometime between now and the birth, you may experience a sudden burst of energy, known as the nesting instinct. Don't overdo things and decide to spring-clean your whole house. Remember that you will shortly need all your energy reserves for the exhausting demands of labour.

As the birth approaches, it is a good time for you and your partner to start making a list of names that you both like.

WEEK 38: INDUCTION/PAIN RELIEF IN LABOUR

You and your body

You will notice that the baby is moving about less now that it is head down in the uterus. You may be feeling tired and rather depressed about the waiting so try to keep busy.

Sometimes labour has to be induced because of a problem such as pre-eclampsia, bleeding, diabetes, or being well past your due date. Induction techniques include:

Pessaries Prostaglandins are naturally occurring hormones which help dilate the cervix. A synthetic form of prostaglandin, either in a pessary or gel, is applied internally to the cervix to soften and thin it. It may require two or three treatments before labour starts.

Artificial rupture of the membranes (ARM) This involves the puncturing of the membranes of the amniotic sac. Once ruptured, prostaglandins from the amniotic fluid are released and labour follows.

Syntocinon drip This is a concentrated synthetic form of oxytocin, a natural hormone that makes the uterus contract. Given through an intravenous drip, it acts quickly and produces contractions that may be stronger than those of natural labour. Some hospitals offer an epidural with this form of induction.

PAIN RELIEF

If you decide to have a completely natural birth make sure that this is marked clearly on your birthplan and inform the medical staff who will be attending you during labour. Remember that you can always change your mind if you find coping with the pain too difficult. If you have decided to opt for some form of pain relief, there are a number of options you can choose from:

Gas and air (Entonox) A mixture of oxygen and nitrous oxide which is breathed in through a mask or mouthpiece and takes the edge off pain. This is the most controllable form of pain relief because you hold the mask or mouthpiece and regulate the gas and air intake. The gas is processed in your lungs so it doesn't affect the baby.

Injections Drugs like pethidine and meptid can be given during the first stage of labour. They will help you relax and relieve pain but they can make your baby sleepy.

Epidural A local anaesthetic is injected into the space between your spinal column and the spinal cord, numbing the nerves that serve the uterus. An epidural or spinal block may be used if a Caesarean delivery is performed because it allows the mother to stay awake while her baby is being delivered.

An anaesthetist is needed to give an epidural injection, which takes around 15 minutes to set up, and then usually requires topping up every hour and a half.

Transcutaneous electrical nerve stimulation (TENS) This is a technique which involves a weak electric current being used to block pain sensations in the brain and to stimulate the release of endorphins, the body's natural painkilling

By holding a mask to your face, you can breathe in oxygen and nitrous oxide for pain relief during contractions.

hormones. TENS is not available at all hospitals so you may need to hire a machine before you go into labour. Your midwife should be able to give you all the necessary details.

An epidural injection into the spinal area helps deaden the nerves around the uterus.

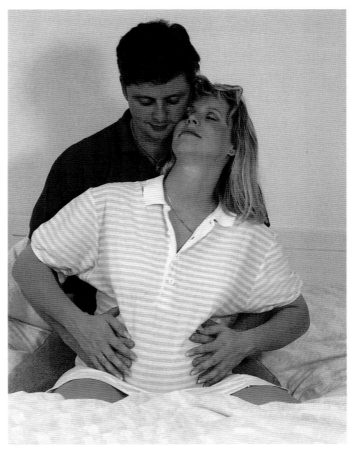

At the most painful times in your labour, lean on your partner for support and encouragement. He can also massage your back if it is really painful.

Pads from a TENS machine can be fitted to your back to ease pain in labour.

Alternative pain relief Both acupuncture and hypnosis can be used effectively to relieve pain during childbirth, but if you are having a hospital birth you will need to ask for permission to have a private practitioner with you during labour.

If used correctly, massage, aromatherapy, and reflexology can all help to ease labour. You should get some expert advice before the birth if you intend to use any of these techniques.

Your growing baby

The baby has put on fat so that it now appears rounded and its skin has a pinkish look. The hair may be as long as 5cm/2in and the nails already need cutting. The vernix, which has been protecting the skin of the growing baby from the amniotic fluid, is beginning to dissolve. At this stage of your pregnancy, the baby now measures about 48cm/19in and weighs around 2.9kg/6½lb.

WEEK 39: COMPLICATIONS DURING BIRTH

The ideal position for your baby to be born is with its head lying down with its back against your abdomen. This way it has less distance to rotate in the birth canal. Sometimes a baby is in an abnormal position which can make birth more complicated, but this does not necessarily mean that it can't be born in the normal way.

An occipito posterior position means that the baby is lying with its back towards your back and, if it fails

to turn, will be delivered normally, but will be born face up. This way of lying often leads to a long, back-aching labour.

In a deep transverse arrest, the baby's head partially rotates in the birth canal and then becomes stuck with its face towards one side. The baby will need to be helped out. This can sometimes also happen if you push too hard by mistake in the second stage of labour.

Disproportion means that the baby's head is too big for your pelvis. A scan will be done to decide whether there is enough room for a normal delivery to take place. If there isn't, your baby will probably be born by Caesarean.

BREECH BIRTH

A small number of babies don't turn in the last weeks of pregnancy. This means that their feet or bottom would come out first so the birth canal will not have been stretched enough when the head, the largest part of the baby's body, is ready to be born. Doctors have different opinions about the best way of delivering a breech baby; some insist that a Caesarean is the safest method, others believe that birth should take place under an epidural, and some think that if the mother remains mobile throughout the first stage of labour the baby will get itself into a good position for birth. It may then be helped out with forceps or by vacuum extraction.

Birth positions

A normal birth

A breech birth

You and your body

The waiting is nearly over and you will probably be feeling both excited and apprehensive. You may be having quite strong Braxton Hicks contractions as the cervix softens in readiness for the birth. Although you may be feeling heavy and weary, don't simply sit around waiting for something to happen. Keep up your social life and talk to other friends from your parent-craft classes who are at the same stage as you.

FORCEPS DELIVERY

In a forceps delivery, your legs will be put up in stirrups and then the forceps, which are like a pair of large, shallow metal spoons, will be inserted into the vagina and cupped around the baby's head. The doctor helps the baby out while you push.

VACUUM EXTRACTION

Vacuum extraction (ventouse) is now used more often than the forceps method. With this technique the doctor places a suction cup on the baby's head and the baby is sucked out as you push down with each contraction.

If the birth canal is not going to be big enough for the baby's head and there is a risk that the perineum may tear, a small cut is made in this area under local anaesthetic.

Your growing baby

The baby is now able to function on its own, although it is still getting nourishment from the placenta. The baby is in position for birth and is about 49cm/19¼in long and weighs around 3.1kg/7lb.

This type of incision is called an episiotomy and is stitched after the birth, again under local anaesthetic.

FETAL MONITORING

This keeps a check on the unborn baby's heartbeat during labour and the birth. Monitoring can be done the low-tech way by simply placing a stethoscope against the abdomen to listen to the baby's heart, or through electronic fetal monitoring (EFM). There are two types of EFM and both give a continuous readout of the baby's heart and uterine contractions; if the EFM method is used then you are having a high-tech birth.

Below: If you need a forceps delivery, your legs will be put up in stirrups.

Above: Electronic fetal monitoring (EFM) involves placing a belt around your bump which is attached to a monitor. This gives a continuous readout of the baby's heart.

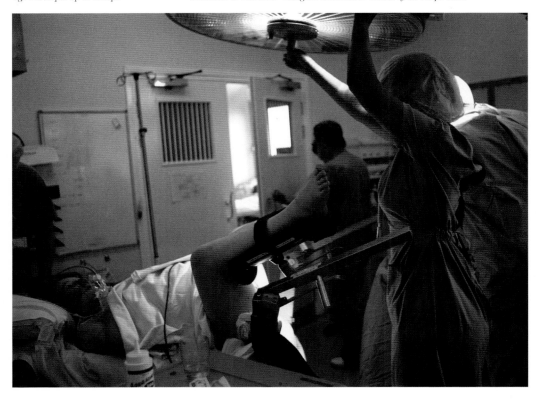

WEEK 40: LABOUR AND BIRTH

It is unlikely that you won't recognize the beginnings of labour as the signs, when they come, are generally unmistakable. There are three main indications that labour is about to start, or has started, and they can occur in any order. Once one or more of these has occurred you should let the hospital or midwife know immediately:

A show The protective plug, which sealed the cervix at the neck of the uterus, comes away and passes down the vagina. It usually appears as a small amount of bloodstained mucus. A show occurs before labour starts or during the first stage.

Waters breaking The membranes of the amniotic sac in which your baby has been floating break, causing either a trickle or a sudden gush of clear fluid from the vagina. If the fluid is yellow, greenish, or brown in colour you will need to go to the hospital straight away because the baby may be in distress. Your waters can break hours before labour starts or when it is well underway.

Contractions The regular tightening of the muscles of the uterus occurs throughout labour. During the first stage, the contractions thin out and dilate the cervix from closed to 10cm/4in open; in the second stage they help to push the baby down the vagina and after the birth they then deliver the placenta (afterbirth). For most women they feel rather like bad period pains. The contractions may also be accompanied by uncomfortable backache, sickness, and diarrhoea.

Your growing baby

Your baby is curled up, head down, in the fetal position with legs drawn up underneath and waiting to be born. He or she measures about 50cm/19¾in and weighs around 3.4kg/7½lb.

You and your body

You will probably be impatient for labour to start as you approach your EDD. If nothing has happened by your due date try not to be too disappointed; only around five per cent of babies actually arrive on the date they were expected. Keep yourself busy and make plans for each day so that you are not just sitting and waiting for something to happen. Once you are close to your EDD you may feel more confident wearing a sanitary towel just in case your waters break.

During the first stage of labour, you can involve your partner by leaning and holding onto him for comfort and also physical support.

Being on all fours during labour will keep the weight of the baby off your back as your partner helps to ease your discomfort.

STAGES OF LABOUR

The first stage There are three stages of labour and the first is usually the longest, lasting generally for up to 12 hours for a first baby. Contractions, which may have started off as mild and infrequent will, by the end of the first stage, be very strong and coming close together. Once they are coming

Tips for labour

● Keep active for as long as you can during the first stage of labour.

● Don't be on your own: get your partner, mother or a friend to stay with you once labour has started.

● If your waters break check that the fluid is clear: yellow, greenish, or brown fluid could mean that your baby is in distress and you should go to the hospital immediately.

● Ask for pain relief if you need it.

● Try different positions to help you cope with the pain of contractions.

● Get your birth partner to make sure your wishes are known to whoever is delivering your baby. You may be too busy coping with contractions to explain clearly what you want.

● Put your baby to the breast soon after the birth. This will stimulate your milk supply and help to speed up the delivery of the placenta.

regularly every 10 minutes, or are each lasting for around 45 seconds, you should start getting ready to go to the hospital, or call the midwife if you are having your baby at home. When you get to the hospital, or the midwife attending you at home

arrives, you will be examined to see how far your cervix has dilated and your blood pressure will be checked.

Although you will be able to carry on fairly normally for quite a lot of the first stage you should have someone with you. You will need to

eat plenty of light snacks during this stage as your body is having to work very hard and will need plenty of energy in order to cope.

Towards the end of the first stage you will go into what is known as the transitional stage which can last for anything up to an hour. During this transitional period your baby moves down the birth canal and you will feel pressure on your back passage which may make you want to start pushing, even though the cervix is not fully dilated. By using the breathing techniques you have been taught you will be able to control this urge.

The second stage Once the cervix is fully dilated and you start pushing the baby out you have entered the second stage. It can last for as little as half an hour or for as long as two hours or more. Once the baby's head is visible to the midwife she will tell you to start pushing. When the head reaches the vaginal opening you will be told to pant in short breaths so that the head can be delivered as slowly as possible. This allows the skin and muscle of the perineum to stretch so that the head can be born. If it seems likely that you will tear badly an episiotomy, a small cut in the perineum, the area between the vagina and anus, may be given. Once the head is born your baby's body will follow quite quickly. As soon as your baby is delivered it will be lifted onto your stomach for you to see it. The umbilical cord will be clamped and cut and the midwife will check the baby to make sure that it is all right and breathing properly. You may want to put your baby straight to the breast. You'll certainly wish to admire it with your partner and welcome your child into the world.

With a water birth, contractions can be eased by the warm water. Your baby can be delivered in the water or outside.

If you have your baby in the water, he will be given to you immediately after the birth for you and your partner to cuddle.

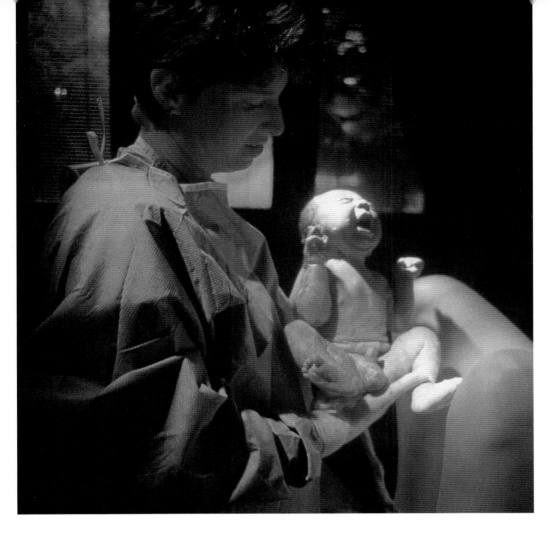

Above: A doctor holding a newborn baby boy, with the umbilical cord still attached, at a home delivery.
Right: A Caesarean is performed when there are risks from natural childbirth. The baby is delivered through an incision.

The third stage The final stage is the birth of the placenta, which usually takes less than half an hour. You may be offered an injection as your baby is being born to speed up the placenta's delivery. The midwife will check to see that the placenta is whole and that nothing has been left inside you. If you had an episiotomy it will be stitched up.

PART TWO

BABYCARE

A NEW BABY can seem rather overwhelming, especially if this is your first experience of motherhood. Suddenly you are responsible for the care and welfare of a very demanding little person who needs looking after almost 24 hours a day. If you have never fed, bathed or changed a baby you need to learn how to carry out these daily routines. This section looks at basic babycare and explains, in simple terms, everything that you are likely to need to know about caring for your baby during the first year of life.

It is important to take care of yourself too, especially in the days after the birth, so your post-natal care is described at the beginning of this section.

Feeding your baby should be a special time for you both, regardless of whether you are breast- or bottle-feeding in the early months. But when things go wrong, or your baby doesn't feed in the way you expect, it can be difficult to know what to do. Breast- and bottle-feeding are discussed here, along with the latest information on when and how to introduce first foods.

When your child is unwell it is quite natural to be concerned. Knowing what to do and when you need to call the doctor comes with experience. In the meantime the section on common childhood ailments such as coughs, colds, teething and sickness tells you how to relieve discomfort and when you should seek medical help. There is also a comprehensive first aid section which explains exactly what you should do if your child has an accident.

Caring for your baby will take up a great deal of your time during the first year, so use the daily routines of bathing, feeding and changing as a time to get to know and enjoy each other.

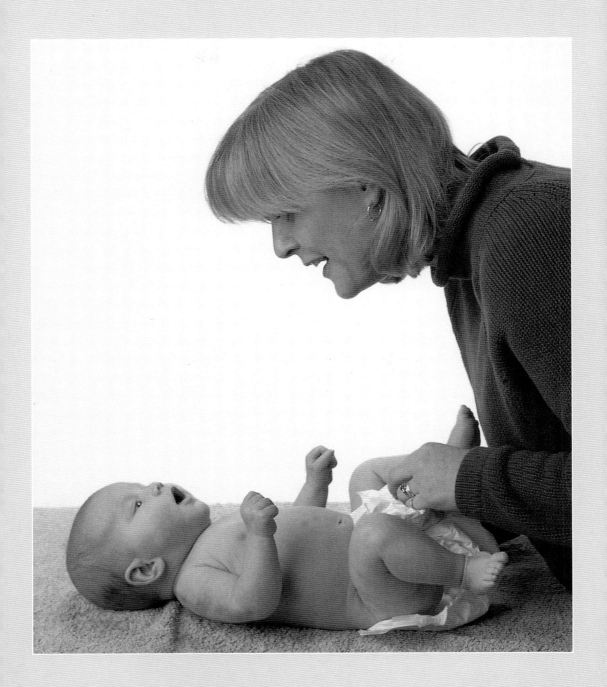

POST-NATAL CARE

Although your new baby will probably give you great emotional satisfaction, you may be physically uncomfortable. Your body has gone through many changes during pregnancy and it will take a while for it to return to its pre-pregnancy state.

Six weeks after the birth your doctor will examine you to make sure that everything is returning to normal; this also gives you a chance to discuss any worries you may have. The doctor will take your blood pressure and check a sample of your urine. Your breasts and abdomen will be examined and the doctor will make sure that any stitches have healed properly. You will probably have an internal examination to check the size and position of your uterus and you may have a cervical smear test if one is due.

If your baby was born in hospital, a midwife or doctor will probably talk to you about contraception before you go home. Alternatively, you can discuss this at your six-week check. Don't take any risks; to avoid getting pregnant again you should use contraception as soon as you resume intercourse. It is an old wives' tale that breast-feeding prevents conception.

If you were not immune to rubella (German measles) during your pregnancy, you will probably be offered the immunization before you leave hospital or at your six-week check-up. Ask your doctor if you are at all unsure about your immunity.

YOUR BODY
Immediately after the birth your breasts will produce colostrum, a high-protein liquid full of antibodies. Then, after the pregnancy hormones decline, your main milk supply should come in around the third or fourth day. At this time the breasts swell, feel hard, and can sometimes be painful. Bathing them with warm water is soothing, and letting the baby have frequent feeds will also help.

This initial swelling subsides after a few days as both you and your baby get used to feeding. However, if you have decided to bottle-feed, your breasts will remain full for a few days until they gradually stop producing milk. Your breasts will probably never be quite as firm as they were before pregnancy, but a well-fitting support bra will help greatly.

After delivery your abdomen will probably be quite flabby and wrinkled because of slack muscles and stretched skin. Gentle post-natal exercises will help tighten up your abdominal and vaginal muscles, so make time to do them every day. If you feel you're not disciplined enough to exercise on your own, join a local post-natal class.

Following the birth you will have a vaginal discharge which is known as lochia. This will be like a very heavy period for a few days, with the flow gradually getting lighter until it disappears within a few weeks. Use maternity pads or large sanitary towels to absorb the discharge because there is a risk of infection if you use tampons in the early weeks after the birth.

Your newborn will find your physical presence very reassuring during the first days after the birth. She will also find your smell comfortingly familiar.

Post-natal exercises

Pelvic floor: Lie flat on the floor with your legs drawn up and slightly apart. Close the back passage by drawing it in, hold for the count of four, then relax. Do as often as possible.

Tummy toner: Sit up with knees bent and feet flat on the floor. Fold arms in front. Lean back until you feel the abdominal muscles tighten, hold, then sit up and relax. Repeat several times.

1 *Curl-ups: This exercise will help strengthen your vertical abdominal muscles. Lie on your back with a pillow under your head, your knees bent and your feet flat on the floor.*

2 *Pull in your abdominal muscles and, raising your head, stretch your arms towards your knees. Hold for the count of five and then relax slowly. Repeat several times.*

Leg slide: Lie with your head on a pillow with the small of your back pressed against the floor and your knees bent. Gently slide one leg away from your body until it is fully extended, keeping the small of your back pressed against the floor for as long as you can. Slowly draw the leg back towards your body and then repeat with the other leg. Do this several times.

Your uterus will take about six weeks to return to its original size. If you are breast-feeding you may feel it contract as you feed the baby.

If your perineum (the skin between the vagina and anus) was bruised during labour, or if you had stitches, you will find that anything that puts pressure on the area painful. Take paracetamol to relieve the pain and ease the soreness with a gel pack held against the perineum or by sitting in warm water. Try drying the area with a hand-held hair dryer, set on cool, rather than

with a bath towel. Do not put the dryer too close to your skin, or use it in the bathroom.

GETTING BACK INTO SHAPE
Despite losing the combined weight of the baby, the placenta, and the amniotic fluid, you will still be heavier than you were before you became pregnant. You may even find that you have to continue to wear maternity clothes for a short while. As your uterus shrinks during the six weeks following the birth you will lose more weight, but you will need

to watch your diet to regain your pre-pregnancy shape. Eat regularly and healthily and don't be tempted, because you're short of time, to snack on foods containing empty calories such as sweets and fizzy drinks. If the weight isn't disappearing as fast as you'd like, ask your health visitor for advice. Do not attempt any diet now or while you are breast-feeding – this would increase stress as your body is struggling to regain its equilibrium. Doing exercises will help you get your figure back, get you moving again, and make you feel fitter.

1 *Waist trimmer: Lie on the floor with your arms away from your side, with your knees bent and feet flat. Pull in your abdominals and, with knees together, roll over to the right. Take your knees back to the middle and pause.*

2 *Rest briefly, then pull in your abdominals again and roll your knees to the left, then back to the middle and pause. Keep your shoulders flat on the floor as you roll from side to side. Repeat six times and work up to 20.*

1 *Foot exercises: These will help improve your circulation and are especially important if you are confined to bed. Lie with your legs straight and knees together and bend and stretch your feet.*

2 *Flex one foot, pulling the toes up towards you while pointing the other foot away from you. Repeat, alternating the feet. Do this exercise quite briskly for about 30 seconds.*

Post-natal depression

Two or three days after the birth you may suddenly feel very tearful and depressed. This is commonly called the "third day blues", or the milk blues, because it usually coincides with the milk coming into your breasts. These feelings are caused by all the hormonal changes that are going on in your body and should disappear after a few days. If they don't go away, however, you need to talk to your health visitor or doctor. You may be suffering from

post-natal depression (PND) which, if left untreated, can go on for several months. Symptoms of PND include feeling unhappy and wretched as well as irritable and exhausted, yet unable to sleep. You may also lose all interest in food, or find yourself eating too much and then feeling guilty afterwards. PND is one of the most common illnesses following childbirth and it is likely that it is related to the huge hormonal changes that take place at the time of the birth, but it is still unclear as

to why it affects some women so badly but not others. If you think you are suffering from PND, don't feel ashamed and don't ignore it. You need help and the sooner you ask for it the sooner you will begin to feel better and able to cope with life again. Post-natal depression is a common condition. Many women are affected by it, and it needs to be treated early on, not ignored in the hope that it will just go away on its own.

Those for strengthening the pelvic floor are among the most important post-natal exercises. The pelvic floor muscles support the bladder, uterus, and rectum, so it is vital that their tone is restored after being stretched during childbirth.

TIREDNESS AND RELAXATION
Tiredness goes hand in hand with being a new mother, but you need rest to help your body recover from childbirth. It is tempting to use the baby's sleep times to catch up on chores, but do try to have a nap or proper rest at least once during the day. You and your child are more important than housework, so find ways to cut down the work. Accept offers of help and, if no one volunteers, don't be afraid to ask people.

Another way to cope with tiredness or stress is relaxation, so try using the ante-natal relaxation exercises to help you now. Also a long, lazy bath with a few drops of relaxing oil in the water will work wonders. For a real treat, ask your partner to give you a massage using a specially formulated oil before you go to sleep.

HAIR AND NAILS
The condition of your hair is likely to change during this time. It may become more greasy, or the opposite may happen and it will become noticeably drier than before. You may also suffer an increase in hair loss or your hair may seem a lot thicker than it did before you became pregnant. Whichever

condition applies to you, wash your hair using a mild shampoo and avoid rubbing or brushing oily hair too much as this will only stimulate the sebaceous glands to produce more oil. Dry hair should be conditioned after every wash and, if possible, allowed to dry naturally.

Your nails are made of the same tissue as your hair, so if you are having problems with one you are likely to have problems with the other. These are due to fluctuating hormone levels and as soon as these settle your hair and nails will return to normal. Meanwhile, include enough protein and B vitamins in your diet because these will help improve the condition of both your hair and nails.

Left: A long, lazy bath with a few drops of oil, such as lavender, in the water will help you to relax.

Below: A stimulating rub with a loofah brush or mitt will help remove dead cells on the skin's surface, and will stimulate the circulation.

Below right: Try using some unscented soap or a soapless cleansing bar if your skin is very itchy.

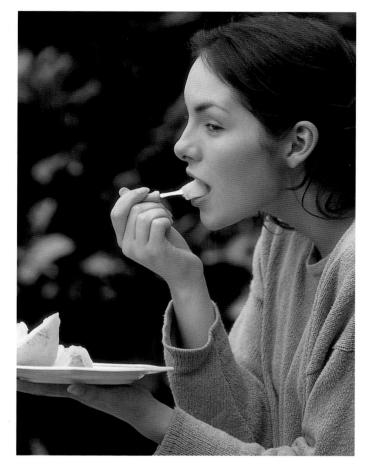

Above: Eating regularly and healthily will help you to regain your pre-pregnancy shape.

CARING FOR YOUR NEWBORN

You may find the first weeks at home with your new baby quite difficult, especially if you are still feeling weak and emotionally down. Don't get upset if the house is a mess; it is much more important for you to spend time with your baby than to do housework. If you are still in your dressing gown at lunchtime don't worry; your baby will not care and it is how he or she feels that matters most at the moment.

Your newborn will seem fragile at first, but is actually quite tough. It is natural to be worried about how to pick your new baby up and hold him without hurting him in any way. Before you pick up your baby make sure that you have his head and neck supported with one hand, then slide the other hand underneath his back and bottom to support the lower part of his body before lifting. Hold your baby firmly against you, either cradled against your chest with one arm still supporting the head and the other holding the bottom and lower back, or cradled in your arms with your baby's head lying in the crook of one arm while your other arm supports his back and legs. Always keep any movements gentle so that you don't hurt or frighten your baby.

THE NEWBORN AT DELIVERY

As soon as the baby is born it will be assessed on the five points of the Apgar Score: heart rate, respiratory rate, colour, activity, and response to stimulation. The baby will be given a maximum of two points for each category, so if he is pink, active, and responsive the score is 10. The Apgar Score is usually done twice – one minute after birth and five minutes after birth – and it may be done again later if there are any problems.

Your baby will also be weighed and measured by the doctor and will probably receive the first of three doses of vitamin K, by mouth, to prevent a rare bleeding illness which occasionally affects newborn babies. A second dose is given at 10 days and a third at six weeks. Vitamin K is given by injection to very premature babies or those who have had a traumatic birth.

After the birth, the umbilical cord will be cut and a plastic clamp placed about 1–2cm/½–1in from the infant's body. Over the next few days

A newborn baby boy's genitals may appear rather big in proportion to the rest of him. This will right itself after a few days.

A newborn baby loses the stump of her umbilical cord usually within the first few days after the birth.

the cord will shrivel up and after about a week it will drop off completely. During this time the area around the cord should be kept dry and clean to avoid the risk of infection. Try to let the air get to the healing navel as much as possible so that moisture from wet nappies doesn't affect it.

Your baby has soft spots known as fontanelles on the top of the head. These are the spaces between the skull bones, where they have not yet joined. There is usually a large one on top of the skull and a smaller one further back. They will gradually fuse over the next two years. The fontanelles are covered with a tough membrane to protect the brain and you should never press them hard. If you notice a bulge or the skin seems

Before you leave the hospital your newborn baby will be given a complete physical examination to check that all the organs and limbs are functioning correctly.

very tight over the fontanelles you should get in touch with your doctor immediately.

Some babies are born with a lot of hair, others arrive almost bald. Any first hair that a baby has will rub off within a couple of months, but this will be replaced with new hair growth. The new hair may be a different colour.

Most white babies are born with eyes that appear to be blue-grey in colour. This is because melanin, the body's natural pigment, is not present in the eyes until some weeks after birth. Babies with brown or black skins may have brown eyes at birth. If your baby's eyes are going to change colour this will gradually happen over a period of weeks or even months.

Although a new baby may cry quite a bit during these early weeks there probably won't be any tears.

Babies often scratch themselves accidentally with their nails when they are very young. Scratch mitts will stop your newborn from catching her face with her fingernails.

How to hold your new baby

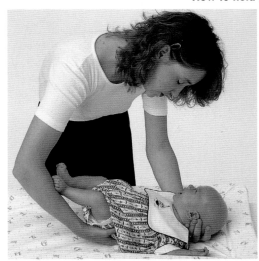

1 *Pick up your newborn baby by sliding one hand under his neck and head and then placing the other hand under his back and bottom to support his body.*

2 *Lift your baby so that he is cradled against your chest with one arm supporting the head and the other holding the lower back. Holding him close to your body will make him feel secure.*

Right: Touch is very important to a newborn and a gentle massage with a special baby oil can be soothing.

Some babies don't produce tears until they are six months old – this is not a cause for concern.

Slightly swollen or bloodshot eyes are common in newborn babies. This is caused by pressure from the birth and will disappear within a week or two. The muscles that control a new baby's eye movements are still very weak so he may look slightly cross-eyed at first. After a month or so the muscles will have developed sufficiently for the eyes to work together. However, even when looking cross-eyed, a baby can focus on things up to 20-25cm/8-10in away, so hold your face close when you are feeding or talking.

Enlarged genitals and breasts are common in both boys and girls when they are first born. In some cases the breasts may even ooze a little milk and baby girls can have a slight vaginal discharge. This is caused by your hormones, which are still in your baby's bloodstream. In a few days these effects will disappear.

GENERAL HYGIENE

Young babies often object noisily to being undressed and immersed in a bath full of water, so don't feel you have to bathe your baby every day if the infant is unhappy about it. A top and tail wash every other day is quite sufficient until you both feel more comfortable. Always start by washing the baby's face with cooled boiled water using several pieces of cotton wool. Never use any kind of soap on the baby's face or near his eyes. If you wipe the eyes, use separate pieces of cotton wool for each one and start from the inner corner wiping

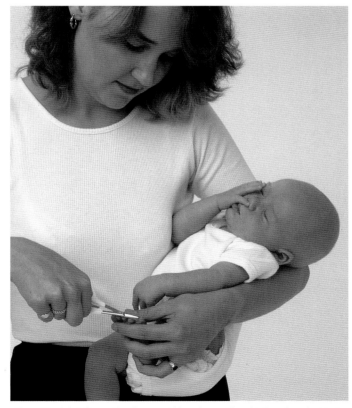

Above: Your baby's fingernails will grow quickly and you will need to keep them short to stop him scratching himself. You may find it easier to cut the nails while your baby is asleep.

outwards. A baby's ears and nose are self-cleaning so never try cleaning inside them with cotton wool or buds. Just gently remove any visible mucus or wax. Once you have washed his face you will need to lift up his head and clean the folds of his neck, making sure that you dry

the area carefully afterwards. Using another piece of cotton wool, wash between your baby's fingers and then dry his hands carefully.

When you have finished the top half you need to remove his nappy, wiping away any solid matter before gently cleaning his bottom. You can

use lotion to do this, or some warm water. Once the area is dry, you can apply a barrier cream to help prevent nappy rash.

Cradle cap is very common in the early months and can sometimes continue for a while. Dry white or yellow scales form a crusty cap on

Topping and tailing

1 *Undress your baby down to his nappy. Using cooled boiled water, and several pieces of cotton wool, gently wash his face. Never use any kind of soap on your baby's face or near his eyes.*

2 *Take a piece of cotton wool and gently lift his chin so that you can wash in the folds of his neck. When you have finished, use another piece of cotton wool and carefully dry between the folds.*

5 *Gently wipe his bottom area with lotion or damp cotton wool making sure that you clean in all the folds and creases of his legs.*

6 *Once you have dried the nappy area, apply a small amount of barrier cream to help prevent nappy rash.*

the scalp. Rub olive oil, baby oil, or a specially formulated treatment into the scalp and then comb out the loosened flakes. Wash the baby's head afterwards with baby shampoo and dry thoroughly. You may need to repeat this treatment several times to remove all the flakes. As soon as the condition is under control you will only need to do this once a week. Cradle cap usually disappears by the time a baby reaches about eight or nine months.

A young baby's nails will grow very quickly and if not cut can cause scratches, especially on his face. You should keep his fingernails and toenails short by cutting them straight across with a pair of blunt-ended scissors. If your baby objects to this, or you find it difficult to cut his nails while he is wriggling about, try doing it while he is asleep or get someone else to hold him steady.

3 *Your baby's ears and nose are self-cleaning, so don't be tempted to clean inside them with cotton buds. Take a dampened cotton bud and carefully remove any visible mucus from his nose.*

4 *Put your baby in a clean vest and then remove his nappy, wiping away any solid matter with a clean corner before placing the dirty nappy in a bag.*

7 *Now that your baby is clean and dry he is ready to have his nappy put on. Place the nappy under his bottom and draw it up carefully between his legs.*

8 *Fasten the nappy securely and once it is firmly in place pull down your baby's vest over the top of it. He is now clean and ready to be dressed again.*

BREAST-FEEDING

Breast-feeding is the ideal way to feed a baby because breast milk is a baby's natural food containing all the required nutrients in the right proportions for the first months of life. But like any new skill, breast-feeding has to be learned and you may find it more difficult than you expected. Don't give up though, because breast-feeding really is best for your baby and for you and, once it is established, it can be a pleasure. If you are having problems, talk to your midwife or health visitor.

Ideally, you should put your baby to your breast as soon after birth as possible. The sucking will start a reaction that leads to the release of the hormones that cause both the milk to be manufactured in the breast and the let-down reflex, which allows the milk to pass through the breast to the nipple.

Immediately after the birth and for the first few days, the breasts

Getting your baby latched on

Make sure that your baby's body is in a straight line with your breast so that she doesn't have to turn her head to feed.

Hold your baby in a comfortable position. Offer her the breast making sure that her mouth is open wide enough.

Allow your baby to feed from one breast for as long as she wants. She will let you know when she has had enough.

produce colostrum, a high-protein liquid full of antibodies. This is followed by the actual milk coming in, which often makes the breasts feel heavy and uncomfortable. This discomfort will soon wear off once breast-feeding has become established.

At the first stage of a feed your baby gets foremilk from the breast; this has a high water content to satisfy thirst. Foremilk is followed by calorie-rich hindmilk which satisfies your baby's hunger and helps her to grow. To make sure that your baby always gets the hindmilk, you should allow her to feed for as long as she wants from one breast before you offer her the other one. If your baby has had enough when she has finished feeding from one breast, remember to start with the other breast at the next feed.

Your breasts produce milk in response to your baby's feeding, so the more your baby feeds the more milk you will produce. By letting your infant feed for as long as she wants you should be able to produce the amount of milk that is needed.

FINDING THE BEST POSITION
Finding the position which best suits both you and your baby is one of the most important factors for successful breast-feeding, so don't be afraid to experiment. Immediately after the birth, when you are still sore, you may find that sitting on a low chair with plenty of soft cushions is more comfortable than sitting in bed. You can raise your knees slightly by resting your feet on a low stool, or put a pillow on your lap to raise your baby and cushion your abdominal muscles.

Hold your baby so that her body is in a straight line with your breast so that she does not have to turn her head to feed. Sit up straight and lean

Breast-feeding techniques

Aim the nipple towards your baby's nose and allow her to take it into her mouth herself. When supporting your breast try not to apply pressure which can block the milk ducts.

Your baby may try to hold your breast or simply clench and unclench her fists while feeding. Her ears will move as she swallows.

When you want to remove your baby from the breast, insert a finger into her mouth to release the suction.

Advantages of breast-feeding

• Breast milk is designed especially for babies and it contains all the nutrients your baby needs. It is always available, at the right temperature, and it is free.
• Breast milk is easy for your baby to digest, so she is less likely to suffer stomach upsets and constipation.

• Breast milk contains antibodies which will help protect your baby against some infections.
• Breast-fed babies are less likely to develop allergies.
• Breast-feeding will help you get your figure back more quickly.

To bring up any wind, either during the feed or once she has finished feeding, lay your baby across your knees and stroke her back gently.

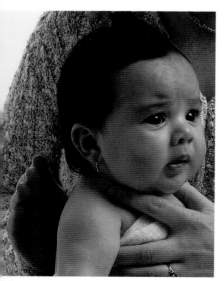

You may prefer to wind your baby by sitting her upright on your knee, supporting her head, and gently patting her back.

slightly forward so that the nipple drops into your baby's mouth. Make sure that she is then properly latched onto the breast. This means that your baby takes as much as possible of the areola (the dark area around the nipple) into her mouth, along with the nipple. The milk ducts lie just under the areola and your baby's sucking action on these effectively draws the milk from the breast. You may well be told to check that your baby's nose is not pushed against your breast so making it hard for her to breathe. However, if your baby is positioned properly, she will be able to breathe easily.

There is no set pattern for feeding. Some babies want to be fed every couple of hours, others can happily go for four to six hours before requiring a feed. Your baby will let you know when she is hungry and your milk supply will be regulated by supply and demand.

EXPRESSING MILK

Expressing milk allows someone else to feed your baby with your breast milk. You can express milk with your hands or you may find it easier to use a breast pump. The best time to express is when you have the most milk, which is either in the morning or, once your baby has dropped her night feed, it may be in the evening. Milk can be expressed from your breast and kept in a sterile container in the refrigerator for up to 48 hours, or it can be frozen and kept for up to six months. Any feeding equipment or containers you use must be sterilized.

BREAST-FEEDING PROBLEMS

If you are concerned that you are not producing enough milk, breast-feeding more often will automatically increase your supply, so don't be afraid to let your baby suck for as long as it is comfortable.

You may have a sleepy baby who needs to be woken for a feed. If your baby needs encouragement, gently brush her mouth with your nipple but don't force it into her mouth. Your baby may fall asleep at the breast after a feed but this only means that she is contented, well fed and doing all right.

Breast-feeding may hurt during the first few weeks because your milk supply has to become established and your nipples are not yet used to your baby's sucking. If the discomfort persists, however, then the positioning of your baby on the breast may not be right and you should experiment. Also check that your baby is latched on properly.

If not, your baby may just be sucking the nipple which means she won't be getting enough milk and the more she sucks the more painful it will actually become.

You may experience engorged breasts. This is when your breasts become over-full and painful. Feeding your baby frequently will help and you can ease the swelling by bathing your breasts with warm water or having a hot bath. Smooth out some milk with your fingers, stroking the breast downwards towards the nipple.

If you experience a shooting pain when your baby sucks, you may have a cracked nipple. If your baby is in the correct position even if your nipples are sore, they shouldn't hurt when you are feeding, so check your positioning. Keep sore nipples clean and dry and let the air get to them as much as possible. A nipple shield which fits over your nipple may help, but don't wear it for more than a day or two. Occasionally sore nipples can be caused by thrush in a baby's mouth. If you think this may be the case, discuss the problem with your doctor.

Finally, some nursing mothers can develop a condition called mastitis. This is an infection of the milk ducts and your breast will be inflamed, hot, and flushed in places. Bathing your breast in warm water, or holding a cold flannel against it, will help to ease any discomfort. You may also need a course of antibiotics to clear up the infection, so consult your doctor.

Sore, cracked nipples and mastitis are usually caused by your baby sucking just the nipple. Make sure your baby takes the nipple and surrounding area well into her mouth when she is feeding.

Breast-feeding equipment

Although no equipment is essential, there are some items that will make life easier, such as feeding bras. There are other things that you may require if you decide to express milk so that you can occasionally bottle-feed. You may need:

• At least two well-fitting cotton nursing bras that allow access to a large area of the breast when your baby is feeding.
• Breast pads for use inside the bra to absorb any leaks of milk.
• Nipple shields to protect your sore nipples.
• Breast shells to fit over the nipple and collect excess milk.
• Breast pump, bottles, and teats if you intend to express breast milk.
• Sterilizing equipment.

Breast milk can be expressed by hand, or using a manual breast pump like this. Electric pumps are also available.

Various accessories may help with breast-feeding. Breast pads will absorb any leakage, freezer bottles can be used to freeze breast milk, and nipple shields may help protect sore nipples.

BOTTLE-FEEDING

If you decide to bottle-feed you should be content with your decision. Do not feel guilty, or think that you are giving your baby second best. Such feelings will only take away the pleasure you should get from feeding your baby. Make the most of each feed by settling comfortably and giving your baby all your attention.

FORMULA MILKS

Formula milk has been specially produced to provide all the vitamins and minerals your baby needs. Most formula milk is made from cow's milk, which has been specially treated to make it easily digestible, and its nutritional quality as near to that of breast milk as possible. There are several brands to choose from and the midwife will be able to advise you. If your baby is known to have a lactose intolerance, or there is a strong family history of allergies that are connected to cows' milk, you may be advised to use an alternative to regular formula milk. Often this is a soya-based milk, but others are available. It is important that these alternatives are only introduced if recommended by your doctor.

Formula milks are available in powder forms, which are made up with cooled boiled water. It is important to follow the instructions on the tin or pack because the amounts have been calculated to make sure that a baby gets the correct balance of nutrients. Never be tempted to add more powder than is recommended because feeds that are too strong can be harmful to your baby. Ready-prepared formula milks are also available in cartons and bottles. These are more expensive than powdered formula but can be useful when you are away from home with your baby.

HOW TO BOTTLE-FEED

Prepare the formula milk according to the instructions, making up enough for 24 hours. Store the bottles in the refrigerator until

Feeding equipment

All feeding equipment needs to be kept scrupulously clean. Bottles and teats should be washed out immediately after use and then sterilized before you make up the next batch of feeds.

You will need to have:
• Enough bottles, teats, and caps to make up feeds for a 24-hour period.
• Bottle brush for cleaning inside all the bottles.

• Sterilizer – there are four main ways of sterilizing feeding equipment: the chemical method, using a container filled with sterilizing solution; an electric steam sterilizer; a microwave steam sterilizer; boiling on the stove.
• Sterilizing solution or tablets for chemical method.
• Bottle warmer – this is optional, but can be very useful, especially when doing night feeds.

A bottle warmer is useful at night.

Sterilizing equipment for bottles.

A microwave steam sterilizer.

Bringing up wind is something a father can do whether you breast- or bottle-feed.

An older baby may prefer to hold the bottle himself, but he will still need to be cuddled and you should check that the teat is always full of milk.

Feeding should always be a special time for a baby as it helps him bond with the people closest to him. Here a father takes his turn at bottle-feeding.

needed and make sure that any unused formula is thrown away after this time. Never reuse leftover milk because it is a potential breeding ground for bacteria. Some babies are quite happy to take their bottles at room temperature but if yours prefers warm milk, heat the bottle either in a normal bottle warmer, or by standing it in a jug of hot water. Always test the temperature on the inside of your wrist to make sure that it isn't too hot before giving the bottle to your baby to drink.

Check that the milk is coming through the teat at the right speed. If your baby is having to work hard to get the milk, the flow is too slow and you need a teat with a bigger hole. If, on the other hand, your baby seems to be gulping a lot and the milk is leaking out of the corner of his mouth, the flow is too fast and the teat should have a smaller hole. If the teat flattens while you are feeding, pull it gently out of the baby's mouth to release the vacuum, then insert it again.

All your baby's feeding equipment must be thoroughly washed before sterilization.

Chemical sterilizing

1 *After washing the equipment fill the sterilizing unit with cold water.*

2 *Add sterilizing tablets to the water and place the bottles, teats and caps in the unit.*

3 *Check bottles are filled with water, then place tray in unit. Leave for time specified.*

Electric steam sterilizer

1 *Wash and rinse the feeding equipment and then place it in the sterilizing unit.*

2 *Add water, taking care to follow the manufacturer's recommendations.*

Place lid on unit and switch on. The steam destroys any bacteria present.

Making up a formula feed

1 *Fill the bottle with the correct amount of cooled boiled water. Never use water that has been boiled more than once.*

2 *Using the scoop provided, measure the required amount of milk, levelling off each scoopful with the back of a knife.*

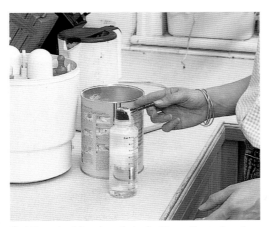

3 *Add powdered formula to the bottle. Never add extra formula as this can make the mixture too concentrated and could be harmful.*

4 *Secure teat and place lid on bottle. Shake until the powder has dissolved. Check the milk temperature before giving it to your baby.*

You may want to encourage feeding by stroking the teat across your baby's mouth. Once his mouth has opened, place the teat between his lips and your baby should start sucking. Keep the bottle tilted so that formula fills the teat completely and your baby doesn't suck in air, which can cause wind. Never leave your baby to feed from a bottle on his own because he could vomit and choke. Don't add solids such as rusk, cereal, or baby rice to bottle feeds – this could cause choking.

The amount of milk your baby needs at feeds will change as he gains weight. At first he may take only a couple of ounces but this will increase. Your health visitor will give you a growth chart to check on progress.

Wind can sometimes be a problem, so try stopping halfway through a feed and wind your baby by holding him against your shoulder, or propping him up on your lap while you rub his back. You may want to do this after the feed has finished as well. The baby may bring back a small amount of milk during or after a feed; this is called possetting and is quite normal. If the vomiting becomes frequent or violent, you need to consult your doctor.

INTRODUCING SOLIDS

Once milk alone no longer satisfies your baby you will need to start introducing solids into her diet. The recommended age for this is six months, but if your baby seems ready for solids before this you should talk to your health visitor or doctor. Your baby will let you know she is still hungry by wanting more after the feed is finished, or she may start chewing her fists. A baby may also begin to demand feeds more often and if she normally sleeps through the night, she may start waking up early wanting to be fed.

Breast and formula milk give babies all they require for the first six months so you don't have to worry if your baby seems satisfied with milk alone until this age. By six months of age, your baby needs the additional nourishment provided by solids, and she also needs to learn how to eat.

HOW TO START

First solids are really just tasters to get a baby used to different textures and flavours; the main nourishment will still come from breast or formula milk. The first food should be bland and smooth, like baby rice mixed with either cooled boiled water, or formula or breast milk. To begin with offer a small amount on the tip of a clean spoon, midway through a feed, once a day. Once your baby has accepted this, you can introduce a small amount of fruit or vegetable purée, for example, banana, potato, or carrot (with no added salt or sugar), mixed with formula or breast milk.

As soon as your baby has got used to taking solids off a spoon, you can begin to introduce new foods and other solids at a second meal. If your baby obviously doesn't like the taste of something don't force matters. Try another food and reintroduce the rejected food at a later stage. At first the baby will simply try to suck anything off the spoon. But it won't take long to master getting the food off the spoon and into the back of her mouth. Once your baby can do this she will be able to cope with lumpier textures, so you can begin to mash rather than purée food. Your baby will also be able to enjoy a wider variety of tastes and textures.

ADVANCED FEEDING

At around eight months, you can introduce food combinations such as baby cereal and fruit, or egg yolk and tomato – remember to remove the seeds from the tomato and to cook the egg thoroughly. Food can be lumpier and more solid so that it encourages your baby to start chewing. Try mincing or mashing the food with a fork.

At nine months and over, your baby is likely to be on three meals a day as well as milk, unsweetened diluted fruit juice, or water. Giving your child food at grown-up

Making your own purée

1 *Steam the fruit or vegetable until it is thoroughly cooked and soft, then place it in the food mill or blender.*

2 *Without adding any sugar or seasoning, blend to a smooth consistency then remove a portion for your baby.*

3 *Pour the remaining purée into an ice-cube tray to freeze in baby-size portions. Label and use within one month.*

meal-times will encourage her to learn social skills by watching others. As her appetite grows you can gradually increase the amount given at each meal. Offer finger foods such as slices of peeled apple, and banana; this will encourage her to feed herself. Always stay with your child while she is eating in case of choking.

As with younger babies, don't force unwanted foods; your child may simply not be ready for that particular taste. Don't ever fight over it. Take the food away, but don't offer alternatives or provide snacks between meals or let the child fill up on drinks, especially non-nourishing drinks, such as squash.

THE VEGETARIAN BABY
The principles of weaning are the same as for a non-vegetarian baby with the first solids being cereal, puréed fruit, and vegetables. However, vegetarian diets tend to be high in fibre and too much fibre is not suitable for young babies. And it can also interfere with the absorption of minerals such as calcium and iron. So your child will require a combination of cereals, milk, and vegetables which contain the right balance of energy and other nutrients for healthy growth. The diet will also need to include iron-rich foods such as dried fruit, fortified breakfast cereals, bread, lentils, eggs and green leafy vegetables. Vitamin C helps the absorption of iron from vegetables so you should give fresh orange juice, fresh fruit, or raw vegetables with every meal.

A vegan diet excludes milk and all dairy products, as well as meat and fish, and it may be unsuitable for babies. If you are considering a vegan diet it is essential that you talk

Equipment

First foods should be mashed with a fork to a smooth purée. Alternatively, press the food with a spoon through a sieve, or process it in a blender or liquidizer. As your baby gets older she will be able to cope with lumpier foods. Your baby should have his or her own feeding utensils, which you will need to keep very clean.

To prepare and feed your own puréed foods you will need:
• Blender or liquidizer.
• Unbreakable bowl, spoon, and feeding cup.
• Bib (preferably two or three) and several face cloths.
• Ice-cube tray or similar for freezing small portions of purée.

Use an unbreakable bowl, plastic teaspoon and feeding cup when weaning your baby.

A blender or sieve will purée first foods. Freeze baby-size portions in an ice-cube tray.

Left: By eight months a baby will be enjoying finger foods. At first he will examine the food, squashing it between his fingers as he explores its texture. Right: Once he's examined the food he will probably concentrate on trying to get it into his mouth.

Below right: Using both his hands to help, he eventually manages to get the food into his mouth. These are the very early stages of how a child learns to feed himself.

to your health visitor or community dietician before beginning to wean your baby onto solid food.

BABY FOODS

You can make your own first foods by puréeing ripe fruit or vegetables. Remove the skin and any seeds or stones, then boil, steam, or microwave until thoroughly cooked. Allow the cooked fruit or vegetable to cool, then purée. Fruits with

seeds such as strawberries will need to be sieved. Make a batch of purée, and freeze in small portions for convenience. Reheat thoroughly before use and allow it to cool before giving it to your baby.

When your baby is older and has progressed to lumpier, mixed foods she can eat the same foods as you, but remove a small portion for your baby before you add any seasoning or sugar.

Warming food for babies in a microwave is not recommended because it can result in uneven heating which could scald the child's mouth. If you have to use a microwave, stir the food well after cooking to ensure the even distribution of heat and allow it to stand for at least one minute. Check the temperature again before offering the food to the child.

Choking

If your baby chokes while eating try to hook out the obstruction with your finger (being careful not to push it further in) while gently slapping her on the back. If this doesn't work, lay your baby face downwards with her chest and abdomen lying along your forearm and your hand supporting her head. Then slap the infant gently on the back to dislodge the obstruction.

The alternative to home-made baby food is to choose from the prepared baby foods that are widely available. One of the advantages of prepared baby foods is that they are quick and convenient. They have been formulated to make sure that, in conjunction with breast or formula milks, a baby receives a nutritionally balanced diet. Available in jars, packs and tins, there are commercially prepared baby foods available for each stage of weaning. Check the labelling for the age range for which it is suitable and, if you wish, whether it is acceptable for a vegetarian diet.

Introduce new combinations of prepared baby food with the same care as you would home-made food. Different food combinations contain several ingredients, some of which may be new to your baby. Always place the amount you require in a dish rather than feeding straight from the tin or jar. The digestive substances in your baby's saliva can

find their way from the feeding spoon into the container, which can make any remaining food unsuitable for another meal. Opened tins and jars should be covered, and can be stored in the fridge for up to 48 hours.

Always feed your baby her food using a plastic spoon. Keep the dish away from her until she learns not to put her hands in it.

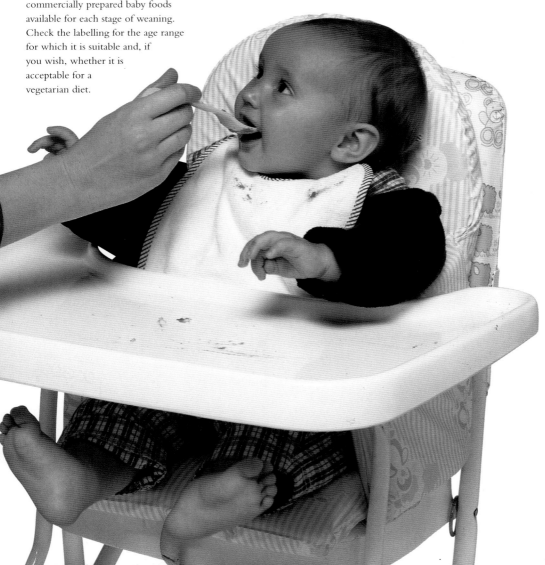

FOODS TO WATCH

You must think carefully about the foods you introduce to your baby's diet. Some must be avoided altogether; others simply need special care in their preparation.

High-fibre foods Babies and young children shouldn't be given high-fibre foods such as bran because their digestive systems are too immature to cope with them.

Salt Never add salt to your baby's food. An infant's system can't cope with more salt than is found naturally in food. Some products, such as crisps, are usually quite salty, so you need to be aware of any salt intake from these foods.

Sugar Sugars occur naturally in fruit and vegetables so you should never add sugar to your baby's food or drinks as this can lead to tooth decay later and the possibility of obesity. Some manufacturers' prepared foods may contain sugars, so read food labels: sugars may be listed as glucose, sucrose, dextrose, fructose, maltose, syrup, honey, or raw/ brown sugar.

Additional fats Babies shouldn't have much additional fat added to their food – although the occasional knob of butter added to mashed potato will do no harm.

Nuts Whole nuts should never be given to a child under five years of age because of the risk of choking. Finely ground nuts may be given to children over six months unless there is a history of nut allergy in your family.

Spices Strong spices such as chillies, ginger and cloves are not suitable to be given to babies.

Eggs Since eggs can cause allergic reactions, start by offering a small amount of well-cooked yolk. Egg white is not recommended for babies under 12 months.

FOOD ALLERGY

If either you or the baby's father have a family history of food allergies, eczema, asthma, or hayfever, your baby may have an intolerant reaction to the following foods: wheat, oats, and barley cereal; citrus fruits, eggs, nuts, and fish; dairy products, including cow's, goat's and sheep's milk. Intolerance to cow's milk is usually the result of an allergy to one of the proteins in milk or an intolerance of lactose (milk sugar). When you buy manufactured food, check the ingredients for foods that may cause an allergic reaction.

Drinks, other than breast or formula milk, should be given in a feeder cup from the age of six months.

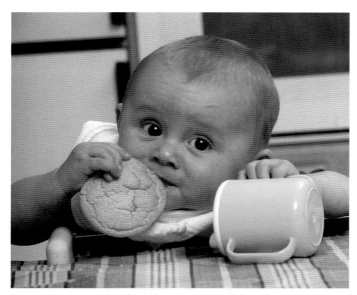

At around one year a baby will be able to manage finger food and a feeder cup without help. Never leave your baby alone when he is eating in case he chokes. Give drinks at the end of a meal or they will fill your baby up before eating.

Vitamin drops

It is recommended that vitamin supplements are given to children from six months if you are breast-feeding. Bottle-fed babies do not usually require supplements until they switch to cow's milk at a year old. These vitamin supplements should be given to children up to the age of five. They are available from your health visitor at the baby clinic or you can get them from the pharmacist.

Symptoms of food intolerance or allergy include diarrhoea, vomiting after eating, or occasionally blood in stools. In extreme cases the reaction can be a generalized blotchy skin rash that occurs within an hour or so of eating the food. Your child's lips may also become swollen, the eyes puffy, and breathing a little wheezy. If breathing becomes restricted you will need to get medical help immediately. The blotchiness and swelling will disappear quickly but it should always be reported to your health visitor or doctor. These extreme reactions are rare, but if they do occur you should make sure that you avoid that particular food in future.

If your child shows an intolerance to any food, it may be that you need to change your child's diet, but this should always be done with the advice of a health professional.

MILK AND OTHER DRINKS

As the amount of food that your baby eats increases, her intake of milk will decrease. However, the recommendation is at least 600ml/ 1pt of breast, formula, or follow-on milk (after six months) a day, until the baby is one year old.

Follow-on milks help to meet the nutritional needs of growing babies from six months to two years. They contain more iron than other milks, plus a healthy balance of other nutrients.

In the past cow's milk was introduced into the diet at around six months, but it is now thought that it is unsuitable until the baby is at least one year old. This is because cow's milk is low in vitamins like C and D, and is particularly low in iron, all of which your baby needs for healthy growth. After a year full-fat milk should be give to the

under-fives as it provides energy, protein, and calcium, even though it has more saturated fat than breast or baby milks. Reduced-fat milks are not suitable as they are low in calories and vitamins. Skimmed milk should not be given to a child until she is at least five years of age. But if your child has a good appetite and varied diet, you may offer semi-skimmed milk at two. Always check with your health visitor first.

If your baby seems thirsty and you are still breast-feeding, your milk should provide all the liquid needed. If your baby remains thirsty you may want to offer cooled, boiled water between feeds. Try giving your baby these additional drinks from a teaspoon; this will make the idea of a spoon familiar before you start weaning on to solids. From the age of six months, any drinks other than breast or formula milk should be offered from a feeder cup.

Any water you give your baby needs to be boiled and cooled until the child is at the age when you no longer sterilize feeding equipment. Only use boiled water or bottled water sold specifically for babies – never make up a feed with, or offer your baby, bottled mineral water.

NAPPIES

Nappies are produced in a variety of types, styles, and sizes, but the basic choice is still between disposable and towelling nappies. Ideally, you should decide which type of nappy you are going to use before your baby arrives. You will need to take into account a number of factors: your lifestyle, the amount of time and money you have available, and the type of washing and drying facilities you will be using. Whichever nappy you choose, the techniques required for changing and cleaning a baby's bottom are the same.

CHANGING

You should change your baby whenever he is wet or dirty. The number of changes may vary from day to day, but generally you will have to change your baby first thing in the morning, after each feed, after a bath, and before bed at night. Get everything you need together before you start so that there is no reason to leave your baby unattended while you are changing the nappy. Make sure that the room where you are changing your new baby is warm and free from draughts. Lie your baby on a folded towel or changing mat, placed on the floor, a table, or on the bed, making sure that a

---

Folding towelling nappies/Triple absorbent fold

This is particularly good for newborn babies because it makes a small, neat shape while giving extra absorbency between the legs.

1 *Fold the nappy into four sections with the two folded edges nearest you and to your left.*

2 *Pick up the top layer by the right-hand corner and pull it out to make a triangle.*

5 *Fold these layers over again to make a thick central panel.*

6 *Place a nappy liner over the top of the central panel.*

Changing equipment:
• Changing mat or towel.
• Clean towelling nappy, nappy liner, pins, plastic pants. Or a disposable nappy.
• Baby lotion or wipes, cotton wool.
• Bowl of warm water.
• Barrier cream.
• Bucket for dirty nappy or a plastic bag for a disposable nappy.

3 *Turn the nappy over.*

4 *Fold the vertical edge into the middle by a third.*

7 *Bring the middle fold between the legs, then fold one corner across your baby's stomach and hold while you bring the second corner across. Pull taut and then pin all three layers together.*

Kite fold

This is suitable from about three months onwards. You can adapt the size of the nappy by varying the depth when you fold the point up, before positioning the liner.

1 *Lay the nappy out flat in front of you so that it is in a diamond shape with one of the corners nearest you.*

2 *Fold the sides into the centre so that you form a kite shape with the nappy.*

5 *Bring the nappy up between the baby's legs and carefully fold one side and then the other into the middle. Secure the nappy with one pin in the centre for a small baby and two pins, one on either side, for a bigger baby.*

wriggling infant cannot roll off if you are changing the nappy on a raised surface.

Remove the soiled nappy. Then clean your baby's bottom thoroughly, wiping away any solid matter with a clean corner of the used nappy, or with a damp tissue or cotton wool soaked in warm water. A baby wipe, or some baby lotion, can be used to finish cleaning the area. Once you have dried your baby's bottom, apply a small amount of a specially formulated barrier cream to protect the skin. Then put on a clean nappy.

WHAT'S IN A NAPPY
You may find the nappy of your new baby is stained dark pink or even

3 *Fold the point at the top down towards the centre so that there is a straight edge along the top.*

4 *Fold the bottom edge up towards the centre, adjusting the fold so that the nappy is the correct size for your baby.*

red. This is because the urine of newborns contains substances called urates. Your newborn's immature bladder cannot hold urine for very long so he may urinate as frequently as 20 times in every 24 hours. This will gradually lessen.

Your baby's first stools will be a blackish-green colour because the meconium from your amniotic fluid is working its way out of his system. Once feeding begins, the stools will change to greenish-brown and then to a yellowish-brown colour. The number of stools passed varies from baby to baby, but generally breast-fed babies pass fewer stools than bottle-fed babies.

DISPOSABLE NAPPIES

There is no doubt that disposables are more convenient than towelling nappies. They are quick and easy to put on and remove and they don't require washing, which is a strong consideration when you think about the extra washing your baby is likely to produce without even including nappies. Their main disadvantages are that they are more expensive than their towelling counterparts and, despite their name, are cumbersome to dispose of. Most end up being wrapped and put in the dustbin; there are special plastic bags that will neutralize strong odours, and these are widely available.

Alternatively, there are a number of portable units available which will wrap and seal the dirty nappy in strong film, so that they can be stored for a number of days and then be disposed of in bulk.

Disposables work by allowing moisture to soak through a top sheet into an absorbent filling, which is protected on the outside by a waterproof backing. They come in a wide range of shapes and sizes. Most disposables have elasticated legs to ensure a snug fit, and reusable tapes so that you can check whether the nappy needs changing and adjust the leg size. Disposables need to be checked frequently because many of them are so good at keeping your baby dry that you may forget to change them.

TOWELLING NAPPIES

These are a once-only buy which makes them more economical than disposables. Towelling nappies come in a variety of absorbencies and qualities. As a general guide the more absorbent the nappy the more expensive it is, so buy the best you can afford. The nappy can be folded in a number of different ways to fit your baby. It is held together with special pins and covered with reusable plastic pants to prevent leakage. One-way liners can be placed inside the nappy to help keep your baby dry; this method also has the added advantage of allowing you to flush any motions down the lavatory with the minimum of bother.

Putting on a towelling nappy

Towelling nappies can be folded in a variety of ways to suit the age and sex of your child.

1 *Fold nappy and place a liner in the centre. Lay your baby on the nappy with top edge at waist. Now bring nappy up between her legs.*

2 *Holding the nappy in place, fold one side over the central panel and secure with a nappy pin.*

3 *Fold the other side into the middle and secure. Always keep your finger between the nappy and your baby's skin when inserting the pin so that there is no risk of pricking your baby.*

4 *Once the nappy is securely in place you may want to put on a pair of protective plastic pants. Try not to get cross if your baby wets her clean nappy immediately and you have to start all over again.*

When working out the price of towelling nappies you need to take into account the cost of washing powder, the electricity used for washing and drying them, sterilizing solution, plastic wraps, nappy liners and clips. Towelling nappies are harder work than disposables because they need washing, so a washing machine and tumble dryer will make life easier for you. The nappies also need to be sterilized, rinsed, washed and dried. Then they should be aired before being reused.

SHAPED WASHABLE NAPPIES

These wash like towelling nappies but are shaped like disposables, with re-sealable fastenings and elasticated legs. They come in various sizes, and require a separate waterproof wrap. All-in-one cloth nappies are similar, but are simpler to use as they come complete with waterproof wraps.

THE ENVIRONMENTAL ISSUE

There is no arguing that disposable nappies are a great convenience for busy parents, but there are costs to the environment. Disposables, despite their name, are not 100 per cent disposable and millions of them are deposited in landfill sites every day where they will take years to break down.

Although, towelling nappies would seem environmentally friendlier, you need to assess the cost of the energy resources required to wash them and the impact on the environment of the sterilizers and detergents needed to clean the used nappy.

Whichever type of nappy you choose, you can arrange for services to handle them. You can have disposables delivered regularly for a nominal charge, at a price reduced for bulk ordering. Or, with towelling nappies, you can use a nappy laundry service and pay to have the used ones picked up and replaced with clean, sterile ones.

NAPPY RASH

Whichever nappy you choose, it is unlikely that your baby will get through the nappy years without experiencing nappy rash at some time. The key to avoiding the problem is cleanliness and frequent nappy changes, so that urine and faeces don't remain in contact with

Putting on a disposable nappy

Disposable nappies are available in a variety of shapes, sizes and absorbencies. Always select the size which is recommended for your baby's weight.

1 *Open out the nappy with the re-sealable tabs at the top. Lay your baby on the nappy so that the top aligns with her waist. Bring the front of the nappy up between her legs.*

2 *Smooth the front of the nappy so that it fits snugly round your baby's waist. Pull the adhesive tabs firmly towards the front of the nappy and fasten them to secure.*

the skin too long. Allow your baby to spend some time naked each day; this will help keep the skin clear. Nappy rash is sometimes caused by the fungus thrush, and if so an antifungal cream will be needed, so consult your doctor if the rash persists.

DRESSING YOUR BABY

There are clothes to fit every size of newborn, from the tiny premature baby to the bouncing 10-pounder. Most baby clothes are sized by the approximate age and height of the child. Your baby probably won't require a great number of first-size clothes and may well grow into the next size within a matter of weeks – some babies are even big enough when born to go straight into second-size clothes.

Dressing and undressing your newborn can be difficult enough without having to worry about doing up complicated fastenings, so keep first clothes simple and save buttons and bows until later. Choose well-designed baby clothes that allow you to dress and undress your baby with the minimum of fuss. Look for garments that have wide, envelope necks that will stretch, so that you can slip them over baby's head easily. Stretchsuits which have fastenings up the inside leg will allow you to change a nappy without having to remove all your baby's clothes. All-in-one bodysuits, which fasten between the legs, will prevent your baby from getting cold around the middle and are ideal if you dress your baby in separates.

If you have a girl you may well be tempted to put her in dresses from the beginning, but dresses are not practical everyday wear for a young baby. They ride up and can be uncomfortable to lie on, they will allow draughts in around her middle, and they get in the way when she is starting to crawl. It is better to save them for special occasions or for when she's older.

Lacy jackets and shawls are best avoided too, as little fingers can get caught in the holes.

As your baby grows, colourful rompers and dungarees can take the place of stretchsuits. They are versatile and are suitable for both boys and girls. Rompers, which are really stretchsuits without feet, are easy to wear as they allow your baby freedom of movement. When you buy dungarees make sure that they have generous turn-ups and adjustable shoulder straps so that you get the maximum wear out of them.

When the weather is warm, babies need to be dressed in clothes that will keep them comfortably cool, and you should always cover their heads with a sun hat if you are out and about. Outerwear for cold days should be roomy enough to fit easily over everyday clothes.

EASY-CARE FABRICS

Your baby is quite likely to get through as many as three or four changes a day so it makes sense to buy clothes made in easy-care fabrics that will wash and wear well. Check the labels before buying and avoid any garments that are going to need special treatment. Choose natural fabrics as these are best for warmth and absorbency. Pure cotton is ideal for your baby's underwear and also her stretchsuits.

Whether you are machine- or hand-washing garments, always follow the instructions on the labels so that your baby's clothes retain their shape, colour, and texture. Avoid using "biological" washing powders as these may irritate your baby's skin. It is important that all clothes are well aired and completely dry before being put away.

FOOTWEAR

It is important that a baby's toes are never restricted by tight footwear. Check regularly that all-in-one-suits, leggings, and tights have enough room in them for the baby to wiggle her toes. Socks, bootees, and tights that have shrunk or been outgrown should be discarded. (The same care should be taken with tight collars, cuffs, mittens and also gloves.)

Your baby will not need proper shoes until she is walking and her feet need protection from the hard ground. If you do put your child in soft shoes before this, these should be made from a lightweight breathable material such as cloth or very soft leather and they must be flexible enough for you to feel her toes through them.

When you come to buy your baby's first shoes always have them fitted at a shop that offers a special fitting service for children. Both your baby's feet should be measured for length and width. If you can afford them, shoes with leather uppers are best. It is essential to check regularly that the shoes still fit and have not become too tight.

For a first layette you will need:

- 3 baby gowns.
- pair of scratch mittens.
- shawl.
- 7 stretchsuits.
- 2 pairs of bootees or socks.
- 4 vests or bodysuits.
- warm outer wear for chilly days.
- sun hat.

How to dress your newborn

Dressing and undressing a newborn can seem difficult at first. Always dress a newborn baby on a flat surface
so that you have both hands free.

1 *Put the all-in-one vest over your baby's head, raising her head slightly. Then widen one of the arm holes with your hand.*

2 *Using your other hand, gently guide the arm through the sleeve. Repeat with the other arm.*

3 *Place your hand under your baby's bottom and pull down the back of the vest.*

4 *Do up the poppers between the legs and make sure that the vest isn't too tight anywhere when fastened.*

5 *Concertina up the leg of the sock and then hold it wide as you ease it over your baby's foot.*

6 *Gently place one foot in the trouser leg and then the other and pull the trousers up.*

7 *Place your hand under your baby's bottom and lift so that you can pull the trousers up over the nappy.*

8 *Adjust the trousers and make sure that the vest is smooth and that there are no puckers that could be uncomfortable to lie on.*

9 *Hold the neck of the T-shirt wide as you slip it over your baby's face and then pull it down over the back of her head.*

10 *Gently ease your baby's arm through the T-shirt's sleeve and then pull the sleeve down.*

11 *Put her other arm into the sleeve, then pull down top and tuck into her trousers. Your baby is now ready to face the day!*

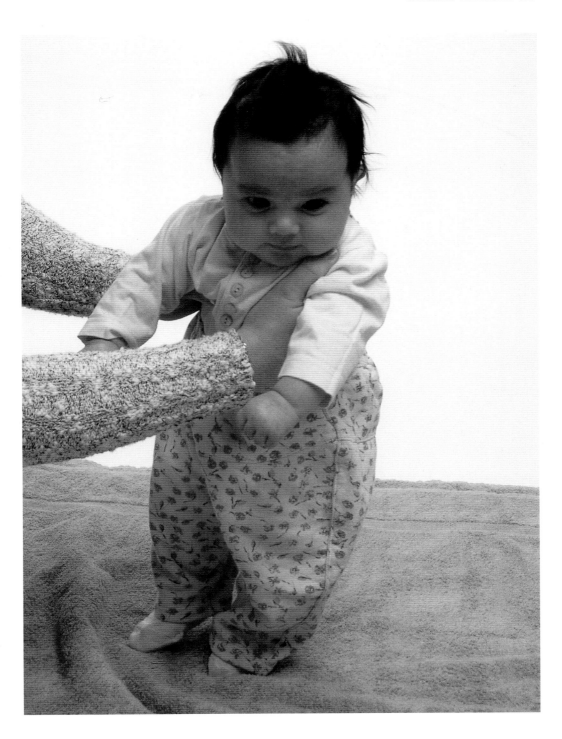

An all-in-one suit with leg fasteners is ideal for a new baby. The leg opening allows you to change the nappy easily without having to remove any of her clothes.

Rompers and a top are ideal for an older baby and are practical for both boys and girls. The romper straps hold the rompers in place even when your baby is being very active and will help prevent gaps occurring around the middle.

A more mobile baby will be happiest in trousers that will protect her legs as she learns to walk. Make sure the trouser legs clear the floor so that she doesn't trip.

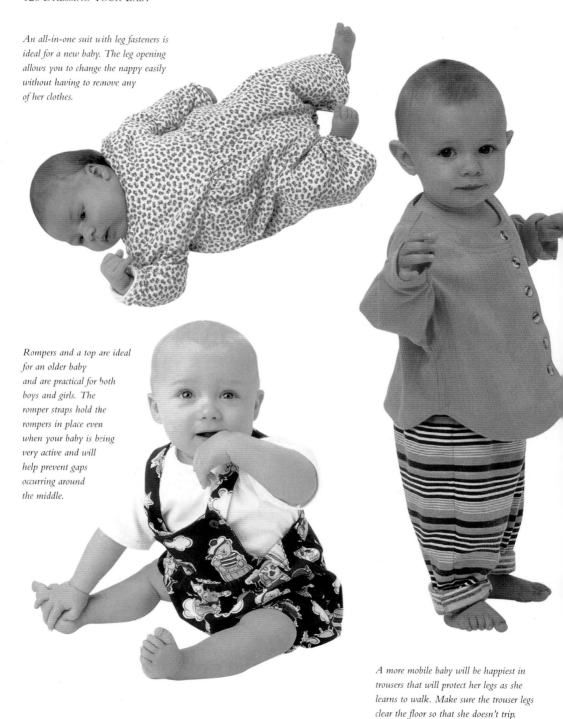

Choose clothes carefully

You will be surprised at how quickly your baby grows during the first 12 months. Select clothes that will mix and match and allow some room for growth. Once she begins to crawl, your baby will need sensible easy-care clothes that will withstand endless washing. Make sure that neck openings are large enough and that garments are easy to unfasten for quick nappy changes. Not all clothes have to be practical; it is nice to buy a couple of special outfits that can be used for parties and days out too.

Dresses look pretty, but are not really practical everyday wear for very young babies or once your baby becomes mobile. Keep dresses for those special occasions.

Rompersuits with short sleeves made in natural fibres are ideal for the summer. Synthetic fibres don't allow the skin to breathe properly and may make your baby feel hot and uncomfortable.

Babies don't need proper shoes until they have started to walk. Soft shoes like these are perfect for little feet in the meantime.

BATHING

When you bath your baby you need to get all you require together before you start. It helps if you can keep all the nappies, pins, pants, and toiletries either in a changing bag or box. A nappy bucket is essential because you'll need somewhere to put the dirty nappy and used cotton wool. A second bucket is also useful for dropping the dirty clothes into as you undress the baby. Any clean clothes and towels should be well aired before you begin and the room where you undress your baby should be warm (a minimum of 21°C/70°F) and draught-free.

When babies are tiny it is easier to bath them in a baby bath on a stand, or one that fits into the big bath, so they will be at a comfortable height for you to hold them. Before undressing your baby, fill the bath with warm water, putting the cold in first then the hot, and mix well. Add any bath preparation at this stage. Test that the water is at the right temperature. A bath thermometer will give you an accurate reading or you can use your elbow.

For bathing you will need:
• Bowl of cooled boiled water, cotton wool and cotton buds (optional) to clean your baby's face before bathing (see topping and tailing).
• Changing mat.
• Bath towel.
• Baby bath preparation.
• Baby shampoo.
• Baby powder.
• Nappy changing equipment and a clean nappy.
• Clean clothes.

1 *Wrap your baby firmly in a towel. Test the temperature of the bath water again then, having tucked his legs firmly under your arm, hold your baby's head over the bath, supporting his neck and back with your hand.*

2 *Wet his head and apply a mild baby shampoo. Wash the hair with gentle circular movements, keeping the water and shampoo well away from his eyes. Once washed, rinse off the shampoo and lift your baby back onto your knee and towel his hair dry.*

3 *Lift your baby gently into the bath, supporting his head and back on your arm, while holding the arm that is the furthest away from you.*

4 *This leaves your other hand free to wash under his arms and in all the folds and creases. When you have finished, lift your baby out of the bath and into a warm towel.*

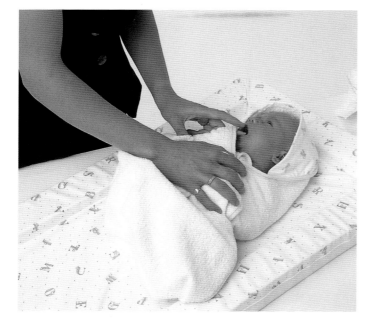

5 *Once you have dried your baby, you may want to apply some baby powder. Put a little powder on your hands and then rub it on to the baby's body, making sure you close the lid tightly after use. Don't sprinkle it on straight from the container in case it gets into your baby's mouth or eyes. It can be dangerous for young infants to inhale powder into their lungs.*

You may find it easier to bath a very young baby in a baby bath. Some of these have their own stand; others, like the one above, fit over a big bath.

A sponge inlay which fits snugly into the bottom of the bath will prevent your baby from slipping, and will make it easier for you to hold him.

Once your baby is old enough to be bathed in the big bath you should cover the taps with a folded towel before putting him in the bath. This will prevent him from accidentally burning himself on the hot tap.

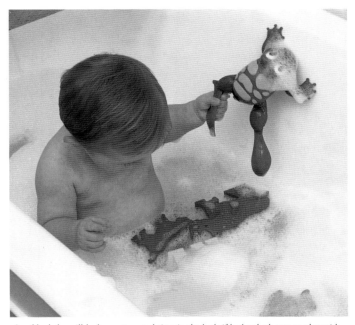

An older baby will be happy to spend time in the bath if he has bath toys to play with. Containers that can be filled and emptied and toys that float and bob about will give hours of fun and entertainment.

Safety notes

Never leave your baby or toddler alone in the bath. It only takes a few seconds for a child to drown in as little as 5cm/2in of water.

• When drying or dressing your baby never leave him unattended on a raised surface. He could easily roll off and hurt himself.

• Always check the temperature of the bath water before putting your baby in the bath.

• If you bath your child in a conventional large bath, place a cover over the taps so that he can't burn himself. A folded towel will do.

• Use a non-slip bath mat in the bath.

• Always put the cold water in first when running the bath.

• If you are using a bath and stand, make sure that it is sturdy and secure before lifting your baby into it.

Above: Your child may enjoy sharing his bath with others, or he may prefer to have a bath alone. If you are intending to bath two or three children together it is often easier to put the smallest into the bath first and then let the others join him one at a time.

Right: Not all children enjoy spending time in the bath. If one child is unhappy about bathtime don't force him to stay in longer than he wants. Always stay in the bathroom with your children so that you can be sure that they are safe.

SLEEPING

Your new baby has no understanding of day and night so during the first weeks of her life she will sleep and wake at random. You may find that she sleeps for 20 hours out of every 24 or for only 12 hours out of 24. Whatever pattern your baby adopts, she will be getting as much sleep as she needs.

Average sleep pattern

Birth	17 hours in every 24	
	Day	**Night**
3 months	5 hours	10 hours
6 months	4 hours	10 hours
9 months	3 hours	11 hours
12 months	2 hours	11 hours

Your baby's biological clock will dictate when she is ready for sleep in the evenings and this is a good starting point for establishing a regular bedtime. From the very

Try not to let your baby fall asleep before putting him in his cot as he may wake feeling distressed if you are not there.

beginning you should make the hour before bed quiet and relaxing. You may choose this time to give your baby a bath, and you will certainly want to feed and change your baby before putting her down in the cot. You may need to rock or sing to the child until sleep comes, especially if she is very young. During the first few weeks your baby may sleep better if swaddled in a blanket or sheet – this will prevent tiny limbs from jerking and twitching. These sudden involuntary movements often wake a very young baby. As your child gets older she will begin to settle on her own and you can help by providing things for amusement, such as a mobile and cot toys. Follow the same routine every night so that

Your baby will enjoy being outside from an early age. Keep her out of direct sun in the shade and have the hood up to protect her from draughts.

the baby begins to associate the cot with night-time and sleep.

A baby's room needs to be warm – around 18°C/65°F – so that the child doesn't wake up cold in the

Cot death

All parents are worried about the possibility of cot death, technically known as Sudden Infant Death Syndrome (SIDS). Although the chance of this happening to your baby is remote, it is sensible to take a few simple precautions that are known to reduce the risk.

• Let your baby sleep in her own cot in your room for the first six months.

• Make sure that your baby sleeps on her back in the 'feet to foot' position, that is with her feet at the foot of the cot so that there is no danger of her wriggling down under the blankets and becoming overheated.

• Keep your baby warm, but do not let her overheat. Check your baby's temperature regularly by feeling the back of her neck or tummy. It is best to

use several lightweight blankets so that you can add or take them away to adjust the temperature. Remember that cot blankets that are folded count as two blankets.

• Use a firm mattress and don't use a duvet, baby nest, cot bumper or pillow.

• Do not smoke near your baby and keep her out of a smoky atmosphere.

• If your baby seems unwell, take her to the doctor immediately.

• Make sure your baby's room is well ventilated. Leave the door ajar or a window open (but ensure that the baby is not in a draught). The temperature in your baby's room should be around 18°C/65°F.

• Don't take your baby into your bed if you have drunk alcohol or taken any form of drugs.

Bedtime tips

- Encourage your baby to sleep while there are background noises going on. This way she won't expect silence at bedtime.
- Put a selection of toys in the cot to provide amusement for an older baby.
- Make night feeds as quick and quiet as possible, keeping the lights low and changing the baby first. Don't do anything stimulating.
- Put the baby down to sleep in the cot at night so that she comes to associate it with sleep.
- Wrap up a newborn baby firmly so that she feels secure.

Put your baby in the "feet to foot" position.

during the day. Stimulate your baby by talking and playing with her in the daytime when she is awake. Keep feeding and changing down to a minimum amount of time during the night so that your baby learns that this is not a time for being sociable.

Above: Older babies often prefer to sleep on their sides. Place the lower arm in a forward position to stop her rolling onto her stomach.

Below: Check your baby's body warmth regularly at night, and remove some blankets if she feels too warm.

night. Put your baby down to sleep in a vest, nappy, and stretchsuit and cover her with a sheet and several layers of blankets. You can check for body warmth during the night by feeling the tummy or the back of the neck, then you can add or take away blankets accordingly. If your baby seems worried by the dark, leave a nightlight on near the cot.

You can help your infant to develop a better sleeping pattern by encouraging her to be more awake

CRYING

Your response to your child's crying and the way that you comfort him can influence the bond that grows between you. There is no risk of spoiling your child by responding to his cries. It is impossible to give a young baby too much love. By going to your baby when he cries you will be showing him that you care and this in turn will help to form a deep, loving relationship between you.

WHY BABIES CRY

Babies cry for a lot of different reasons and you need to understand what makes your baby cry so that you can provide comfort. Your newborn may cry a lot because this is the main means of communicating with you. The infant needs to be able to let you know that the world he is now in is a strange and sometimes frightening place. Once he has adapted to the new environment and you have developed a routine that

takes account of his likes and dislikes, the amount of crying will gradually start to decrease.

Hunger is the most common cause of crying and you will soon learn to recognize when your baby is hungry. The first action is to feed on demand – a young baby may need feeding every two or three hours.

Being too hot or too cold can also make a baby cry. A young baby can't regulate his own temperature and he can easily become too hot or too cold, so it is important to keep a check on an infant's temperature. You should make sure that your baby's room is kept at a constant 18°C/65°F. Wet or dirty nappies do not cause crying except when the wet nappy gets cold.

Your new baby will probably hate being undressed, even in a warm room. This is because the feel of clothing on the skin creates a secure feeling, so when it is removed the infant cries. Keep undressing to a

Crying cures

• Movement soothes a baby so try rocking him or walking around holding him on your shoulder.
• Put your baby in a bouncing seat that will move very gently.
• Push him backwards and forwards in the pram.
• Put the baby in his car seat and go for a drive.
• Talk, sing, or croon soothingly.
• Put on the radio or TV or turn on the vacuum cleaner.
• Distract the baby with a noisy toy.
• Play calm music.
• Carry a young baby next to your body in a sling.

minimum in the first few weeks. Top and tail rather than bath your baby so that you only need to remove a bit of clothing at a time. When you do undress him completely, wrap him in a towel to give him a feeling of security.

Pain is a definite cause of crying, but it may be hard for you to locate the cause of the actual pain. If you

Not being allowed to do what he wants, when he wants, can lead to a child's tears of frustration.

Waiting for a bottle to cool down can be tiresome and can lead to angry tears from a hungry baby.

can, remove the source of the pain –
for example an open nappy pin. If
you can't find a reason for the pain,
don't just leave your baby to cry;
pick him up and comfort him.
Stay with your baby until he is
completely calm. If your baby seems
feverish or just generally unwell,
always seek medical advice.

Any baby will normally start
crying when he is tired. If you think
that this is the cause, put your child
down to sleep in a dimly lit, warm
room. If necessary, rock or sing a
soothing song to him until he has
completely calmed down and starts
to become sleepy.

*Tiredness is a common reason for tears
before bedtime.*

*The discomfort of wind after a feed can
cause a baby's tears.*

Sometimes it all gets too much for a young child and the only way to show his feelings is to scream.

COLIC

Young babies sometimes have prolonged periods of crying during the day which are often attributed to colic. These crying spells often take place around the time of the evening feed, although they can happen at any time of day. Colic, if it is going to occur, usually starts within the first three weeks after birth and normally lasts until around three months, although it can go on for longer. It generally stops as abruptly as it starts, having caused your baby no harm.

Although no one knows exactly what colic is, or what causes it, many doctors believe that it is a type of stomachache that occurs in spasms, and makes the baby draw up her legs in pain. The pattern of crying would indicate cramp-like pains; the baby is miserable and distressed, then calms down for a few minutes before starting to scream again. This may continue for several hours at a time, which can become very wearing and upsetting for both of you.

POSSIBLE CAUSES

Colic has been blamed on many things and it is worth investigating all the possibilities if your baby suffers from it. Since colic affects both bottle- and breast-fed babies the method of feeding is not thought to be the cause. However, if you are breast-feeding it could be something that you are eating that is causing the problem. Try cutting out of your diet anything you have eaten during the previous 24 hours that you think might have affected your baby. It has been suggested that the amount of feeds offered – both too little and too much – could be to blame, or that the milk, if bottle-feeding, could be too hot or too cold, or the feeds too weak or too rich. Remember, when you make up bottle feeds it is essential to follow the manufacturer's instructions.

Other possible causes are constipation, diarrhoea, indigestion or intestinal cramps. Vigorously crying babies are almost always healthy, but if your baby looks pale or ill, seek medical advice.

There may also be a link between tension and colic, which can lead to a chain reaction. The end of the day is usually a busy time in a household and you may be tired and tense as you try to prepare the baby for bed, tidy up, and get a meal ready. Your baby is sensitive to your moods and may respond to tension by crying which, of course, increases your anxiety, with the result that the crying becomes prolonged and ends when you are both exhausted.

WHAT TO DO

There is no reliable treatment for colic and, although there are some over-the-counter medicines available, you should always consult your doctor before giving them to your baby. On a practical level you can rearrange your day by preparing the evening meal earlier, so that you have time to spend comforting your baby during this crying period. Although there is little you can do to ease your baby's discomfort completely, holding her against you, so that there is gentle pressure and warmth on her stomach, and rubbing her back soothingly may be of some help. Try to share the comforting with your partner to spread the strain, and remember that colic doesn't last for more than a few months so, although it is awful at the time, it will not last for ever.

Colic can start as early as three weeks and may last until your baby is three months old. Be patient; it will pass and it won't do your baby any harm.

TEETH

At around six months your baby's milk teeth will start to emerge and by the age of two-and-a-half all 20 first teeth will usually have appeared. Every tooth has two parts: the crown, which can be seen in the mouth; and the root, which anchors

Your baby's first teeth will start to emerge at around six months old, and you should start to clean them as soon as they appear in the gums.

the tooth to the jaw. The outside of the tooth is made of enamel, which protects the crown and provides a strong surface for chewing. Because the enamel is not fully formed when the teeth first come through, calcium and other minerals are required over the next 6–12 months to strengthen it. These minerals are found in the saliva and plaque in your child's mouth and, under normal conditions, will steadily accumulate in the teeth. But calcium and phosphates in the enamel frequently come under attack from acids that are formed by the bacteria living in plaque. These bacteria use carbohydrates, such as sugar, to generate the acid.

Your baby needs carbohydrates, but food and drink containing a lot of simple sugars such as sucrose, fructose, and glucose will speed up the production of the acids which can damage

When he is teething your child will chew anything, even his fingers. Try offering her finger foods, such as a stick of raw carrot, as something different to chew on.

teeth. It is not just the amount of sugar he eats that affects your child's teeth, it is also the frequency of his consumption of sugary food and drink. Drinks taken slowly, or sugary foods eaten over a long period of time, keep the sugar content of the

Chewing and biting on things is often one of the first signs of teething in a baby, and this may occur some weeks before any teeth appear.

Before you start trying to brush your baby's teeth, it is a good idea to let him play with his toothbrush so that he becomes familiar with it and does not cause a fuss when you put it in his mouth.

Your child will find it good fun attempting to brush his own teeth from a very early age.

You will need to clean your child's teeth until he is old enough to do it himself. A fluoride toothpaste will help protect his teeth and gums.

mouth high, which means that calcium and phosphates are being removed for longer and less time is available to replace them. Generally, the lower the sugar content of food and drink the better they are for the teeth because it is the total sugar levels, not just added sugar, that counts. This is why you should never add sugar to your baby's food or drinks and you should always dilute concentrated drinks and give them in a trainer cup rather than a feeding bottle.

CLEANING TEETH

As soon as your baby's first teeth appear, you should clean them every morning and night. Cleaning them before bed is especially important because the flow of protective saliva decreases when your baby is asleep, which means that any sugar in the mouth allows the plaque to stay

acidic for a prolonged period. In the morning, brush your baby's teeth to remove any build-up of plaque that has occurred during the night.

The main point of cleaning teeth is to remove as much plaque as possible, and toothpaste does this with the aid of abrasives; there are toothpastes specially formulated to be suitable for young children. A pea-sized amount of toothpaste on the brush is all that is required to clean a mouth full of teeth. You'll probably find it easiest at first to use your finger wrapped in a soft cloth and then, when your baby has got used to the idea of having his teeth cleaned, you can start to clean his teeth with a soft baby toothbrush.

Since the introduction of fluoride toothpastes, children's teeth have been healthier. Fluoride, which is present in most toothpastes, works by making the enamel stronger

As your child starts to get teeth she will experiment with the chewing action on her favourite toys.

against attack from plaque. The amount of fluoride children should use varies according to their age and the fluoride levels already present in the water.

THE DENTIST

Take your baby with you when you go for your own dental check-ups so that he will become familiar with the dentist and the surgery. By getting your child used to having his teeth inspected before he needs treatment, he will then experience no alarm at the thought of going to the dentist. A child usually won't need to have an actual dental check-up until he is about three years of age, when your dentist will check to see that the teeth are developing properly. The dentist will also be able to advise you about any special protective treatments available for your child.

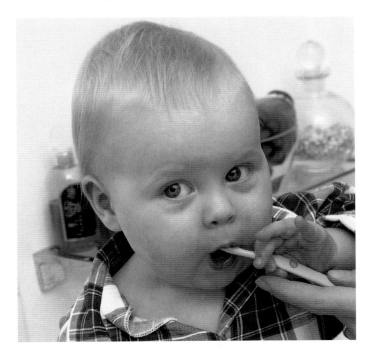

Cleaning your young baby's new teeth at bedtime is essential to prevent the build-up of plaque as he sleeps.

IMMUNIZATION

Diseases such as measles, mumps, whooping cough, rubella (German measles), diphtheria, tetanus, polio, and Haemophilus influenzae type b (HiB) – a cause of meningitis – can be very serious and, in very young children, even fatal. Immunization offers long-lasting protection against these diseases. If you are concerned about the immunizations, or are worried about allergic reactions, or if there is a family history of convulsions, don't just decide not to have your child immunized, talk to your doctor.

The five-in-one vaccination, which immunizes against diphtheria, whooping cough (Pertussis – the medical name for whooping cough), tetanus, polio and Hib is usually given as one injection at two months, three months, and four months of age. In addition, a new pneumococcal vaccine, which protects against pneumococcal infections has been introduced at two, four and 13 months. The menC vaccine that protects against meningitis C is given at three and four months, and then as a combined injection with HiB at 12 months. With all of these it is important to complete the course to ensure the maximum immunity. MMR immunizes against measles, mumps, and rubella and is given in one injection at 13 months.

Your newborn baby may also be offered immunization against tuberculosis (TB) with a BCG vaccine if you are in or from a high-risk area, or if you come from a family that has a history of TB.

SIDE-EFFECTS

After any immunization it is quite normal for the skin around the site of the injection to become red and sore or slightly swollen. Your child may feel a bit off-colour for a while and may run a slight temperature. If you are at all worried about your child you should ask your doctor or health visitor for advice.

Any side-effects from the five-in-one vaccine are usually mild. Your baby may become slightly feverish and appear unhappy for up to 24 hours after the injection. Very occasionally a convulsion occurs as a result of the fever, but this is over very quickly and has no lasting effect.

The MMR immunization has no immediate side-effects, although some children develop a mild fever and rash seven to 10 days after the injection, while others sometimes get a very mild form of mumps. If either of these reactions occur they are not infectious.

If your baby is feverish or acutely unwell, or has had a severe reaction to an earlier immunization, you should not have her immunized again without talking first to your doctor. Always tell the doctor who is doing the immunization if your baby

is taking medication or if she has a severe allergic reaction to eggs. If the baby is vomiting or has diarrhoea it may be better to put off having the vaccination until she is better.

OTHER COMPLICATIONS

Many parents worry about the possibility of more serious effects from these vaccines, especially from the MMR and whooping cough vaccines.

The whooping cough part of the five-in-one vaccination is the one that has in the past been linked to brain damage, but research has shown that there is no link between this and the vaccine.

Parents may be concerned about the suggested link between the MMR vaccine and autism, or the vaccine's possible link to the increase in Crohn's disease, but recent research has shown that there is no evidence to support these fears.

THE DISEASES

Immunizations have developed over the years and many diseases that were formerly feared are no longer threats. This is the result of a sound immunization programme which has been applied to virtually all children.

Often parents are vague about the actual disease themselves, so it is worth familiarizing yourself with the conditions and their symptoms.

Immunization timetable

At 2 months:		At 3 months:	
Diphtheria		Diphtheria	
Whooping cough		Whooping cough	
Tetanus	5 in 1 injection	Tetanus	5 in 1 injection
HiB		HiB	
Polio		Polio	
Pneumococcal		Meningitis C	

Diphtheria starts with a sore throat and then quickly develops into a serious illness which blocks the nose and throat, making it difficult and sometimes nearly impossible for a child to breathe. It can last for weeks and can often be fatal.

Tetanus is caused by germs from dirt or soil getting into an open wound or burn. It attacks the nervous system, causing painful muscle spasms. Immunization has made it rare, but there is still a real chance of getting it and it can be fatal.

Whooping cough is a highly infectious disease that causes long bouts of coughing and choking. These bouts can occur up to 50 times in one day and the cough can last two to three months. Whooping cough can cause convulsions, ear infections, pneumonia, bronchitis, and even brain damage. It can prove fatal, especially in children who are under one year of age.

Bacterial meningitis develops rapidly and can cause serious illness within a few hours. If left untreated seizures can occur, followed by loss of consciousness leading to coma, and in some cases it can be fatal. Even when children recover there is a risk of long-term problems such as deafness and epilepsy.

Pneumococcal infection can lead to meningitis, septicaemia (blood poisoning) and pneumonia if it enters the blood stream it.

Polio attacks the nervous system and causes muscle paralysis. If it affects the breathing the sufferer will need help to breathe and could even die. Thankfully, polio is rare in most Western countries because of immunization, but there is still a risk of contact with the disease through foreign travel, which is why immunization is still important. Adults should check to see if they need a polio booster when they take their baby for immunization.

Tuberculosis (TB) usually affects the lungs; symptoms include a cough, fever, or night sweats. Children are vulnerable and develop TB meningitis more often than adults.

Measles can be much more serious than people think because it is the disease most likely to cause encephalitis (inflammation of the brain). It begins like a bad cold with a fever and then a rash appears, which is often accompanied by a bad cough. Measles can cause ear infections, convulsions, bronchitis, and pneumonia. It can sometimes be fatal.

Mumps is usually a mild illness, but it can have serious complications that affect both boys and girls, and it can cause permanent deafness.

Rubella (German measles) is a mild disease, but one which can harm an unborn baby if a woman catches it when she is pregnant. The risk is particularly high during the first four

At two months your child will be given his first immunizations. Although they will probably cause some momentary discomfort it will all soon be forgotten with a cuddle.

months of pregnancy. Babies whose mothers get rubella during pregnancy can be born deaf, blind, and with heart and brain damage.

At 4 months:
Diphtheria
Whooping cough
Tetanus   } 5 in 1 injection
HiB
Polio
Meningitis C and Pneumococcal

At 12 months:
HiB   } combined
Meningitis C

At 13 months:
Measles   }
Mumps   } MMR one injection
Rubella   }
Pneumococcal

CHILDHOOD ILLNESSES

Knowing what to do when your child is ill and when you should call the doctor is something that comes with experience. Common symptoms that indicate that your child is unwell include sickness, diarrhoea, or a high temperature. These may be accompanied by unusual behaviour such as listlessness, refusing to eat, and crying for no apparent reason. However, it is not always easy to tell when a very young baby is unwell so you should trust your instincts – you know your baby better than anyone. Signs indicating that a baby is ill and you should call the doctor include refusing feeds, a fit or convulsion, extreme drowsiness, difficulty in breathing, severe diarrhoea, vomiting, high fever and the appearance of unusual rashes.

DEALING WITH ILLNESS

Fever occurs when the body temperature rises above normal and is usually caused by an infection. If your child is feverish he will need a lot of cold fluids to drink and a dose of paracetamol syrup to bring his temperature down (aspirin should not be given to children under the age of 12, unless specifically prescribed by your doctor).

If your child is very feverish, keep him in bed and cool him down. This can be done by sponging him all over with tepid water, then covering him with a light sheet and making sure that he drinks plenty of liquids. Alternatively, put a cool fan next to the bed – but safely out of reach.

The easiest way of detecting feverish illness is by taking your child's temperature. This can be done by using a digital thermometer which is placed under your baby's arm (remember this is about 0.6°C/1°F lower than internal body temperature). Older children can hold it under their tongue. You can also use an ear thermometer or hold a fever strip on your child's forehead. Whichever method you use, make sure that you start with a low reading. A normal temperature is 37°C/98.6°F, but a child's can vary between 36°C/96.8°F and 37.5°C/99.5°F. You must phone your doctor if the temperature goes over 39°C/102°F, or if it remains above normal for more than two days.

Medicines for young children usually come in liquid form and can be given to them by dropper, or by using a specially designed spoon; older children can manage with an ordinary spoon. It is important that you know what the medicine is, what it does, and the correct dosage before you give it to your child. If you are in any doubt, check the details with your pharmacist.

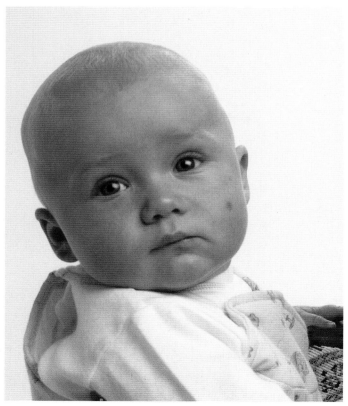

You are the best person to judge whether your child is unwell as you know him better than anyone else. As you become more experienced as a parent you will know whether you need to call the doctor. If you are unsure, it is always better to seek medical advice.

It may be easier to take a young baby's temperature using a fever strip. Place the strip on your child's forehead and hold it there for 15–20 seconds to get the necessary reading.

A more accurate way of taking a temperature is with an ear thermometer, or with a digital thermometer placed in the armpit and held in position for two or three minutes.

SPECIFIC CONDITIONS:

COUGHS AND COLDS

Colds are caused by air-borne viruses, not bacteria, so antibiotics can't be used to help relieve the symptoms. If your child is suffering from a blocked or runny nose, you may need to buy a nasal decongestant or your doctor may prescribe some nose drops, particularly if the cold is hindering your baby's feeding. Seek advice from your doctor or health visitor if a cold is affecting your child's breathing. It is better to be safe than sorry.

Irritating coughs often occur with a cold so if your child has a dry cough ask your pharmacist to recommend a soothing linctus that is suitable for children.

Although a fever strip is not as accurate as a thermometer, it is useful for a quick assessment. It will show a raised temperature so that you can take the appropriate action.

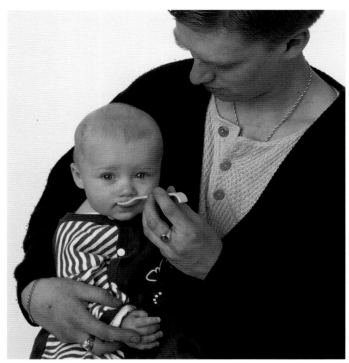

Medicines for young children usually come in liquid form and can be given on a teaspoon. Sit your baby on your knee and hold his hands out of the way as you spoon the medicine into his mouth.

If your child appears hot and feverish you can help to cool him down by wiping his forehead with a face cloth that has been wrung out in cold water.

EAR INFECTIONS

Problems with a child's ears often accompany a cold. One of the first signs is if your baby starts pulling at one of his ears, which might appear red, but he may also just cry a lot and seem generally unwell. Paracetamol syrup will help relieve the pain, but an antibiotic may also be required to clear up any infection, so you will need to consult your doctor for advice. Do not take your child swimming with an ear infection.

CONSTIPATION AND DIARRHOEA

If a child is having difficulty passing stools because they are hard, the problem is most likely to be constipation. A change in diet will be necessary. Including more water, fruit, vegetables, and fibre will help solve the problem. If the problem continues to persist, a mild laxative may be required. Consult your health visitor or doctor for advice.

Diarrhoea is the frequent passing of loose, watery stools. If a baby is being bottle-fed or being weaned, you should omit one or two milk feeds and solids and offer plenty of clear fluids instead, including an oral rehydration mixture if the loose stools continue. Breast-fed babies can continue their milk feeds as normal.

You should contact your doctor if the diarrhoea persists after a period of 12 hours, or if it is accompanied by vomiting because the baby could become dehydrated.

TEETHING

The first signs of teething in a young child are often a red area on his cheek, excessive dribbling, and he starts chewing on his fingers. A teething gel, containing a local anaesthetic, will help to give some relief, but you will need to watch out for any sign of allergic reactions to the gel. These can include a noticeable reddening or swelling of the gums.

VOMITING

If your baby starts to vomit frequently or violently, and if there is any other sign of illness, you should always contact your doctor immediately as young babies can very quickly become dehydrated if they are sick.

Older children can be sick once or twice without suffering any lasting effect. Give your child plenty of clear fluids to drink and don't bother about trying to offer him any tempting food until he feels better.

CHILDHOOD DISEASES

There are a number of diseases that affect most children. If treated promptly, they pose no serious threat and will probably give immunity to the sufferer. The key thing for the parent is to recognize the condition as close to its onset as possible and take the appropriate action.

GERMAN MEASLES (RUBELLA)
This is usually a mild illness which causes few problems. It is rare for a child to get German measles in the first six months if the mother has had the infection or has been immunized. The incubation period is 10–21 days and the virus is spread through the coughing and sneezing of an infected person. It is infectious from the day before the rash appears and for two days after its appearance. It is very important to keep your child away from any woman who might be pregnant if you suspect German measles because it can seriously damage an unborn baby.
Symptoms: The first sign is usually a rash that starts on the face and then spreads to the trunk. The spots are pink, pinpoint in size, separate (not blotchy), and are not raised above the level of the skin. The rash is not

Some babies are born with slight jaundice, a yellowing of the skin, which may need treatment with ultra-violet light. It is usually carried out in the post-natal ward.

The polio vaccine will probably be given to your baby on a spoon at the same time as he has his other injections.

itchy and lasts for only two or three days. It may be accompanied by a slightly runny nose and a little redness around the eyes and swollen glands in the neck, the back of the head, and behind the ears. These may remain swollen for a few days.

Treatment: Check your child's temperature at least twice a day and give plenty of fluids if the temperature is at all raised.

Call the doctor: If you think your child has German measles, contact your doctor to confirm it. Do not take your child to the surgery because of possible contact with a pregnant woman.

MEASLES

It is rare for a child under six months to get measles if the mother had measles as a child, because the mother's immunity is passed on to the baby. The incubation period is 10–15 days and your child is infectious about six days before the rash appears and for five days afterwards. The virus is spread through droplets from the nose and throat of an infected person.

Symptoms: The first symptoms are a slightly raised temperature, runny

One of the first signs of measles are Koplik's spots which appear inside a child's cheeks. The spots are small and red and have a white centre.

nose, cough, redness of the eyes, lethargy, and loss of appetite. Two or three days later white spots about the size of a pinhead, with a surrounding red area, can be seen on the inside of the cheeks. These last for a few days then a blotchy, slightly raised, red rash appears behind the ears and on the face and then spreads to the chest during the next 24 hours. By the third and fourth day it will have spread over the arms and legs and will have reached the feet. The rash is not itchy but it will be accompanied by a high temperature. As the rash fades so the temperature falls.

Treatment: Bring the fever down. If your child's eyes become crusted, wipe them gently with cotton wool dipped in cooled boiled water. Your child can get out of bed as soon as she is feeling better.

Call the doctor: If your child is no better three days after the rash develops; if the child's temperature rises very rapidly; if earache or breathing difficulties develop.

MUMPS

This affects the glands in the neck and in front of the ears and causes swelling. Sometimes mumps causes inflammation of the testicles, but this is rare in boys before puberty. Mumps is unlikely to affect a baby under the age of six months. The incubation period is 12–21 days. Mumps is spread by droplet infection and it is infectious from two days before the swelling appears and until it disappears.

Symptoms: Pain and swelling in one or both of the parotid glands which are situated just in front of the ears. The swelling makes the face appear puffy and reaches its maximum in about two days. It subsides within about five days.

With mumps, your child's face will become swollen and he may find it hard to swallow. Make sure he drinks plenty of liquids and give him jelly and ice cream to eat.

Treatment: Give a suitable painkiller to reduce discomfort. Give your child easy-to-swallow foods such as ice cream and jelly and plenty of liquids, but avoid acidic drinks. If opening the mouth is painful, try getting her to drink through a straw. Warmth will help to soothe the swelling, so heat a soft cloth and hold it gently to her cheeks.

Call the doctor: If your child develops bad pains in her stomach or, if a boy, has a red testicle. Your doctor should be told if you suspect that your child has mumps.

WHOOPING COUGH

This can occur at any age and is one of the most serious common infectious diseases. The incubation period is 7–10 days and the germ is spread through droplet infection. A child is infectious from about two days before the onset of the cough until about three weeks later.

Symptoms: Whooping cough starts with a slight cough and sneezing and is often mistaken for an ordinary cold. It develops into severe bouts of 10–20 short, dry coughs which occur during the day and night – these are often worse during the night. In children over 18 months of age a long attack of coughing is followed by a sharp intake of breath which may produce the crowing or whooping sound. Not all children develop the whoop. During bad bouts of coughing your child may vomit, become red in the face and sweat. The cough can last for two to three months.

Treatment: Stay with the child during her coughing fits because they are distressing and she will need you to comfort her. Try lying her face-down across your lap while she coughs. Sleep with her at night when the cough is at its worst. Keep a bowl near her in case of vomiting and clean it afterwards with disinfectant so that the infection isn't spread. Try to keep your child entertained to distract her from coughing.

Call the doctor: Immediately if you suspect that your child has whooping cough. The doctor may prescribe a cough suppressant and an antibiotic. A very young baby may need to be admitted to hospital if the coughing is affecting breathing.

CHICKENPOX

This is a highly infectious but usually mild disease in childhood (it can be serious if it occurs during adulthood). It is caused by one of the herpes group of viruses and is transmitted through direct contact with an infected person. The incubation period is 14–21 days and it is most infectious before the rash appears, which makes it difficult to isolate an infected child from others.

Symptoms: Chickenpox often starts with a fever, which may be accompanied by a headache and is then followed by a rash. Sometimes the only sign is the rash, which appears mainly on the trunk and

then spreads to the rest of the body and may even occur in the mouth. The rash consists of small red spots that quickly turn into itchy blisters. These gradually dry to form crusts which can remain for a few weeks. New spots appear in batches so an area may be covered in both crusty spots and new blisters. Scars only occur if the spots are scratched or if they become infected. Your child is infectious to other children until new blisters have stopped appearing,

which normally takes about one week.

Treatment: Treat any fever as previously described. Keep your child's nails very short to prevent her from scratching and infecting the spots. Apply calamine lotion to help reduce the itchiness. A handful of bicarbonate of soda added to a cool bath will also ease itchiness.

Call the doctor: If the itchiness is really causing a serious problem or if any of the spots have become infected or are very painful.

Your child will probably feel miserable if he has chickenpox. Try to prevent him from scratching the spots as this will lead to scarring. Applying some calamine lotion to the spots will help reduce the itchiness and irritation.

LEARNING WITH TOYS

Playing with toys is important in a child's development because through play they learn about themselves and the world in which they live. During the first few months your child isn't capable of manipulating objects so he learns through sight, sound, and touch. A young baby likes to see things from close up and will enjoy objects that are colourful and that move or make a noise. A baby doesn't need a lot of toys because in these early months you will be his best plaything and your baby will be endlessly fascinated by your face and will study it during feeding. Sing and talk to your baby because, even though he can't understand, he will love the sound of your voice. As your baby gets older he will start imitating you and making different sounds. Encourage him by playing games such as Pat-a-cake or singing "Old MacDonald had a farm" and getting him to help with the animal noises. Your child may be able to remember simple concepts too, such as putting things in and taking them out of a container. Bath toys will give a lot of pleasure as your baby learns the fun of playing in water.

Toys will help your child learn to develop new skills, and they offer stimulation at each stage of development. For example, a very young baby will gain a lot from a simple pram toy; he can see it, touch it, suck, and smell it and by doing so will be discovering a number of new sensations. It won't take long to learn that a toy pushed out of the pram will just disappear. By performing this trick over and over again your baby will start to realize that he can make things happen which influence his world.

In the first year, toys can be used to help a child to learn hand and eye co-ordination, recognition, and then crawling and walking. As a child gets older, toys become useful props in imaginative games that teach him how to communicate with others, and help him to discover different aspects of life.

A baby will enjoy a play mat that offers her different textures to play with. She will also be fascinated by the bright colours and bold designs featured on the mat.

An activity gym will keep a baby amused from a young age. At first he will just look at the hanging objects, but he will soon start to reach for the toys.

Left: An activity centre is always fascinating to a young baby and this one can be used as a walker too. Toys which will help your child to balance as she begins to pull herself up and then take her first steps will give her confidence.

Below: Although there are many attractive, well-designed toys available, don't be surprised if your baby decides that a wooden spoon and a metal pan are her favourite play things.

There are so many toys to choose from that it's often difficult to decide which ones are right for a child at any particular stage. You should always buy the correct toys for the age of your child. Toys designed for an older child may well have loose parts on which a baby could choke. You should check all the toys a child plays with regularly to make sure that there are no loose or broken parts that could hurt him.

Toys for 0-6 months

- Mobile
- Rattle
- Soft toys
- Baby mirror
- Squeaker
- Baby gym
- Play mat

Toys for 7-12 months

- Cloth or card books
- Big ball
- Soft blocks
- Beakers
- Bath toys
- Pop-up toys
- Musical toys
- Push-along toys

Your young baby will enjoy looking at a toy hung from the pram or above the cot.

This rollaball can be rolled along and will help your baby's hand/eye co-ordination.

Simple toys which are colourful, tactile and chewable will interest a young baby.

As your baby learns to co-ordinate his hands, he will like to hold and feel toys that are easy to handle. This frog also has a baby-safe mirror. Your baby will be fascinated by his own reflection.

A play telephone with push buttons that make different noises will intrigue your baby and keep him amused for hours.

This colourful activity octopus has eight different-textured tentacles for your young baby to grasp and pull at. The caterpillar can be bent into different positions.

Your older baby will enjoy playing with different-sized, coloured stacking beakers.

This stacker has different coloured rings to help an older baby recognize colours and learn how to stack the rings.

This shape sorter offers your child the opportunity to explore different shapes as well as colours.

Once your baby can sit unaided he will enjoy toys such as this train that he can push along the floor.

A simple shape sorter will give your older baby hours of entertainment as he discovers how to put the squares into the holes and then watch them drop inside.

All babies enjoy an activity centre and one that can be fixed to the side of the cot will keep your baby amused when you put him down for a rest.

Pull-along toys will develop and encourage your baby's mobility. They will also help him gain confidence as he learns how to push and pull the toy back and forth along the length of the floor.

BABY MASSAGE

Touch is an important part of your baby's physical and emotional growth, and massage is an ideal way of extending your natural inclination to caress and cuddle your baby. Massage has been used on babies in India and Africa for hundreds of years, not only to help form a bond between mother and baby, but also as a means of relieving colic, helping the digestive system, and making the developing muscles supple. It is thought that gentle stroking encourages the abdominal walls to relax, which helps to alleviate wind and ease colicky pain; massaging the young limbs will also help to strengthen them.

There are a number of specific massage techniques that can be learned, but initially your instinctive touch will be enough, just as long as you are gentle and don't try to manipulate your baby's limbs. You need to be sensitive to your baby's moods and should only massage her when she is content, perhaps between feeds or after a bath. Before you undress your baby for massage, make sure that the room is very warm and draught-free – this is important because babies lose their body heat 10 times more quickly than adults.

Remove any rings or bracelets before you begin and make sure that your fingernails are short and that there are no jagged edges that could scratch or irritate your baby. Relax your hands by stretching and shaking them, then warm them up by rubbing them together. Place a small amount of baby oil on your hands and, with your fingertips, gently massage the baby's skin using light, rhythmic movements. Start at the head and gradually work down to the feet.

Remember, a newborn needs only a feather-light, extremely gentle touch, and you must be careful when stroking the head and around the still-healing navel. The tiny infant will naturally revert to the fetal position, so you shouldn't try to straighten out her arms and legs too much. As your baby gets older you can start to apply a slightly firmer touch, using the whole of your hand in the massage. When you have finished and your baby is dressed, allow her to have a sleep if that is what she seems to want.

Massaging tips

- Don't attempt to massage your baby if she is tired, hungry, or fretful.
- Allow yourself plenty of time so that the massage is not hurried or stressed.
- Get everything you need ready before you begin.
- Don't massage for more than 10 minutes or your baby will start to become bored.
- Talk or sing to your baby during the massage so that it is a pleasurable experience.
- If your baby isn't enjoying the massage, stop immediately and try again another time.

How to massage your baby

1 *Your baby will love the feel of massage. Place him on a towel in a warm room. Take some warmed baby oil into your hand and lightly massage his chest with circular movements.*

2 *Move on to the arms. Gently squeeze down his arms from the shoulder to the wrist. If your baby is happy repeat again up to three times.*

3 *Turn him onto his stomach and, with a hand on each side of his body, massage him from his bottom up to his shoulders, crossing your hands from side to side. Work down again and repeat.*

4 *Placing your hands on either side of his shoulders, bring your thumbs together and gently massage around your baby's neck and shoulders with a circular movement.*

5 *Move both your hands down to your baby's sides and softly knead his skin for a short time between your fingers. Repeat up to three times if he is happy.*

6 *Move your hands into the centre of your baby's back and do some light kneading movements with your fingers up and down the length of his spine.*

To finish your baby's massage, make some soft circling strokes with both hands up and down the back.

TRAVELLING WITH A BABY

The secret of successful travelling with children, no matter how long or short your journey, is careful planning. Young children are surprisingly adaptable, so providing that you take the essentials – food, nappies, and a favourite toy or two – your child should be quite happy to go with you.

The car is probably the easiest form of transport with a baby as you can use it as a kind of nursery on wheels, packing into it everything that you and your child are likely to require. Prepare a survival kit for the journey before you set off and keep it where it is easily accessible. The kit should include spare nappies, a change of clothes, baby wipes, changing equipment, and a mat or towel. If you are bottle-feeding or giving solids, you will also need to include some feeds plus some feeding equipment.

From birth your child should travel in the car in an approved safety restraint suitable for his age and weight. These restraints must be fixed and used properly to obtain maximum protection for your child in the event of an accident.

An older baby will need to be kept amused on the journey and the easiest way to do this is with a selection of toys. Choose toys that have been specially designed for use in the car, or ones which have suction pads that will stick on the window or the back of the front seat. These are better than loose toys, which you may find you have to retrieve each time they are dropped.

Try to make the journey as relaxed as possible by checking the route before you leave and allowing extra time to get there. This way you won't arrive late and anxious because you've had to make a number of unscheduled stops. If you are going on a long journey consider travelling at night. If you are fortunate, your child will be soothed by the motion of the car and will sleep for at least half the journey.

If the journey you are taking involves public transport, you will need to be selective about what you take with you as you'll have to transport your luggage as well as your baby. Take a similar survival kit to the one already mentioned, but make sure it is packed into an easy-to-carry holdall. If possible, take a lightweight pushchair, which you can fold with one hand, leaving the other free, or put your baby in a baby carrier, either strapped on your front if he is still very young, or on your back if he is old enough to sit up on his own.

If you are booking a seat on a train, coach or plane, always mention the fact that you are travelling with a young child when you arrange your ticket and ask for the most convenient seating accommodation available. If the rail or coach station has a lot of steps to be negotiated ask one of the staff to help you, or find out if there is a lift you can use.

Some airlines have sky cots and others will allow you to take a buggy onto the plane as hand luggage. They may even allow you to use your car seat (if it is of a suitable type) as a restraint for your child. Ask the airline or your travel agent what facilities are available for babies and older children before you set off.

Whichever method of transport you use, always shield your child from the sun, and make sure that any exposed skin is protected by a high-factor sunscreen. Keep your baby as comfortable as possible by putting him in clothes that are loose and easy to change. A number of layers of fairly thin clothing are best as this will allow you to add or take away a layer depending on how warm it is. Cars can get very hot in the summer, with the temperature creeping up considerably without you realizing it, so keep a constant check on your child while travelling.

Once your baby can support his head, you can put him in a carrier on your back. But always make sure that it is a comfortable fit.

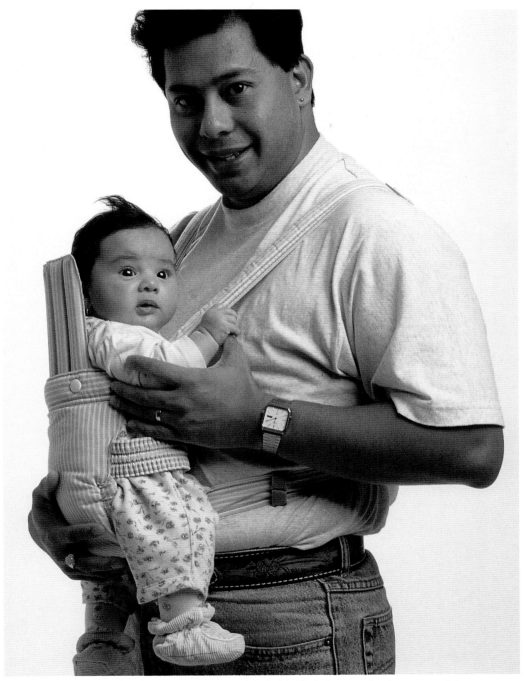

A baby sling is an ideal way for either parent to carry a young baby, both inside the house, or when they are out and about.

KEEPING YOUR CHILD SAFE

Although there is no such thing as a completely safe home, many accidents can be prevented by taking a few safety precautions. High-risk areas can be made safer by installing devices that have been specially designed to prevent your child getting into danger.

HALL, STAIRS AND LANDING

The most common accident in these constantly used corridor areas is a child falling down the stairs, so keep staircases blocked off at both the top and bottom.

What you can do:

• Ensure that there is no loose floor

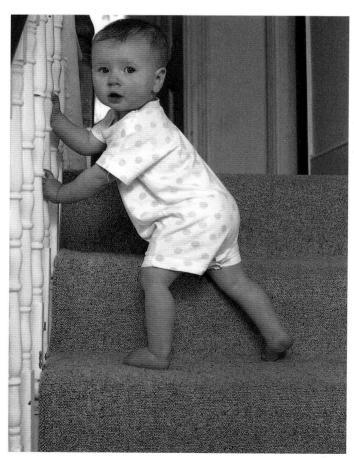

Stairs can be hazardous for your child and should ideally be blocked off top and bottom. Always accompany your child on the stairs and teach him to hold on as he climbs.

covering or any trailing wire at the top of the stairs on which either you or a child could trip.

• If you have carpet on the stairs make sure that it is securely fitted and in a good state of repair.

• Make sure that the gaps between the stair spindles are no more than 10cm/4in so that a child's head cannot get stuck between them.

• Fix gates at the top and bottom of the stairs to prevent young children from having access to them.

• Check that the lighting is good, so that there is no risk of tripping on some unseen object on the stairs.

• Fit safety film or safety glass to any glass doors in these areas.

• Make sure that the front-door latch and letterbox are out of reach.

LIVING ROOMS

These rooms are more difficult to keep safe because the environment is constantly changing as people come in and out and items are moved. Frequent safety checks are needed because the danger areas change as your child becomes more mobile. Try looking at the room from your child's level. One of the biggest dangers in the living area is fire.

What you can do:

• Install a circuit-breaker.

• Install smoke alarms throughout your home.

• Fit all fires with guards.

• Use electrical plug socket covers to prevent a child poking something into the socket.

• Unplug electric fires when they are not in use.

• Make sure that all fabrics and upholstery are made from fire-resistant materials.

• Keep matches, lighters and cigarettes out of reach and regularly empty ashtrays.

A safety gate is an essential piece of baby equipment. Fitted to the top or bottom of the stairs it will prevent your baby from climbing the stairs and falling. Placed across a doorway it will keep your child out of a room, such as the kitchen, where he could be in danger.

As your baby becomes more mobile he will use anything he can hold on to when pulling himself up. Once he is standing, things that were safely out of the way while he was still only sitting or crawling can now be reached.

Ideally, don't smoke at all!
• Fit safety protectors to the corners of tables and cupboards.
• Use mats instead of tablecloths so that your child can't pull things off the table on top of her.
• Place all ornaments and breakables out of reach.
• Check the floor regularly for small objects that could be swallowed.

KITCHEN

This is potentially the most dangerous room in the house for a young child. The most common accidents to occur in the kitchen are scalds from hot water, burns from cookers, and poisoning from cleaning products. What you can do:
• Keep the doorway blocked with a safety gate so that your child can't get in unnoticed.
• Put all sharp objects, such as knives, well out of reach of children.
• Fit safety catches to all low-level

cupboards, drawers, the fridge, and also the freezer.
• Use a shortened coiled kettle flex.
• Cook on the back rings of the hob with the pan handles facing inwards.
• Use a pan guard on the cooker.
• Never leave containers of hot liquid, such as cups or pots of tea, where your child can reach them.
• Make sure that all household chemicals and cleaning materials are kept out of reach and that their lids are always tightly screwed on.

Kitchen cupboards have a fascination for most young children. Safeguard your child by fitting cupboards with safety catches so that he can't open them.

BATHROOM

Among the most common accidents to happen in the bathroom are scalds from hot water, falls in the bath or shower, poisoning from medicines, and cuts from razors, scissors and broken glass.
What you can do:
• Make sure that all medicines and other dangerous objects, such as razors, are locked away in a cabinet which is placed out of easy reach of a child.
• Use a non-slip mat in the bottom

of the bath to prevent your child from slipping.
• Fit a lock to the toilet seat.
• Make sure that your child cannot reach the bathroom window by climbing on the toilet or the bath.
• Always run cold water into the bath before adding hot water and then check the temperature before putting your child into the tub.
• Make sure the water thermostat is not too high. The water should not be above 37°C/98°F.
• Hang a towel over the taps to prevent a child burning herself.
• Check that a child can't reach the door lock and lock herself in.

NURSERY

This is the one room where a child will spend time alone, so regular

Equipment

• Make sure any equipment you buy conforms to the safety regulations established by the European Union (EU) and the British Standards Institute (BSI).
• Only use equipment for the age of the child it has been designed for.
• Second-hand equipment needs to be checked thoroughly for safety.
• Always use safety straps when you put your baby in a pram, pushchair, highchair, or bouncing cradle.
• Never put a bouncing cradle on a raised surface because your baby's active movements could easily make it fall off.
• When travelling in a car, always put your baby in a car seat approved for the child's weight and age.
• Use child locks on the doors.
• Don't leave your child alone in the car, even if she is firmly strapped into her seat.

safety checks need to be carried out as your child grows and becomes more adventurous.

What you can do:

• Make sure that your baby's cot and mattress conform to safety standards and that the mattress fits snugly into the cot base.

• If your child sleeps in a bed, always use a bed barrier and make sure there is a safety gate fitted at the top of the stairs.

• Use a cot light, nursery light, dimmer, or plug light to give your child reassurance at night and to allow you to look in on her without causing any disturbance.

• Install a nursery listening device so that you can monitor your child.

• Place a thermometer in the nursery to help you keep a check on the temperature. The room needs to be around 18°C/65°F.

• If you, or your partner, must smoke, protect children from coming into contact with cigarette smoke, which could put them at risk from coughs, chest infections, and even cot death. There is also some evidence linking passive smoking with the development of childhood asthma.

• Fit any windows with locks.

• Make sure you place the cot or bed away from the window.

OUTSIDE

Many accidents happen outside the home. Even if you have your own garden you should never leave a young child outside unattended.

What you can do:

• Keep all garden tools and chemicals locked away.

• Fit locks to garden sheds and garage doors.

• Make sure that the gate to the road outside is secure.

• Always use a harness and reins, or a wrist link, when you are out on the pavement with your child.

• Make sure that the surface under any play equipment is safe for children to fall on.

• Cover up a pond or a water butt.

A bouncing cradle can be used from around three weeks, and your baby will enjoy reclining in the soft fabric seat. He will quickly learn that by kicking his legs hard he can make the cradle bounce.

Many infant carriers double as car safety seats for at least the first six months. They are usually light and portable so that a newborn will fit into them snugly.

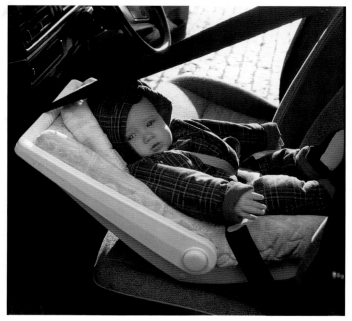

The rear-facing infant carrier can be fitted on both the front passenger seat and the rear seat. If fitted in the front of the car the safety airbag must be disabled first.

FIRST AID

Many accidents can be dealt with when and where they occur. Adults with a sound knowledge of first aid can not only calm a distressed child, but they can also help to limit the effects of an accident, aid recovery, and could save a child's life. First of all you need to assess the situation and establish whether basic first aid is sufficient to treat the injury, or whether you think professional help might be required.

Any minor cuts that a young baby suffers usually can be dealt with on the spot from your first aid box.

GETTING MEDICAL HELP

If your child is unconscious or you think that he may have suffered spinal injury, after a fall, for example, always call an ambulance. If there is even a small possibility of spinal injury, do not attempt to move your child as this could cause severe damage. The best thing you can do is to keep your child warm, still, and calm until the ambulance arrives.

Time is of the essence in dealing with an emergency case that requires immediate medical attention. Should you need to get your child to the hospital urgently, and he can be moved safely, it may be quicker to take him there yourself. If possible, find someone else to drive, so that you can sit with your child in the back seat and give first aid if required. Although it is difficult, it is most important that you try to remain calm and to reassure your child. If you are unsure where the nearest hospital emergency department is, however, or have no suitable transport, then you should call an ambulance; the driver will quickly take you to the nearest suitable hospital.

If you fear that your child has injured his neck or back, call an ambulance and do not move him unless he is in immediate danger. If your child must be moved, you need extra pairs of hands to help turn him onto his back in one movement while holding his neck, shoulders and hips steady.

BREATHING

If your child has stopped breathing, start CPR at once and continue until breathing resumes. Get someone else to call an ambulance.

Rescue breaths:

1 Position – lay your baby or child on his back on a firm surface.

First aid kit checklist

It is important to have a fully stocked first aid kit in your home and you should also carry a basic kit in the car. You can buy ready-made kits, or you can make up your own by buying the items separately and storing them in an airtight container, out of the reach of children. You should check the contents regularly and replace items as they are used, so that you will always be ready for an emergency. Your home first aid kit should contain:

- assorted plasters
- cotton wool
- sterile gauze dressings
- sterile eye pad
- roll of 5cm/2in gauze bandage
- crepe bandages
- triangular bandage
- safety pins
- surgical tape
- scissors
- blunt-ended tweezers
- paracetamol syrup
- antiseptic solution or wipes
- calamine lotion
- clinical thermometer or fever strip
- doctor's telephone number
- details of your nearest hospital casualty department

4 Check breathing – once his airway is open he may breathe spontaneously. Place your ear near the mouth and look along the body for movement. If there is no breathing after five seconds, give two rescue breaths.

5 With a baby, cover his nose and mouth with your lips and breathe gently into his lungs until the chest rises. With a child, tilt his head back and bring the chin forward. Pinch his nostrils, take a deep breath and seal your lips around the child's mouth. Blow steadily until his chest rises.

6 Monitor recovery – your child's chest should rise as you blow air into the lungs, and fall when you take your mouth away. Look for this each time you raise your head to take a new breath of air. Then check for signs of circulation. These include

2 Remove any obvious obstruction, but do not try to clear the mouth by sweeping with your fingers.

3 Open his airway – if your child is unconscious the airway may be blocked or narrowed, making breathing difficult or impossible. With a baby, tilt his chin using one finger. With a child, place one hand on the forehead, gently pushing his head backwards while you tilt his chin with the other hand.

any movement, coughing, or normal breathing. If your child's chest fails to rise the airway may not be fully open, so readjust the position of his head and jaw and try again. Check a baby's pulse on his upper arm. With a child, check the pulse in his neck. If the heart is not beating, external chest compression is needed.

EXTERNAL CHEST COMPRESSION
If your baby is under one year old and there are no signs of circulation start chest compressions:
1 Place two fingers on the middle of your baby's breastbone, just below the nipples. (Use the heel of your hand on an older child.)

2 Use your fingers to compress the chest to one-third of its total depth. Do this five times in three seconds, making the compressions smooth and rhythmic.
3 Give one rescue breath into his lungs and then five more chest compressions.
4 Continue with five compressions followed by one rescue breath until the heart starts beating, or emergency help arrives.
5 Check every few minutes to see if the heart has started beating again. When it does start you must stop the chest compressions immediately.
6 Continue with rescue breaths until your baby begins to breathe on his own.

UNCONSCIOUSNESS AND THE RECOVERY POSITION
If a baby is unconscious but breathing, cradle him in your arms, tilting his head so that his airway is kept open, and phone for medical help. An older child should be put in the recovery position. This prevents the tongue from slipping back into his throat and obstructing his airway, and avoids choking if he vomits. Put your child into this position if unconscious, but still breathing:
1 Lie your child on his back, face turned towards you, keeping the chin pulled down.
2 Place the arm near you at right angles to his body, elbow bent, with the palm upwards.
3 Fold the other arm over your child's chest with the back of his hand against his opposite cheek.
4 Lift the furthest knee, keeping this foot flat on the ground.
5 Keeping your child's hand pressed against his cheek, pull on the thigh furthest away from you, to roll him towards you.
6 Tilt your child's head back with his hand supporting it. Adjust his upper leg so that it supports his body.

7 Cover the child with a blanket and stay with him until help arrives, checking constantly for breathing and heartbeat.

CUTS AND GRAZES
You should seek medical help if there is a serious risk of infection, even with small wounds. But treat minor wounds yourself:
1 Clean the wound and surrounding area under running water.
2 Use an antiseptic cream or saline solution to reduce the risk of infection.
3 Apply a plaster or dressing once the surrounding area is dry.
Never:
• use a tourniquet.
   Larger, more serious wounds must be treated immediately to control the bleeding and to minimize the risk of infection. Once the blood flow has been stemmed you should take your child to hospital:
1 Control any severe bleeding by applying direct pressure to the wound. If possible use an absorbent sterile dressing.
2 If the wound is on an arm or leg, raise and support it.
3 Cover the wound with a sterile dressing and attach it firmly with a bandage or adhesive tape to help control the bleeding.

BURNS AND SCALDS
Burns are caused by dry heat from flames and hot electrical equipment. Scalds are the result of wet heat, such as steam or boiling water. There is always a risk of infection with both burns and scalds because of the damage they do to the skin.
1 Cool the damaged area under cold running water for at least 10 minutes.
2 Try to remove anything that might constrict the area if it swells, for example, rings or tight clothing.

3 Cover with a sterile dressing.
4 Always seek medical advice for all minor burns and scalds.
Never:
• apply butter, oil or grease to the damaged area.
• burst any blisters.
• use adhesive dressings or tape.
• remove anything that is sticking to the burn.

BRUISES AND SWELLING
If your child falls and hits himself, or receives a blow, bleeding may occur under the skin that causes swelling and discoloration. This should fade over about a week. You should hold a cloth that has been wrung out in cold water, or wrapped around an ice pack, to the bruised area for about half an hour to help reduce the swelling.

STRAINS AND SPRAINS
A strain is a tear or rupture of a muscle which causes swelling and discomfort. A sprain is more serious because it involves damage to the joint itself or the ligaments that surround it. Symptoms of a sprain include swelling, acute pain, and restricted movement. Both strains and sprains require the same treatment:
1 Avoid any activity that may overstrain the injured area until the swelling has gone down. Do not massage the injury because this may cause further damage.
2 Cool the injury with a cold pack, a bag of ice wrapped in a towel, or a cold, wet towel. This will reduce the pain and control inflammation.
3 Use a bandage to apply gentle compression to the injured area. This will give support and help to lessen inflammation.
4 Raise and support the injured area as this will help reduce swelling.

APPLYING A BANDAGE
Select the width of bandage appropriate to the area to be covered.
1 Support the injured limb while you are bandaging.
2 Start below the injury site, and wrap the bandage around the limb, using a spiral action, overlapping by two-thirds each time.
3 Secure with a safety pin or some adhesive tape.
4 Check to make sure the bandage isn't restricting the circulation.
5 Bandage injured joints by wrapping the bandage around the joint in a figure-of-eight pattern, overlapping by two-thirds each time.
Never:
• bandage too tightly because this can affect the circulation. If the fingers or toes of the bandaged limb are cooler or darker than the other limbs the bandage is too tight. It should be removed and reapplied, fixing it in position more loosely.
• ignore a limb injury. Always seek medical help if the leg is too painful to take your child's weight, if he is not using his arm, or if any swelling hasn't gone down after 48 hours.

BROKEN BONES
Technically, a broken or cracked bone is a fracture. All fractures should be treated with great care because any undue movement could cause further damage:
1 Keep your child still and cover with a coat or blanket.
2 Remove anything that might constrict any swelling around the injured area.
3 Get medical assistance.

BITES AND STINGS
Bites from mosquitoes and midges or stings from wasps and bees can be extremely painful, causing hard, red, swollen lumps which itch intensely. A small number of people are allergic to wasp and bee stings. If your child appears to be having difficulty breathing as the result of a sting you must seek medical help immediately. In ordinary circumstances:
1 If the sting has been left in the skin, remove it with tweezers, taking care not to squeeze the poison sack because this would force the remaining poison into the skin.
2 Apply a cold compress to the site for quick relief from pain.
3 Massage sting-relief cream into the area for longer-term relief.

EYE INJURIES
Eyes are delicate organs which can be damaged very easily, so immediate first aid treatment is required if an injury occurs:
• Remove any foreign object from your child's eye using a damp piece of cotton wool. If you can't do this or the pain remains after the removal, cover the eye with a clean pad and then take your child to hospital.
• If your child's eye has been injured by a blow, apply a sterile dressing, and take him to hospital for immediate treatment.
• Chemicals that are splashed into the eye should be washed out completely by flooding the eye with some clean, cold water for at least 15 minutes. Then cover the damaged eye with a clean pad and get your child to hospital.

CHOKING
This happens when a foreign object gets lodged in the throat and obstructs the airway.
For a baby:
1 Lay your baby face downwards, with the chest and abdomen lying

Choking

If your baby is choking, you will need to take immediate action. Lay a young baby face down with her chest and abdomen lying along your forearm with your hand supporting her head. Slap her gently on the back several times.

With an older baby or toddler the action would be slightly different. You will need to lay her across your knees, with her head facing downward. To remove the obstruction, slap her firmly between the shoulder blades.

along your forearm and your hand supporting his head.

2 Slap him gently on the back.
Note: if your baby or child doesn't start breathing normally once the blockage is completely removed, call an ambulance and begin artificial ventilation immediately.
For a child:

1 Lay your child across your knee, with his head down, and slap him sharply and firmly between the shoulder blades.

2 If the above fails to remove the blockage, use your finger to try to hook out the object, taking care not to push it further down your child's throat.

CROUP

Croup is a noisy barking cough that may be accompanied by fever and, in severe cases, your child may breathe with a grunting noise called "stridor". Croup can be quite frightening for both you and your child, so it is very important to stay calm and to reassure him. To help remedy the situation:

• Treat simple croup with warm drinks and paracetamol syrup to bring down any fever.

• Ease severe croup by getting your baby or child to inhale steam from a kettle, or sit near a running hot tap in the bathroom or near wet towels over a radiator. Make sure that he

cannot scald himself on the source of the steam.

• If your child is very distressed or has trouble breathing or swallowing, call your doctor immediately, or take him to hospital.

DROWNING

If possible get your child out of the water straightaway, otherwise you will need to give emergency first aid in the water.

1 Empty your child's mouth and, if his breathing has stopped, start to give him recuse breaths. Do not attempt to remove any water out of your child's stomach or from his lungs.

2 If you carry your child, keep his head lower than the rest of his body to reduce the risk of him inhaling any water.

3 Lay him down on a coat or blanket. Open the airway and check his breathing and pulse.

4 Once your child is breathing normally again, remove all his wet clothes and cover him with some warm, dry ones. Give him a reviving hot drink.

5 Always take him to hospital for a thorough check-up, even if he seems to be fine and to have recovered.

ELECTRIC SHOCK

Most electrical accidents occur in the home, so it is vitally important to ensure that household appliances are wired correctly and kept out of the reach of young children. Severe injuries and even death can result from electric shock. But if a shock does still occur:

1 Switch off the current and pull out the plug before touching the child. If this is not possible, use something wooden, such as a broom handle or chair that will not conduct the electricity, to move him right away from the power source.

2 Check his breathing and heartbeat. If your child is unconscious, place him in the recovery position.

3 Treat any burns.

4 Cover your child to keep him warm and reassure him by talking to him calmly.

5 Phone to get some medical assistance immediately.

Never:

• touch your child until the power source has been turned off.

• apply water to a burn that occurs from an electric shock while your child is still attached to the source of the electricity.

NOSEBLEEDS

Bleeding often follows a blow to the nose, or may occur as a result of blowing the nose too hard. Sometimes there is no apparent reason for the nosebleed. The flow of blood can be quite heavy, which can be frightening, although it is not usually a serious problem:

1 Sit your child upright with his head positioned slightly forward. Putting the head back can sometimes cause choking and cause some discomfort.

2 Get your child to breathe through his mouth while you pinch the soft part of his nose firmly for 10 minutes until the flow of blood slows down and stops.

3 If your child's nose is still bleeding, hold a very cold cloth or an ice pack wrapped in a cloth to his nose for a couple of minutes, then pinch his nose again.

4 Try to ensure that your child avoids blowing his nose for several hours after a nosebleed has finally been staunched.

POISONING

This occurs when harmful substances are inhaled or swallowed. It is important to keep all such substances locked away and out of reach of young children.

Always be on the alert and see that your child does not eat any poisonous berries or plants in the garden, or when you are out in the countryside. If you suspect poisoning, ring for an ambulance and then take immediate action:

1 Check breathing and be ready to resuscitate if necessary.

2 If your child is breathing, but is unconscious, place him in the recovery position and then phone for help immediately.

3 If his lips or mouth show signs of burning, cool them by giving water or milk to sip slowly.

4 Keep the bottle or container the poison was in, or a similar berry or fruit to take to the hospital. This will enable the medical staff to administer the correct antidote to your child as fast as possible.

Never:

• try to give fluids to your child if he is unconscious.

• try to make your child sick. This can be extremely dangerous as the poison could find its way into his lungs and cause severe damage to these organs as well as endangering his breathing.

SHOCK

Severe bleeding, burns, and even fear can bring about a state of shock. You can recognize shock by an extreme loss of colour along with cold and clammy skin. The child may also be shivering and sweating at the same time. This may be accompanied by rapid breathing and dizziness, and possibly by vomiting.

Shock often occurs after a major accident, so all the casualties must be treated for shock, even if they are not showing any of the listed symptoms. In extreme cases shock can be fatal, so it requires some immediate action and should always be taken seriously:

1 Lay your child down on his side and make sure that his breathing isn't restricted.

2 Loosen any restricting clothing at his neck, chest, and waist. Then cover your child with a blanket or a coat, but take care not to allow him to overheat.

3 Try to get your child to remain still and to be calm while you seek medical help.

PART THREE

THE FIRST YEAR

YOUR NEWBORN arrives in the world a helpless, totally dependent baby, yet, with your help, within a year she will have learned all the basic skills that she needs to build on for her future growth and development. This section takes you, month by month, through the first year of a child's development. It is, however, important to realize that your child is unique, so there is little point in comparing her with others in anything other than a general way at this stage.

You will want to help and encourage your child as she masters each new skill. Understanding how she learns to talk, crawl, walk and play will enable to you to assist her at each stage. The five senses – hearing, vision, taste, smell and touch – are all extremely important from the time your child is born. As each sense develops, your child will be discovering something new about the world in which she's living.

Being able to participate in this fascinating time in your child's life is a very special privilege. You will be part of the most exciting process in the world: the development of your child from a helpless baby to a confident, independent toddler.

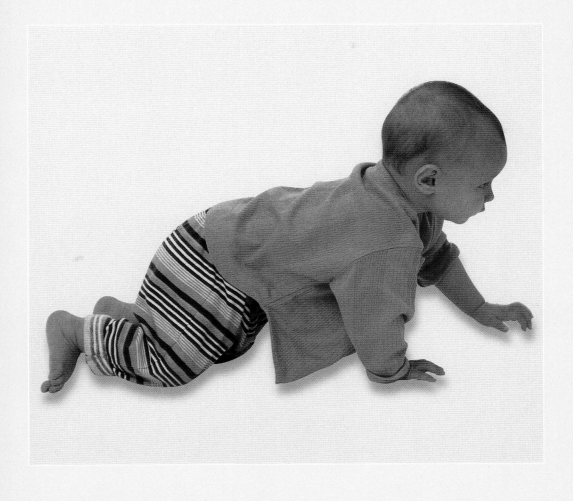

NEWBORN

Your newborn baby will probably look wrinkled and slightly blotchy at first. When he is born his skin may have a bluish tinge and the legs may even be a different colour to the rest of his body. This will only last for a short time, until oxygen from the lungs has had time to reach the bloodstream. You may also find patches of dry skin. Eyes may be reddish and slightly swollen and your baby may still be covered with vernix, the greasy white substance which has been protecting the skin from becoming waterlogged by the amniotic fluid. There may also be a covering of lanugo, fine hair which covers the shoulders, upper arms, and legs.

Your baby's head may look too big for his body. It is usually about one-quarter of the total body length and it may be a slightly odd shape because of the pressure that was put on it during the birth. His features may also appear slightly flattened from being squeezed through the pelvis. Your baby's head may be covered with very thin hair or have a thick thatch that stands up on end.

Milestones

Your child is immediately able to:
• Hear and respond to noises.
• Focus on objects that are within 20–30cm/8–12in.
• Grip your finger tightly.
• Suck vigorously.
• Make walking movements when held on a hard surface.
• Turn towards you when you stroke his cheek.

An increase in female hormones from the placenta just before birth affects both boys and girls and your baby's genitals may be enlarged and breasts may appear slightly swollen.

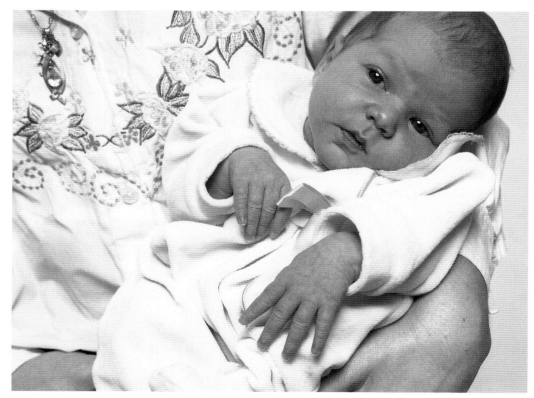

When a baby is born he can be between 45–55cm/18–22in long and weigh anything between 2.5–4.5kg/5½–10lb.

It is quite usual for the breasts of both boys and girls to have a milky discharge; girls may have a slight vaginal discharge as well. All these features will disappear over the next few weeks.

SIZE

Although the average weight of a baby at birth is 3.4kg/7½lb, wide variations occur so, assuming that your baby was born around the estimated date of delivery (EDD), it could weigh anything between 2.5–4.5kg/5½–10lb. Your baby's weight is determined by a lot of factors, including your size and the size of your partner, how much weight you put on in pregnancy, and your general health.

Your baby is quite likely to lose weight during the first week. This is because it takes a little while for regular feeding to become properly established. Once an infant is feeding well his weight should remain stable for a couple of days and then, within seven to 10 days, he will regain his birth weight. A baby's weight gain is one of the easiest ways of telling whether he is thriving.

The average length of a newborn is between 48–51cm/19–20in, but as with weight, this can vary, although most babies are somewhere between 45–55cm/18–22in.

REFLEXES

A baby is born with a number of reflexes. The rooting reflex means that your child's mouth automatically searches for your nipple; grasping is seen when your baby demonstrates a surprisingly strong grip. When on his back, your baby may adopt the tonic neck reflex – the head is turned to one side and the arm and leg on that side are extended while the opposite ones are flexed. A loud noise or the sensation of falling causes the startle or Moro reflex: the newborn extends legs, arms, and fingers, arches the back and throws the head back and then draws back the arms, fists clenched, into the chest. All these initial reflexes will gradually diminish over the next weeks and months as voluntary movements take their place.

In addition to these reflexes, every baby is born with the ability to suck, swallow, and gag so that they can feed as soon as they are born. The gagging reflex prevents a baby from choking on too much liquid and allows the child to get rid of any mucus that may be blocking up his airways.

Your newborn will probably hiccup and snuffle a lot at first. Hiccups occur because the baby's breathing rhythm is still rather jerky.

The cord which attached your baby to the placenta is cut at birth but a small sharp stump remains for a week or so. This will dry up and drop off leaving a healed navel.

They don't hurt, or even particularly bother the baby in fact, so you need not worry about them at all. Your baby will also make some snuffling noises. This is from learning to breathe through his nose and because the nasal passages are still very small. As the nose gets bigger the snuffling will stop.

All babies are sensitive to bright lights and this may make them sneeze when they first open their eyes. This is because the light stimulates the nerves in their nose as well as their eyes. Sneezing is also a way of clearing the nasal passages and it will prevent any dust from getting into the baby's lungs.

CRYING

Your baby may make his first cry as soon as his chest has been delivered, others wait until they have been born or until they start to breathe normally. These first cries are often not much more than a whimper and the full-bodied cry follows later. A baby may look red and angry while crying, but this is quite normal. Crying is a baby's way of communicating as well as a means of exercising his lungs.

Hunger is the main reason for a newborn to cry, but being lonely, wet, or tired will also make a baby cry. Some babies cry because they don't like being undressed, others

when they are immersed in water. Some babies are more fretful than others so they cry more. You will quickly learn to recognize why your baby is crying and the best way to soothe him.

NEWBORN TESTS

The first test your baby will be given is the Apgar test. The scores are recorded at one minute after birth and then again at five minutes and they reflect your newborn's general condition. Babies who score between 7 and 10 are in good to excellent condition, those who score between 4 and 6 are in fair condition, but may need some resuscitative

A newborn baby might initially have a stepping reflex, but this will soon be replaced by voluntary movements.

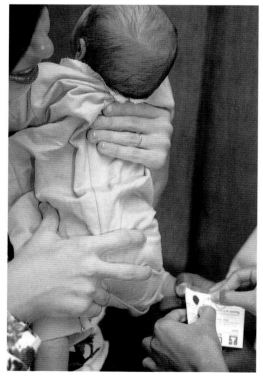

When a baby is six or seven days old he will be given the Guthrie test to test for a range of rare diseases.

Apgar table			
Score	**0**	**1**	**2**
Appearance (colour)	pale or white	body pink, extremities blue	pink
Heart rate	not detectable	below 100	over 100
Grimace (reflex irritability)	no response to stimulation	grimace	cough, sneeze
Muscle tone	flaccid (no or weak activity)	some movement of extremities	moving
Respiration (breathing)	none	weak, gasping, irregular	crying, regular

measures. Babies who score under 4 will need some immediate emergency treatment.

Sometime, soon after the birth, your baby will be thoroughly checked over. A doctor will check your baby's head circumference, the fontanelles, and the roof of the mouth to see if there are any abnormalities. The doctor will listen to the heart and lungs and feel your baby's abdomen to check that the internal organs such as kidney, liver, and spleen, are the right shape and size. The genitals are also checked for abnormalities and, if your baby is a boy, the doctor will look to see that both testicles have descended. Hips will be checked for possible dislocation and all the limbs will be inspected to see they are the right length and are moving correctly. The doctor will run his thumb down the baby's spine to make sure that the vertebrae are in place. The baby's reflexes will also be checked.

The Guthrie test is usually done in the first 10 days after birth. A blood sample will be taken from the baby's heel. The blood is then tested for phenylketonuria (PKU), a rare disease which causes severe mental handicap, and for thyroid deficiency.

SPECIAL CARE

If your baby is born several weeks early, the birth weight is low, or your child needs extra care for any other reason, he may be put in the Special Care Baby Unit (SCBU). Here the infant will be monitored so that he gets all the special treatment required. It can be distressing to see your baby in a special care unit, especially if he is surrounded by an array of strange equipment. Ask the staff to explain what the equipment is for and why your baby needs it. Try to spend as much time as you can with your baby in special care because, even if you can't pick him up and hold him, your baby will be able to hear your voice and it will soothe him. You will probably be able to touch your baby through the side of the incubator.

If your baby is born early, he may have to go into the Special Care Baby Unit. Don't be afraid to ask about all the equipment he is attached to, and let him know you are there by touching and talking to him.

ONE MONTH

Your child may be able to:
- Lift her head briefly while lying on her stomach.
- Focus on your face while feeding.
- Respond to a small bell being rung by moving her eyes and head towards the source of the sound.
- Follow with her eyes an object which is moved in an arc 15–25.5cm/ 6–10in away from her face.
- Turn her head towards you when you speak to her.

Even at this early age your baby will be interested in things around him.

Your baby's movements are still dominated by the primary reflexes so when placed on her back your infant will adopt the tonic neck reflex posture, with her head to one side and the limbs on that side extended while the ones on the other side are flexed. If you place your baby on her front her head will turn to one side, then she will pull her knees under the abdomen and hold her arms close to her body, with her hands curled into fists. The fingers and toes will fan out when she straightens her arms or legs. If you hold your baby to stand on a hard surface she will press down and make a forward walking movement.

Although your baby was born with vision and can see colours and shapes at close range, her sight is still immature. Images which offer a high contrast and simple patterns, for example black lines on a white background, are easier for a baby to understand than paler, more complicated designs. Hold your baby upright or in a half reclining position

A young baby will often hold his arms close to his body and clench and unclench his fists when lying on his back.

if you are showing her something; this will help to keep the child's interest and will stop her dropping off to sleep. Cot books, with bold patterns and shapes which attract very young eyes, placed where a baby can see them, will help develop visual powers.

Babies can recognize their mother's smell from the earliest days and your baby will be able to distinguish between the smell of your breast milk and that of any other mother. She can also tell the difference between the smell of formula or cow's milk and your milk.

MINOR BLEMISHES

Occasionally babies may be born with some minor skin blemishes. These are usually harmless and require no treatment; they disappear on their own as the skin matures. *Milia* are tiny white spots on the face, caused by blocked oil glands. They should fade after a few days. *Stork marks or bites* are red marks which occur around the back of the neck, on the eyelids, or across the bridge of the nose. They usually disappear in the first few months. *Strawberry marks* are raised red marks that sometimes appear in the days after the birth and they may grow rapidly during the first few weeks. These usually disappear after about six months, although they can last until the child is much older. Treatment may be required if the mark has not disappeared by the time your child is in her teens. *Port wine stains* are red or purple marks that are usually found on the face and neck. These are permanent and will require treatment once your child is older.

Urticaria, or nettle rash has a raised white centre surrounded by an

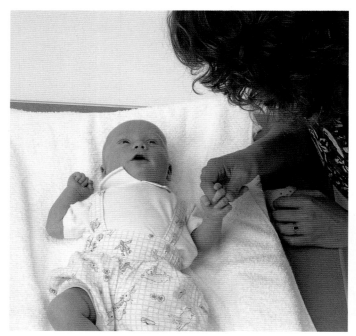

When you are changing your baby, always make time to play and talk to him.
This will make him feel secure and at ease.

FRESH AIR

A baby needs fresh air, so if you have a garden or secure outside area and the weather is warm enough you can let your infant sleep outside in the pram from the first week or so providing that she is well covered up and away from draughts. When it is hot, use a canopy rather than the pram hood so that the air can circulate, and make sure that the pram is in the shade. When outside, protect your baby from cats and

inflamed red area and quite commonly occurs during the first weeks. This rash doesn't require any treatment and will usually clear up after the first month.

INFECTION

Thrush is a fungal infection that produces white patches on the baby's tongue, the roof of her mouth, and in her cheeks. It can be caught from unsterilized feeding teats and dummies or from the mother if she was suffering from vaginal thrush at the time of the birth. Thrush can also appear on the baby's bottom as a red rash which spreads from the anus over the buttocks. Oral thrush is treated with anti-fungal drops and thrush on a baby's bottom needs to be treated with antibiotic cream. Both can be obtained from your doctor.

Above: White patches on the tongue are
one indication that your baby has thrush.
This is easily treated.

insects with a fine mesh pram net. If you have no place to leave the baby outside, put her in the cot or crib and open the window to let fresh air into the room. Don't leave a baby in her cot or pram for too long when she is awake because she will get bored. Babies need other activities to stimulate them as well as exercise.

Taking your baby on outings in a baby sling or carrier is another way of giving your baby fresh air and a convenient way for you to carry her

if you don't want to push a pram. Your baby will enjoy being close to you and will be able to see the world from a different viewpoint.

NOISE

There is no need to tiptoe around or to get people to whisper while your baby is asleep. If you do, it could mean that your baby won't be able to go to sleep if there is any noise and will wake at the least little sound, which can cause sleep

problems when your child is older. A very young baby will quickly learn to sleep through the everyday noises that go on in a home, such as the television and vacuum cleaner. Sudden loud noises may wake your baby, but reassurance and a cuddle should soon settle her down again.

When newly born your baby's vision is not well developed, so hold her up to talk to her and let her focus on your face.

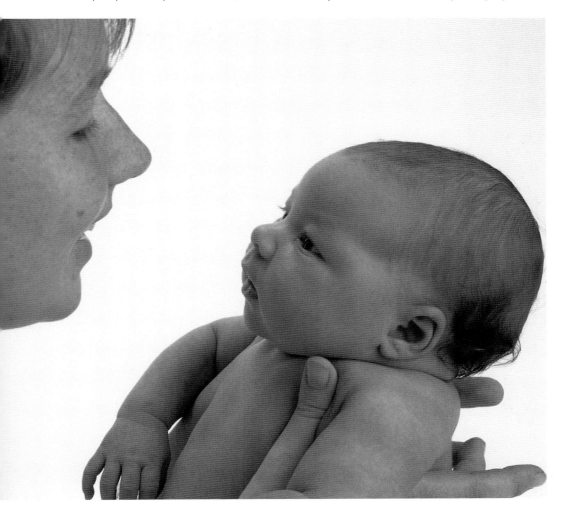

TWO MONTHS

Your baby is developing quickly and, although you may not realize it, he is already trying to talk to you by making a number of vowel sounds and throaty gurgles. At first it may not seem as though these noises are actually directed at you because your baby will enjoy practising these vocal exercises as much for his own benefit as for yours. Each new noise is helping your baby discover which combinations of throat, tongue, and mouth actions make which sounds. As your baby masters each new sound you will begin to notice that he uses them to communicate vocally with you.

CRYING

Your baby now stays awake for longer periods between feeds and is usually more awake in the evenings. It is quite likely that your baby will use some of this extra waking time to cry. Of course not all babies are the same and yours may cry very little, but on average babies usually cry for two to three hours a day and

Milestones

Your child may be able to:
- Smile.
- Begin to make cooing noises.
- Lift his head 45° when lying on his stomach.
- Grasp a rattle for a few seconds if one is put in his hand.
- Follow an object which is moved in a 180° arc above his face.

much of this takes place in the evening. Often this is blamed on colic, thought to be a type of stomach or abdominal ache occurring in spasms, which makes a baby draw up

At two months, your baby will start to smile at you and will turn her head to follow objects moved above her head.

his legs in pain as he screams. No
one knows exactly what colic is, but
if it is going to occur it usually starts
within the first three weeks of birth
and lasts until around three months,
although it can go on longer. There
is no reliable treatment for colic and,
although there are some over-the-
counter medicines available, you
should consult your doctor before
giving them to your baby.

Colic isn't always the cause of
excessive crying; some babies cry for
no obvious reason for some time
each day. If your baby does this you
may be able to offer comfort by
rocking, letting him suck, or by
distracting him with a toy. Don't

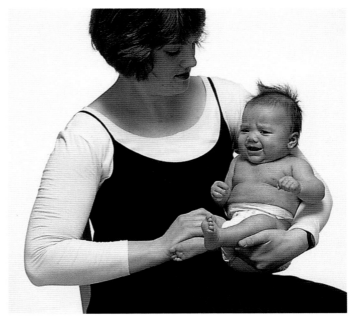

When you support your baby in a sitting position, she can hold her head up for a minute.

Holding and cuddling your young baby is an important part of her getting to know you.

leave him to cry for more than a few minutes; at this age crying is the only way to let you know that he is miserable and needs comforting.

LEARNING CONTROL

Your baby is gradually gaining control of his body. When you place the child on his stomach he will be able to lift his head, keeping the nose and mouth free to breathe. If held in a sitting position, your baby will be able to hold his head up for about a minute, and if you touch his hand with a rattle your baby will jerk his hand towards it. This is the first stage of learning when he reaches out to hold something.

SIX TO EIGHT WEEK DEVELOPMENT CHECK

The ages at which developmental screening takes place vary within each health authority and with the individual needs of the child. But in general, you can expect your child to have an initial developmental check sometime between six and eight weeks. This will be carried out

Immunization

Your baby will be offered the first round of immunizations at two months. He'll be given two injections, usually into the upper thigh. After the immunization your child may feel a bit off-colour for up to 24 hours and may even run a temperature. Rarely, a convulsion may occur as a result of the fever, but this is over quickly and has no lasting effect. It is also quite normal for the skin around the site of the injection to become red and sore or slightly swollen. If you are at all worried about your child's reaction, contact your doctor immediately.

Learning head movements

1 *At this stage of development, your baby is gaining control of her body. When lying on her stomach, with her arms supporting her, she can start to lift her head.*

2 *As she manoeuvres herself into position, she pushes hard with her legs and starts to put her weight on her arms.*

3 *As she raises her head, pushing up with her arms, she will find she can hold it up, keeping her nose and mouth free to breathe.*

Make sure you allow enough time to play and have fun with your baby, so that you can really get to know her.

at the child health clinic by a doctor or health visitor, or at your doctor's surgery. These checks are part of the child health surveillance programme and their aim is to detect any problems early, to prevent illnesses, and to promote good health. If the checks detect any early signs of delayed development, or health or behaviour problems, treatment can be begun at once. A number of routine checks take place between now and when your child reaches school age. They are all important because the checks are designed to reveal hidden disabilities as well as more obvious ones.

This early check will include measuring your baby's weight, length and head circumference and noting the changes since birth. You will probably be asked questions about how your baby is feeding and sleeping. General progress will be assessed and the doctor may also carry out a series of tests to evaluate your baby's head control, use of hands, vision, hearing, and social interaction. You may be given guidance about what to expect during the next month in relation to feeding, sleeping, and development. You may also be asked questions about how you, the baby, and the rest of the family are managing with your new baby at home. This is the time to voice concerns or problems that have been worrying you.

At six to eight weeks your baby will be given a developmental check-up at the health clinic or your doctor's surgery. This will detect any early problems.

THREE MONTHS

Below: As you pull your baby up at this age, he will now be in more control of his head movements.

Your baby will probably have begun to control her head movements, so that when held in a sitting position she can keep her head up for several seconds before it drops forward. As her neck strengthens your baby will be able to look around and turn her head to watch something moving within 15–20cm/6–8in.

EARLY LEARNING

As babies begin to understand their own body, they will spend hours studying and moving their fingers. Their hands have opened out now and they can clasp and unclasp them, pressing the palms together. Babies enjoy playing with them and may even be able to hold a small toy for a few seconds. When your baby is lying down you will probably notice that her arms and legs make a lot of

Below: When your baby lies on the floor, he will often raise her head for several seconds before it drops forward.

Below: As your baby sits up, he can hold his head steady more easily because his neck has strengthened.

Bottom: Your baby will be fascinated by any toys in bright, primary colours that are hung over her cot.

Milestones

Your child may be able to:
- Smile and coo when she sees you.
- Control her head.
- Show anticipation when she is about to be fed by licking her lips.
- Enjoy looking at brightly coloured objects such as a mobile hanging over the cot.
- Play with her hands.
- Hold a small toy for a few seconds.

movement. She will kick vigorously, usually with alternate legs, but occasionally with both legs together.

The first smiles are reflexive, but they very quickly become social and the baby will smile at you in response to your smile or voice. The smiles will come in clusters, four or five at a time, followed by a pause of maybe half a minute before the next cluster. The baby will also respond vocally when you speak to her.

Talk to your baby and she will answer you back in her own way, using her lips and tongue as she coos and tries to imitate you. She uses her whole body to express the way she feels, making excited movements when pleased, expressing happiness and delight with gurgles and squeals. When she is angry, uncomfortable, or lonely she will tell you by crying loudly and angrily. To encourage your baby, you should respond to her behaviour with exaggerated gestures and praise, using a slow singsong voice and lots of repetition.

A baby will react to familiar situations and will show excitement when she recognizes preparation for things that she enjoys. She responds with obvious pleasure to friendly handling, especially when it is accompanied by play and a friendly voice. Bathtime and other caring routines, where she has your undivided attention for quite a while, are likely to become her favourite times of the day.

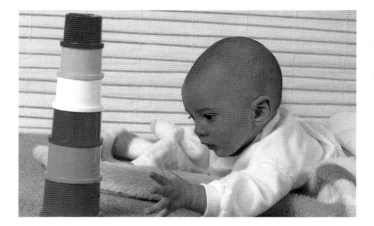

Left: Plastic stacking toys in bright colours will soon attract the attention of your inquisitive baby who will try to grasp hold of them.

Below: Lying on his back, your young baby will enjoy kicking vigorously with alternate legs and sometimes with both legs together.

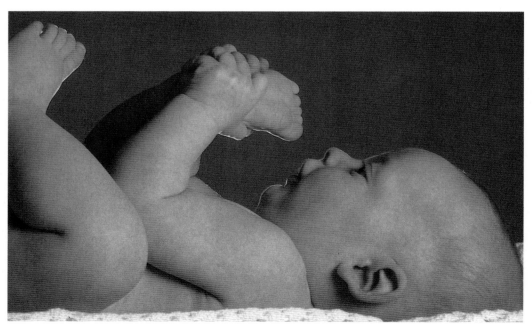

If you haven't already done so, introduce a regular bedtime routine now so that your child starts to realize that a bath, a story, and a cuddle are a prelude to being put into the cot to sleep. By about three months many babies begin to sleep for long periods at night. If your baby has started to sleep through the night you will probably find that she needs less sleep during the day and that her daytime sleep is not as deep as it was. You may find that your baby is more easily disturbed by household noises now. Encourage her to stay awake during the day by stimulating her with different toys and by playing and talking with her.

Immunization

At three months your baby will have the next round of injections on the immunization programme. If there was any adverse reaction after the first injections tell your doctor.

Your baby is now using her whole body to show her feelings, and will start to recognize her favourite toys.

FOUR MONTHS

Your baby is developing rapidly. He is awake for much longer and during these waking periods will want to be sociable and will respond with delight to conversations with you and enjoy playing simple games.

You can encourage your baby's development by spending time responding to these early attempts at sociability. Make a point of showing your baby different objects and talk about them. Your baby will also enjoy seeing and talking to himself in a mirror. Place the mirror about 15–20cm/6–8in away so that he can keep his image in focus.

Motor development and learning progress at the same rate between four and five months. Hand and eye co-ordination is being learned and your baby may be able to reach out and grasp an object. He will try hard to learn how to sit because he will have discovered that sitting up gives him a different view of the world. At first he will need you to help him balance, but as his confidence grows he will learn to adjust his legs and to use his hands to keep himself upright.

GETTING READY FOR SOLIDS
Babies get all the nourishment they require from breast or formula milk during their first six months, although you may notice that your baby begins to show the physical signs that he's getting ready for solids before this.

A baby needs to be able to have control over his head before he can move on to solid food. Even strained or puréed first foods should not be given until he can hold his head

At four months your baby will try to sit up with your help.

Milestones

Your child may be able to:
• Lift his head up 90° when he is on his stomach.
• Raise himself up a little way, supported by the arms, when lying on his stomach.
• Laugh out loud.
• Hold his head steady when he is held upright.
• Roll over in one direction.
• Reach out for an object.

As your baby gains control over his head he will be able to hold it at different angles.

As he gets more active your baby will probably start to learn how to roll over in one direction. First, he will grab his foot with his hand and lift that leg up.

When your baby is lying flat on his stomach, he will now be able to raise his head up 90° and support himself more sturdily on his arms.

He'll then push down this leg, and helped by his bottom arm, roll his body over in one direction.

Your baby will now start to reach out for interesting toys and often try to put them in his mouth.

A young baby is fascinated by mirrors, but at distances she can only make out vague shapes.

If you place your baby 15–20 cm/6–8 in away from a mirror, she will be able to focus on her image and chat to herself.

upright when he is sitting propped up. A baby needs to be able to sit up unaided before chunkier foods that require chewing are given to him. This doesn't usually happen until about seven months.

First solids, given at around six months, are little more than tasters that get a baby used to the idea of sucking from a spoon rather than from the breast or bottle. To be able to do this the tongue thrust reflex, which the baby was born with, must have disappeared. This is the reflex that causes the tongue to push any foreign matter out of the mouth and prevents very young babies from choking. To be able to eat from a spoon your baby also needs to be able to draw in his lower lip.

Another fairly obvious sign to look out for which shows that your baby is ready for solids is if he shows any interest in the food that you are eating. If your baby watches intently while you eat and shows excitement or tries to grab your food, then he is probably telling you that he is now ready for more grown-up food himself.

Although it is recommended that babies are not given solids before six months, if you feel your child is ready before this ask your health visitor or doctor for advice.

THUMB SUCKING
Your baby will suck anything he can get into his mouth and now that he has some control over his hands, his fingers and thumbs will be preferred and he will suck them for pleasure and also for comfort. He may suck his whole hand, or one or two fingers, or he may prefer his thumb. This is quite normal and is not a sign of emotional distress, nor will it, at this age, damage the alignment of permanent teeth. If your baby is breast-fed you need to make sure that he isn't sucking his thumb to compensate for suckling he is no longer getting at the breast, otherwise there is no harm in letting your child suck his thumb. Most children grow out of this habit over the next year or two, although a child who uses sucking his thumb as reassurance to get to sleep may take a little longer to break the habit. This is nothing to worry about.

Immunization
At four months your baby will have the third round of immunizations. After this he will not have any further immunizations until he is one year old.

You can now give some solids to your baby if she can hold her head upright and if food isn't rejected by her tongue.

Your baby will try to stand with help, but he shouldn't put too much weight on his legs.

FIVE MONTHS

Your baby's grasp of basic concepts is growing and she is thinking much faster. It is thought that a baby when she is first born will take between five and 10 minutes to get used to something new; by three months a baby may take between 30 seconds and two minutes and by six months she will take only 30 seconds. Your baby will begin to learn about cause and effect by carrying out simple experiments, such as throwing a toy out of her pram. Initially she will believe that it has vanished and won't

Milestones

Your child may be able to:
• Hold her head steady when upright.
• Keep her head level with her body when pulled into the sitting position.
• Pay attention to a small object.
• Squeal with delight.
• Be able to say vowel-consonant combinations such as "ah-coo".

At five months, your baby will be able to lift her head up from a lying position and hold it steady.

She will love to suck things, and will often put her hands or feet in her mouth.

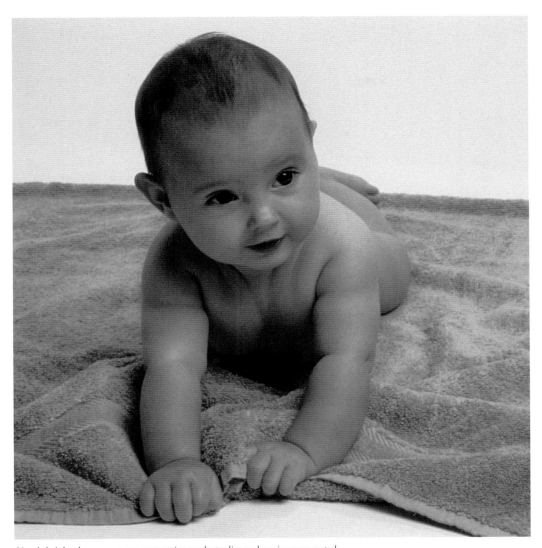

Your baby's head movements are now getting much steadier as she gains more control.

understand where it has gone. If you pick up the toy and return it she will be both puzzled and delighted. She will do the trick again and again until she begins to realize that, by dropping the toy and getting it back, she is beginning to take control of her world by making things happen.

You can encourage your baby with her experiments by playing games such as peek-a-boo, or hiding an object that was in front of her and then making it reappear again. At this age your baby won't attempt to recover what you have hidden because she thinks that the object no longer exists because she can't see it.

It will be several months before she learns that this really isn't the case and starts looking for the hidden object herself.

TEETHING

There is no fixed time for your baby to start teething, but on average a baby's first tooth appears sometime

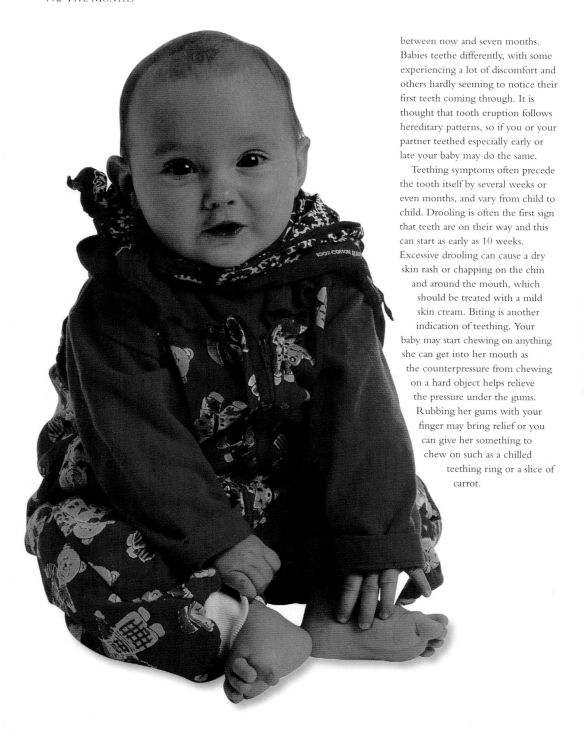

between now and seven months. Babies teethe differently, with some experiencing a lot of discomfort and others hardly seeming to notice their first teeth coming through. It is thought that tooth eruption follows hereditary patterns, so if you or your partner teethed especially early or late your baby may do the same.

Teething symptoms often precede the tooth itself by several weeks or even months, and vary from child to child. Drooling is often the first sign that teeth are on their way and this can start as early as 10 weeks. Excessive drooling can cause a dry skin rash or chapping on the chin and around the mouth, which should be treated with a mild skin cream. Biting is another indication of teething. Your baby may start chewing on anything she can get into her mouth as the counterpressure from chewing on a hard object helps relieve the pressure under the gums. Rubbing her gums with your finger may bring relief or you can give her something to chew on such as a chilled teething ring or a slice of carrot.

Delight your growing baby with different types of toys to keep her interested and fully stimulated.

Inflammation of the tender gum tissue often occurs when a tooth is coming through so your baby is likely to have red, sore gums before a tooth erupts. Ear pulling and cheek rubbing may also be a sign of teething as pain can travel along the nerve pathways to these areas. This is particularly common when the molars are coming through. If your child seems to be in pain you can give her the recommended dose of paracetamol. However, never attribute illnesses such as diarrhoea, fever, or earache to teething: if you are concerned seek medical advice.

Your baby will often prefer a simple toy like this rattle as it is easier for her to manage and play with.

SIX MONTHS

Your child is beginning to show a greater interest in what is going on around him. He will turn his head quickly to familiar voices and will examine things that interest him for longer periods. If your baby hasn't started on solids yet, now is the time to introduce them.

THE BABY TAKES CONTROL

Your baby is rapidly becoming more mobile and will probably be able to pull himself into the sitting position if both hands are held. When lying on his stomach, he may find that kicking will push him along, usually backwards at first. If he becomes frustrated because he can't get to where he wants to go, don't be too eager to help him: encourage him by placing a toy just out of reach, or by placing your hands against his feet so that when he kicks he has something to push against. If you pick him up and place him where he wants to go he will not learn how to achieve this for himself.

Your baby's ability to reach and grasp is becoming more accurate and you can help him improve these skills by passing objects in such a way that he has to reach up or down or to the side for them. Toys strung across his cot or playpen will allow him to practise using these skills. Your baby will hold objects in the palm of his hands, and will be able to pass them from one hand to the other. You can encourage him by giving him two toys simultaneously, one in each hand, so that he has to reach out with both hands. If you offer him a rattle, shake it to make a noise as you hand it to him; he will reach for it immediately and then shake it deliberately to make the same noise.

Visually your baby is keenly aware of everything that is going on around him and will move his head and eyes eagerly in every direction to which his attention is attracted. He will follow what you are doing, even if you are busy on the other

Milestones
Your child may be able to:
• Laugh, chuckle, and squeal aloud and scream with annoyance.
• Use whole hand to grasp objects and can pass them from one hand to the other.
• Move his eyes in unison and turn his head and eyes towards something that attracts him.
• Play with his feet as well as his hands.
• Can manipulate small objects.
• Start to be wary of strangers.

Right and opposite: If you have a very active baby it is best not to put her in her high chair at meal times until her food is ready to eat or has cooled, as she will only get restless and may have a temper tantrum because she can't easily move around. A quieter baby will probably be quite happy to sit in her chair and play for a while with a stimulating toy that you have given her. If she is content to sit quietly and amuse herself until you can feed her, it will also give you peace of mind that she is safe and not getting into any other mischief as you prepare her food and drink.

side of the room. His eyes should now move in unison. If your child appears to have a squint (with an eye turned inwards or outwards all the time) you should discuss this with your doctor who may suggest that he sees an eye specialist.

Your child is now very chatty and will vocalize tunefully both to himself and others in a singsong manner using vowel sounds and single and double syllables such as a-a, adah and er-leh. He laughs, chuckles, and squeals with delight when playing and will express anger or annoyance with loud screams.

INTELLIGENCE

Assessing a child's IQ (intelligence quotient) when he is very young is difficult, and the motor development tests that can be used to evaluate IQ in the first year do not usually correlate well with a child's IQ later on. It is recognized that intelligence can be influenced by many factors, including stimulation, health and diet, and social aspects such as poverty. Even trauma can play a part. At this stage in your child's development you can encourage his physical, social, and intellectual growth by raising him in a stimulating environment and spending as much time as you can playing, reading, and talking to him.

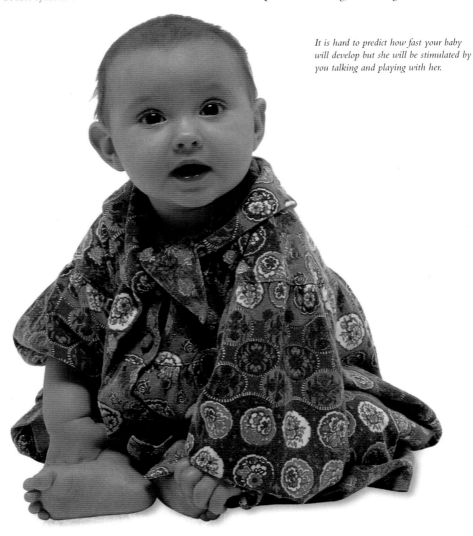

It is hard to predict how fast your baby will develop but she will be stimulated by you talking and playing with her.

Always buy toys that suit the age of your baby. This one has bend projections that he can easily grasp.

Once you have helped your baby to sit up, she will often sit quite happily and watch you as you move around the room.

SEVEN MONTHS

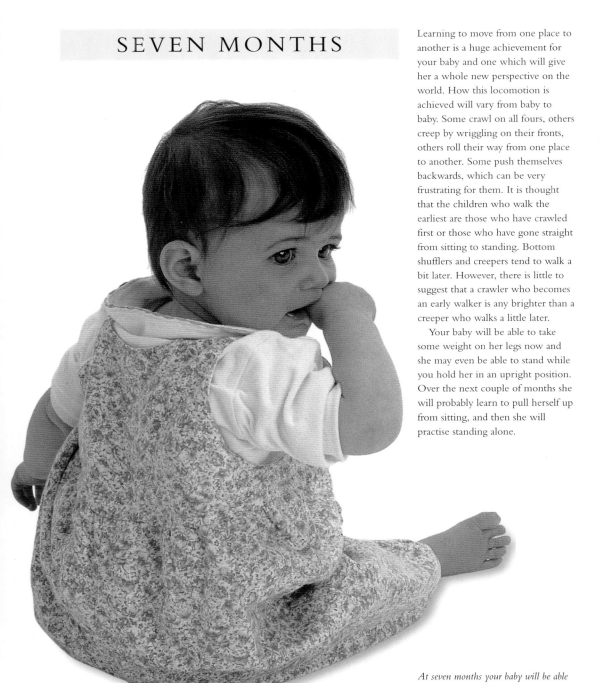

Learning to move from one place to another is a huge achievement for your baby and one which will give her a whole new perspective on the world. How this locomotion is achieved will vary from baby to baby. Some crawl on all fours, others creep by wriggling on their fronts, others roll their way from one place to another. Some push themselves backwards, which can be very frustrating for them. It is thought that the children who walk the earliest are those who have crawled first or those who have gone straight from sitting to standing. Bottom shufflers and creepers tend to walk a bit later. However, there is little to suggest that a crawler who becomes an early walker is any brighter than a creeper who walks a little later.

Your baby will be able to take some weight on her legs now and she may even be able to stand while you hold her in an upright position. Over the next couple of months she will probably learn to pull herself up from sitting, and then she will practise standing alone.

At seven months your baby will be able to sit up and turn at the waist. She will also like to suck her thumb.

Your baby is developing a mind of her own and will often try to wriggle free when picked up or held.

DEXTERITY

Your baby may start to show a preference for using her right or left hand at this age. Offer her a toy held straight in front of her and see which hand she uses to reach for it. If your baby regularly uses the same hand she is beginning to show a preference, but this is by no means a final choice. Very often the hand she uses at seven months is not the same as the one she prefers at nine months

Milestones

Your child may be able to:

• Put weight on legs when upright.

• Sit with minimal support.

• Look for a dropped object.

• Babble combining vowels and consonants such as "ga-ga", "ma-ma" and "da-da".

• Feed herself with finger foods.

• Begin to crawl.

Your baby is now very much on the move and will be beginning to crawl everywhere quite quickly.

Your baby will hold toys in both hands with much more dexterity now. She will also still enjoy sucking them.

Try and talk to your baby as much as you can as he will reply with babble that mixes both vowels and consonants.

or a year. Once your baby is able to use two hands in a coordinated way, give her something which needs one hand to hold it and another to make it work – a pot with a lid that comes off is ideal – and see which hand she uses for which action. This will give you a better idea of whether your baby is likely to be left- or right-handed, although her final choice may not be made until she reaches two years of age.

You may notice that your baby no longer grasps things in the centre of her palm to hold them. She now uses her fingers and thumb so that her grip has become very much more refined. Now that she can operate her fingers and thumb independently, rather than using them as a rake, she can pick up an object as small as a raisin to examine it.

You can encourage the baby by allowing her to feed herself. Give her a bowl and spoon and let her get on with it. At first it is a good idea for you to have a spoon too, so that you can give her the occasional mouthful while she is still working out how to get the food from the bowl, onto the spoon and into her mouth. Finger foods will help your baby learn how to get food into her mouth using her fingers.

At around the time your baby starts to show hand preference her language also starts to become more fully developed and she will babble a lot more using both vowel sounds and consonants. Her cries also change to include both low- and high-pitched sounds and she will start to make different movements with her tongue and mouth.

As his hand movements improve, your baby will start to grasp toys, such as soft bricks, with his fingers and thumb.

You can encourage your baby to eat solids by allowing him to hold the spoon and feed himself.

EIGHT MONTHS

By eight months your baby will probably have started to be selective about the people with whom he is sociable. The outgoing friendliness of the earlier months may have been replaced by a certain wariness, especially of strangers. If you leave your baby with someone he doesn't know he may now burst into tears, whereas before he would have been perfectly happy, as long as he was being entertained and was warm and comfortable. This wariness of strangers often occurs at about the same time that your baby is making a surge in his development. About a month after this, your baby may start to show distress, sometimes known as separation anxiety, when you leave the room. This distress at being separated from you or your partner will probably peak at around 15 months and then gradually subside.

If your baby does suffer from separation anxiety it can be misery for both of you. The best way of easing his distress is to leave him in a familiar environment with, if possible, a familiar person or relative.

Favourite and familiar toys can also be a source of comfort.

When you are leaving your baby to go out, try to leave quickly without making a fuss and keep your goodbyes down to a minimum.

As the bond grows stronger between you and your child, he will appreciate as much attention as you can give him.

Milestones

Your child may be able to:

• Stand up while holding on to something firmly.

• Get himself into a sitting position from his stomach.

• Pick up a small object. such as a raisin with, his hand.

• Turn round in the direction of a familiar voice.

• Move himself towards an out-of-reach toy.

DISCOVERING GENITALS

It is normal for your baby to start to show an interest in his genitals at around this age. This interest is an inevitable and healthy part of your baby's development in the same way that his fascination with his fingers and toes was earlier. There is no physical or psychological harm in your baby handling his genitals and you should never make your child feel bad or think about punishing him because he is doing so.

A boy is capable of having an erection from before birth; this is simply the normal response to the touch of a sensitive organ. A baby girl has clitoral erections from a very young age too, although these are much less obvious.

INTRODUCING BOOKS

From eight months onwards, your baby's behaviour will become more flexible and he will begin to use his own initiative in a relationship. He will give you toys as well as taking them and may start playing simple games with you. For the first time he will want to share his interest in an object with another person. This is a good time to introduce him to books, which you can sit and read together. At first he will only be interested in the rhythm and sound of the words and the colour and pattern of the pictures in the book. By speaking slowly in a singsong manner, with exaggerated emphasis in the right places, and encouraging your child to join in with simple sounds such as "moo" when he sees the picture of a cow, you will make reading a shared, enjoyable experience.

DEVELOPMENTAL CHECK

At between six and nine months your baby will be given another developmental check by your doctor

Your baby will happily respond to your games and will often try playful actions like grabbing your hair.

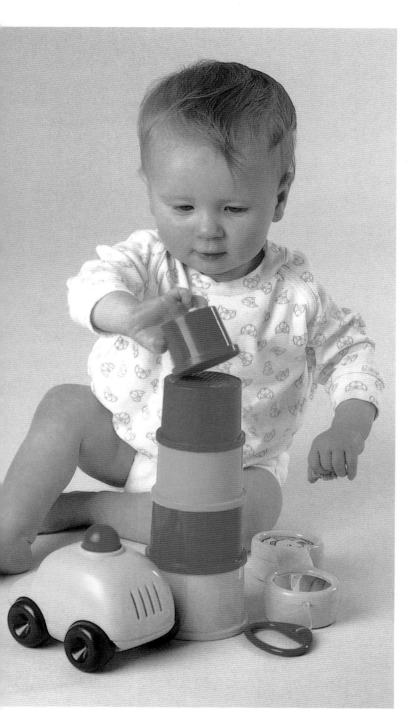

Left: As the grasping action is much more developed, your child will enjoy handling and playing with stacking toys. He may need guidance from you as to the order the shapes go in, and which colour should go next.

Opposite: A car or any toy with wheels is likely to be a particular source of interest for your baby. He may just want to sit and play with it, and only go after it if you join in and spend time pushing it back and forth to him.

or health visitor. She will be looking to see how your baby is developing and also checking that nothing has been missed in any previous health checks. Your baby's pelvis and legs will be examined to make sure there is no congenital dislocation of the hips. If your baby is a boy, his testicles will be checked to make sure they are well down in the scrotum. A distraction test for hearing will be carried out. This involves making a noise for two seconds with something like a bell or rattle out of your baby's sight to see whether he turns towards the sound. His eyes will be checked to see that there is no sign of a potential squint. You will probably be asked if your baby has ever had any breathing problems such as wheezing, and his heart and lungs may be checked with a stethoscope. He may be weighed and his height measured and the circumference of his head checked.

If you are worried about any part of your child's development you should talk about your concerns now with your doctor. The health visitor or doctor will be able to help with any questions you may have and can also offer advice if you are experiencing problems with feeding your child or with his sleeping.

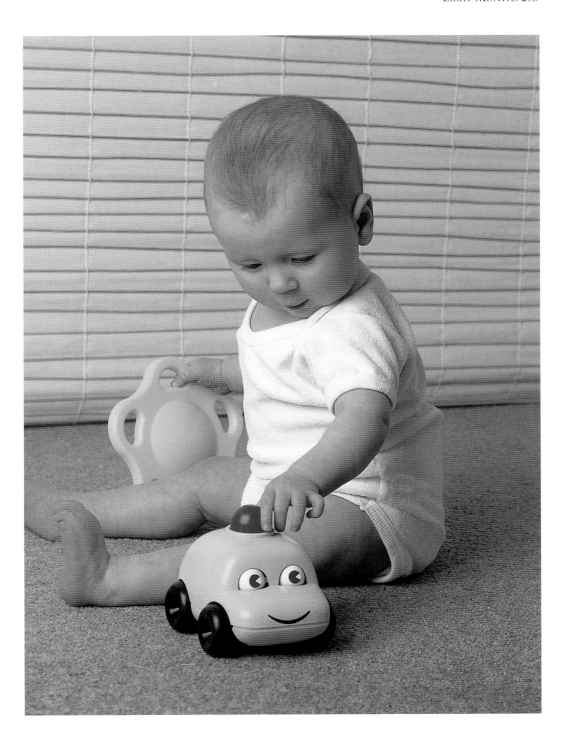

NINE MONTHS

A nine-month-old baby is capable of showing a wide range of emotions from happiness to fear, anger, and sadness and she will use these as a means of expressing feelings at any given moment. Your child needs you to be in tune with her feelings and to understand what she is trying to express, otherwise she will become frustrated. She may begin to show signs of early independence, but she will still want the reassurance of knowing that you are nearby and ready to help out if required.

MOVEMENT

Your baby can now sit alone for 10–15 minutes at a time and lean forward to pick up a toy without falling over. She can also turn her body and will stretch out for something at her side. She will spend time manipulating a toy with her hands and is able to pass the toy from one hand to the other, turning it as she does so. She uses a pincer grasp, using her finger and thumb, to pick up small items. She will poke at things with a forefinger and may even start to point. You will notice that she still cannot put down a toy she is holding. She will still drop it or press it against a hard surface to release it. If she drops a toy she will look where it has fallen, even if it has completely disappeared from view.

Your child is now very active and she will begin to move herself across the floor either by

Your baby is now constantly on the move and will use her hands to help push her forward as she crawls along.

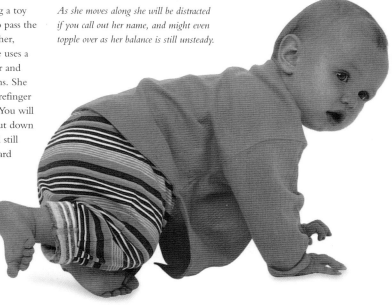

As she moves along she will be distracted if you call out her name, and might even topple over as her balance is still unsteady.

As she pushes forward with her arms, her legs will move back and forth to propel her along.

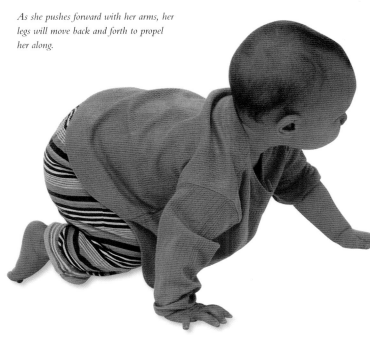

Milestones

Your child may be able to:
• Look for an object that she dropped out of view.
• Pull herself into a standing position.
• Pick up small objects using her finger and thumb.
• Enjoy games such as pat-a-cake.
• Wave goodbye.
• Cruise around the furniture.

crawling, or by shuffling or rolling if she can't yet crawl. She will try to pull herself to standing while holding on to something and may manage to hold herself upright for a few moments before sitting down with a bump. She won't be able to lower herself in a controlled way into a sitting position. If you hold her in a standing position she will probably make purposeful stepping movements with alternate feet as though practising walking.

ACTIVITY

You will notice that your child is becoming a lot more vocal now. She will shout for your attention, stop, listen for your response, and, if she doesn't get it, she will shout again. She will hold long conversations with you, babbling in a loud, tuneful way using strings of syllables such as "dad-da", "ma-ma", "aga-aga", over and over again. She not only uses this babble as a means of interpersonal communication to show friendliness or annoyance, but also as a way of amusing herself.

After crawling for a while, your baby may try to push herself up, but will not be able to balance properly yet.

She likes to practise imitating adult sounds, not just talking but also smacking her lips, coughing and making "brrr"-type noises.

By now your baby will be able to bite and chew her food well and she will be able to feed herself with some finger foods. She will probably try to grasp hold of the spoon as she is being fed. Let her have her own play spoon so that she can continue to practise feeding herself between the mouthfuls of food you are giving to her.

Your baby will probably enjoy games such as "peek-a-boo" and looking for something that you've half hidden while she watched. She will be delighted when she discovers the item and will show it to you with great glee. You may even be able to get her to look for something that you've completely hidden, but she won't necessarily be able to find it and this may cause her some distress and even annoyance.

If your baby seems at all worried by these first simple games you will need to encourage her to take part in them by responding to all her efforts with obvious surprise or delight. She will be happy

All toys will be held firmly now by your baby, who will use a pincer grasp with her finger and thumb.

Your baby's fascination with her toes will continue and she will often be found playing with them.

Right: As bonding with her father continues, your baby will enjoy being lifted up in the air and other games with him.

when you show her how much you enjoy her cleverness because she will enjoy your approval.

As your baby starts to become more confident, the games to play will become more adventurous. She will let you know when she is ready to progress to the next stage.

Below: Your baby will not play with an older brother at this stage, but she will be interested in toys he is showing her.

Standing up will be a problem unless there is a support nearby. If he lets go he will sit down with a bump.

TEN MONTHS

You will probably have discovered by now that your child has a sense of humour. At 10 months, your baby will not only enjoy playing games with you but will also rock with laughter at some of his own antics. For example, he will enjoy splashing in the bath and this will become even more fun if he gets you wet too. The more you protest the more he will enjoy splashing you. You may also find some of the things you do make your baby laugh uproariously. Appearing around a door saying "boo" can make him squeal with laughter and he will enjoy this game over and over again. Your baby may also enjoy teasing you in return by offering you a toy and snatching it back before you can take it.

Traditional nursery rhymes and games can give your child endless fun. Try saying: "Round and round the garden, like a teddy bear, one step, two step, tickly under there!" as you run your fingers around his palm, then up his arm and end with a tickle. Another favourite is Humpty Dumpty. Build up to a climax at the point Humpty is going to fall off the wall and pretend to let

Your child is now developing rapidly and will be trying to stand. He won't be able to do it on his own and will need your support.

Milestones

Your child may be able to:

- Move around the furniture.
- Understand the word "no", but not necessarily obey it.
- Stand alone for a few seconds.
- Use the word "dada" to get his father's attention.
- Hold a feeder cup to drink from it.
- Roll a ball back to you.

He might try a few faltering steps, but can't easily manage these and will need to hold onto one of your hands as he moves forwards.

Supports, such as a chair, will be used by your child to pull himself up as he learns to stand.

your baby fall too. The baby has probably reached what is sometimes known as the joint-attention stage. This is when a child is able to concentrate on more than one thing at a time. You can encourage this by pointing out things while also giving your baby some information. For example, you can show your child a cat, then tell him that when a cat speaks it says "miaow". Later, when he sees a cat again, you can ask him what the cat says. This is a great way of sharing knowledge and making learning fun.

ESTABLISHING ROLES

Along with this sense of humour, new mobility, and the desire to share with you, comes a real talent for getting into trouble. Your baby's curiosity will lead him into all sorts of dangers and you will need to be constantly on your guard so that he isn't allowed to hurt himself. Your baby, on the other hand, may see thwarting your efforts at keeping

him out of mischief as a great way of getting a response from you. For the first time since your child was born you may begin to think about using some form of discipline.

Discipline doesn't mean rules and punishment, it means teaching the concept of right and wrong. It will be a long time before your child fully grasps the idea of what is involved, but by teaching him now, through your example and guidance, you will be helping him towards eventual self-control and showing him that he needs to have respect for other people.

It is important to remember that a baby cannot be bad because babies and toddlers do not know right from wrong. They learn about their world through experimentation, and by observing and testing adults. Introducing the concept of things being right or wrong at this early age is the first step to helping your child develop from a naturally self-centred baby to a more sensitive and caring

child. The most effective discipline is neither uncompromisingly rigid nor too permissive. Either of these extremes can leave a child feeling that he is unloved.

You need to set limits and standards that are fair and enforce them firmly, but lovingly. Never threaten to withdraw love from your child as this will badly effect his self-esteem and it is important that he knows he is loved even when you don't approve of his behaviour.

Don't smack your child. Smacking has been shown not to be an effective way to discipline a naughty child. It has many negative aspects, including teaching the child violence and that using force is the best way of ending a dispute or getting what you want.

Opposite: A container with various slots for different shapes will keep a child amused as he tries to work out which one should go in the right hole.

A young baby 'cruises' around furniture using it for support as he moves around.

If a stool is at the right level, your baby may use it as a means of pulling himself up, and as a table to leave some of his toys there in easy reach.

ELEVEN MONTHS

Many babies speak their first word at around 11 months, although some speak as early as nine months and others don't say a word until well after a year. This is a remarkable achievement when you consider that not very long ago your child didn't even know how to smile. These first words take the longest to learn and you will need to be patient while you wait for your child to produce another new one. Sometimes these first words are learned as infrequently as one a month from now on, until your child has a vocabulary of around 10 words. After this the rate usually increases quickly, but this stage isn't reached until around 15 months of age.

DEVELOPING SPEECH

You can help your child to build up her vocabulary by saying the names of things in which she expresses an interest. By now she can probably point at items that she wants because she will have already discovered that pointing is an effective means of communicating with you. When you pick up the item and hand it to the child you probably tell her what it is.

Milestones

Your child may be able to:
- Say the word "mama" to attract your attention.
- Stand on her own.
- Take her first steps.
- Respond to a simple command which isn't accompanied by gestures.
- Say her first word other than "mama" and "dada".

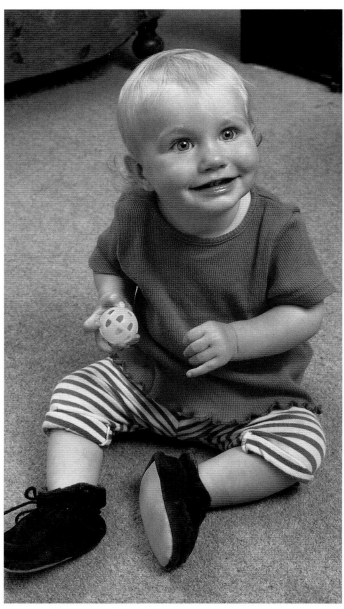

At 11 months your child will be much more responsive and will start reacting to simple questions and commands.

For example, your child points at an apple, you pick up the apple and hand it to her saying something like: "You want this apple?" By doing this you are teaching your child new words; although she may not remember them straightaway, in time each word will become part of her vocabulary.

Don't worry if you are the only person who can understand your baby's first words. It is not unusual for others outside the family to be baffled by the way a baby speaks. It may well be two or three years before your child can be easily understood outside the immediate family. It is important not to keep correcting your child's pronunciation.

This will knock her confidence and she may become worried about trying to use new words. However, don't revert to using her wrongly pronounced words simply because they sound really cute. If you imitate her errors, the child will carry on using the incorrect words for much longer than she would otherwise have done.

MOBILITY

Your baby may have started to pull herself up onto her feet; she may even be walking by holding onto the furniture. This is known as "cruising' and is a natural prelude to learning to walk. Don't be tempted to rush out and buy shoes at the first

sign of walking because the child doesn't need shoes yet, in fact they would not be good for her feet at this stage. A child needs to wear shoes when she is walking confidently and her feet will need protection when she goes outside.

Learning to walk is a matter of trial and error. You can't really do anything to help your child apart from making sure that the area she is learning to walk in is as safe as possible. But even when you have removed all the obvious hazards in your child's path you need to stay close at hand to make sure that she doesn't hurt herself.

A child is bound to experience falls while as she learns to walk and

developing baby will now start to share things and will happily hand [t]oys, such as a ball.

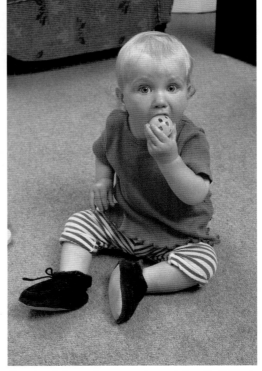

Even though she now has some teeth, your baby will still like the sensation of putting different objects in her mouth.

Right: Your baby will be particularly responsive playing games now. If you keep hiding a toy and then making it re-appear it will keep her happily amused for quite a while.

Below left and right: Your child will enjoy standing upright with some help from you. Provided she can hang onto something with one hand, she will eagerly pick up toys from the floor to show you, wave around or suck.

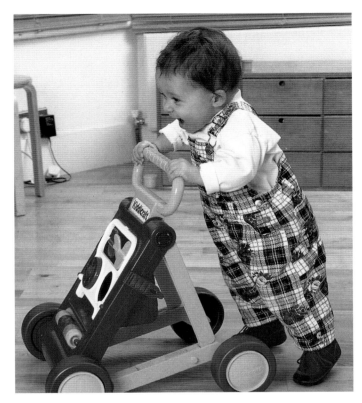

your reaction to these mishaps can colour your child's response to them as well. If you rush over in a panic every time she stumbles and demand to know if she is all right she may well shed more tears than she would if she'd really hurt herself. This over-reaction on your part may also make her lose her sense of adventure and make her afraid of attempting other normal physical development hurdles. By remaining calm and reacting with an "up you get, you're all right" sort of attitude, your child is likely to deal with minor tumbles in a matter-of-fact way.

Left: By pushing a baby walker, your baby can walk happily around the room. Keep an eye on her so that you can help if she gets stuck in a corner. It takes time for a child to learn how to walk backwards. Below: A child will place her favourite toys on a low-level table and play with them there. When she is bored she may just leave them and go off to do something else more interesting.

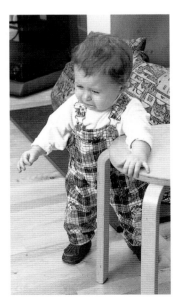

TWELVE MONTHS

You are the parent of a year-old child. One by one all the skills that will make your baby a self-dependent and integrated member of society are being perfected. You are both teacher and observer. And now the changes come very quickly indeed.

GROWING SKILLS

If your baby isn't actually walking he should be well on his way to doing so by the end of the first year. He will probably be able to pull himself to his feet and navigate by holding onto the furniture. He will certainly be crawling, bottom shuffling, or rolling, and he will be able to get around at quite some speed. He will be able to sit for long periods and can now get into the sitting position from lying flat.

Your baby's grasp is now more refined and he will be able to pick up small objects using the thumb and the tip of the index finger. He will drop and throw toys deliberately and enjoy watching them as they fall. If a toy rolls out of sight he may look for it. He uses both hands to hold toys, but he may start to show a preference for using one hand rather than the other. When your child wants to show you something he will point using his index finger. He's curious and will want to explore everything, so make sure that your home is a safe place. This doesn't mean restricting your baby to such an extent that he becomes frustrated. Try to compromise by leaving some safe cupboards for him to get into and locking the others.

When the baby is outside he will watch people, animals, or cars with prolonged, intent regard. He will be able to recognize familiar people or animals from around 6m/20ft and will probably greet them vocally with great enthusiasm. The child responds to his own name and can understand other words such as the

Milestones

Your child may be able to:
- Indicate what he wants in other ways instead of crying.
- Stand on his own.
- Walk a little way unaided.
- Wave goodbye to you, close relatives and friends.
- Say "mama" and "dada" with discrimination.
- Roll a ball back to you.

At 12 months your child will be able to let you know what he wants by pointing or reaching towards an object.

All children vary when they first start walking, but your child may well be taking his first few steps now, so you should give him every encouragement.

names of family members. He may be able to understand instructions such as "give it to Mummy", and he may even do as you ask.

You may find that your baby holds out his arm or leg when you ask him to while you are bathing or dressing him. You will see through his actions that he can understand much of what you say even though he can't yet express himself verbally. He babbles to himself and to you, making a lot of speech-type sounds and if he hasn't already said his first word then he soon will.

EATING HABITS

Your baby will be joining in family meals and will probably be eating a mashed-up version of whatever everyone else eats. He is still too young to eat spicy or seasoned food, so remove his portion before adding salt and pepper and other seasoning. He enjoys finger foods but will want to imitate others at mealtimes by using a spoon. It will be difficult for him to get food onto the spoon and then the spoon into his mouth, so he may well revert to using his fingers after a few attempts.

Your child will be able to drink from a feeder cup by himself and will probably be able to drink from an ordinary cup with your help, but he's still too young to manage this on his own. If you are weaning, or are about to wean your baby off his bottle or the breast, you may want to start giving him cow's milk as his main drink. This should only be introduced into your baby's diet after the age of one year and you should always give him whole, pasteurized milk. Skimmed milk has too much protein and sodium content for babies and should not be introduced into your child's diet before the age

of five. Semi-skimmed milk can be given from two years, but only if the child is eating a very varied and adequate diet.

Your baby may be reluctant to give up the bottle because it may be a source of emotional comfort, but it is recommended that a child stops drinking from a bottle at around a year because of the adverse effect it can have on his teeth. If you don't feel that he is ready to give up his bottle completely, try to limit the number of times he has a bottle each day. Encourage him to drink from a trainer cup at meal-times and offer

him a bottle between meals and at bedtime. When you give a bottle during the day, fill it with water rather than juice or milk, because this will help reduce your child's interest in it. Insist that he drinks from it while sitting in an adult's lap and when he wants to get down take the bottle from him. Don't allow him to take his bottle to bed or to walk about with it. By restricting the use of a bottle like this you will limit the amount of potential harm it can do to his teeth.

Your baby may have as many as four or five teeth and you should

Toys such as a cuddly, soft panda will soon become a firm favourite with your child as he will enjoy its furry texture.

When your child has a favourite cuddly animal he will love to carry it around, hug and squeeze it, and may want to take it with him wherever he goes.

have been cleaning them from the time they appeared. These first teeth can be cleaned with a soft baby toothbrush and a pea-sized amount of children's toothpaste. If your baby is cutting teeth and is fretful, offer him a cold teething ring or a piece of raw carrot to chew on.

YOUR CHILD AND OTHERS
Even though he is confident and outgoing with you, your baby may still be wary of strangers. He may also suffer from shyness. This is an inherited trait which he will have got from either you or your partner, even though neither of you may appear to display the trait yourselves. Shyness can be modified, but it is rarely possible to eradicate it altogether. If you build up your child's confidence with praise and encouragement this

will help him to feel more comfortable with others and this may eventually help to diminish any shyness.

It is possible that what you consider to be shyness is actually just a normal lack of sociability. At this age your child is not ready to make friends, and he probably won't be until he is at least three years old. Until then the social limit will probably be parallel play, which is when he plays side by side with another child. Don't try to force him to play with others – pushing him may make him withdraw from social situations completely.

Don't expect a child to share his toys at this age.

Right now the only things that matter are his own needs and desires. Other children are seen as objects not people. If he displays aggressive behaviour towards other children, like biting or hitting, you need to respond immediately by removing him from the scene of the incident. Explain calmly why he shouldn't have behaved like that, then give him something to play with or point out a new object to distract him and change the subject. Of course he won't really understand what you are saying but, if you use this approach every time it happens, he will eventually understand that hitting and biting other people are just not acceptable behaviour.

Opposite: Although your child will be perfectly happy when being held by you, he may be shy and withdrawn with other people he doesn't know.
Below: Your baby will interact quite happily with his father and will keep experimenting with touch.

UNDERSTANDING YOUR CHILD'S DEVELOPMENT

SIGHT AND VISION

Although your baby practised the blinking reflex by opening and closing her eyes while in the womb, the first time she actually uses her eyes for seeing is at the moment of birth. As soon as she is born she is capable of distinguishing objects and most colours, but is only able to focus on items that are 20–30cm/8–12in away. These things will look fuzzy.

A newborn is very sensitive to bright lights and will blink and screw up her eyes if a light is shone in her face. Movement will attract a baby from birth and you may notice that yours actively seeks out moving objects. She will probably show a preference for an object which has a highly contrasting pattern rather than one which is just a solid block of colour. As your baby begins to control her eye movements she will start tracking moving objects, which is an indication that her vision is developing well.

YOUR BABY'S WORLD

At first your face will be of more interest to your child than anything else. It is thought that a baby is born with a simple mental template of the human face and will actively search out and stare at any human face during the first couple of months. When she is first born, whether she is able to recognize you by your individual features is open to debate, but she will certainly know the general shape of your head and hairline and by two months will have started to recognize your features.

Your baby will soon become interested in other things and by six to eight weeks will be concentrating on details, scanning faces and objects so that she can take in as much information as possible. At this age she may find it hard to disengage her attention when she is watching something and she may need you to distract her before she can remove

A newborn baby's vision will be fairly limited and initially he will only be able to see a fuzzy image of you.

her gaze. But by three to four months the pathways in the brain for voluntary action begin to take over and your baby starts to disengage her attention on her own.

By three months a baby can perceive colours fully, with all their different shades, and will be able to focus at different distances and to see things in 3D. From seven to eight months, as she begins to interpret what she sees, your baby starts to realize that things don't necessarily cease to exist just because she can't see them anymore. A toy dropped over the edge of

Your young baby will become fascinated by different objects and will become difficult to distract from whatever is capturing her attention.

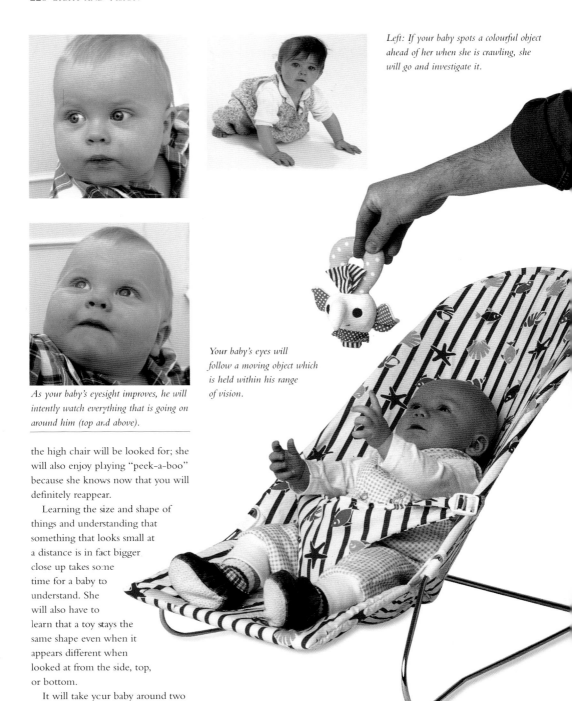

Left: If your baby spots a colourful object ahead of her when she is crawling, she will go and investigate it.

As your baby's eyesight improves, he will intently watch everything that is going on around him (top and above).

Your baby's eyes will follow a moving object which is held within his range of vision.

the high chair will be looked for; she will also enjoy playing "peek-a-boo" because she knows now that you will definitely reappear.

Learning the size and shape of things and understanding that something that looks small at a distance is in fact bigger close up takes some time for a baby to understand. She will also have to learn that a toy stays the same shape even when it appears different when looked at from the side, top, or bottom.

It will take your baby around two years to have good vision and to be

How you can help

• Give your baby plenty of stimulating things to look at.

• Hold an item within her range of vision and move it slowly in an arc so that she can follow it with her eyes.

• Play games like "peek-a-boo" and "hide-and-seek" with a toy or by hiding under a large cloth or blanket.

• Check that your child doesn't have a squint. If you are concerned, talk to your doctor.

able to see almost as clearly as an adult does. Her vision will continue to develop until she is four to five years of age.

A SQUINT

Many babies are born with what may appear to be a slight squint and this often remains until they have learned to control the muscles around the eyes. It is quite difficult for a baby to hold both eyes in line with each other to focus on an object, and you may notice that when your baby stares at you one of her eyes wanders out of focus. A wandering eye usually rights itself by the time a baby reaches three to four months of age, but you should always point it out to your doctor or health visitor as it may be necessary for your child's eyes to be checked thoroughly by an orthoptist.

A real squint is when the eyes never focus together on an object and, rather than moving together and then one wandering off, they are often out of alignment with each other. A squint needs to be treated from an early age so you must talk to your doctor as soon as you notice it in your child.

A brightly coloured mobile, moving in the breeze and suspended or held from above, will delight your child and keep him amused for a long time.

HEARING

During the last three months in the uterus a baby will have been hearing a variety of different noises. By the time a baby is born, he will already be familiar with his mother's voice, the beating of her heart, and the sound of the amniotic fluid in which he has been floating. His ability to hear at birth is almost as good as an adult's. His hearing threshold, however, is lower, so your baby will be startled by loud, unfamiliar noises, although he will probably sleep happily through a constant loud sound such as a blaring television or loud music.

A very young baby will prefer to hear rhythmic noises that may not seem soothing to you: the noise of a washing machine or tumble dryer, the hum of the vacuum cleaner or hair dryer. These will probably reassure him and may even lull him to sleep, perhaps because he heard such sounds before birth and he finds them both comforting and familiar. Your own child will quickly associate you and your voice with comfort – it is thought that an infant of only a few days old can actually recognize his mother's voice.

Your baby will respond to all the human voices he hears and will turn towards the sound of people talking and appear to listen intently. If he is spoken to in the exaggerated, high-pitched tone and rhythmic singsong manner, known as "motherese" that adults often instinctively adopt for babies, you will notice that your baby pays particular attention. He may even lose interest if the speaker reverts to a normal tone.

It is through hearing others speak that your baby will eventually learn to form the words which will make up early vocabulary. He will start to understand what is being said long before he can actually make the noises himself; if he has a hearing

How you can help

- When the baby is very young, try not to let him become startled by sudden noises which make him cry.
- Talk to your child, using "motherese", the high-pitched, singsong voice that babies find appealing.
- Introduce him to many different sounds from an early age.
- Let him sleep where he is happiest rather than insisting that he should be in a quiet room on his own.

defect this knowledge and the eventual ability to speak will be affected. As your baby gets older he will start looking for the source of the different sounds that he hears and will respond with pleasure to familiar voices, words, and tunes.

HEARING TESTS

Your baby will be offered a newborn hearing test either before you leave the maternity unit where he was born, or in the weeks after the birth at your doctor's surgery or baby clinic.

From an early age your baby will respond to your voice and be interested in toys you are showing him.

He will turn towards any new or interesting noise that you make with a toy even if it is coming from behind him.

In some areas the test may be carried out at home. You should mention if there is a close family history of hearing problems. If there is any concern, your baby can be referred to a hearing clinic.

At seven or eight months, your baby will have his next developmental check and this will include a screening test of his hearing carried out by your health visitor. By now the response to sounds should be obvious, turning his head when you speak to him and responding to different noises of varying pitch and intensity. Both ears will be tested to identify anything previously missed. If your child is deaf or partially deaf, his speech may not progress past the babbling stage and you may notice that he becomes quieter as he gets older. Any concerns about your child's hearing should be discussed with your doctor as soon as they occur.

Your baby will study your expression and listen intently to your voice before trying to imitate you.

SMELL, TASTE, TOUCH

SMELL

Newborn babies are very sensitive to smell and can remember certain smells almost from the moment they are born. They recognize their parents' natural smell and a breast-fed baby can distinguish the smell of her mother's milk from that of any other woman's just a few hours after birth. In fact, your baby will start sucking in her sleep if she smells your milk.

A bottle-fed baby will quickly learn to identify her own mother's smell and the smell of any other family members who also feed her. The smell of people who are familiar to her will help your baby distinguish between family members and people strange to her.

As your baby grows, certain smells will become associated with specific things. For example, food smells will suggest meal-times and perhaps happy social occasions, while the smell of bath preparation and baby powder will become associated with bathtime and bed. Smells that your baby finds unpleasant will make her turn her head away even when she is only a few days old.

Your baby will use her sense of smell with her other senses to learn about the world around her.

From a young age, a baby has a highly developed sense of smell and she will delight in a sweet-smelling flower.

Taste is very important to a baby and she will experiment with the sensation of sucking her toys.

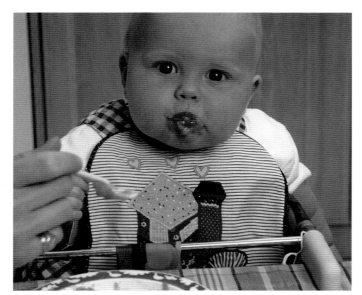

From the moment he is born, your baby will be able to react to bitter tastes and show a preference for sweet foods.

How you can help

• Spend time cuddling and talking to your baby so that she really gets to know you.

• Offer your child a wide variety of tastes once she is old enough to take solids, but avoid foods that are seasoned or spicy.

• Don't encourage your child to have a sweet tooth.

• Remember that a young baby cannot control her temperature as well as an older child, so you need to keep a constant check on her to make sure she isn't too cold or if she is becoming overheated.

• Your baby's skin is very sensitive so check that her clothes aren't tight or rubbing her skin.

TASTE

Smell and taste are intrinsically linked so it is no surprise that a baby is born with the ability to differentiate between tastes. From birth your baby's taste buds can detect sweet, sour, bitter, and salty. When offered any of these tastes she will give a definite and consistent reaction to each one. Her taste buds will become more refined with age, but even as a newborn baby she will show appreciation for sweet flavours and grimace when experiencing salty or bitter tastes.

All babies seem to be born with a preference for a sweeter taste, probably because breast milk is slightly sweet and it is important that she likes its flavour. This natural preference for sweet things won't harm your baby's teeth providing that you don't indulge her by giving her sweetened juice to drink, or adding sugar to her food when you start to wean her. When you start to introduce solids into your baby's diet it is better to encourage her to eat bland foods at first and then savoury foods and to keep sweet things to a minimum. Your baby will quickly develop her own tastes and you can help by giving her a varied diet once she is old enough to take solids. By the time she is around a year old she will use her experience of different foods she has tried to help her distinguish between the more subtle flavours. For example, one brand of baked beans will taste different to another and at a year old your child will be able to taste the difference.

TOUCH

Your baby uses touch immediately after birth. This provides her with a means of finding out about her new environment through the textures that her skin comes into contact with, like her clothes, your clothes, and skin. Your baby can also feel through her skin whether her environment is warm or cold, wet or dry. She feels pain and discomfort and, because a young baby has more sensitive skin than an adult, you need to treat her gently.

As she matures, your baby will use touch in different ways to help her learn. Touch-sensitive nerve endings are concentrated at the end of the fingertips and around the lips, and a young baby will use her hands and mouth for exploring new objects. Gradually, after a few weeks touch will also become associated with feelings and your baby will start to connect the feeling of your nipple in her mouth or your arms around her and associate them with warmth and security. One of the most important sensory experiences for your baby is through her tongue and mouth so that sucking is not only a means of obtaining nourishment, but is also a great source of comfort for her.

Your young baby will reach out and touch different objects, such as this furry panda, to get used to the different sensations.

When you undress your baby you may notice that she becomes increasingly tense as you remove each layer of clothes and she may actually cry when you remove the garment nearest to her skin, usually her vest. This is not because you are clumsy, but because she physically misses the feel of her clothes against her skin. She should stop crying as soon as you dress her again. Between two and three months your child begins to use touch as a means of exploring and she will use her hands to hit out at things that are near her. By around five months she will have mastered hand and eye co-ordination and will learn by feeling and putting things in her mouth.

BONDING

Touch plays an important part in the main bonding process. This is the formation of a close emotional relationship between you and your baby which will provide her with the love, comfort, and security that she wants.

Although your baby is born with a deep-rooted psychological need to have a close interaction with you this doesn't always happen immediately. A child's bonding with her mother is often a gradual process which may not be fully completed until the baby is a few months old.

At a few months old a young baby will react to bright toys such as this octopus which has two different materials on the undersides of its legs. He will enjoy the feel of soft textures.

TALKING

Your child is born with the potential to learn to speak and a receptiveness to the influences that will help him communicate. A baby starts to learn about language while he is still in the womb, which is when he first begins to identify the voice of his mother. As a newborn he will prefer his mother's voice to any other because it will already be familiar and he will quickly associate it with warmth, comfort, and feeding.

Even a very young baby will be receptive to the sound of his mother's voice because he will have heard it in the womb.

A newborn baby's brain is tuned to pick out the texture, pattern, and rhythm of language and he will pay more attention to voices talking than any other sounds he hears. From the moment he is born your baby understands speech sounds in a way that allows him to segment the speech he hears into sound units.

Before he can speak fluently a baby has to go through distinct stages of development. In the beginning your baby's vocal skills will consist of cries and burps. The inability to speak in the early months does not actually hinder a baby's ability to become a talker. He uses this time to learn how to control his mouth and his tongue. You may notice that from a very early age your baby will move his mouth a lot, pushing his lips forwards and backwards in a kind of rhythm.

CONVERSATIONS
One of the skills your baby has to acquire before speech is the ability to interact with people. He will begin to learn about this process very early on and by three months he will already be using communicative gestures. Try raising your eyebrows to him and then watch as he imitates you. This is the first stage of learning about holding a conversation. These gestures will be accompanied by different noises as your baby begins to develop control over dozens of separate muscles that are involved in making speech sounds. When your baby coos and gurgles at you he is learning to coordinate tongue movements while taking air in. When you respond to these early noises you will instinctively use a high-pitched, rhythmic singsong tone, repeating words in such a way that you capture your baby's attention.

Chat to your baby when you hold him as he will find the sound of your voice soothing and comforting.

By around five or six months, your child will be concentrating on one-syllable words such as "ba" or "ma" which he will repeat over and over again, often when he is on his own. This use of early sounds is known as babbling, and is not yet being used as a form of communication. This is your baby's way of learning how to make new sounds. Soon after he has learned to babble you will notice that your baby starts to use his eyes to communicate with you and to direct your attention towards something that he wants.

This communication is soon followed by what is called declarative pointing: pointing as a form of interacting, rather than just as a basic means of asking you to pass him

If you speak to your new baby in a high-pitched, singsong voice you will immediately get his attention.

Even at the young age of eight weeks your baby will respond to your voice and attempt to smile at you.

something he can't reach for himself. After a month or two your baby's babbling will start to flow like speech, rising and falling as if he were holding a conversation. Although he is still not able to form words, he will understand simple words that are made clear, for example, "bottle" when you point to his feeding bottle. Understanding more than he is able to say will continue throughout baby- and toddlerhood until he can speak fluently.

FIRST WORDS
By the end of his first year your baby will probably produce his first word.

It may not seem recognizable as a word to you, but it will be a sound that he uses for one specific object, for example, "ine" for when he wants an orange. It is certainly no accident that "mama" and "dada" are often among the first recognizable words that a new baby says, because first words are simple and are associated with things that are special to a child.

Once speech has begun with your baby, he will continue to produce a handful of new words each month with the majority of this early communication being simple nouns or proper names.

How you can help
• Always respond to your baby's attempts at communicating with you.
• Don't be embarrassed to use high-pitched speech; it is the language your child likes best.
• Talk to your baby as you go about your daily routine and remember to speak clearly using simple words.
• Be consistent, using the same words for the same thing every time.
• Look at simple picture books with your baby. By telling him what is in each picture you will be increasing his understanding of words.

A mother can help her child learn to talk properly by repeating words and by pointing out objects and saying the word.

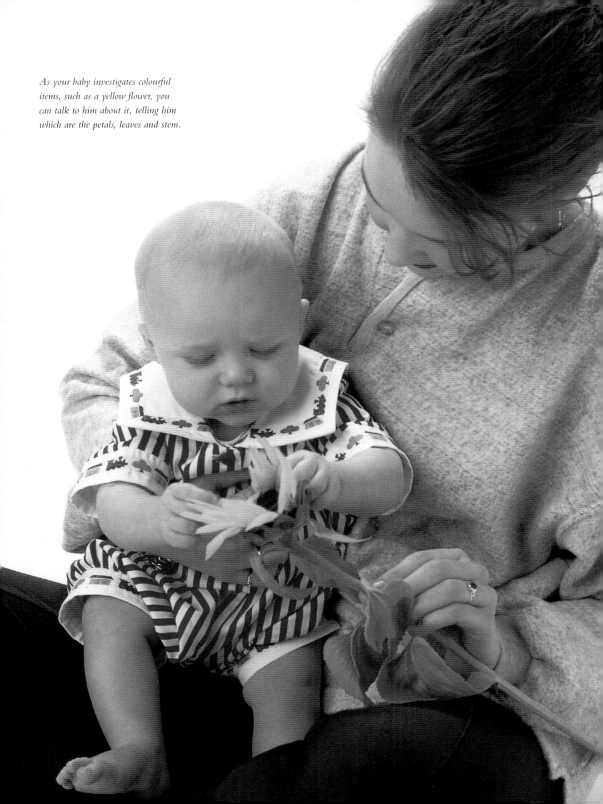

As your baby investigates colourful items, such as a yellow flower, you can talk to him about it, telling him which are the petals, leaves and stem.

SOCIAL BEHAVIOUR

A newborn baby doesn't appear very sociable to the outside world because she doesn't smile or respond verbally until some weeks after birth. But her parents' reactions to the baby's ordinary behaviour lead to the development of social mannerisms. For example, wind may cause your baby to appear to smile at an early age and you respond by smiling back. Your baby will eventually realize that this movement of her mouth makes you react in this way and so will use it deliberately in the future. It is this early, simple form of communication that is the basis for your child's social development.

All babies' early social learning comes from imitating the people with whom they have the most contact, generally their mother and father. A newborn of only a few hours can imitate some adult gestures such as poking her tongue out or yawning. This ability to imitate is one of the most important tools your baby has to help her learn about life.

Through imitation your baby will eventually start communicating. You will speak to her and she will respond with "coos" and will wriggle her body in delight. This first stage of conversation will eventually develop into the ability to talk and listen. These early conversations often start during feeding, because the rhythm of feeding initiates your baby into the basics of dialogue. A baby sucks in her mother's milk in bursts with pauses in between. It is during these pauses that her mother usually fills in the gap by talking happily to her.

IMITATION BECOMES CHOICE
Social interaction between you and your baby becomes increasingly intentional on her part during the first two months of life, with much of your baby's behaviour geared towards making you react. These early conversations and the ability to imitate are just two ways of getting you to respond; the other very effective way is crying. Initially, your baby's cries are a reflex to pain, hunger, or discomfort. But crying assures a baby of adult response, especially her mother's. Her cries will increase her mother's heart rate and, if breast-feeding, her mother will automatically start producing milk. Within a few weeks a baby will have learned to expect certain reactions to her crying, such as being fed or picked up.

At around six weeks your baby will learn to smile properly, another social skill which she will be able to use to her advantage. Although her

When young babies are placed together, they don't play with each other as they haven't yet learned how to interact. Instead they will just play on their own.

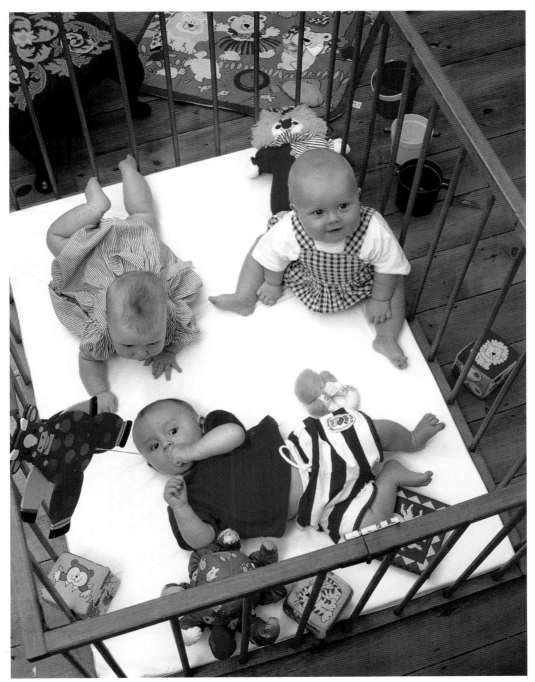

If you put two or three babies together in a playpen they will not play together as they haven't learned how to socialize.

first smiles are simply facial grimaces, your response will be such that she soon discovers that by using her facial muscles in this way she is guaranteed to get you to smile back. A baby will quickly learn to repeat an action if she gets a positive reaction. However, if she regards the response she receives as negative she is less likely to repeat the action.

By three months your baby will be able to show her enjoyment of people and surroundings. She will respond to friendly adults and generally not mind who is with her as long as they are paying attention to her. She will enjoy activities such as having a bath and often show pleasure when she realizes that bathtime has arrived. Feeding will be a great source of emotional pleasure and your baby will study your face unblinkingly while she feeds.

At around four months your baby will cry more deliberately. She will probably pause after crying to see if anyone is coming in response, before crying again. She has learned that crying brings attention and this new ability to manipulate is the start of some exciting discoveries.

CHANGING BEHAVIOUR PATTERNS
Somewhere after six months your child may change from a social, happy baby, who will go to anyone and reward complete strangers with smiles, to one who overnight has become wary of people she doesn't know. Your baby has reached the stage when she needs time and space to handle each new sight and sound, and a stranger may present her with too many new, unfamiliar things to be taken in at one time. This new wariness leads to what is known as "stranger anxiety". It often manifests itself as loud protestations when your baby is about to be separated from you. She is at the stage of

As your baby will feel safe with you, try to show her different toys and items to interest her and attract her attention.

development when she is becoming more sensitive to change and appears to be suddenly more dependent. She may try to avoid upsetting or stressful events by crying, clinging to you, or turning away from what is upsetting her. Towards the end of her first year she may start to use objects such as a favourite blanket, bottle, or thumb as a comforter.

Over the next six months your baby will probably show an increasing reticence with strangers but will be very responsive to people with whom she is familiar. She may become very clinging so that any separation from you is accompanied by real distress. This attachment may cause you problems, but it is in fact an important stage of development. She now recognizes individuals as people and is beginning to develop selective, permanent relationships. She will use these relationships as a safe base from which to explore the world. Now that she is getting older, your baby will use her developing

A baby will sit with her brother because he is familiar. She will be interested in his toys but won't play with him.

vocal skills to create noise – this guarantees the attention that gives her the reassurance she needs. She may use mimicry to make you laugh and the more you show your appreciation the more she will repeat the antic which is amusing you. This is her first real control over her social environment.

By the time she is a year old, your child will probably have grasped the idea that she exists as an entity. She may even begin to use a word or

Your baby will sit quite happily on your knee, but may be wary of moving to his grandmother who is less familiar to him.

A baby will soon learn to recognize his older sister and will happily let her help him to stand up.

sound to describe herself as a means of expressing this. Her social skills, however, are still very limited and she will show little interest in anyone outside her immediate circle of well-known people. Other children hold very little appeal for your child at this age and are more likely to be treated as inanimate objects rather than playmates.

It will be another year or two before your child has enough social understanding to develop friendships with other toddlers.

How you can help

- Encourage your baby to imitate you by exaggerating your responses to her actions.
- Smile at your baby to let her know how pleased you are when she smiles at you.
- If she becomes wary of strangers don't force her to be sociable.
- When you have to leave your baby, say goodbye quickly; don't prolong the parting.

MOBILITY

All babies go through the same stages of mobility, but how fast they move from one to another varies considerably. Your baby may walk independently before he is a year old, or he may be content to shuffle along on his bottom or hands and knees until well after this. Your baby's mobility takes place in a set order, starting at his head and working down to his toes. He won't be able to sit upright or crawl until he can hold up his head, and he won't be able to walk until he can move his body along, either by crawling or doing a bottom shuffle.

Finally, your baby will learn to control his arms and legs before gaining control of his hands and feet. At each stage it will take time for the movements he has learned to progress from being awkward, rather clumsy and uncoordinated to the smooth, controlled movements he will ultimately achieve.

MAKING PROGRESS

A newborn baby has no control over his head, which will flop around if left unsupported. By about eight weeks, control of the head and neck begins and you may notice your baby practising lifting his head and holding it for a few seconds before letting it flop down again. At around three months most babies are able to hold their heads up steadily so that they can look around and examine the world about them.

The next stage in mobility comes when your baby starts to roll around, first from side to back and then, a few weeks later, from back to side. The way a baby rolls is highly individual and your baby will roll when he's ready and in his own way. Rolling is another way of practising control over his body and your baby will do it over and over again until he's mastered what to him is a new movement. The result of this

How you can help

• Hold your baby upright so he can bounce his legs up and down on your lap to help strengthen his muscles.

• Sitting a little way away from your baby, persuade him to come to you. Do this to encourage both crawling and walking.

• Once he can sit upright, you can help your baby learn to balance by placing toys slightly out of reach so he has to stretch out for them.

• To get your baby to twist around, place a toy behind him and then support him as he turns.

• Push-along toys will encourage your baby to crawl and walk.

movement will change your baby's view of the world and once he has discovered this, rolling becomes a new function: a means of getting closer to something that he wants. Your baby will have been using his legs to push with since he was born, although the first stepping movements he made as a newborn were a reflex

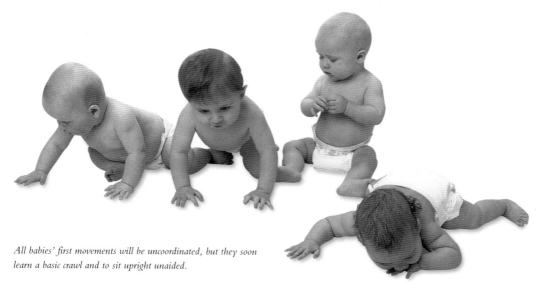

All babies' first movements will be uncoordinated, but they soon learn a basic crawl and to sit upright unaided.

When your baby is placed on his stomach at a few months old he will attempt to crawl.

He will lift up his arms and legs in the swimming motion that is the prelude to crawling.

Before she's a year old, your baby will start to stand and balance holding onto a chair if you hold it steady for her.

She will grasp firmly onto the bottom part of the chair and start to pull herself up. Try to encourage her as much as possible.

As she straightens into an upright position, she will need support from the chair you are holding.

Now she is standing confidently, she will start to look around her to see what else is going on in the room.

As your baby starts to crawl, he will move towards interesting toys.   *When he is nearer the toys, he will probably reach out for them.*

action. At around four months if you put your baby down on his abdomen, he will be able to lift his shoulders, arms, and legs off the floor and move them in a swimming-type motion, and by around five-and-a-half months your baby should be able to sit with some support, his back straight and shoulders braced. By around six months he will probably be able to support himself in a crawling position, although he won't be able to go anywhere just yet. By seven months he will be able to sit upright using his arms for support. Once he has done this he will quickly learn to sit unaided, and he will also enjoy standing and bouncing vigorously while you hold him.

By eight or nine months he will have learned to control his movements and he will be able to move his arms and legs in order to propel himself either backwards or forwards. Once he has mastered this he will be off and it will only be a matter of time before he starts trying to stand up on his own. By about nine months he will be able to sit and reach in front, upwards, to the side and behind him without falling over.

As soon as he has learned to crawl at around nine months he will be ready to start pulling himself up into a standing position using you, or the furniture, for support. At this stage he will not have mastered sitting down so when he wants to sit he will simply let go and land down on the floor with a resounding bump. He probably won't be able to control his sitting movement until he is 11 to 12 months old.

Before he's a year old your baby will start to cruise around the furniture, taking little sideways steps. Once he can move around like this with some confidence he will let go with one hand. As soon as he is able to let go with his remaining hand, perhaps to cross a gap in the furniture, he will begin to get the confidence to walk about unaided.

Your baby's first steps on his own will be very wobbly and ungainly, with his feet placed wide apart to help him balance. But once he becomes more mobile his legs will straighten and he'll become steadier on his feet.

By eight or nine months your baby will be able to crawl around on the floor.

Your baby will try to stand with your help.

Lift him up supporting his arms.

Once up, he will need your hand to balance.

A baby walker can help a child to take her first steps and practise walking.

Once crawling your baby will go all over.

Other types of baby walker can be sat in and propelled along by your child's feet.

A young baby will enjoy a baby bouncer, but make sure it is firmly attached.

Your child's first steps are often wobbly and his movements may seem awkward.

PLAY

Introduce your baby to games by teaching him nursery rhymes like "This little piggy went to market".

A baby is born with the potential to learn and play. She can see, hear, and feel. She is aware of her environment and will respond from birth to brightly coloured, moving objects and to sounds. She learns all the time and play is one of the ways in which she develops new skills, while toys are the play tools that she uses to stimulate herself at each stage of development. Toys don't have to be elaborate; your child will invent her own games and use everyday objects as toys when she is young. Watching you and trying to imitate your voice and facial expressions will provide hours of entertainment in the early months. Ultimately, the toy that a child enjoys and plays with most will give her the greatest learning experience, and in the first weeks of life this "toy" will be you.

Your child will change rapidly during the first year so that a toy that entertains her at two months will not appeal to her when she is a year old. As she develops, your child will need different stimuli and the choice of toys for each stage of development should reflect these different needs. It is also very important that the toys you give a child are appropriate to this age. A toy designed for a younger child will be boring, while a toy for an older child may be too complicated and may even be dangerous if it contains small pieces on which a young baby could choke.

BIRTH TO THREE MONTHS
During the first few months, your baby is developing her basic senses – touch, sight, and sound. She needs toys which will stimulate these senses

Your child will be fascinated by nursery rhymes that involve actions that use his hands.

Because the end of "round and round the garden" includes tickling your baby, he will associate it with fun and ask for more.

As your child develops she will start to enjoy playing games with you such as "peek-a-boo".

As you teach her the game, she will enjoy "hiding" behind the chair and peeking out at you from behind the legs.

Games to play

• Gently bounce your baby up and down on your knee in rhythm to a nursery rhyme.

• Hold her palm open and play "round and round the garden" ending up with a tickle under her arm.

• Use her toes to play "this little piggy went to market".

• Take your baby as your partner and dance around the room with her in your arms.

You can buy your baby many expensive toys, but she'll still enjoy playing with simple kitchen utensils. Always make sure they have no sharp edges.

and give experience of colours, textures, materials and shapes. A good first toy is a mobile, hung where your baby can study it at leisure. It doesn't have to be expensive – one made from pictures cut from a magazine and suspended from a coat hanger will be just as effective as one you buy. Once your baby begins to wave her hands around and tries to swipe at things, she will enjoy toys that make a noise or that react to her actions, a rattle for example. This will give your child a sense of control as well as encouraging the development of manual skills and hand and eye co-ordination.

A newborn baby's hands are usually held closed in fists, but she will gradually relax them so that if you place an object in her open palm she will close her hand around it for a few seconds. The strong grasp reflex she was born with will have disappeared so that she will probably drop the object within a few seconds. By the age of two or three months

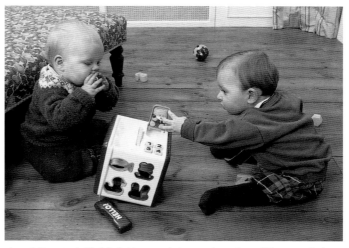

An activity centre is ideal for babies around nine months as they will love to push the buttons and manipulate all the different shapes and knobs.

she will try reaching out to touch things. These first grasping movements are important steps learning hand-eye co-ordination.

Once your baby is old enough to sit in a bouncing cradle she will be able to see more of the world around

her and her hands will be free to explore. A toy fastened across the front of the cradle will encourage her to bring her hands forward to try and hit it to make it move. Once she has done this, she will want to do it again and again; gradually she sees that she is responsible for making this happen and her movements become more deliberate.

A newborn is acutely aware of sounds and will already have become familiar with your voice while in the womb. Talking and singing to your baby from the time she is born will encourage her to listen and help her develop her own speech later. As she gets older, hold her on your lap and try having a conversation with her. Say something, then wait until your baby makes a noise in response. Her response will be slow at first so allow her plenty of time. These conversations will help her learn about taking turns, listening, and copying – all essential parts of communication. Once your baby has got used to life outside the womb,

As she starts to move around, your baby will get pleasure from pushing a baby walker. She will also enjoy trying to put plastic shapes in the right holes on the walker.

she will find touch and the freedom to move her limbs exciting. Different textures will give her new sensations of touch, so offer her various things to feel that will give her experience of rough, soft, silky, or smooth textures. Bathing and changing times will provide an opportunity for your baby to explore touch and sensation. She will like the feeling of not being hampered by nappies and clothing and should enjoy the sensation of warm water next to her skin. Try tickling her gently, blowing raspberries on her abdomen, and kissing her toes when she is undressed.

THREE TO SIX MONTHS

As your baby grows and her movements become more controlled, she will reach out for things and take them in her hands. Her grip becomes stronger and she will be able to hold a wider variety of items. This means that she will start to experience the difference between things that are light and heavy, soft and hard. Her curiosity will be endless and every object will be a plaything. She may prefer to use her mouth rather than her hands to explore things at this age, so it is important to make sure that she can't get hold of anything which could do her any harm.

Your baby will probably play happily for short periods on her own, but she needs you to encourage her. When you play with your baby get her to do things for herself; allow her to use her hands and eyes to work out what she wants to do with the toy she is holding. It is better to give your child only a few selected items to play with at this age because she won't be able to concentrate on more than one thing at a time.

A stimulating, inviting environment is important for all creative play. Toys that are piled up in a jumble are not as inviting to a child as toys which are laid out for her in an attractive, inviting way.

SIX TO TWELVE MONTHS

Once your baby can support herself sitting up and has started to make her first attempts at moving around, she will want toys that she can manipulate. This is the ideal time to give your child an activity centre with lots of different knobs and handles for her to twist and turn. By around seven or eight months she

will want to find out what things can do and will bang objects on the ground or table to find out if they make a noise or wave them in the air to see what happens.

As her manipulative skills develop she will learn that she can use her hands and arms simultaneously and will start to bang things together. She will be able to reach out to you with both arms when she wants to be picked up. It takes a while longer for her to learn how to let go of items she is playing with, but you can encourage her by giving her an object, then holding out your hand and asking for it back.

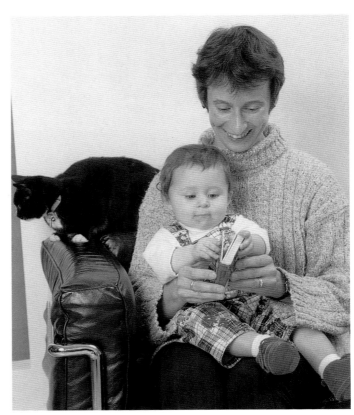

A young baby will enjoy being read to from a simple board book and will be interested in touching the pages. She will soon learn how to recognize the book's pictures.

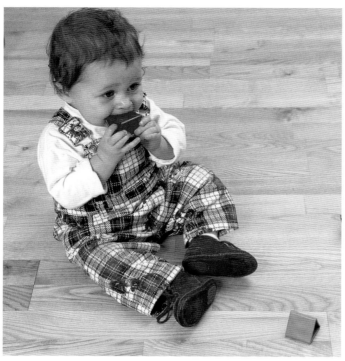

Your child will often put different things in her mouth to investigate them.

Once she's got the hang of this game she will love it and keep you busy for hours!

As she becomes more mobile, your baby will want to be into everything and her natural curiosity could lead her into danger, so you need to pay constant attention to safety. One of your baby's favourite pastimes will be emptying things out of containers. She will take things out of cupboards with just as much enjoyment as she will empty shapes out of a shape sorter. Once she has emptied a container she will want to examine the contents in great detail and will bang things together and may put them in her mouth before discarding them and moving on to the next object. When she has mastered this

she will soon learn that she can put things back into the container and will spend ages tipping things out and putting them back again. She will try doing this with different objects and may discover that some of them don't fit. As your child plays she will be learning about the nature of the objects, how they behave, and their relative size and shape.

Water play can be introduced now and your baby will enjoy filling and emptying plastic beakers while she is having her bath. Give her toys which have different sizes of holes in them so that she can spend time sprinkling or pouring the water from one container into another.

Once your baby has started to crawl, give her toys that roll and move when they are pushed along so that she can go after them. Later, as she starts taking her weight on her legs, you can encourage her and help her balance with sturdy push-along

A baby walker will help your child to walk and some double as an activity centre.

toys, such as a brick trolley. This will give her something to hold onto until she feels confident enough to let go and walk unaided.

BOOKS

It is never too early to introduce your baby to books. Start at an early age with brightly coloured rag books that your baby can chew as well as handle, or simple board books. At first she will enjoy these books as objects to be explored but, if you sit her on your knee and talk to her about the pictures in the book, she will soon learn to recognize them. Encourage her by making the noises of any animals pictured in the books and then getting her to do the same.

Games to play

• "Pat-a-cake, pat-a-cake, baker's man" is a rhyme to which your baby will enjoy clapping. When you get to "prick it and pat it and mark it with ..." use your baby's own initial and then her name when you come to "put in the oven for ...".

• Blowing bubbles using either a made-up solution and a wand or washing-up liquid and your hands.

• "Peek-a-boo": use your hands to cover your face; then later hide and seek: hide objects under a soft cloth for your baby to find.

• Hold your baby's hands securely and rock her gently backwards and forward while singing "Row, row, row the boat ...".

• Sit your baby on your knee facing towards you and hold her firmly by the hands as you bounce her in time to "Humpty Dumpty". When you get to the big fall allow your baby to drop through your knees while holding her firmly.

By just giving your baby one toy at a time to play with, she will be able to concentrate on it more fully.

PART FOUR

COOKING FOR BABIES AND TODDLERS

A baby has specific nutritional requirements, very different from those of an adult. Many new parents are apprehensive of their ability to cater for their baby's needs – especially when children have a mind of their own, and can reject the carefully chosen and prepared food. This section sets out to explain the latest guidelines for feeding babies and young children. It explains clearly which are the highly nutritious foods, packed with the protein and vitamins that an active child needs, and warns against foods that do not provide enough calories or that may cause allergic reactions.

We all know commercially prepared food can be bad for us and it is sometimes hard to judge how much salt and sugar has been added. Home cooked food is delicious, and can be just as quick to make. This section is packed with recipes, each fully illustrated and set out clearly, step by step. Many recipes have been specially created to work for the entire family with only a little adaptation. The same basic ingredients and methods of preparation can be tailored to create three meals: for a baby, a fussy toddler and for two hungry parents. This section is also packed with tips to help make meals a calm, pleasant time, where you can relax and enjoy your family's company.

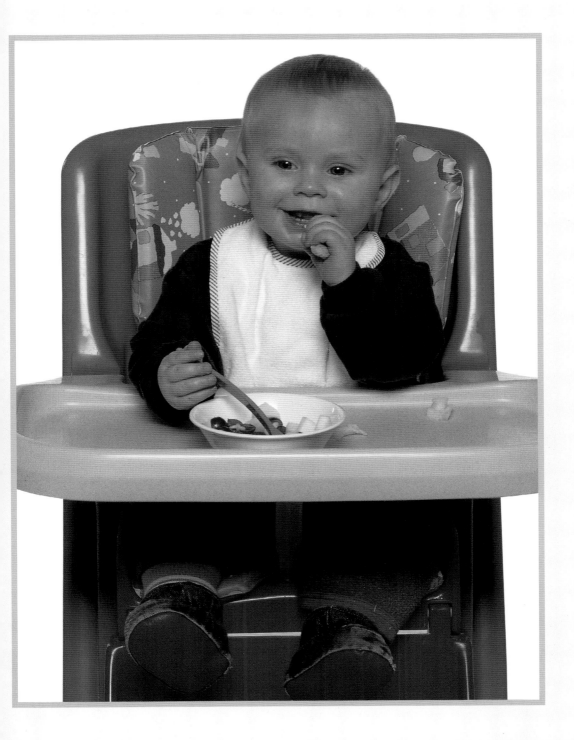

INTRODUCTION

Part Four, Cooking for Babies and Toddlers, aims to explain all you need to know about feeding your young family. Set out in three easy-to-use sections, it is packed with over 200 recipes, all beautifully illustrated with colour pictures – from first purées to tempting toddler meals then moving on to food for all the family.

In the very early days all a baby needs is milk, but as it grows so too will its nutritional needs. By four months most babies will have doubled their birth weight and will be ready to begin mini-mouthfuls of smooth purée.

Although this marks an exciting time in your baby's development it can also cause immense worry for a new parent. We all want to provide the best for our child and what better start in life than to begin laying the foundations for a healthy diet? But what do you do if your child just refuses to eat? This section has practical tips that may provide some of the answers.

If your child has any food allergies or sensitivities, read each recipe to make sure that it doesn't contain a problem ingredient.

FIRST FOODS

Section one covers everything you need to know about introducing those first spoonfuls of smooth puréed foods: including when to begin weaning, the signs to look out for, what foods to serve and when, basic equipment, plus sound nutritional advice, helpful guidelines on food preparation and masses of colourful and exciting recipes to tempt your baby.

You will almost certainly find that health professionals, friends and relatives will offer you differing, perhaps contradictory, advice. Some will be useful, while some will turn out to be outdated or inappropriate: the difficulty is sorting through the confusion to find something reliable. This section draws upon current dietary information to provide helpful advice on feeding your baby.

FOOD FOR TODDLERS

In the second section we move on to feeding an energetic toddler. By this stage your baby will probably have tripled her birth weight and will have begun to feed herself and may be developing strong likes and dislikes. Many young children go through a stage of extreme food fads, causing frustration and worry for parents. Again, we have included down-to-earth tips and practical advice on coping with a fussy eater, plus lots of easy recipes to tempt your child.

FAMILY MEALS

In the third section the recipes have been devised to feed the whole family from one basic set of ingredients prepared at the same time. With step-by-step instructions we illustrate how to mash food for your baby, make a mini-meal for your fussy toddler and how, by adding a few extra ingredients, to simultaneously transform this simple meal into something more exciting for Mum and Dad.

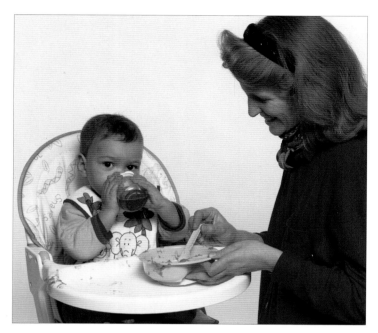

Above and below: *Start with simple vegetable purées. Sit your baby in a high-chair with a strap, or on your lap with a dish towel to protect your clothes.*

about 50 per cent of energy as fat. As your child progresses to a mixed diet, the proportion of energy supplied by fat decreases and is replaced by carbohydrate. However, it is important that the energy is provided by fat up to the age of two, as too much carbohydrate may be too bulky for a young infant.

Adequate energy is necessary to sustain growth. Fat is a very useful source of energy and the main source of the fat-soluble vitamins, A, D, E and K, while also providing essential fatty acids that the body cannot make itself. It is best to obtain fat from foods that contain other essential nutrients, such as full-fat (whole) milk, cheese, yogurt, lean meat and small quantities of oily fish.

Try to include a portion of carbohydrate in every meal once your child is over nine months: for example, bread, potatoes, rice or pasta for energy. Encourage young

FOOD AND YOUR CHILD

Childrens' nutritional needs are very different from our own. Forget about low-fat, high-fibre diets. Young children require nutrient-dense foods to meet their rapid levels of growth. Requirements for protein and energy are high in proportion to the child's size. Tiny tummies mean children are unable to eat large quantities of food, while at the same time they are usually very active. Their appetites can vary enormously, but the range of foods that they will eat may be very limited. Consequently, it is vital that the foods which are eaten contain a variety of nutrients, in combination with calories, while still fitting in with family meals. High-fibre foods can be very filling without providing sufficient levels of protein, vitamins and minerals.

For young infants fat is the major source of dietary energy: both breast milk and infant formula contribute

Below: *Babies are easily encouraged to take pleasure in their food, however simple. Give your baby finger food as well as a spoon and bowl.*

children to eat a variety of fruit and vegetables. As with adults, try to keep salt intakes to a minimum; fried foods or very sugary foods should be discouraged and served only as a special treat. As children approach school age they should gradually be pushed towards a diet that is lower in fat and higher in fibre, in line with the guidelines for adults.

Snacks are also important as young children require high calorie levels and cannot meet this requirement in three meals a day. Try to encourage healthy snacks such as mini ham sandwiches, cubes of cheese or wedges of apple instead of chocolate biscuits.

Obviously, having a healthy, well-balanced diet is essential for any age group, but acquiring social skills is also important. Our children learn from us and so it is vital to eat together as a family, if not every day, then as often as possible. It is never too early for the youngest member of the family to start learning how to behave at the table – though to begin with it will probably be a messy experience. Your child will soon regard family meals as a sociable and enjoyable time.

We hope that this book will make meal-times fun for the entire family and help to minimize any problems you may come up against when feeding your baby and toddler.

Below: *Don't deprive the children of cakes at party-time, but include some healthy dips and savouries, too.*

Above: *Giving your child the best possible start in life is a major concern, but good food planning is easy to achieve.*

FIRST FOODS

Introducing your baby to the delights of solid food heralds the beginning of a new and exciting stage in your baby's development. You will know she is ready when she seems unsatisfied after a milk feed, or shows an interest in what you are eating. Although it will be a few months yet before she is able to share in family meals fully, the foods that you give your baby now are important not only for their nutritional benefits but also in laying down the first foundations for a healthy diet through childhood and beyond.

Start your baby with baby rice that is barely warm and only slightly thicker than milk – then move to bland mashed vegetables and fruits. For those first spoonfuls, sit your baby on your lap in a familiar position, but once she is accustomed to the idea, put her in a baby chair on the floor, or in a portable car seat. It won't be long before she is ready for a high-chair. Remember that hygiene is still very important, and you should continue to sterilize equipment until your baby is six-and-a-half months old.

Weaning from Milk Feeds to Solids

Most babies are ready to begin those first few mini-mouthfuls of mashed or puréed foods at around six months and will soon progress to a mixed diet of solid foods. By this age, babies need the extra energy, protein, iron and other essential nutrients that are found in solids in order to help them develop and grow. Your baby will also be progressing from sucking to biting and chewing – as many breast-feeding mothers find out!

Remember that every baby has individual needs, so don't be surprised if your baby seems ready for solids a little earlier or later than other babies of the same age. Don't feel pressurized by friends with young babies, or helpful relatives. Be guided by your own baby.

Below: *Your baby will very quickly take an interest in your hand and the spoon, and will play as she eats.*

Right: *When the signs are right, start your baby with a few mouthfuls of mashed vegetables or fruit after a milk feed, or in the middle of one, if this works better. If the food is hot, make sure you stir it and test it before giving it to your baby.*

Below right: *When your baby starts picking up food and putting it into his mouth, he is ready to try solid foods.*

WHAT TO LOOK OUT FOR

If your baby:
- still seems hungry after you have increased the milk feed
- wants feeding more frequently
- shows a real interest in the foods that you are eating
- picks up food and puts it in his or her mouth, wanting to chew
- can sit up

If your baby is showing some or all of these signs, then he or she is probably ready to begin solids. Some babies may show these signs earlier than six months, but the majority should not be given solid foods before six months as their digestive systems can't cope. Be guided as well by any family history of allergies, eczema or asthma. Studies suggest that babies fed on breast or formula milk a bit longer are less likely to develop such complaints.

In the early days of weaning, your baby is not dependent on solid food for the supply of nutrients as this is still met by milk feeds. Don't worry if she only takes a taste of food to begin with – the actual experience of taking food off a spoon is the most important thing at this stage. However, as your baby grows older, solid foods are essential for supplying all the vital minerals and vitamins she needs.

WHAT ABOUT MILK FEEDS?

During the early stages of weaning, solids are given in addition to normal feeds of breast or formula milk. As mixed feeding continues, your baby will naturally cut down on the number of milk feeds, but milk will remain an important part of a child's diet.

Up to six months your baby should be having four to five milk feeds a day, and by age one your baby needs at least 600ml/1 pint full-fat (whole) milk a day. Milk will still contribute 40 percent of the energy she uses up. Health professionals recommend that children should not be given cow's milk as their main drink until after 12 months, due to low levels of iron and vitamins C and D. Mothers may be advised to go on to fortified formula when breast feeding has finished. Small amounts of cow's milk may be used in cooking from six months, but it is better to use formula milk.

Above: *Bottles are a wonderful aid, but try to wean your baby off them by age one, or the sucking habit can be difficult to break.*

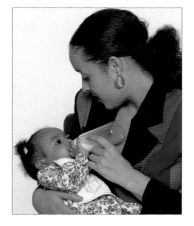

Above: *Every baby is different. There is no need to be worried if your baby seems ready for solids earlier or later than other babies.*

Full-fat cow's milk can be given to children between one and two, while semi-skimmed (low-fat) milk can be gradually introduced to those over two, providing the child eats well. Skimmed milk should not be given to children under five.

Only give pasteurized milk to children. UHT or long-life milk is a useful standby for holidays and travelling as it doesn't need to be refrigerated. However, once opened treat it as full-fat pasteurized milk.

Some people prefer to give goat's or sheep's milk believing it is less allergenic and offers additional nourishment, although this cannot be substantiated. Goat's milk is deficient in folic acid and must not be given to babies under six months. Boil goat's milk before use, as it may be sold unpasteurized.

WEANING FROM BREAST OR BOTTLE

You can go on breast feeding your baby, as well as giving solid food, for as long as you wish. However, many mothers are quite relieved when their baby is happy to try a feeder cup or bottle along with their lunch-time "solid" meal. Once solids become established the number of daytime milk feeds naturally tails off, with just the special morning and evening comfort feeds continuing until you and your baby are ready to stop.

Whether bottle or breast and bottle feeding, try to wean your baby off the bottle completely by the age of one. Otherwise your baby may find it difficult to give the bottle up, and comfort sucking on a teat can be a hard habit to break.

Once your baby can sit up, you can introduce a lidded feeding cup, initially at one meal a day, then at two and so on. But do make sure that you cuddle your baby while giving a drink, so that the baby still enjoys the closeness and security of being with her mother or father. There may be a few setbacks when your baby is teething or unwell, but be guided by your baby.

Above: *It won't all happen at once: a mixed period of feeding with breast, bottle and simple solids is perfectly natural and healthy.*

Introducing Solid Food

Many parents find that around late morning, after their baby's morning sleep, is the best time to introduce solids. The baby is happy and nicely hungry without being frantic. Offer a small milk feed to take the edge off her immediate hunger and make her feel secure, and then go on to offer solid food. Finish with the rest of the milk feed or "second side".

SITTING COMFORTABLY

If you are feeding a slightly younger baby, you might like to hold her securely on your lap while offering the first spoonfuls. However, most babies will be comfortable fed in a high-chair.

FIRST SPOONFULS

Baby rice is often the most successful first food because its milky taste and soft texture seem vaguely familiar to the baby. Begin by trying a teaspoonful of bought baby rice, add a little previously boiled water, expressed breast milk or formula milk as the pack directs, and mix to make a smooth runny purée, slightly thicker than milk. Test the temperature on the edge of your lip, it should be just lukewarm – too hot and you may put the baby off solids completely. Offer tiny amounts on the end of a sterilized teaspoon. Go at your baby's pace and don't try to hurry things.

Above: *First baby rice will be barely warm, and only very slightly thicker than milk.*

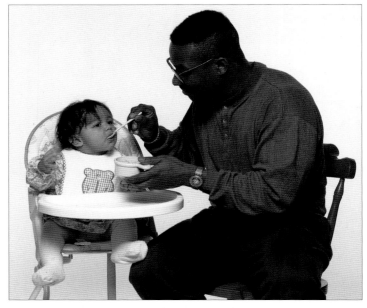

Above: *At about six months your baby will be ready to sit safely in a high-chair. You should always use a strap to make sure she is safely fastened in.*

Learning to eat from a spoon is quite a skill, and your baby may start spitting out the food until she has mastered the technique of taking food off the spoon and transferring it to the back of her mouth. It is possible that she may not like the taste of the food. If you started with baby rice, then go on to potato or parsnip purée mixed into the baby rice. If your baby seems reluctant, then abandon the feed and go back to breast or bottle feeding – your baby may simply not be ready for solids yet.

You could try solids again a few days later – there's plenty of time. Never force-feed and never add solid foods to a baby's bottle, as it can lead to choking, which can be dangerous.

BABY APPEARS TO GAG

Some babies just cannot cope with solids at first and may seem distressed and almost gag on the food.

Try thinning down the food even more, as it may be too thick. Alternatively, you may be putting too much on the spoon: try offering your baby a little less. If neither of these seems to help, stop solids and breast or bottle feed as usual, giving your baby plenty of reassuring cuddles. Try again in a few days' or weeks' time.

INTRODUCING VEGETABLES

After rice, gradually introduce mashed or puréed potato, carrot, parsnip and swede (rutabaga), or puréed apple or pears. As always, be guided by your baby: this is a slow process so don't try to hurry your baby if she is not ready, or you will run the risk of discouraging her altogether.

SPOON FEEDING FOR THE FIRST TIME

1 Sit your baby on your lap in a familiar position. Always test the temperature of the food.

2 Offer the spoon to your baby. Go slowly and if the spoon or food is rejected try again another day.

3 When your baby has taken her first solid food, sit her quietly for a little while in an upright position.

After a week or two your baby may be ready to try two mini-meals a day. Increase the amount of food to 10ml/2 tsp, even 15ml/3 tsp if your baby seems ready. You may be able to slightly reduce the amount of formula or breast milk you use to make the purée, so that it is not quite so sloppy. If your baby likes the flavour, then offer it again for a few meals before introducing a new taste. If your baby spits it out, then go back to baby rice or try mixing the new flavour with a little baby rice so that it is milder and more palatable.

Try to follow your baby's appetite and pace; most babies will stop when they have had enough. Don't be tempted to persuade your baby to finish off those last few spoonfuls. It's a bad habit to force or encourage anyone to clear the plate if they are full. If you do it with a baby, she'll probably be sick!

Adopt a feeding schedule to suit you both. In the early days it may be easier to give the baby breakfast before older children get up, or after they're at school, when the house is quieter. Six to eight weeks into solid feeding, your baby will probably be ready for three small meals a day. Again, be guided by her needs and appetite, so don't introduce a third meal until you feel she is really ready. Aim to feed your baby at roughly equal time intervals that will eventually coincide with as many family meals as possible.

TIPS

- Take advice from your doctor or health visitor, particularly if your baby was premature.

- Sterilize all equipment before use up to the age of about six-and-a-half months.

- Don't force your baby if she doesn't seem ready for solids – be guided by her and let it happen at its own pace.

- Maintain milk feeds and offer plain boiled water or very diluted fruit juice as well.

- Try one taste at a time and continue with this until your baby is accustomed to it. If she doesn't like it, don't offer it again for a few days.

- Allow plenty of time for feeding, particularly at first.

- Choose a time of day when you and your baby are relaxed.

- Talk to your baby quietly and encourage her to eat.

- Never leave your baby alone when feeding her.

- Remember, babies don't mind repetition – they've been living on milk for months!

Above: *You can build up the diet from baby rice to items like mashed or puréed carrot, parsnip, apple or pear, gradually leaving more texture as your baby seems ready.*

EQUIPMENT

Choose a small plastic spoon, preferably with a shallow bowl that is gentle on your baby's gums. Look out for packs of weaning spoons in pharmacies or baby-care shops. If you don't want to buy a lot of equipment right away, you may find it useful to mix small quantities of baby rice in the sterilized cap of a bottle. Alternatively, use a small china ramekin or plastic bowl. Plastic bowls with suction feet or insulated linings are also perfectly adequate and will be useful later on when your baby gets bigger. All equipment must be scrupulously clean (and sterilized if your baby is under six-and-a-half months old).

Below: *This shallow bowl with a spoon would be the perfect starter set.*

Above, left and below: *Any small dish, or even the lid of a baby's bottle, can be used for mixing and feeding.*

Below: *A bib is even more essential once your baby is taking solid foods.*

Left: *A bowl with an insulated lining is a good idea for a baby who takes her time eating.*

Below: *Your baby will graduate from bottles with teats to cups and beakers with tight-fitting lids. There is a variety of types, but you will find one the toddler likes.*

FEEDING TWINS

Probably the easiest way to feed twins is to sit the babies side by side and offer food from one bowl. Twins can get rather frustrated if you have to keep picking up different bowls and spoons. Try to be adaptable and if you find a way that works then stick with it. Encourage finger foods slightly earlier: perhaps a mini ham sandwich, cooked broccoli floret or carrot stick.

Wait until each child has finished their main course before offering dessert, as the slow eater will be distracted and want to go on to dessert too.

Looking after twins can be exhausting so you may find serving sandwiches for lunch an easier option, and this will give you a chance to eat something too. Serve cooked food for the evening meal.

DRINKS

Although your baby will need less milk for nourishment, she will still need something to drink, especially in hot weather. Always offer at least two drinks during the day and also a drink with every meal.

You can give:

- breast, formula milk or, at over one year, full-fat (whole) cow's milk
- cooled boiled water
- well-diluted pure unsweetened fruit juice

Above: *Dilute juices with boiled and cooled water.*

Above: *If you have twins, put their chairs side by side at meal-times.*

Below: *Drinks fill up the baby's tummy – so offer drinks after food.*

You can stop boiling the water for the baby's drinks when you stop sterilizing her feeding equipment, but always make sure you provide water from the mains supply and allow the tap to run before using it. Never use water from the hot tap.

If you have a water softener make sure that you use a tap connected directly to the mains supply and independent of the water softener. Artificially softened water is not recommended as salts are added during the softening process. Check with your doctor or health visitor before giving a baby bottled water, as the mineral content varies and you will need to choose a low-mineral brand such as those that are labelled "spring water". As a general rule, bottled water is not really necessary unless you are on holiday (vacation) where it is unsafe to drink the water.

Some fruit drinks contain a lot of added sugar, so check the label for sucrose, glucose, dextrose, fructose, maltose, syrup, honey or concentrated fruit juice. If you do give concentrated drinks to your baby, make sure you dilute them correctly, and do not give them too often. Pure fruit juices contain no added sugar. At first, dilute them with one part juice to three parts water. The amount of water can be reduced as the child matures. Offer drinks at the end of meal times once your baby has settled into three meals a day.

Never allow a baby to use a bottle of juice as a comforter or go to sleep with a bottle in his mouth, as this can result in serious tooth decay.

Sterilizing and Food Preparation

For babies older than six months, it isn't necesssary for the first solids to be completely smooth and soft, and you can start introducing some texture quite quickly, depending on your baby's preferences. Fork-mashing is simple and easy, but there are several useful pieces of kitchen equipment to help you with larger quantities.

For ease and speed, an electric liquidizer is by far the best. You may be able to buy a liquidizer attachment for your mixer, or purchase a free-standing liquidizer unit. A food processor works well, but make sure the food is blended to the required smoothness before offering it to your baby, as processors can miss the odd lump, especially when processing small quantities. A hand-held electric multimixer has the bonus of reducing washing up by mixing foods in the serving bowl. If you prefer to purée food by hand, then a sieve (strainer) or hand mill are both perfectly adequate and are much cheaper alternatives.

Above: *There is a huge range of brand-name food processors and blenders on the market, many of which have attachments for puréeing.*

Left: *The basics – manual mashers, or a sieve – take longer but will do the job just as well.*

Above: *A purpose-designed liquidizer will make perfect purée in seconds. This is the right tool for making large batches.*

Above: *This hand-held blender takes a little longer, but the results are just as reliable. They are easy to clean and store.*

Above: *Making purée manually the old-fashioned way – with a sieve and spoon – is time-consuming but highly satisfying.*

FOOD HYGIENE

Young babies can easily pick up infections, so it is vitally important that all equipment is scrupulously clean before use.

• Always wash your hands before handling food or feeding equipment.

Above: *Rule one – always wash your hands with soap and warm water before feeding your baby or handling food.*

• Items such as bottles, feeding spoons and serving bowls should be sterilized until your baby is six-and-a-half months old. Sterilize equipment by boiling it in a pan of water for 25 minutes, immersing it in a container of cold water with sterilizing fluid or a tablet, or by using a steam sterilizer. Larger items such as a sieve, knife, pan, blender or masher, or plastic chopping board should be scalded with boiling water.

Above: *Scald larger objects such as chopping boards, spoons, sieves and pans with boiling water to sterilize.*

• Sterilize all baby equipment until your baby is six-and-a-half months; milk bottles, teats and so on should be sterilized until she begins to use a cup.

Above: *Boiling for 25 minutes is still the simplest way of sterilizing baby equipment.*

Right: *Always cover baby food at all times – even when stored in the refrigerator.*

Below: *Always keep the surfaces around where your baby eats scrupulously clean.*

• Never use equipment used for the family pet when preparing baby food. Keep a can opener, fork and dish specifically for your pet, and make sure other members of the family are aware of this.

• Once cooked, cover all baby food with a lid or plate and transfer to the refrigerator as soon as possible. Food should not be left for longer than 1½ hours at room temperature before either refrigerating or freezing.

SOLUTION STERILIZER

STEAM STERILIZER

1 Fill the sterilizer to the required height with cold water, and add sterilizing tablets or liquid.

2 Pack the items to be sterilized into the container. Bottles will fit into the spaces provided.

1 Measure the specified amount of water into the base of the steamer as directed in the instructions.

3 Make sure no air gets trapped in the container – or these pockets will not be properly sterile. Push everything down with the "float".

4 Place the lid on and leave for the length of time specified in the instructions. Rinse everything afterwards in boiling water.

2 Pack the bottles and teats into the container: steamers have less capacity for dishes, which will need to be boiled separately.

Left: *There is a wide range of sterilizing equipment to choose from. This group, all specially designed for bottles and teats, comprises two steam sterilizing units that operate electrically and a traditional container that holds the bottles efficiently in cold water sterilizing solution.*

STERILIZING IN THE MICROWAVE

Microwave ovens are not suitable for general day-to-day sterilizing without special equipment, and many health authorities and mother-and-baby experts recommend against using the microwave for this purpose. However, microwave sterilizing units can be purchased for sterilizing bottles, and if you are using one, the manufacturer's instructions should be followed closely.

Right: *This purpose-designed sterilizing unit is specially made for microwave use. Add about 5mm/¹/4in water to the base before putting in the bottles.*

BATCH COOKING

Cooking for a baby can be very frustrating. Those spoonfuls of lovingly and hygienically prepared food, offered with such hope and spat out so unceremoniously can leave you feeling quite indignant.

Save time by cooking several meals in advance. Freeze mini-portions in ice-cube trays, great for those early days when you need only one cube for lunch, and flexible enough for later on when your baby's appetite has grown to two or three cubes per meal.

Spoon the mixture into sterilized ice-cube trays and open freeze until solid. Press the cubes into a plastic bag, seal, label and return to the freezer. Keep single batches of food in the same bag so that the different flavours don't combine.

Recycle yogurt containers, cottage cheese containers with lids, small plastic boxes with lids, or use disposable plastic cups and cover them with clear film (plastic wrap). Sterilize the containers using sterilizing fluid or tablets. Cover all prepared foods and label them clearly so that you know what they are and on which date they went into the freezer.

Most foods should be used within three months if stored in a freezer at – 18°C/0°F. Defrost plastic boxes in the refrigerator overnight. Ice cubes can be left to defrost at room temperature in a bowl or on a plate, loosely covered with clear film.

BATCH COOKING TIPS

1 It is just as quick (and very much cheaper in the long run) to make a larger batch of purée as a smaller quantity for a single meal.

2 Freeze in meal-size portions in sterilized ice-cube trays: these can later be put into freezer bags for storing.

3 Make sure the bags are carefully labelled and dated. Keep only for the period specified in your freezer handbook.

Reheating, Freezing and Using a Microwave

HOW TO REHEAT BABY FOOD
Although reheating food sounds relatively straightforward, it is vitally important that the following rules are followed, as tepid food provides the perfect breeding ground for bacteria, especially if left uncovered in a warm kitchen and reheated several times.
● Don't reheat food more than once. It is a health risk, and can be dangerous.

● If you have a large batch of baby food, then reheat just a portion in a pan and leave the remaining mixture in a covered bowl in the refrigerator. If your baby is still hungry after the feed, then reheat a little extra again, with the remaining mixture left in the refrigerator.
● Reheat small quantities of baby food in a sterilized heat-proof container, covered with a saucer or

small plate and put into a small pan half filled with boiling water. Alternatively, spoon larger quantities straight into a pan, cover and bring to the boil.
● Make sure food is piping hot all the way through to kill any bacteria. Food should be 70°C/158°F for a minimum of 2 minutes. Take off the heat and allow to cool. Test before serving to your baby.

REHEATING TIPS

1 Reheat small quantities in a sterilized bowl, covered with a dish or foil.

2 Place the bowl into a pan half filled with boiling water. Make sure the food is cooked through.

3 For larger quantities, put the food straight into the pan and bring to the boil.

FREEZING

● When using a freezer for storing home-made baby foods, use up the foods as soon as possible, as the texture preferred by the child will change very quickly as she develops.
● Keeping a well-stocked freezer of basic provisions can be a life-saver: there is nothing worse than going shopping with small children, especially when they're tired, and freezing will save you trip after trip.
● Make sure to always label foods so you know exactly when they went into the freezer, and double check against this handy list of storage dates:

Meat and poultry

Beef and lamb	4–6 months
Pork and veal	4–6 months
Minced (ground) beef	3–4 months
Sausages	2–3 months
Ham and bacon joints	3–4 months
Chicken and turkey	10–12 months
Duck and goose	4–6 months

Fish

White fish	6–8 months
Oily fish	3–4 months
Fish portions	3–4 months
Shellfish	2–3 months

Fruit and vegetables

Fruit with or without sugar	8–10 months
Fruit juices	4–6 months
Most vegetables	10–12 months
Mushrooms and tomatoes	6–8 months

Dairy produce

Cream	6–8 months
Butter, unsalted (sweet)	6–8 months
Butter, salted	3–4 months
Cheese, hard	4–6 months
Cheese, soft	3–4 months
Ice cream	3–4 months

Prepared foods

Ready-prepared meals, highly seasoned	2–3 months
Ready-prepared meals, average seasoning	4–6 months
Cakes	4–6 months
Bread, all kinds	2–3 months
Other yeast products and pastries	3–4 months

Chart published by kind permission of the Food Safety Advisory Centre

Above: *Many parents will find a microwave helpful and time-saving if used carefully. It can be used for heating milk and drinks (for toddlers – not newborns), for defrosting, reheating and cooking preprepared foods.*

USING A MICROWAVE

Health advisers do not recommend using a microwave for reheating, as the food heats up unevenly, but if you decide to microwave baby food, then make sure you stir the food thoroughly after cooking. Leave the dish to stand for 2–3 minutes before stirring again so that "hot spots" are well stirred into the mixture, and always check the temperature before serving. Choose the type of dish carefully as some ceramic dishes can get very hot; plastic or pyrex dishes are the most successful in the microwave, heating food quickly but staying relatively cool themselves.

1 Cover with clear film (plastic wrap), pierce and place in the oven.

2 When cooked, remove from the microwave oven and stir.

MICROWAVING TIPS

● Never warm milk for a newborn or young baby in the microwave.

● For older children, warm milk in a bottle without the teat or in an uncovered feeder beaker for 30–45 seconds. Stir well and always test the temperature of the milk (*not* the temperature of the container) before serving to make sure that the milk is an even and comfortable temperature. Seek advice from your doctor or health visitor.

● To defrost ice cubes of baby food, press three into a baby dish, cover with clear film (plastic wrap) and thaw in the microwave on Defrost (30%) for 1–2 minutes. Stir well then re-cover and microwave on Full Power (100%) for 1 minute. Stir well to avoid hot spots, then test the temperature.

Choosing a High-chair

There is a surprisingly wide choice of high-chairs available in a range of finishes, colours and price levels, so make sure you shop around before you buy. Those shown here are just a selection of the many different chairs that are available.

CONVERTIBLE CHAIRS

Designed for babies between four weeks and six months, these chairs can convert from a high-chair into a swing, and some models will also convert into a baby chair and rocker too. It is best to buy one of these when the baby is very young so that you get maximum use from it. The only disadvantage may be the space required for the frame. The ease in converting from one type of chair to another varies from model to model, so you would be well advised to practise in the shop before choosing which one to buy. Most chairs have white painted frames.

THREE-IN-ONE CHAIRS

Various designs on the market convert into a separate chair, chair and table or high-chair. Some simply clip apart, while others require a little help with a screwdriver. There are good rigid structures available with a wide range of decorative seat patterns. They are available in wood or white finishes. The low chair is suitable for children up to four years old if used without the tray.

ELEVATOR CHAIRS

These chairs are slightly more expensive, but will convert from a high-chair to a low chair. Some models have adjustable tray settings to fit a growing child. The frames are mostly available in white metal, with attractive seating.

Three-in-one-type

Elevator type

TIPS

● For maximum use of a high-chair, buy a booster cushion for the early days when your baby first begins to use the chair. Adjust the tray position as well, if possible.
● Check that the high-chair is easy to clean – dried-on food in cracks can be impossible to clean off. Look out for possible dirt traps on the seat or around the tray fixing.
● Make sure that the chair is sturdy and rigid – it will need to withstand considerable wear.

Above: *A portable clip-on chair.*

● If using a clip-on high-chair make sure that the table is suitable and will be able to withstand the weight of your child. Never, in any circumstances, fix on to glass.

FOLDING CHAIRS

These less expensive chairs, available in wood or white finishes, usually fold up in a scissor movement. Some can be folded crossways for packing into the boot (trunk) of the car. Before buying, check how easy they are to fold out and up, and make sure the frame is rigid when opened out.

Folding type

COUNTRY-TYPE CHAIRS

These are sturdy wooden high-chairs usually with a wooden tray and attractive spindle features. The seat can be hard for the baby, so it is best to buy a fitted chair cushion.

PORTABLE CHAIRS

There are two main types available:
● A very simple cloth tie, useful for visiting friends or eating out, as it will fold up and fit in a bag. However, it is not really suitable for everyday use as the child is literally tied on to the chair and so cannot reach the table to feed himself.
● Clip-on seats where the frames are placed under and over the edge of a dining table. Check that the table is strong enough and is not likely to overbalance before you put your baby in the chair.

1 Undo the tray catches by pressing both sides at once, and fold the tray upwards.

3 This allows you to fold the chair over on to itself: the design is incredibly neat and compact.

TIPS

● Always use a safety harness. Although most high-chairs have a three-point lap strap, you will probably have to buy straps that will go around your baby's body and clip on to the chair. It is amazing how quickly a baby learns to wriggle out of a high-chair when you're not looking.
● Never leave a child in a high-chair unattended.

2 Undo the side catches that keep the frame rigid so the chair can scissor in two.

4 It is now ready for storing, putting out of the way, or placing in the boot (trunk) of the car.

Above: *Always strap your baby in tightly.*

STAGE 1: FIRST TASTES – EARLY WEANING

OFFICIAL GUIDELINES NOW RECOMMEND THAT WEANING TAKES PLACE AT SIX OR SIX-AND-A-HALF MONTHS, BUT THERE ARE SOME BABIES WHO SHOW INTEREST IN EATING SOLIDS AT AN EARLIER AGE. YOU SHOULD NOT INTRODUCE SOLID FOODS BEFORE YOUR BABY IS 17 WEEKS OLD – AND BE SURE TO ASK YOUR DOCTOR OR HEALTH VISITOR FOR ADVICE BEFORE STARTING EARLY WEANING. BEGIN BY OFFERING ONLY A TEASPOONFUL OF BABY RICE OR VERY SOFT RUNNY PURÉE ONCE A DAY. MILK IS STILL PROVIDING YOUR BABY WITH ALL HER NUTRITIONAL NEEDS, BUT THESE EARLY FOODS WILL BE THE FOUNDATIONS ON WHICH LATER EATING HABITS ARE BUILT, SO IT SHOULD BE A POSITIVE EXPERIENCE.

Suitable Foods

FOODS TO INCLUDE
- baby rice mixed with water, breast or formula milk.
- mild-tasting fork-mashed vegetables – beginning with potato then carrot, parsnip, or swede (rutabaga).
- mild, naturally-sweet fruit purées made with eating apples or pears.

Below: *If your baby seems ready to start taking solids at around four to five months old, start with a teaspoon and build gradually to two and finally three meals a day.*

Baby rice

Apple

Swede (rutabaga)

Pear

Potato

Carrot

Parsnip

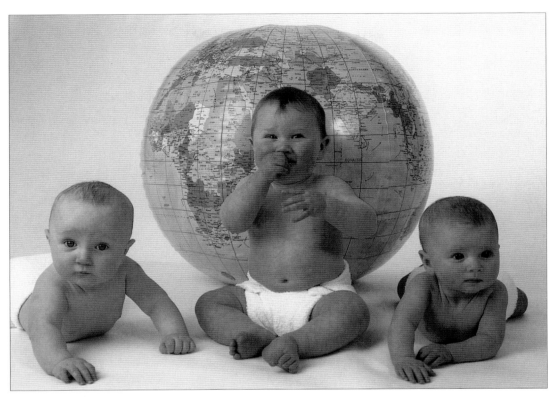

FOODS TO AVOID

- highly spiced foods
- salt as this causes the kidneys to overwork. Avoid seasoning with salt or adding stock cubes, bacon and salami to foods
- cows' milk (give breast or formula milk feeds instead)
- foods containing gluten, found in wheat, oats, rye and barley (check pack labels)
- eggs
- meat, fish, poultry
- citrus and berry fruits – can result in allergic reactions in some babies
- nuts, either whole or ground
- honey
- fatty foods

Right: *Adult favourites – but these must be avoided at this age, even as treats.*

Note: If you have a family history of allergies, your doctor or health visitor may also advise you to avoid other foods. Check with them.

Above: *A world of foodstuffs opens up over the months: but introduce them gradually, and at the right time.*

Baby Rice

Mix 5–15ml/1–3 tsp rice with cooled boiled water, formula or breast milk as the pack directs. Cool slightly and test before serving.

Left: *Plain baby rice will be the staple for your baby for the first few weeks of solids – then gradually add flavour and variation.*

Vegetable Purées

Makes: 175ml/6fl oz/³⁄₄ cup

1 Peel 125g/3½oz potato, parsnip, carrot or swede (rutabaga) and chop into small dice.

• **To microwave**: put the vegetable or vegetables in a microwave-proof bowl with 30ml/2 tbsp formula or breast milk. Cover with clear film (plastic wrap), pierce and cook on Full Power (100%) for 4 minutes. Leave to stand for 5 minutes, then press through a sieve (strainer) and mix with 30–45ml/2–3 tbsp formula or breast milk. Cool and serve as above.

2 Steam over a pan of boiling water for 10 minutes, until soft.

3 Press through a sieve (strainer), mix with 60–75ml/4–5 tbsp formula or breast milk, depending on the vegetable used. Spoon a little into a bowl, test on a spoon and cool if needed. Cover the remaining purée and transfer to the refrigerator as soon as possible. Use within 24 hours.

Fruit Purées

Makes: 120ml/4fl oz/½ cup

1 Peel, quarter and core 1 dessert apple or 1 ripe pear.

2 Thinly slice and put in a small pan with 15ml/1 tbsp water, formula or breast milk. Cover and simmer for 10 minutes, until soft.

● **To microwave:** place the apple or pear in a microwave-proof bowl with water, formula or breast milk. Cover with clear film (plastic wrap), pierce and cook on Full Power (100%) for 3 minutes. Leave to stand for 5 minutes, then press through a sieve (strainer). Cool and serve as above.

3 Press through a sieve (strainer). Spoon a little purée into a serving bowl, test on a spoon and cool if needed. Cover, transfer to the refrigerator, and use within 24 hours.

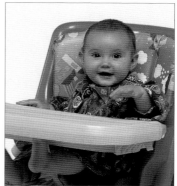

Top: *Pear and apple purée (top) will bring a smile to any baby's face (above).*

STAGE 2: AROUND SIX TO SIX-AND-A-HALF MONTHS

IF YOU BEGIN WEANING AT SIX MONTHS, START WITH BABY RICE AND RUNNY VEGETABLE AND FRUIT PURÉE. IF YOU HAVE ALREADY INTRODUCED YOUR BABY TO SOLIDS, INCREASE THE VARIETY OF FOODS OFFERED AND START TO COMBINE FOOD TASTES. PURÉE CAN BE A THICKER COARSER TEXTURE, BUT MAKE SURE THERE ARE NO PIPS (SEEDS) OR BONES. ALWAYS CHOOSE THE BEST, FRESHEST INGREDIENTS AND MAKE SURE UTENSILS ARE SCRUPULOUSLY CLEAN.

Suitable Foods

FOODS TO INCLUDE

- wide selection of vegetables, including fresh or frozen peas, corn, cauliflower, broccoli, cabbage, spinach, celery, mushrooms and leeks
- fruits – banana, apricots, peaches, plums, strawberries, raspberries, melon (Warning: offer tiny amounts of soft berry fruits as some children may be allergic to them.)
- chicken
- mild-tasting fresh or frozen fish – plaice, cod, haddock, trout
- small quantities of very lean red meat
- small quantities of split peas and red lentils, and very well-cooked or canned whole chickpeas and beans
- gluten-free cereals – rice, cornflour (cornstarch)

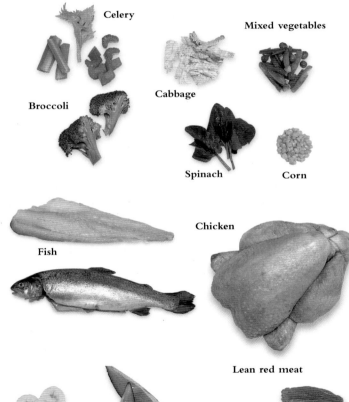

Celery

Mixed vegetables

Cabbage

Broccoli

Spinach

Corn

Fish

Chicken

Lean red meat

Plums

Apricots

Banana

Melon

Above: *Every day brings a new taste: these young gourmets can't wait!*

FOODS TO AVOID
- gluten-based cereals, wheat flour and bread
- cow's milk and milk products
- eggs
- citrus and berry fruits
- nuts, ground or whole
- honey
- fatty foods
- salt and highly spiced foods

Below: *Even healthy adult foods such as wholewheat bread and oranges should be avoided.*

Chickpeas

Cocoa

Split peas

Cornflour (cornstarch)

Lentils

Rice

Going Vegetarian

A vegetarian diet can provide all the necessary nutrients for health and vitality, but it is important to balance the baby's diet to ensure that she receives adequate supplies of protein, vitamins D and B12, calcium and iron.

The basic guidelines are the same as for weaning any other baby: introduce flavours slowly and be guided by your baby. The biggest differences are obviously in the type of foods offered. Instead of obtaining protein from meat and fish, your baby will receive it from other protein-rich food. These include eggs, beans, peas, split lentils, and grains, finely ground nuts or nut creams, sunflower seed spread, milk and dairy products, and vegetarian cheese where available.

Vegetarians need to make sure that sufficient iron is included in their baby's diet. If she is over six months, offer prune juice, puréed apricots, molasses, refined lentils and cereals, particularly fortified breakfast cereals. Green vegetables and well-mashed beans, if over eight months, are also a good source of iron. Vitamin C aids the absorption of iron from plant sources, so make sure you serve fresh green vegetables or fruit in the meal. Your doctor may also think it is beneficial for your baby to take vitamin drops.

If you plan to bring the baby up as a vegan and so omit dairy products and eggs from the diet, then it is vital to consult your doctor or dietician.

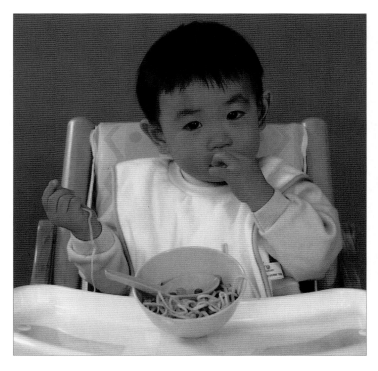

Vegetarian diets tend to be bulky and lower in calories than a diet containing meat, so make sure you include foods that are protein and calorie rich, with little or no fibre, such as eggs, milk and cheese. These can be mixed with smaller quantities of vegetables, fruit and cereals. Fibre-rich foods can also be difficult for a child to digest as many nutrients

Above: *Raising your child as a vegetarian takes special planning and care to make sure all the necessary nutrients are included.*

may pass straight through the body. To ensure your baby is getting the correct amount of vitamins, minerals and food energy her diet should include foods from the four groups on the opposite page.

Oranges

Carrots

Cucumber

Grapes

Cereals and grains: baby rice no earlier than 17 weeks; pasta, bread, oats and breakfast cereals from 6 months.

Fruit and vegetables: begin with potato, carrot, apple and pear at 6 to 6½ months, progressing to stronger-flavoured foods such as broccoli, beans, oranges and plums as your baby develops.

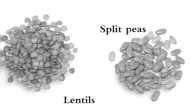

Dairy produce: including milk, cheese, fromage frais and yogurt from 6 months.
Note: Make sure cheese is rennet-free. If you are unsure, ask the delicatessen assistant, or check the packet if pre-packed.

Split peas

Lentils

Beans, peas and lentils: split and softly cooked lentils from 6–6½ months. Gradual introduction of tofu, smooth peanut butter, hard-boiled egg from 6 months. Well-cooked, mashed dried beans and peas and finely ground nuts from nine months. Do not give whole nuts to the under-fives.

To make sure your baby is thriving and happy, irrespective of the type of diet, make sure you check your baby's weight at regular intervals at the health clinic.

Baby dhal

Autumn Harvest

Makes: 600ml/1 pint/2½ cups

115g/4oz carrot

115g/4oz parsnip

115g/4oz swede (rutabaga)

115g/4oz potato

300ml/½ pint/1¼ cups formula milk

1 Trim and peel the carrot, parsnip, swede and potato, and place in a colander. Rinse under cold water, drain and chop.

2 Place the chopped vegetables in a pan with the formula milk, then bring to the boil, cover and simmer for 20 minutes, or until they are very soft.

3 Purée, mash or sieve (strain) the vegetables until they are smooth.

4 Spoon a little into a bowl. Test the temperature and cool if necessary, before giving to the baby.

5 Cover the remaining food and transfer to the refrigerator as soon as possible. Use within 24 hours.

• Suitable for freezing.

TIP
Thin the purée down with a little extra formula milk if your baby prefers a very soft purée.

Mixed Vegetable Platter

Makes: 600ml/1 pint/2½ cups

115g/4oz carrot

175g/6oz potato

115g/4oz broccoli

50g/2oz green cabbage

300ml/½ pint/1¼ cups formula milk

1 Peel the carrot and potato. Rinse, chop and place in a pan. Wash the broccoli and cabbage and cut the broccoli into florets and the stems into thin slices. Shred the cabbage finely.

2 Add the milk to the carrot and potato, bring to the boil, then cover and simmer for 10 minutes.

3 Add the broccoli stems and florets and cabbage, and cook, covered, for 10 minutes, until all the vegetables are tender.

4 Purée, mash or sieve (strain) the vegetables until smooth.

5 Spoon a little into a bowl. Test the temperature and cool if necessary, before giving to the baby.

6 Cover the remaining food and transfer to the refrigerator as soon as possible. Use within 24 hours.

• Suitable for freezing.

Carrot, Lentil and Coriander Purée

Makes: 600ml/1 pint/2½ cups

350g/12oz carrots
175g/6oz potato
50g/2oz/¼ cup red lentils
2.5ml/½ tsp ground coriander
300ml/½ pint/1¼ cups formula milk

1 Trim and peel the carrots and potatoes and then chop into small cubes and place in a pan. Rinse the lentils thoroughly, discarding any black bits.

2 Add the lentils, coriander and milk to the pan and bring to the boil, then cover and simmer for 40 minutes, until the lentils are very soft. Top up with a little extra boiling water if necessary.

TIP

The mixture thickens on cooling so any remaining mixture will need to be thinned slightly with a little formula milk before reheating for the next meal.

3 Purée, mash or sieve (strain) the mixture until smooth.

4 Spoon a little into a bowl. Test the temperature and cool if necessary, before giving to the baby.

5 Cover the remaining purée and transfer to the refrigerator as soon as possible. Use within 24 hours.

• Suitable for freezing.

Red Pepper Risotto

Makes: 600ml/1 pint/2½ cups

50g/2oz/¼ cup long grain rice

300ml/½ pint/1¼ cups formula milk

75g/3oz red (bell) pepper

75g/3oz courgette (zucchini)

50g/2oz celery

1 Place the rice and milk in a pan, bring to the boil and simmer, uncovered, for 5 minutes.

2 Discard the core and seeds from the pepper and trim the courgette and celery. Place the vegetables in a colander and rinse under cold water, then chop them into small pieces.

3 Add the vegetables to the rice mixture, bring to the boil, cover and simmer for about 10 minutes, or until the rice is soft.

- Suitable for freezing.

4 Purée, mash or sieve (strain) the rice mixture until smooth.

5 Spoon a little into a bowl. Test the temperature and cool if necessary, before giving to the baby.

6 Cover the remaining food and transfer to the refrigerator as soon as possible. Use within 24 hours.

Parsnip and Broccoli Mix

Makes: 600ml/1 pint/2½ cups

225g/8oz parsnips

115g/4oz broccoli

300ml/½ pint/1¼ cups formula milk

1 Trim and peel the parsnips and place in a colander with the broccoli. Rinse the parsnips and broccoli under cold water. Chop the parsnips and cut the broccoli into florets, slicing the stems.

2 Put the parsnips in a pan with the milk, bring to the boil, then cover and simmer for about 10 minutes.

3 Add the broccoli and simmer for a further 10 minutes, until the vegetables are soft.

4 Purée, mash or sieve (strain) the vegetable mixture to make a completely smooth purée.

5 Spoon a little into a bowl. Test the temperature and cool if necessary, before giving to the baby.

6 Cover the remaining purée and transfer to the refrigerator as soon as possible. Use within 24 hours.

• Suitable for freezing.

Turkey Stew with Carrots and Corn

Makes: 600ml/1 pint/2½ cups

175g/6oz potato

175g/6oz carrot

115g/4oz turkey breast, skinned and boned

50g/2oz/⅓ cup frozen corn

300ml/½ pint/1¼ cups formula milk

1 Trim and peel the potato and carrots, rinse under cold water and then chop into small cubes.

2 Rinse the turkey and cut into thin strips. Place in a small pan with the potato and carrot.

TIP
Bring the mixture to the boil in a flameproof casserole and transfer to a preheated oven 180°C/350°F/Gas 4 and cook for 1¼ hours if preferred.

3 Add the corn and milk. Cover and simmer for 20 minutes, until the turkey is cooked. Purée, mash or sieve (strain) the mixture until smooth.

4 Spoon a little into a bowl. Test the temperature and cool if necessary, before giving to the baby.

5 Cover the remaining food and refrigerate. Use within 24 hours.

• Suitable for freezing.

Chicken and Parsnip Purée

Makes: 600ml/1 pint/2½ cups

350g/12oz parsnips

115g/4oz chicken breast, skinned and boned

300ml/½ pint/1¼ cups formula milk

1 Peel the parsnips, and trim the woody tops and bottoms. Rinse and chop roughly.

2 Rinse the chicken under cold water and cut into small pieces.

3 Place the parsnips, chicken and milk in a pan. Cover and simmer for 20 minutes, or until the parsnips are tender.

4 Purée, mash or sieve (strain) the mixture until smooth.

5 Spoon into a bowl. Test the temperature and cool if necessary, before giving to the baby.

6 Cover the remaining purée and transfer to the refrigerator as soon as possible. Use within 24 hours.

• Suitable for freezing.

TIP

For a very smooth purée, drain all the liquid into a liquidizer and add half the solids, blend until smooth, then add the remaining ingredients. If using a food processor, add all the solids and a little liquid, process until smooth, then add the remaining liquid.

Cock-a-Leekie Casserole

Makes: 600ml/1 pint/2½ cups

50g/2oz leek

275g/10oz potatoes

115g/4oz chicken breast, skinned
 and boned

300ml/½ pint/1¼ cups formula milk

1 Halve the leek lengthways and
 rinse under running water to
remove any dirt or grit.

2 Peel potatoes and cut into small
 dice. Rinse the chicken and cut
into pieces and thinly slice the leek.

3 Place the vegetables and chicken
 in a pan with the milk.

4 Bring the mixture to the boil,
 cover with a lid and simmer
gently for 20 minutes, until the
potatoes are just tender. Purée, mash
or sieve (strain) the mixture until it is
completely smooth.

5 Spoon a little into a bowl. Test
 the temperature and cool if
necessary, before giving to the baby.
Use within 24 hours.

• Suitable for freezing.

TIP
You can vary the texture of this
recipe depending on how you
purée the mixture. A fine sieve
(strainer) produces the finest
consistency, then a food processor,
while a food mill gives the coarsest
texture. Starchy vegetables thicken
the purée and bind it together. Any
root vegetable can be used for this
recipe, but make sure it is
thoroughly cooked before blending.

Trout and Courgette Savoury

Makes: 600ml/1 pint/2½ cups

275g/10oz potatoes

175g/6oz courgettes (zucchini)

115g/4oz pink trout fillet

250ml/8fl oz/1 cup formula milk

1 Peel the potatoes, trim the courgettes and rinse under cold water. Dice the potatoes and cut the courgettes into slices.

2 Place the vegetables in a pan. Rinse the trout and arrange on top, then pour over the milk. Bring to the boil, cover and simmer for 15 minutes, until the potatoes and fish are cooked.

3 Lift the trout out of the pan and peel off the skin. Break it into pieces with a knife and fork, checking carefully for any bones.

4 Purée, mash or sieve (strain) the fish, the vegetables and the liquid until quite smooth.

5 Spoon a little into a bowl. Test the temperature and cool if necessary, before giving to the baby.

6 Cover any remaining food and transfer to the refrigerator as soon as possible. Use within 24 hours.

• Suitable for freezing.

Fisherman's Pie

Makes: 600ml/1 pint/2½ cups

350g/12oz potatoes

90g/3½oz brick frozen skinless cod

25g/1oz/¼ cup frozen peas

25g/1oz/2 tbsp frozen corn

300ml/½ pint/1¼ cups formula milk

1 Peel and rinse the potatoes and cut into even pieces. Place in a pan with the fish, peas, corn and milk.

2 Bring to the boil, cover and simmer for 15 minutes, until the potatoes are very tender.

3 Lift the fish out of the pan and break into pieces with a knife and fork, checking carefully and removing any small bones.

4 Purée, mash or sieve (strain) the fish, vegetables and cooking liquid until completely smooth.

5 Spoon a little into a bowl. Test the temperature and cool if necessary, before giving to the baby.

6 Cover the remaining purée and place in the refrigerator as soon as possible. Use within 24 hours.

• Suitable for freezing.

Apple Ambrosia

Makes: 300ml/½ pint/1¼ cups

1 eating apple

25g/1oz flaked rice

300ml/½ pint/1¼ cups formula milk

1 Quarter, core and peel the apple. Slice thinly and place in a pan with the rice and milk.

2 Bring to the boil then simmer over a gentle heat for 10–12 minutes, until the rice is soft, stirring occasionally with a wooden spoon.

3 Purée or mash the apple and rice mixture until completely smooth.

4 Spoon into a bowl. Test the temperature and cool if necessary, before giving to the baby. Cover the remaining purée and transfer to the refrigerator as soon as possible. Use within 24 hours.

VARIATION
Chocolate Pudding
Cook the rice as above but without the apple. Stir 25g/1oz milk chocolate dots and 15ml/1 tbsp caster (superfine) sugar into the hot rice and then purée or mash until smooth. Spoon into small dishes and cool as necessary.

Fruit Salad Purée

Makes: 350ml/12fl oz/1½ cups

1 nectarine or peach

1 dessert apple

1 ripe pear

25g/1oz fresh or frozen raspberries
  or strawberries

1 Halve the nectarine or peach,
  discard the stone (pit), then peel
and chop. Peel, quarter and core the
apple and pear and slice thinly.

2 Put the prepared fruits, the hulled
  raspberries or strawberries and
15ml/1 tbsp water in a pan. Cover
and simmer for 10 minutes, until the
fruit is soft.

3 Press the mixture through a
  sieve (strainer) or process and then
sieve (strain) to remove the berry pips
(seeds). Discard the pips.

4 Spoon a little into a baby bowl.
  Test the temperature and cool if
necessary, before giving to the baby.

5 Cover the remaining purée and
  transfer to the refrigerator as soon
as possible. Use within 24 hours.

- Suitable for freezing.

TIP
Babies tend to eat smaller
quantities of dessert, so it is best
to open freeze purée in a sterilized
ice cube tray. Transfer the cubes
to a plastic bag once frozen.

VARIATION
Peach and Melon Blush
To make 175ml/6fl oz/¾ cup, take
1 ripe peach and ¼ ripe Charentais
melon. Peel and halve the peach,
discard the stone (pit) and cut up
the fruit. Scoop the seeds out of the
melon and cut away the skin.
Roughly chop the melon into pieces.
  Purée or sieve (strain) the fruit until
completely smooth. Spoon a little
into a bowl and serve.

STAGE 3: SEVEN TO NINE MONTHS

FROM SEVEN TO NINE MONTHS IS A RAPID DEVELOPMENT PERIOD FOR YOUR BABY. BY EIGHT MONTHS, BABIES ARE USUALLY QUITE GOOD AT HOLDING THINGS, SO LET YOUR BABY HOLD A SECOND SPOON WHILE YOU ARE FEEDING HER, TO HELP DEVELOP CO-ORDINATION. THIS IS THE FIRST STEP TOWARDS SELF-FEEDING. ALL THE RECIPES FROM THE PREVIOUS SECTION CAN STILL BE MADE FOR YOUR GROWING BABY; JUST ADJUST THE TEXTURE SO THAT FOODS ARE SLIGHTLY COARSER.

Suitable Foods

FOODS TO INCLUDE
- wheat-based foods, pasta, bread – first fingers (thin slices) of toast or bread sticks
- breakfast cereals such as those made up with cows' milk
- cow's milk and dairy foods, e.g. yogurt, cottage cheese, mild Cheddar and Edam cheese
- red meat, but make sure you trim off fat and gristle
- hard-boiled egg yolk
- citrus fruits
- fingers of cooked carrot, broccoli
- smooth peanut butter

Breakfast cereal

Breakfast cereal

Mild cheeses

Yogurt

Lean red meat

Cottage cheese

Cooked egg yolk

Citrus fruit

Pasta

Bread

Peanut button

Fish

Broccoli and carrot

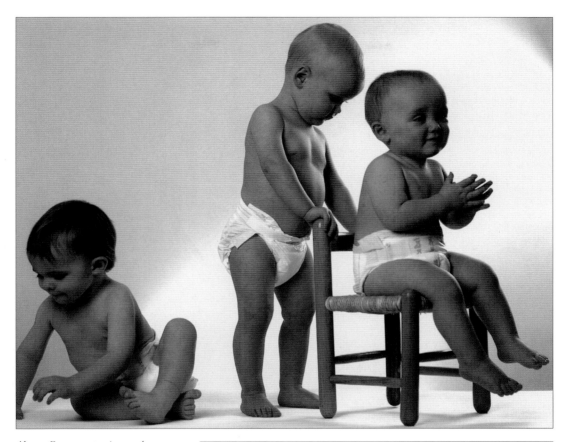

Above: *From seven to nine months your baby will develop rapidly.*

FOODS TO AVOID
- egg white
- whole or chopped nuts
- canned fish in brine
- organ meats – liver, kidney
- chillies and other very spicy foods
- salty foods
- sugary foods

Right: *There is still a wide range of fatty, salty and spicy foods that must be avoided.*

Shepherd's Pie

Makes: 600ml/1 pint/2½ cups

2 tomatoes
¼ onion
225g/8oz potato
50g/2oz button (white) mushrooms
115g/4oz lean minced (ground) beef
250ml/8fl oz/1 cup water
15ml/1 tbsp tomato ketchup
pinch of dried mixed herbs

1 Make a cross cut in each tomato, put in a small bowl and cover with boiling water. Leave to stand for 1 minute and then drain and peel off the skins. Cut into quarters and scoop out the seeds.

2 Finely chop the onion, chop the potato and slice the mushrooms.

3 Dry-fry the beef in a pan for 5 minutes, stirring until browned all over.

• Suitable for freezing.

4 Add the tomatoes, potato, mushrooms and onion and cook for a further 3 minutes. Stir well to blend all the flavours together.

5 Add the water, ketchup and herbs. Bring to the boil, then reduce the heat, cover and simmer for 40 minutes, until the meat and vegetables are tender.

6 Process or mash the meat and vegetables just enough to give the desired consistency.

7 Spoon a little into a bowl. Test the temperature and cool if necessary, before giving to the baby.

8 Cover the remainder and refrigerate. Use within 24 hours.

Braised Beef and Carrots

Makes: 600ml/1 pint/2½ cups

175g/6oz potato

225g/8oz carrots

¼ onion

175g/6oz stewing beef

300ml/½ pint/1¼ cups water

pinch of dried mixed herbs

1 Preheat the oven to 180°C/
350°F/Gas 4. Peel and chop the
potato, carrots and onion, and place
in a flameproof casserole.

2 Rinse the beef, cut away any fat
and gristle and cut into small
cubes using a sharp knife.

3 Add the meat, water and herbs
to the casserole, bring to the boil
and then cover and cook in the oven
for 1½ hours, or until the meat is
tender and the vegetables are soft.

4 Process or mash the ingredients
to the desired consistency and
spoon a little into a bowl. Test the
temperature and cool if necessary,
before giving to the baby.

5 Cover any unused food and
transfer to the refrigerator as soon
as possible. Use within 24 hours.

● Suitable for freezing.

TIP
Replace the carrots with any other
root vegetable, such as parsnip or
swede (rutabaga), if wished.

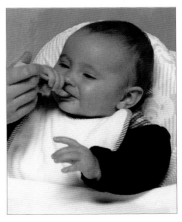

Lamb Hotpot

Makes: 600ml/1 pint/2½ cups

115g/4oz potato
115g/4oz carrot
115g/4oz swede (rutabaga)
50g/2oz leek
115g/4oz lamb fillet
300ml/½ pint/1¼ cup water
pinch of dried rosemary

1 Peel the potato, carrot and swede, then rinse and chop into small cubes. Halve the leek lengthways, rinse well and slice. Place all the vegetables in a pan.

2 Rinse the lamb under cold water and chop into small pieces, discarding any fat.

3 Add the meat to the pan with the water and rosemary. Bring to the boil, cover and simmer for 30 minutes or until the lamb is thoroughly cooked.

4 Process or mash the ingredients to the desired consistency.

5 Spoon a little into a bowl, test the temperature and cool if necessary, before giving to the baby.

6 Cover the remaining food and transfer to the refrigerator as soon as possible. Use within 24 hours.

• Suitable for freezing.

Lamb and Lentil Savoury

Makes: 600ml/1 pint/2½ cups

115g/4oz lamb fillet

115g/4oz swede (rutabaga)

1 celery stick

25g/1oz/2 tbsp red lentils

15ml/1 tbsp tomato ketchup

350ml/12fl oz/1½ cups water

1 Rinse the lamb under cold water, trim off any fat and chop into small pieces. Peel the swede, place in a colander with the celery and rinse with cold water. Chop into cubes and place in a pan.

2 Put the lentils in a sieve (strainer) and rinse under cold water, picking out any black bits. Add to the pan with the lamb and ketchup.

3 Add the water and bring to the boil, then cover and simmer for 40 minutes, or until the lentils are soft. Top up with extra water during cooking if necessary, then process or mash just enough to give the desired consistency.

4 Spoon a little into a bowl, test the temperature and cool if necessary, before giving to the baby.

5 Cover the remaining food and transfer to the refrigerator as soon as possible. Use within 24 hours.

● Suitable for freezing.

VARIATION

Substitute green lentils or split peas for the red lentils and a small courgette (zucchini) for the celery stick.

Country Pork and Runner Beans

Makes: 450ml/³/₄ pint/1⁷/₈ cups

115g/4oz lean pork

115g/4oz potato

115g/4oz carrot

75g/3oz runner (green) beans

pinch of dried sage

350ml/12fl oz/1½ cups water

1 Rinse the pork under cold water, trim away any fat and gristle and chop into small cubes.

2 Peel the potato and carrot, trim the beans, rinse and chop.

TIPS
If runner beans are unavailable use French (green) beans, sugar snap peas or broccoli. Look out for ready-prepared diced pork in the supermarket. Cut into smaller pieces and be sure to remove any gristle before cooking.

3 Put the pork, potato and carrot in a pan with the sage and water. Bring to the boil, cover and simmer for 30 minutes.

4 Add the beans and cook, covered, for a further 10 minutes, until all the vegetables are tender.

5 Process or mash to the desired consistency, then spoon a little into a bowl. Test the temperature before giving to the baby.

6 Cover and transfer the remaining food to the refrigerator. Use within 24 hours.

● Suitable for freezing.

VARIATION
Instead of the pork, use any lean meat in this recipe, such as chicken or turkey. Add broad (fava) beans, with the outer skin removed, in place of the runner beans.

Pork and Apple Savoury

Makes: 600ml/1 pint/2½ cups

175g/6oz lean pork

175g/6oz potato

175g/6oz swede (rutabaga) or parsnip

¼ onion

½ eating apple

300ml/½ pint/1¼ cups water

pinch of dried sage

1 Preheat the oven to 180°C/350°F/Gas 4. Rinse the pork under cold water, trim away any fat and gristle, then chop. Peel and chop the vegetables. Peel, core and chop the apple.

2 Put the meat, vegetables, apple, water and sage in a flameproof casserole, cover and bring to the boil, stirring once or twice.

3 Cover and cook in the oven for 1¼ hours, until the meat is tender, then process or mash to the desired consistency.

4 Spoon a little into a bowl, test the temperature and cool if necessary, before giving to the baby.

5 Cover the remaining food and transfer to the refrigerator as soon as possible. Use within 24 hours.

● Suitable for freezing.

TIP
The mixture can be cooked in a pan on the stove for 40 minutes, if preferred.

Nursery Kedgeree

Makes: 600ml/1 pint/2½ cups

50g/2oz/¼ cup long grain rice

25g/1oz/2 tbsp frozen peas

350ml/12fl oz/1½ cups formula milk

90g/3¼oz brick frozen skinless cod

2 hard-boiled egg yolks

1 Place the rice, peas, milk and fish in a pan, bring to the boil, cover and simmer for 15 minutes, until the fish is cooked and the rice is soft.

2 Lift the fish out of the pan and break into pieces with a knife and fork, checking for bones.

3 Stir the fish into the rice mixture and add the egg yolks.

TIP

Peas can be quite difficult to mash down. Check before giving to the baby as whole peas are difficult for her to chew.

4 Mash with a fork to the desired consistency. Alternatively blend in a food processor or liquidizer, or press through a sieve (strainer).

5 Spoon a little into a bowl, test the temperature and cool if necessary, before giving to the baby.

6 Cover the remaining kedgeree and transfer to the refrigerator as soon as possible. Use within 24 hours.

• Suitable for freezing.

Mediterranean Vegetables

Makes: 600ml/1 pint/2½ cups

3 tomatoes

175g/6oz courgettes (zucchini)

75g/3oz button (white) mushrooms

115g/4oz red (bell) pepper

20ml/4 tsp tomato ketchup

250ml/8fl oz/1 cup water

pinch of dried mixed herbs

40g/1½oz dried pasta shapes

1 Make a cross cut in each tomato, put in a small bowl and cover with boiling water. Leave for 1 minute, then drain and peel off the skins. Cut into quarters and scoop out the seeds from the tomatoes.

2 Trim the courgette and mushrooms and cut away the core and seeds from the pepper.

3 Rinse and slice the courgette and mushrooms. Chop the pepper.

4 Put the vegetables in a pan with the ketchup, water and herbs. Cover and simmer for 10 minutes, or until tender.

5 Meanwhile cook the pasta in boiling water for 8–10 minutes, until tender. Drain.

6 Mix the vegetables and pasta together and process or mash.

7 Spoon a little into a bowl, test the temperature and cool if necessary, before giving to the baby.

8 Cover remaining mixture and refrigerate. Use within 24 hours.

● Suitable for freezing.

TIP
For adventurous eaters add ½ clove crushed garlic at Step 3.

Pasta with Sauce

Makes: 600ml/1 pint/2½ cups

115g/4oz carrot

50g/2oz Brussels sprouts

25g/1oz green beans

25g/1oz/2 tbsp frozen corn

50g/2oz dried pasta shapes

350ml/12fl oz/1½ cups formula milk

50g/2oz Cheddar or mild cheese

1 Peel the carrot, discard any discoloured outer leaves from the sprouts and trim the beans. Rinse and then chop into pieces.

2 Place the prepared vegetables, corn, pasta and milk in a pan, bring to the boil and then simmer, uncovered, for 12-15 minutes, until the pasta is cooked.

TIP

Vary the vegetables depending on what you have in the refrigerator.

3 Grate the cheese and add to the vegetables, stirring until the cheese has completely melted.

4 Process or mash just enough to give the desired consistency, then spoon a little into a bowl. Test the temperature and cool if necessary, before giving to the baby.

5 Cover the remaining food and transfer to the refrigerator as soon as possible. Use within 24 hours.

• Suitable for freezing.

Apple and Orange Fool

Makes: 250ml/8fl oz/1 cup

2 eating apples

5ml/1 tsp grated orange rind and
    15ml/1 tbsp orange juice

15ml/1 tbsp custard powder

5ml/1 tsp caster (superfine) sugar

150ml/¼ pint/⅔ cup formula milk

1 Quarter, core and peel the
apples. Slice and place the apples
in a pan with the orange rind
and juice.

2 Cover and cook gently for 10
minutes, stirring occasionally
until the apples are soft.

3 Blend the custard powder and
sugar with a little of the milk to
make a smooth paste. Bring the
remaining milk to the boil and stir
into the custard mixture.

4 Return the custard to the pan
and slowly bring to the boil,
stirring until thickened and smooth.

5 Process or mash the apple to the
desired consistency. Add the
custard and stir to mix.

6 Spoon a little into a bowl, test
the temperature and cool if
necessary, before giving to the baby.

7 Cover the remaining fool and
transfer to the refrigerator as soon
as possible. Use within 24 hours.

• Suitable for freezing.

Orchard Fruit Dessert

Makes: 450ml/¾ pint/1⅞ cups

1 ripe pear

225g/8oz ripe plums

15ml/1 tbsp caster (superfine) sugar

15ml/1 tbsp custard powder

150ml/¼ pint/⅔ cup formula milk

1 Quarter, core, peel and slice the pear. Wash the plums, then cut in half, stone (pit) and slice.

2 Put the fruit in a pan with 15ml/1 tbsp water and 10ml/ 2 tsp of the sugar. Cover and cook gently for 10 minutes, until soft.

3 Blend the custard powder, remaining sugar and a little of the milk to make a smooth paste.

4 Bring the remaining milk to the boil and gradually stir into the custard mixture. Pour the custard back into the pan and bring to the boil, stirring, until it is both thickened and smooth.

5 Process or mash the fruit to the desired consistency and stir in the custard. Spoon a little into a bowl, test the temperature and cool if necessary, before giving to the baby.

6 Cover the remaining custard and transfer to the refrigerator as soon as possible. Use within 24 hours.

- Suitable for freezing.

Peach Melba Dessert

Makes: 175ml/6fl oz/¾ cup

1 ripe peach

25g/1oz fresh or frozen raspberries

15ml/1 tbsp icing (confectioners') sugar

115g/4oz Greek (US strained plain) yogurt

1 Halve the peach, discard the stone (pit), then peel and slice. Place in a pan with the raspberries and 15ml/1 tbsp water.

2 Cover and cook gently for 10 minutes, until soft.

3 Purée and press through a sieve (strainer) to remove the raspberry pips (seeds).

TIP
The finished dessert is not suitable for freezing, but the sweetened fruit purée can be frozen in sections of an ice-cube tray. Defrost cubes of purée and mix each cube with 15ml/1 tbsp yogurt.

4 Set aside to cool, then stir in the sugar and swirl in the yogurt. Spoon a little into a baby dish.

5 Cover the remaining dessert and transfer to the refrigerator. Use within 24 hours.

VARIATION
Bananarama
To make a single portion, use ½ a small banana and 15ml/1 tbsp of Greek (US strained plain) yogurt. Mash the banana until smooth and add the yogurt. Stir to mix and serve immediately. Do not make this dessert in advance, as the banana will discolour while standing.

STAGE 4: NINE TO TWELVE MONTHS

GRADUALLY PROGRESS FROM MINCED (GROUND) TO CHOPPED OR ROUGHLY MASHED FOOD. BY NOW YOUR BABY WILL BE ABLE TO JOIN IN WITH FAMILY MEALS AND EAT A LITTLE OF WHAT YOU ARE EATING. ENSURE THAT YOUR BABY IS EATING THREE MAIN MEALS AND TWO TO THREE SNACK MEALS PER DAY. YOUNG CHILDREN DEVELOP AT AN INCREDIBLY FAST RATE AND SO NEED TO EAT LITTLE AND OFTEN TO SUSTAIN ENERGY AND GROWTH LEVELS. AGAIN, FOODS FROM THE PREVIOUS SECTIONS CAN STILL BE SERVED TO YOUR BABY; JUST ADJUST THE TEXTURES AS NECESSARY.

Suitable Foods

FOODS TO INCLUDE
- whole eggs
- finely ground nuts
- more flavourings – stock (bouillon) cubes if part of a family-size casserole
- greater selection of finger foods – slices of peeled fruit (such as dessert apple or pear), raw carrot and cucumber sticks, small squares of cooked chicken

- selection of foods from the four main food groups – carbohydrates (cereals, bread, potatoes, rice, pasta); fruit and vegetables; protein (meat, poultry, fish, eggs, beans, peas, lentils, tofu, nuts); milk and milk products (cheese, yogurt, butter).

Apple, carrot and cucumber

Ground nuts

Whole egg

Left: *Finger foods – such as chopped raw vegetables and fruit pieces – come into their own at this age, and children love to help themselves.*

Above and below right: *Active children develop at a fast rate and need to eat little and often to sustain their energy levels.*

Below: *Though now a very small list, there are still some foods it is important to omit.*

FOODS TO AVOID
- keep salt to a minimum and omit if possible
- sugar: add just enough to make the food appetizing without being overly sweet
- honey
- fat: trim visible fat off raw meat, grill rather than fry
- organ meats – liver, kidney

I can feed myself!

Encouraging your baby to feed herself can be a truly messy business. Some babies are interested from a very early age, and those little fingers seem to move like lightning grabbing the bowl or the spoon you're using to feed them with. Give your baby a second spoon to play with, leaving you more able to spoon in the lunch.

As your baby grows, offer her a few finger foods to hold and hopefully eat, while you continue to feed from a spoon. Cooked carrot sticks, broccoli and cauliflower florets are soft on a young mouth and easy to chew. As your baby grows, you can introduce bread sticks and toast fingers.

Encourage your baby to pick up foods, and as her co-ordination improves and she gets the idea, more food will actually go where it is intended. Try to cut down on the mess by rolling up your baby's sleeves and covering clothes with a large bib, preferably with sleeves.

Above: *A bib with sleeves.*

Remove any hair bands and have a wet flannel at the ready.

Although it is tempting not to allow a baby to feed herself, try not to be frustrated by the mess. Babies that are encouraged to feed themselves will probably be more adventurous later on, and you will probably find there is less mess than with a baby who is always spoon fed

TEACHING YOUR BABY TO FEED HIMSELF

1 Cover your baby well – this can be very messy! Give him a spoon of his own to play with.

2 While you are feeding your baby, allow him to play with the food – with his hands or the spoon.

3 Let your baby use the cup and spoon by himself. Don't worry about spillage – there are bound to be lots of slips at this stage.

4 Keep tissues or a damp flannel available and clean as you go. Be patient and take things slowly.

and keeps grabbing at the bowl. In addition, she will be able to join in your family meals and also give you the chance to eat your own meal before it gets cold.

WHAT TO DO IF YOUR CHILD CHOKES

• Don't waste time trying to remove food from your baby's mouth unless it can be done easily.
• Turn your baby, head down, supporting her head with your forearm and slap firmly between the shoulder blades.
• If this does not work, try again.
• Don't hesitate to ring your doctor or emergency services if worried.

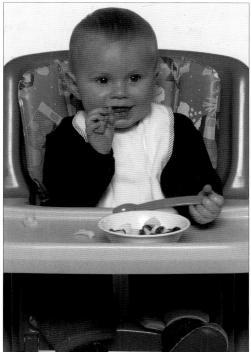

Left: *It is a real delight when your baby can begin to eat independently. Not only can you start to eat with your baby, and relax a little more, but he will also enjoy setting his own pace and eating his meal in the order he chooses. At this stage, the family can usually return to eating together around the table as a group.*

Above: *Don't be afraid to take quick, firm action in an emergency.*

COPING WITH THE MESS

As babies grow so too does the amount of mess! It is incredible how just a few tablespoons of lunch can be spread across so many surfaces and so many items of clothing.
• Choose a large bib. Fabric bibs with a plastic liner are the most comfortable for babies to wear when tiny, moving on to a plastic pelican-style bib to catch food as they grow older. Check the back of your baby's neck as these can rub.

Above: *A hard plastic "pelican" bib.*

• If you plan to feed your baby in the dining room, then protect the carpet with an old sheet, pieces of newspaper, or a plastic tablecloth or groundsheet. It is vital to take this with you if visiting friends.
• Give your baby a second spoon or small toy to play with so that she doesn't try to grab the laden spoon that you are holding.

Above: *A plastic tablecloth or groundsheet on the floor will prevent carpet stains.*

FINGER FOODS

Finger foods are not only fun to eat but help your baby's co-ordination. Snacks play an important part in a young child's diet as appetites may be small, but energy and growth needs are great. Choose foods that are nutrient dense and avoid sweet sugary snacks such as chocolate biscuits (cookies).

Grapes

Plums

Celery

Carrots

Mini-sandwiches

Chicken pieces

Fish fingers (breaded fish sticks)

Toast triangles

Cheese cubes

Ham

Marmite fingers

Above: *Your baby can eat at his own pace until he is full.*

TIPS

● Make sure the baby is comfortable either on your lap or strapped into a baby chair or high-chair.
● Check the temperature of the food and make sure it is not too hot.
● Change the texture of the food: some babies like quite wet mixtures, some hate lumps, some like a few lumps for interest, others prefer food they can pick up – mini ham sandwiches, thick slices of grilled fish fingers (breaded fish sticks), even picking up peas and corn.
● Encourage your baby to feed herself; don't worry about the mess – your baby is still learning – but just mop up at the end.

● Try to keep calm. If your baby keeps spitting food out, you may find it less upsetting to offer bought food rather than home-made so you don't feel you've wasted time cooking.
● Try not to let your baby see you're upset or annoyed. Even a one-year-old can sense the power she can have over you.
● If solid meals are well established, give her a drink at the end of the meal so that she is not full with milk before she begins.
● Avoid biscuits (cookies) and sweet things – your baby will soon learn that if she makes a fuss when the savoury is offered, dessert will soon follow.

● Remember no baby will starve herself. Often babies who have been good eaters become more difficult to feed. Continue offering a variety of food and don't despair.

Above: *Give drinks at the end of the meal, or they will fill your baby up before he eats.*

Coping with a fussy eater

All children are fussy eaters at some stage. If meal-times are always calm and plates always clean, then your family must be one in a million. Even very young children learn the power they have over their parents, and meal-times give them a great opportunity to exercise it.

THE BABY SEEMS TO HAVE A SMALL APPETITE

Babies' appetites, like adults', vary enormously. Don't force feed your baby; if she's been eating well and then turns her head away or starts spitting out the food, it's a clear indication that she's had enough, even if the amount seems very small to you. Resist the temptation to encourage your baby to clear the dish: it is never helpful to force children of any age, and can be extremely counter-productive. Towards the end of the first year, a baby's weight gain usually slows down, and babies who have been good eaters become more difficult to feed. If you're worried, talk to your health visitor or doctor and regularly check your baby's weight.

Above: Don't worry when you encounter resistance in feeding: there never has been a baby that likes all foods, all the time.

Left: If you have any serious anxieties, see your doctor or health visitor and get your baby's weight checked regularly.

The Importance of a Varied Diet

Once your baby progresses to more varied fruit and vegetable purées you are really beginning to lay down the foundations for a healthy eating pattern and sound nutritional habits that will take your baby through childhood and into adult life.

It is vitally important to include portions of food from each of the four main food groups – carbohydrates such as cereal, pasta and bread; fruit and vegetables; protein such as meat, fish and eggs; milk and milk products – every day. Don't forget to make sure that the types of food you choose are suitable for the age of your child.

Left: *Your baby is now at the age where the diet can and should be as diverse as any adult's. Variety is crucial for health reasons, and also has the benefit of allowing you many options for encouraging and maintaining the kind of interest in all types of food that will ensure good eating habits develop for the future.*

Group 1: *Cereals, bread, potatoes, rice and pasta.*

Group 2: *Fruit and vegetables* – bland tastes to start, such as potato, swede (rutabaga) and parsnip, then stronger flavours and a wider variety.

Group 3: *Meat and meat alternatives* – meat, poultry, fish, eggs, peas, beans, lentils, tofu, finely ground nuts.

Group 4: *Milk and milk products* – milk, including soya milk, cheese, yogurt (plain at first, then flavoured).

Group 5: *Sugars.*

Group 6: *Fats and oils.*

There are two more food groups that add palatability to the diet as well as contributing energy.

It is not recommended that you add sugar to baby foods or give lots of sugary drinks, particularly in the early days of weaning. Many of us have an inherent need for sweetness, but to cater to this without building in bad habits, try and include foods in the diet that are naturally sweet. Choose dessert apples instead of very sharp cooking apples, and mix bananas or ripe apricots with sharper-tasting fruits.

For those foods that are very sharp try to add 5ml/1tsp sugar per portion, so they become palatable without being overly sweet. Given the choice, your baby would prefer sweet flavours to savoury, so make sure you include a good range of tastes in the diet. Too much sugar or too many sweetened foods or drinks at this stage could lead to tooth decay

before the teeth are even through. Try to avoid offering biscuits (cookies) as a mid-morning or afternoon snack. Instead, encourage your baby to eat:

- a piece of banana
- a plain bread roll
- a few triangles of toast
- a milky drink
- a small container of yogurt

Watch the amounts of fat and oil you include in the diet. Avoid frying, especially when preparing first foods, as young babies have difficulty digesting such foods. As your baby develops, you can spread toast fingers with a little butter or margarine as easy-to-hold finger food. Maintain the milk feeds and introduce full-fat (whole) cow's milk after one year as the main drink of the day. Don't be tempted to serve skimmed (skim) milk, as the valuable fat-soluble vitamins A and D will be lost, and your baby may not get the energy needed for growth.

HOME-MADE OR MANUFACTURED FOODS?

Most parents use a combination of the two. Bought baby foods are convenient and often easier to use if going out for the day or until your baby's meals coincide with those of the rest of the family. Dried baby foods can be useful

Above: *A piece of fruit or chopped vegetable is always preferable to a biscuit.*

in the very early days, when your baby is eating only a teaspoon of food at each meal. On the other hand, home-made foods can be batch-cooked or made with some of the ingredients from the main family meal and are often less trouble than you might expect. Added to this is the satisfaction of knowing your baby has eaten a wholesome meal and hopefully is acquiring a taste for home cooking.

Left: *Home-made foods have the advantage that you know exactly what is in them. But there are some excellent products available for purchase that can save you time and effort and add hugely to your repertoire without any loss of dietary value.*

Lamb Couscous

Makes: 750ml/1¼ pint/3 cups

115g/4oz carrot

115g/4oz swede (rutabaga)

¼ onion

175g/6oz lamb fillet

5ml/1 tsp oil

10ml/2 tsp vegetable purée (paste)

30ml/2 tbsp currants or raisins

300ml/½ pint/1¼ cups water

50g/2oz couscous

1 Peel the carrot, swede and onion, rinse and chop. Rinse the lamb, trim off any fat, and chop.

2 Heat the oil in a pan, and fry the lamb until browned.

3 Add the vegetables, cook for 2 minutes, then stir in the vegetable purée, currants and water. Cover and simmer for 25 minutes.

4 Put the couscous in a sieve (strainer) and rinse under cold running water. Cover and steam the couscous over the lamb pan, for 5 minutes.

5 Chop or process the lamb mixture to the desired consistency. Fluff up the couscous with a fork and add to the lamb mixture stirring well.

6 Spoon a little into a bowl, test the temperature and cool if necessary, before giving to the baby.

7 Cover the remaining food and transfer to the refrigerator as soon as possible. Use within 24 hours.

- Suitable for freezing.

TIP
Look out for vegetable purée in tubes on the same shelf as the tomato purée in the supermarket.

Paprika Pork

Makes: 600ml/1 pint/2½ cups

175g/6oz lean pork

75g/3oz carrot

175g/6oz potato

¼ onion

¼ red (bell) pepper

5ml/1tsp oil

2.5ml/½ tsp paprika

150g/5oz/⅔ cup baked beans

150ml/¼ pint/⅔ cup water

1 Preheat the oven to 180°C/ 350°F/Gas 4. Rinse the pork under cold water, pat dry and trim away any fat or gristle. Cut the pork into small cubes.

2 Peel the carrot, potato and onion. Cut away the core and remove any seeds from the pepper. Put into a colander, rinse under cold water, then chop into small pieces.

3 Heat the oil in a flameproof casserole, add the pork and fry for a few minutes, stirring until browned. Add the vegetables, cook for 2 minutes, then add the paprika, baked beans and water.

4 Bring back to the boil, then cover and cook in the oven for 1¼ hours, until the pork is tender.

5 Chop or process the casserole to the desired consistency, then spoon a little into a bowl. Test the temperature and cool if necessary, before giving to the baby.

6 Cover the remaining food and transfer to the refrigerator as soon as possible. Use within 24 hours.

• Suitable for freezing.

TIP

If using a food processor to chop the baby's dinner, drain off most of the liquid. Process, then stir in enough liquid for desired texture.

Chicken and Celery Supper

Makes: 600ml/1 pint/2½ cups

175g/6oz chicken thighs, skinned and boned
¼ onion
225g/8oz carrots
75g/3oz celery
5ml/1 tsp oil
10ml/2 tsp vegetable purée (paste)
250ml/8fl oz/1 cup water

1 Rinse the chicken under cold water, pat dry, trim off any fat and cut into chunks.

2 Trim and rinse the vegetables and cut into small pieces.

3 Heat the oil in a pan, add the chicken and onion, and fry for a few minutes, stirring until browned. Add the carrots, celery, vegetable purée and water. Bring to the boil, cover and simmer for 20 minutes, until tender.

4 Chop or process the mixture to the desired consistency. If using a food processor, process the solids first and then add the liquid a little at a time.

5 Spoon a little into a bowl, test the temperature and cool if necessary, before giving to the baby.

6 Cover the remaining casserole and transfer to the refrigerator as soon as possible. Use within 24 hours.

• Suitable for freezing.

TIP

For extra flavour, add home-made stock instead of the water, or use commercial stock, but make sure it does not have a high sodium level.

Cauliflower and Broccoli with Cheese

Makes: 600ml/1 pint/2½ cups

175g/6oz cauliflower

175g/6oz broccoli

175g/6oz potato

300ml/½ pint/1¼ cups formula milk

75g/3oz Cheddar or mild cheese

1 Rinse the vegetables, then break the cauliflower and broccoli into florets. Slice the tender stems, but cut out and discard the woody core of the cauliflower. Peel and chop the potatoes into cubes.

2 Place the vegetables and milk in a pan, bring to the boil, cover and simmer for 12–15 minutes, until quite tender.

3 Grate the cheese and add to the vegetables, stirring until the cheese has melted.

4 Process or mash the mixture to the desired consistency, adding a little extra milk if necessary.

5 Spoon a little into a bowl, test the temperature, and cool if necessary, before serving to the baby.

6 Cover the remaining food and transfer to the refrigerator as soon as possible. Use within 24 hours.

• Suitable for freezing.

Tagliatelle and Cheese with Broccoli and Ham

Makes: 600ml/1 pint/2½ cups

115g/4oz broccoli

50g/2oz thinly sliced ham

50g/2oz Cheddar or mild cheese

300ml/½ pint/1¼ cups formula milk

50g/2oz tagliatelle

1 Rinse the broccoli and cut into small florets, chopping the stalks. Chop the ham and grate the Cheddar cheese.

2 Pour the formula milk into a pan, bring to the boil and add the tagliatelle. Simmer uncovered for 5 minutes.

3 Add the broccoli and cook for 10 minutes, until tender.

TIP

Pasta swells on standing, so you may need to thin the cooled leftover mixture with extra formula milk before reheating.

4 Add the ham and cheese to the broccoli and pasta, stirring until the cheese has melted.

5 Chop or process the mixture to the desired consistency and then spoon a little into a bowl. Test the temperature and cool if necessary, before giving to the baby.

6 Cover the remaining food and transfer to the refrigerator as soon as possible. Use within 24 hours.

• Suitable for freezing.

Baby Dahl

Makes: 600ml/1 pint/2½ cups

50g/2oz/¼ cup red lentils

¼ onion

2.5ml/½ tsp ground coriander

1.25ml/¼ tsp turmeric

350ml/12fl oz/1½ cups water

75g/3oz potato

75g/3oz carrot

75g/3oz cauliflower

75g/3oz green cabbage

1 Rinse the lentils under cold water, discarding any black bits.

2 Chop the onion and add to a pan with the lentils, spices and water.

3 Bring to the boil, cover and simmer for 20 minutes.

4 Chop the potato, carrot and cabbage. Break the cauliflower into small florets.

5 Stir the vegetables into the pan. Cook for 12–15 minutes.

6 Chop or process the dahl to the desired consistency, adding a little extra boiled water if necessary.

7 Spoon a little dahl into a bowl, test the temperature and cool if necessary, before serving to the baby.

8 Cover the remaining dahl and transfer to the refrigerator as soon as possible. Use within 24 hours.

- Suitable for freezing.

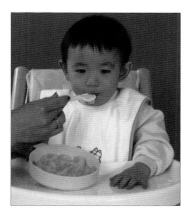

Fish and Cheese Pie

Makes: 450ml/¾ pint/1⅞ cups

225g/8oz potato

50g/2oz leek

50g/2oz button (white) mushrooms

90g/3½oz brick frozen skinless cod

250ml/8fl oz/1 cup formula milk

50g/2oz grated Cheddar,
  or mild cheese

1 Peel the potato, halve the leek and trim the mushrooms. Place all the vegetables in a colander and rinse well with cold water, drain, then chop the vegetables.

2 Place the vegetables in a pan with the frozen cod and milk. Bring to the boil, cover and simmer for 15 minutes, until the fish is cooked and the potatoes are tender when pierced with a knife.

3 Lift the fish out of the pan with a slotted spoon and break into pieces with a knife and fork, checking carefully for bones.

4 Return the fish to the pan and stir in the grated cheese. Chop or process the mixture to give the desired consistency.

5 Spoon a little into a bowl, test the temperature and cool if necessary, before serving to the baby.

6 Cover the remaining fish pie and transfer to the refrigerator as soon as possible. Use within 24 hours.

• Suitable for freezing.

Fish Creole

Makes: 450ml/³⁄₄ pint/1⁷⁄₈ cups

50g/2oz celery

50g/2oz red (bell) pepper

300ml/½ pint/1¼ cups water

50g/2oz/¼ cup long grain rice

10ml/2 tsp tomato ketchup

90g/3½oz brick frozen skinless cod

1 Trim the celery and discard the core and seeds from the pepper. Rinse and chop the vegetables.

2 Bring the water to the boil in a pan and add the vegetables, rice, ketchup and cod.

3 Bring back to the boil, then reduce heat, cover and simmer for 15 minutes, until the rice is tender and the fish is cooked.

4 Lift the fish out of the pan with a slotted spoon. Use a knife and fork to check for bones.

6 Spoon a little fish mixture into a small bowl, test the temperature and cool if necessary, before giving to the baby.

7 Cover the leftover fish creole and transfer to the refrigerator as soon as possible. Use within 24 hours.

• Suitable for freezing.

5 Stir the fish back into the pan and then chop or process.

Chocolate Pots

Makes: 2

5ml/1 tsp cocoa

5ml/1 tsp caster (superfine) sugar

150ml/¼ pint/⅔ cup formula or
  cow's milk

1 egg

1 Preheat the oven to 180°C/
350°F/Gas 4. Blend the cocoa
and sugar with a little of the milk in a
small bowl to make a smooth paste.
Stir in the remaining milk and then
pour the mixture into a pan.

2 Bring just to the boil. Beat the
egg in a bowl, then gradually stir
in the hot milk, mixing well until the
mixture is smooth.

3 Strain the mixture into two
ramekin dishes to remove any
egg solids.

4 Place the dishes in a roasting pan
or shallow cake tin (pan). Pour
boiling water into the pan to come
halfway up the sides of the dishes.

5 Cook in the oven for 15–20
minutes, or until the custard has
set. Leave to cool.

6 Transfer to the refrigerator as soon
as possible. Serve one dessert and
use the second within 24 hours.

Vanilla Custards

Makes: 2

1 egg

5ml/1 tsp caster (superfine) sugar

few drops vanilla essence (extract)

150ml/¼ pint/⅔ cup formula or
  cow's milk

1 Preheat the oven to 180°C/
350°F/Gas 4. Using a fork, beat
the egg, sugar and vanilla essence
together in a bowl.

2 Pour the milk into a small pan
and heat until it is just on the
point of boiling.

3 Gradually stir the milk into the
egg mixture, whisking or
beating until smooth.

4 Strain into two ramekin dishes
and place in a roasting pan. Add
enough boiling water to come
halfway up the sides of the dishes.

5 Bake for 15–20 minutes, or until
the custard has set. Cool and
serve as for **Chocolate Pots.**

Marmite Bread Sticks

Makes: 36

little oil, for greasing

150g/5oz packet pizza base mix

flour, for dusting

5ml/1 tsp Marmite (yeast extract spread)

1 egg yolk

1 Brush two baking sheets with a little oil. Put the pizza mix in a bowl, add the quantity of water as directed on the package and mix to make a smooth dough.

2 Knead on a lightly floured surface for 5 minutes, until smooth and elastic.

3 Roll out to a 23cm/9in square. Cut into strips 7.5cm × 1cm/3 × ½in, twisting each to give a corkscrew effect. Arrange on the baking sheets, slightly spaced apart.

4 Mix the Marmite and egg yolk together and brush over the bread sticks. Loosely cover with oiled clear film (plastic wrap) and leave in a warm place for 20–30 minutes to rise.

5 Meanwhile preheat the oven to 220°C/425°F/Gas 7. Bake the bread sticks for 8–10 minutes, until well risen. Loosen but leave to cool on the baking sheet.

6 Serve one or two sticks to the baby. Store the rest in a plastic box for up to three days.

• Suitable for freezing up to three months in a plastic bag.

Bread Fingers with Egg

Makes: 16

2 slices bread

1 egg

30ml/2 tbsp formula or cow's milk

little butter and oil, for frying

1 Trim the crusts off the bread, then cut each slice in half.

2 Beat the egg and milk in a shallow dish and dip the bread, one slice at a time, into the egg until coated on both sides.

3 Heat a little butter and oil in a frying pan. Add the bread and fry until browned on both sides.

4 Cool slightly, cut into fingers and serve to the baby as finger food or as part of a meal.

Cheese Straws

Makes: 42

little oil for greasing

175g/6oz/1½ cups plain (all-purpose) flour

75g/3oz/6 tbsp butter or margarine, cut into pieces

115g/4oz grated Cheddar or mild cheese

1 egg, beaten

1 Preheat the oven to 200°C/ 400°F/Gas 6. Brush two baking sheets lightly with oil.

2 Place the flour in a bowl, add the butter or margarine and rub in until the mixture resembles fine breadcrumbs. Stir in the grated cheese.

3 Reserve 15ml/1 tbsp beaten egg and then stir the rest into the pastry mixture. Mix to a smooth dough, adding water if necessary.

4 Knead lightly and roll out on a floured surface to a rectangle 30 × 20cm/12 × 8in. Brush with the remaining egg.

5 Cut into strips 7.5 × 1cm/ 3 × ½in and place on the baking sheets, spaced slightly apart.

6 Bake in the oven for 8–10 minutes, until golden brown. Loosen from but leave to cool on the baking sheets.

7 Serve one or two sticks to the baby and store the rest in a plastic box for up to 1 week.

• Suitable for freezing up to three months in a plastic box, interleaved with baking parchment.

TIP

Begin making these with mild cheese, and as your child gets more adventurous, change to stronger flavoured cheese.

Mini Cup Cakes

Makes: 26

50g/2oz/4 tbsp soft margarine

50g/2oz/¼ cup caster (superfine) sugar

50g/2oz/⅓ cup self-raising (self-rising) flour

1 egg

1 Preheat the oven to 180°C/350°F/ Gas 4. Place 26 paper mini muffin cases on a large baking sheet.

2 Put all the ingredients for the cake into a mixing bowl and beat together well until smooth.

3 Divide the mixture among the cases and cook for 8–10 minutes, until well risen and golden.

4 Transfer the cakes to a wire rack and leave to cool completely, then peel the paper off one or two cakes and serve to the baby.

5 Store the remaining cakes in a plastic box for up to three days.

● Suitable for freezing up to three months in a plastic box.

TIP

Cut a cup cake in half crossways and spread one half with a little sugar-free jam. Replace top half and serve to the baby.

Shortbread Shapes

Makes: 60

little oil, for greasing

150g/5oz/1 cup plain (all-purpose)
flour

25g/1oz/3 tbsp cornflour (cornstarch)

50g/2oz/¼ cup caster (superfine) sugar

115g/4oz/½ cup butter

extra sugar, for sprinkling (optional)

1 Preheat the oven to 180°C/
350°F/Gas 4. Brush two baking
sheets with a little oil.

2 Put the flour, cornflour and
sugar in a bowl. Cut the butter
into pieces and rub into the flour
until the mixture resembles fine
breadcrumbs. Mould to a dough
with your hands.

5 Offer the baby one or two shapes
and store the rest in a plastic box
for up to one week.

3 Knead lightly and roll out on a
floured surface to a 5mm/¼in
thickness. Stamp out shapes with
small cookie or petits fours cutters.

4 Transfer to the baking sheets,
sprinkle with extra sugar, if
liked, and cook for 10–12 minutes,
until pale golden. Loosen with a
knife and leave to cool on the baking
sheets, then transfer to a wire rack.

TIP
These biscuits (cookies) will keep
well in the freezer for three
months. Pack in rigid plastic boxes
and thaw in a single layer. If you
prefer, you can freeze them before
baking. Wrap well to prevent them
taking up flavours from other food.

FOOD FOR TODDLERS

Once your child has reached 12 months he or she will be enjoying a varied diet, and eating habits and their personal food preferences will be developing. It is now vitally important to lay the foundations of a good and well-balanced eating regime.

This is a time when food fads may also develop. Try to weather this period of fussy eating – all children will experience it at some time, and even good eaters will go through a picky stage. Hopefully, the fad will go as quickly as it came, but while it lasts, meal-times can become a nightmare.

Coping With a Fussy Eater

We all have different sized appetites whatever our age, and young children are no exception. Children's appetites fluctuate greatly and often tail off just before a growth spurt. All children go through food fads; some just seem to last longer and be more difficult than others.

A toddler's appetite varies enormously, and you may find that she will eat very well one day and eat hardly anything the next. Be guided by your toddler, and try to think in terms of what the child has eaten over several days rather than just concentrating on one day.

At the time, it can be very frustrating and worrying. Try not to think of the food that you have just thrown away, but try to think more in the long term. Jot down the foods that your child has actually eaten over three or four days, or up to a week. You may actually be surprised that it isn't just yogurts and crisps after all!

Once you have a list, you may find a link between the foods your child eats and the time of day. Perhaps your child eats better when eating with the family, or when the house is quiet. If you do find a link, then build on it. You might find that your child is snacking on chocolate, doughnuts or soft drinks when out with friends, and that fussiness at home is really a full tummy. Or it may be that by cutting out a milk drink and a biscuit (cookie) mid-morning and offering a sliced apple instead, your child may not be so full at lunchtime. Perhaps you could hide the biscuit tin (cookie jar) once visitors have had one, so that tiny hands can't keep reaching for more.

If your toddler seems hungrier at breakfast, then you could offer French toast, a grilled sausage or a few banana slices with her cereal.

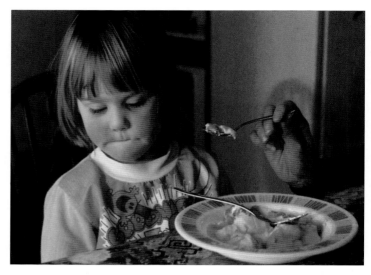

Above: *Don't panic about food rejection. Be patient and keep a journal listing what your child actually does eat.*

Right: *Fresh, healthy snacks of fruit, such as apples, will preserve your child's appetite for main meals.*

Although this may all sound very obvious, when rushing about caring for a toddler and perhaps an older child or new baby as well, life can become rather blurred, and it can be difficult to stand back and look at things objectively.

REFUSING TO EAT

A child will always eat if she is hungry, although it may not be when you want her to eat. A child can stay fit and healthy on surprisingly little. Providing your child is growing and gaining weight, then don't fuss, but if you are worried, talk to your doctor or health visitor. Take the lead from your child, never force feed a child and try not to let meal-times become a battleground.

MAKING MEAL-TIMES FUN

Coping with a fussy eater can be incredibly frustrating. The less she eats, the crosser you get, and so the spiral goes on as your toddler learns how to control meal-times. To break this vicious circle, try diffusing things by involving your child in the preparation of the meal. You could pack up a picnic with your child's help, choosing together what to take. Then go somewhere different to eat – it could be the back garden, the swings or even the car. Alternatively, have a dollies' or teddies' tea party or make a camp under the dining table or even in the cupboard under the stairs.

Even very young children enjoy having friends round for tea. If your child is going through a fussy or non-eating stage, invite over a little friend with a good appetite. Try to take a back seat, and don't make a fuss over how much the visiting child eats compared to your own.

Above: *Changing the scene and breaking routine can help greatly.*

Below: *Making the meal a special event can distract the child from any eating worries.*

Above: *Getting your child to help you cook the food will encourage her to eat it, too.*

Above: *Children are more likely to eat with friends of their own age around them.*

10 TIPS TO COPE WITH A FUSSY EATER

1 Try to find meals that the rest of the family enjoys and where there are at least one or two things the fussy child will eat, as well. It may seem easier to cook only foods that your child will eat, but it means a very limited diet for everyone else, and your child will never get the chance to have a change of mind and try something new.

2 Serve smaller portions of food to your child.

3 Invite round her friend with a hearty appetite. A good example sometimes works, but don't comment on how much the visiting child has eaten.

4 Invite an adult who the child likes for supper – a granny, uncle or friend. Sometimes a child will eat for someone else without any fuss at all.

5 Never force feed a child.

6 If your child is just playing with the food and won't eat, quietly remove the plate without a fuss and don't offer dessert.

7 Try to make meal-times enjoyable and talk about what the family has been doing.

8 Try limiting snacks and drinks between meals so your child feels hungrier when it comes to family meal-times. Alternatively, offer more nutritious snacks and smaller main meals if your child eats better that way.

9 Offer drinks after a meal so that they don't spoil the appetite.

10 Offer new foods when you know your child is hungry and hopefully more receptive.

Above: Remember to give drinks after the meal, not before.

EATING TOGETHER

Sharing meals as a family should be a happy part of the day, but can turn into a nightmare if everyone is tired or you feel as though the only things your children will eat are chips (french fries). There is nothing worse than preparing a lovely supper, laying the table and sitting down with everyone, and then one child refuses to eat, shrieks her disapproval or just pushes the food around the plate. However hard you try to ignore this behaviour, the meal is spoiled for everyone, especially if this is a regular occurrence. It's not fair on you or anyone else.

If you feel this is just a passing phase, then you could try just ignoring it and carry on regardless. Try to praise the good things, perhaps the way the child sits nicely at the table or the way she holds a knife and fork. Talk about the things that have been happening during the day, rather than concentrating on the meal itself. Try to avoid comparing your child's appetite with more hearty eaters. With luck, this particular fad will go away.

However, if it becomes a regular thing and meal-times always seem more like a battleground than a happy family gathering, perhaps it's time for a more serious approach.

First steps

• Check to see if there is something physically wrong with your child. Has she been ill? If she has, she may not have recovered fully. If you're worried, then ask your doctor.

• Perhaps your child has enlarged adenoids or tonsils which could make swallowing difficult, or perhaps she has a food allergy, such as coeliacs disease – an intolerance to gluten, which may be undiagnosed, but which would give the child tummy pains after eating. Again, check with your doctor.

• Is your child worried or stressed? If your family circumstances have changed – the arrival of a new baby, or if you've moved recently – your child may be unhappy or confused.

• Is your child trying to get your attention?

Above: Good seating of the right height will contribute to comfort and relaxation.

Secondly

Look at the way in which you as a family eat. Do you eat at regular times? Do you sit down to eat or catch snacks on the move? Do you enjoy your food, or do you always feel rushed and harassed? Children will pick up habits from their parents – bad ones as well as good. If you don't tend to sit down to a meal, or you have the habit of getting up during meal-times to do other jobs, then it's hard to expect your child to behave differently.

Finally

Talk things over with the whole family. If you all feel enough is enough, then it's time to make a plan of action. Explain that from now on you are all going to eat together where possible, when and where you say so. You will choose the food, there will be three meals a day and no snacks. Since milk is filling and dulls the appetite, milky drinks will only be given after a meal; during the meal water or juice will be provided.

It is important to involve the entire family in this strategy so that there is no dipping into the biscuit tin (cookie jar) or raiding the cupboard for crisps (potato chips) after school. Make sure that the fussy eater is aware of what is going to happen and give a few days' notice so that the idea can sink in.

Once you have outlined your strategy, work out your menus and

Happy Families

stick to them. Include foods your child definitely likes, chicken or carrots for instance, and obviously avoid foods your child dislikes although you could introduce some new foods for variety. Set yourself a time scale, perhaps one or two weeks, and review things after this period has elapsed.

PUTTING THE PLAN INTO ACTION

Begin your new plan of action when the entire family is there to help, such as a weekend, and stick to it. Make a fuss of the plans so it seems more like a game than a prison sentence. Add a few flowers to the table or a pretty cloth to make it more special.

Begin the day with a normal breakfast, but give the fussy eater the smallest possible portion. If the child eats it up, then offer something you know your child likes, such as an apple, a few raisins or a fruit yogurt.

As the days progress, you could offer a biscuit (cookie) or milkshake as a treat.

Give plenty of encouragement and praise, but be firm if the child plays up. If she behaves badly, take her to a different room or to the bottom of the stairs and explain that the only food is what is on the table. Sit down with the rest of the family, leaving the fussy eater's food on the table, and try to ignore the child.

If the child changes her mind just as you're about to clear the table, then get the other members of the family to come back and wait until the fussy eater has finished.

Continue in this way with other meals. Don't be swayed if your child says she will eat her food watching TV or if she wants her dessert first. Explain that she must eat just like everyone else or go without.

If she begins to cry, sit her down in another room and return to the table. This is perhaps the hardest thing of all.

After a few days, there should be a glimmer of progress. Still offer tiny portions of food, followed by foods that you know your child will eat as a treat. Keeping to a plan like this is hard, but if the entire family sticks together and thinks positively, then it is possible. Keep to the time span you have decided, then suggest you all go to your local pizza or burger restaurant, and let the fussy eater choose what she likes.

Fat Cat

Veggie Burger

Tuna Fish Cakes

A Balanced and Varied Diet

Give your child a selection of foods in the four main food groups daily:

Cereal and filler foods: include three to four helpings of the following per day – breakfast cereals, bread, pasta, potatoes, rice.

Fruit and vegetables: try to have three or four helpings per day. Choose from fresh, canned, frozen or dried.

Meat and/or alternatives: one to two portions per day – meat (all kinds, including burgers and sausages), poultry, fish (fresh, canned or frozen), eggs (well cooked), lentils, peas and beans (for example, chickpeas baked beans, red kidney beans), finely chopped nuts, smooth peanut butter, seeds, tofu, and Quorn.

Dairy foods: include 600ml/1 pint of milk per day or a mix of milk, cheese, and yogurt. For a child who stops drinking milk, try flavouring it or using it in custards, ice cream, rice pudding or cheese sauce. A carton of yogurt or 40g/1½oz of cheese have the same amount of calcium as 190ml/⅓ pint of milk.

THE IMPORTANCE OF BREAKFAST

Breakfast is a vitally important start for any young child. Count back: your child may have had a meal at 5 o'clock the previous day, and if she misses breakfast at 8 o'clock she will not have eaten for 15 hours. Allow time to sit down, and don't rush your child. Offer milk and cereals, orange juice diluted with a little water, not squash (orangeade), a few slices of fruit and half a piece of toast, preferably spread with smooth peanut butter or Marmite.

Above: *Cereal and filler foods, such as bread, pasta and rice.*

Above: *Fruit and vegetables, including frozen, dried and canned goods.*

Above: *Meat and meat alternatives, such as beans, peas, lentils and nuts.*

Above: *Dairy foods such as milk, cheese and yogurt.*

Marmite toast

Sliced pears

FATS

As adults we are all aware of the need to cut down on our fat consumption, but when eating together as a family, bear in mind that fat is a useful source of energy in a child's diet. The energy from fat is in concentrated form, so that your child can take in the calories she needs for growth and development before her stomach becomes overfull. Fat in food is also a valuable source of the fat-soluble vitamins, A, D, E and K, as well as essential fatty acids that the body cannot make by itself.

In general, fat is best provided by foods that contain not just fat but other essential nutrients as well, such as dairy products, eggs, meat and fish. Full-fat (whole) milk and its products such as cheese and yogurt, and eggs contain the fat-soluble vitamins A and D, while sunflower (sunflower-seed) oil, nuts and oily fish are a good source of various essential fatty acids.

It is wise to cut down on deep frying and to grill (broil) or oven bake foods where possible. All children love crisps (potato chips), but keep them as a treat rather than a daily snack.

Above: *Keep sweets and chocolate as treats – give fruit and vegetables as snacks.*

FRUIT AND VEGETABLES

Fresh fruit and vegetables play an essential part in a balanced diet. Offer fresh fruit, such as slices of apple or banana, for breakfast and the evening meal, and perhaps thin sticks of raw carrot and celery for lunch. Instead of biscuits (cookies), offer your child raisins, apricots, satsumas, carrots or apple slices if she wants a mid-morning or afternoon snack. Keep the fruit bowl within easy reach so your child may be tempted to pick up a banana as she walks through the kitchen.

Above: *A good mixture of the four basic food types will provide maximum energy and vitality for growing children.*

SNACKS

Young children cannot eat enough food at meal-times to meet their needs for energy and growth, and snacks can play a vital part in meeting these needs. However, keep biscuits and crisps as a treat. They contain little goodness and are bad for the teeth. At meal-times keep sweets (candy) out of sight until the main course has been eaten.

Bread sticks

Raisins

Melon

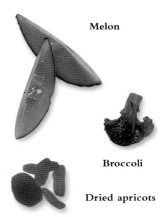

Broccoli

Dried apricots

LUNCH SPECIALS

Now that your baby has progressed from puréed to chopped food, you can begin to cook more grownup lunches. Try to introduce a range of different foods to give a balanced diet and a variety of tastes, but don't be disheartened if there are a few hiccups along the way.

Sticky Chicken

Serves 2–4

4 chicken drumsticks

10ml/2 tsp oil

5ml/1 tsp soy sauce

15ml/1 tbsp smooth peanut butter

15ml/1 tbsp tomato ketchup

small baked potatoes, corn and
   tomato wedges, to serve

1 Preheat the oven to 200°C/ 400°F/Gas 6 and line a small shallow baking tin (pan) with foil. Rinse the drumsticks under cold water, pat dry and peel off the skin. Make three or four slashes in the meat with a sharp knife and place in the tin.

TIP
If more convenient, use the peanut butter and ketchup mixture over chicken thighs or kebabs instead.

2 Blend the remaining ingredients and spread thickly over the top of the chicken drumsticks. Cook in the oven for 15 minutes.

3 Turn the drumsticks over and baste with the peanut butter mixture and meat juices.

4 Cook for a further 20 minutes or until the juices run clear when the chicken is pierced with a knife.

5 Cool slightly, then wrap a small piece of foil around the base of each drumstick. Arrange on plates and serve with small baked potatoes, hot corn, and tomato wedges.

Coriander Chicken Casserole

Serves 2

2 chicken thighs

¼ small onion

1 small carrot, about 50g/2oz

50g/2oz swede (rutabaga)

5ml/1 tsp oil

2.5ml/½ tsp ground coriander

pinch of turmeric

5ml/1 tsp plain (all-purpose) flour

150ml/¼ pint/⅔ cup chicken stock

salt and pepper (optional)

mashed potatoes and peas, to serve

1 Preheat the oven to 180°C/350°F/Gas 4. Rinse the chicken under cold water, pat dry and trim away any excess skin if necessary. Chop the onion, carrot and swede.

2 Heat the oil in a frying pan, add the chicken and brown on each side. Add the vegetables.

TIP
Chop the meat for very young toddlers. Serve older children the whole thigh to make them feel more grown up, then help with cutting.

3 Stir in the coriander, turmeric and flour, then add the stock and a little salt and pepper, if liked. Bring to the boil, then transfer to a casserole.

4 Cover and cook in the oven for 1 hour. Spoon on to serving plates or into shallow dishes, cool slightly and serve the chicken casserole with mashed potatoes and peas.

Chicken and Cheese Parcels

Serves 2

1 boned and skinned chicken breast, about 150g/5oz

25g/1oz Cheddar or mild cheese

1 slice lean ham, cut into 4 strips

15ml/1 tbsp oil

new potatoes, broccoli and carrots, to serve

1 Rinse the chicken under cold water, pat dry with kitchen paper and cut in half crossways. Place each half between two pieces of clear film (plastic wrap) and flatten with a rolling pin until each piece is about 10cm/4in square.

2 Cut the cheese in half and place a piece on each escalope (US scallop). Wrap the chicken around the cheese to enclose it completely.

3 Arrange two pieces of the ham crossways over each of the parcels, securing them underneath with cocktail sticks (toothpicks). Brush the chicken parcels with oil.

TIP
You could wrap the parcels with halved rashers (strips) of rindless streaky (fatty) bacon, if preferred.

4 Place on a piece of foil and chill until ready to cook.

5 Preheat the grill (broiler). Cook the chicken for 10 minutes, turning once, until browned. Remove the cocktail sticks, cool slightly, then arrange on two plates and serve with new potatoes, steamed broccoli florets and sliced carrots.

Peppered Beef Casserole

Serves 2

115g/4oz lean braising steak

¼ small onion

¼ small red (bell) pepper

¼ small yellow (bell) pepper

5ml/1 tsp oil

30ml/2 tbsp canned red kidney
  beans, drained and rinsed

5ml/1 tsp plain (all-purpose) flour

150ml/¼ pint/⅔ cup lamb stock

15ml/1 tbsp tomato ketchup

5ml/1 tsp Worcestershire sauce

45ml/3 tbsp couscous

a few drops of oil

40g/1½oz/3 tbsp frozen peas

salt and pepper (optional)

1 Preheat the oven to 180°C/
350°F/Gas 4. Rinse the meat
under cold water and pat dry. Trim
away any fat and cut into small cubes.

2 Chop the onion, remove the seeds
and core from the peppers and cut
into small cubes.

3 Heat the oil in a pan, add the beef
and onion and fry gently until
browned, stirring frequently.

4 Add the peppers and kidney beans,
then stir in the flour, stock, tomato
ketchup, Worcestershire sauce and a
little salt and pepper if liked.

5 Bring to the boil, stirring, then
transfer to a casserole dish, cover
and cook in the oven for about 1½
hours, or until the meat is tender.

6 Just before serving place the
couscous in a bowl, cover with
boiling water and leave to soak for
5 minutes. Drain into a sieve (strainer)
and stir in a few drops of oil.

7 Bring a pan of water to the boil,
add the peas, and place the sieve of
couscous over the pan. Cover and
cook for 5 minutes.

8 Spoon the casserole on to two
plates or dishes. Fluff up the
couscous with a fork, drain the peas
and spoon on to the plates. Cool
slightly before serving.

Lamb Stew

Serves 2

115g/4oz lamb fillet
¼ small onion
1 small carrot, about 50g/2oz
½ small parsnip, about 50g/2oz
1 small potato
5ml/1 tsp oil
150ml/¼ pint/⅔ cup lamb stock
pinch of dried rosemary
salt and pepper (optional)
crusty bread, to serve

1 Rinse the lamb under cold water and pat dry. Cut away any fat from the meat and cut into small cubes. Finely chop the onion, then dice the carrot and parsnip and cut the potato into slightly larger pieces.

2 Heat the oil in a medium-size pan, add the lamb and onion, and fry gently until browned. Add the carrot, parsnip and potato, and fry the lamb and vegetables for a further 3 minutes, stirring.

3 Add the lamb stock, dried rosemary and a little salt and pepper, if liked. Bring to the boil, cover and simmer for 35–40 minutes, or until the meat is tender and moist.

4 Spoon the stew into shallow bowls and cool slightly before serving with crusty bread.

Mexican Beef

Serves 3–4

¼ small onion

1 strip red (bell) pepper

½ small courgette (zucchini)

115g/4oz lean minced (ground) beef

1 small garlic clove, crushed

45ml/3 tbsp canned baked beans

45ml/3 tbsp beef stock

15ml/1 tbsp tomato ketchup

18 corn chips

25g/1oz/¼ cup grated Cheddar or
  mild cheese

green salad, to serve

1 Finely chop the onion and dice
the pepper and courgette.

2 Dry fry the onion and meat in a
medium-size pan, stirring until
browned all over.

3 Stir in the remaining ingredients
and bring to the boil, stirring.
Cover and simmer the mixture for
15 minutes, stirring occasionally.

4 Place the corn chips on plates,
spoon on the mixture and
sprinkle the grated cheese over the
top. Serve with a green salad.

Lamb and Celery Casserole

Serves 2

115g/4oz lamb fillet

¼ onion

1 small carrot, about 50g/2oz

1 celery stick

25g/1oz button (white) mushrooms

5ml/1 tsp oil

bay leaf

10ml/2 tsp plain (all-purpose) flour

175ml/6fl oz/¾ cup lamb stock

salt and pepper (optional)

mashed potatoes and baby Brussels
  sprouts, to serve

1 Preheat the oven to 180°C/
350°F/Gas 4. Rinse the lamb
under cold water and pat dry, then
trim off any fat and cut into small
cubes. Chop the onion and carrot,
rinse the celery and mushrooms, pat
dry and slice thinly.

2 Heat the oil in a frying pan, add
the lamb, onion and bay leaf and
fry gently until the lamb is browned,
stirring frequently. Add the remaining
vegetables and fry for a further
3 minutes, until they are softened
and lightly browned.

VARIATION
For a more unusual flavour,
substitute fennel for the celery.
Its slight aniseed taste goes well
with lamb.

3 Stir in the flour, then add the
stock, and a little salt and
pepper, if liked. Bring to the boil
and then transfer to a casserole,
cover and cook in the oven for 45
minutes or until the meat is tender.

4 Spoon the casserole on to plates,
discarding the bay leaf. Cool
slightly, then serve with mashed
potatoes and tiny Brussels sprouts.

Shepherd's Pie

Serves 2

½ small onion

175g/6oz lean minced (ground) beef

10ml/2 tsp plain (all-purpose) flour

30ml/2 tbsp tomato ketchup

150ml/¼ pint/⅔ cup beef stock

pinch of mixed herbs

50g/2oz swede (rutabaga)

½ small parsnip, about 50g/2oz

1 medium potato, about 115g/4oz

10ml/2 tsp milk

15g/½oz/1 tbsp butter or margarine

½ carrot

40g/1½oz/3 tbsp frozen peas

salt and pepper (optional)

1 Preheat oven to 190°C/375°F/ Gas 5. Finely chop the onion, and place in a small pan with the mince and dry fry over a low heat, stirring, until the mince is evenly browned.

2 Add the flour, stirring, then add the ketchup, stock, mixed herbs and seasoning, if liked. Bring to the boil, cover and simmer gently for 30 minutes, stirring occasionally.

3 Meanwhile, chop the swede, parsnip and potato, and cook for 20 minutes, until tender. Drain.

4 Mash with the milk and half of the butter or margarine.

5 Spoon the meat into two 250ml/8fl oz/1 cup ovenproof dishes. Place the mashed vegetables on top, fluffing them up with a fork. Dot with butter or margarine.

6 Place both the pies on a baking sheet and cook for 25–30 minutes, until browned on top and bubbly.

7 Peel and thinly slice the carrot lengthways. Stamp out shapes with petits fours cutters. Cook in a pan of boiling water with the peas for 5 minutes. Drain and serve with the shepherd's pies. Remember that baked pies are very hot when they come out of the oven. Always allow to cool slightly before serving to children.

Tuna Fish Cakes

Serves 2–3

1 large potato, about 225g/8oz
knob (pat) of butter or margarine
10ml/2 tsp milk
5ml/1 tsp lemon juice
100g/3½oz can tuna fish
40g/1½oz/3 tbsp frozen corn, defrosted
flour, for dusting
1 egg
60ml/4 tbsp ground almonds
50g/2oz green beans
½ carrot
6 frozen peas
15ml/1 tbsp oil
salt and pepper (optional)

1 Peel and cut the potato into chunks and then cook in a pan of boiling water for about 15 minutes until tender. Drain and mash with the butter or margarine and milk.

2 Add the lemon juice and a little salt and pepper, if liked. Drain the tuna fish and stir into the potato with the defrosted corn.

3 Divide the mixture into six and pat each portion into a fish shape with floured hands.

4 Beat the egg in a dish and place the ground almonds on a plate. Dip the fish cakes into the egg and then into the almonds, making sure they are completely covered. Place on a floured plate and chill until ready to cook.

5 Trim the beans, and peel and cut the carrot into sticks a little smaller than the beans. Cook in a pan of boiling water with the peas for about 5 minutes.

6 Meanwhile heat the oil in a frying pan, and fry the fish cakes for 5 minutes, until golden brown and crisp, turning once.

7 Drain and arrange on serving plates with pea "eyes" and bean and carrot "pond weed". Cool slightly before serving.

Fish and Cheese Pies

Serves 2

1 medium potato, about 150g/5oz

25g/1oz green cabbage

115g/4oz cod or hoki fillets

25g/1oz/2 tbsp frozen corn

150ml/¼ pint/⅔ cup milk

15ml/1 tbsp butter or margarine

15ml/1 tbsp plain (all-purpose) flour

25g/1oz/¼ cup grated Red Leicester
  or mild cheese

5ml/1 tsp sesame seeds

carrots and mangetouts (snowpeas),
  to serve

4 Strain the fish and corn, reserving
the cooking liquid. Wash the
pan, then melt the butter or margarine
in the pan. Stir in the flour, then
gradually add the reserved cooking
liquid and bring to the boil, stirring
until thickened and smooth.

5 Add the fish and corn with half of
the grated cheese. Spoon into two
small ovenproof dishes.

6 Mash the potato and cabbage
with the remaining 10ml/2 tsp
milk. Stir in half of the remaining
cheese and spoon the mixture over
the fish. Sprinkle with the sesame
seeds and the remaining cheese.

7 Cook under a preheated grill
until the topping is browned.
Cool slightly before serving with
carrot and mangetout vegetable fishes.

1 Peel and cut the potato into
chunks and shred the cabbage.
Cut any skin away from the fish
fillets and rinse under cold water.

2 Bring a pan of water to the boil,
add the potato and cook for
10 minutes. Add the cabbage and
cook for a further 5 minutes until
tender. Drain.

3 Meanwhile, place the fish fillets,
the corn and all but 10ml/2 tsp
of the milk in a second pan. Bring
to the boil, then cover the pan and
simmer very gently for 8–10 minutes,
until the fish flakes easily when
pressed with a knife.

Surprise Fish Parcels

Serves 2

½ small courgette (zucchini)
175g/6oz smoked haddock or cod
1 small tomato
knob (pat) of butter or margarine
pinch of dried mixed herbs
new potatoes and broccoli, to serve

1 Preheat the oven to 200°C/
400°F/Gas 6. Tear off two pieces
of foil, then trim and thinly slice the
courgette and divide equally
between the two pieces of foil.

2 Cut the skin away from the fish,
remove any bones, cut into two
equal pieces and rinse under cold
water. Pat the haddock dry and place
on top of the courgettes.

3 Slice the tomato and arrange
slices on top of each piece of
haddock. Add a little butter or
margarine to each and sprinkle with
mixed herbs.

4 Wrap the foil around the fish and
seal the edges of each piece to
make two parcels, then place the
parcels on a baking sheet and cook
in the oven for 15–20 minutes,
depending on the thickness of the fish.

5 To test if they are cooked, open
up one of the parcels and insert a
knife into the centre. If the fish flakes
easily, then it is ready.

6 Cool slightly, then arrange the
parcels on plates and serve with
new potatoes and broccoli.

Cowboy Sausages and Beans

Serves 2

3 chipolata sausages

¼ small onion

1 small carrot, about 50g/2oz

1 strip red (bell) pepper

5ml/1 tsp oil

200g/7oz can baked beans

10ml/2 tsp Worcestershire sauce

fingers of toast, to serve

2 Finely chop the onion, then dice the carrot and the pepper, discarding the core and seeds.

3 Heat the oil in a frying pan, add the sausages and the chopped onion and fry until browned.

TIP
Check the beans towards the end of cooking – you may need to add a little extra water.

4 Add the remaining ingredients and stir in 30ml/2 tbsp water. Cover and cook for 15 minutes, or until the carrot is cooked.

5 Spoon on to serving plates or into dishes, cool slightly and serve with fingers of toast.

1 Press the centre of each sausage, twist and cut in half to make two small sausages.

Mini Toad-in-the-Hole

Serves 2

3 chipolata sausages

5ml/1 tsp oil

60ml/4 tbsp plain (all-purpose) flour

1 egg

60ml/4 tbsp milk

salt

baked beans and green beans, to serve

1 Preheat the oven to 220°C/ 425°F/Gas 7. Press the centre of each sausage with your finger, twist and then cut in half. Brush two 10cm/4in tartlet tins (muffin pans) with oil. Add the sausages and cook for about 5 minutes.

2 Place the flour, egg and a pinch of salt in a bowl. Gradually whisk in the milk, beating until a smooth batter is formed.

3 Pour into the tins, quickly return to the oven and bake for 15 minutes, until risen and golden.

4 Loosen with a knife and turn out on to serving plates. Cool slightly and serve with baked beans and steamed green beans.

Pork Hotpot

Serves 2

175g/6oz lean pork
¼ small onion
5ml/1 tsp oil
5ml/1 tsp plain (all-purpose) flour
40g/1½oz/3 tbsp frozen corn
pinch of dried sage
150ml/¼ pint/⅔ cup chicken stock
1 medium potato, about 150g/5oz
1 carrot, about 75g/3oz
knob (pat) of butter or margarine
salt and pepper (optional)
broccoli and Brussels sprouts, to serve

1 Preheat the oven to 180°C/ 350°F/Gas 4. Rinse the pork under cold water, pat dry, trim away any fat and cut into small cubes. Peel and finely chop the onion.

2 Heat the oil in a frying pan, add the cubed pork and onion and fry until golden brown, stirring.

3 Add in the flour and stir until blended, then add the corn, dried sage, stock and a little salt and pepper, if liked. Bring to the boil and then turn the mixture into a shallow ovenproof dish.

4 Peel and thinly slice the potato and carrot. Arrange slices so that they overlap on top of the pork mixture. Dot with butter or margarine. Cover with foil and cook in the oven for about 1 hour, until the potatoes are tender.

5 Remove the foil and brown under the grill (broiler) if liked. Spoon on to serving plates, cool slightly, then serve with steamed broccoli and Brussels sprouts.

TIP

If you are cooking for only one child, make the hotpot in two dishes. Cool one, cover with clear film (plastic wrap) and freeze for up to three months.

Pork and Lentil Casserole

Serves 2

175g/6oz boneless spare-rib pork
  chop

¼ small onion

1 small carrot, about 50g/2oz

5ml/1 tsp oil

1 small garlic clove, crushed

25g/1oz red lentils

90ml/6 tbsp canned chopped
  tomatoes

90ml/6 tbsp chicken stock

salt and pepper (optional)

swede (rutabaga) and peas, to serve

1 Preheat the oven to 180°C/
350°F/Gas 4. Trim off any
excess fat from the pork and cut in
half. Finely chop the onion and dice
the carrot.

2 Heat the oil in a frying pan, add
the pork and onion and fry until
the pork is browned on both sides.

3 Add the garlic, lentils and
carrots and stir gently to mix.

4 Pour in the chopped tomatoes,
stock and seasoning, if liked,
and cook briefly to bring to the boil.
Transfer to a casserole, cover and
cook in the oven for 1¼ hours.

5 Spoon portions on to serving
plates or shallow dishes and cool
slightly. Serve with diced buttered
swede and peas.

TIP

Teaching a child to use a knife and
fork can be frustrating. Spare-rib
pork chops are wonderfully tender
when casseroled and so very easy
to cut with a child's knife.

Sticky Ribs and Apple Slaw

Serves 2

225g/8oz short pork ribs

10ml/2 tsp oil

10ml/2 tsp tomato ketchup

10ml/2 tsp hoisin sauce

1 medium potato, scrubbed but not peeled

knob (pat) of butter or margarine

For the Apple Slaw

½ carrot

½ eating apple

25g/1oz white cabbage

10ml/2 tsp sultanas (golden raisins)

30ml/2 tbsp mayonnaise

carrot slices, tomato wedges and celery sticks, to serve

4 Meanwhile peel the carrot, and peel, quarter and core the apple. Coarsely grate the apple and carrot and finely chop the cabbage.

5 Place in a bowl with the sultanas and mayonnaise and mix well.

6 Arrange the ribs on serving plates. Halve the baked potato, add a little butter or margarine to each half and serve with the pork ribs, together with star-shaped carrot slices, celery sticks and tomato wedges and spoonfuls of coleslaw.

TIP

Check the temperature of the ribs before serving, as they stay very hot for a surprisingly long time. Nothing will put a child off more than food that is very hot. Toddlers prefer their food to be lukewarm.

1 Preheat the oven to 200°C/ 400°F/Gas 6. Rinse the pork ribs under cold water, pat dry and put on a roasting rack set over a small roasting pan. Mix the oil, ketchup and hoisin sauce, and brush over the ribs, reserving any extra mixture.

2 Pour a little boiling water into the base of the roasting pan. Prick the potato all over with a fork and then place in the oven with the spare ribs, preferably on the same shelf.

3 Cook for 1 hour, turning the pork ribs once during cooking and brushing with any of the remaining ketchup mixture.

Mini Cheese and Ham Tarts

Makes 12

For the Pastry

115g/4oz/1 cup plain (all-purpose) flour

50g/2oz/4 tbsp margarine

For the Filling

50g/2oz/½ cup mild cheese

2 thin slices ham, chopped

75g/3oz/½ cup frozen corn

1 egg

120ml/4fl oz/½ cup milk

pinch of paprika

salt and pepper

carrot and cucumber sticks, to serve

1 Preheat the oven to 200°C/400°F/ Gas 6. Place the flour in a bowl, add the margarine and rub in with your fingertips until the mixture resembles fine breadcrumbs.

2 Stir in 20ml/4 tsp water and mix to a smooth dough. Lightly knead and roll out on a floured surface.

3 Stamp out twelve 7.5cm/3in circles with a fluted cookie cutter, re-rolling the pastry as necessary. Press into a tartlet tin (muffin pan).

TIP

Encourage children to eat more vegetables by serving them with a yogurt dip flavoured with tomato purée (paste).

4 Grate the cheese, mix with the ham and corn, and divide among the pastry cases.

5 Beat together the egg, milk, salt and pepper and pour into the tarts. Sprinkle with paprika.

6 Cook in the oven for 12–15 minutes, until well risen and browned. Serve warm with carrot and cucumber sticks.

GOING GREEN

GETTING CHILDREN TO EAT MORE THAN A FEW FROZEN PEAS AND THE ODD CARROT CAN BE AN UPHILL BATTLE. ENCOURAGE THEM TO BE A LITTLE MORE ADVENTUROUS BY MIXING THEIR FAVOURITE FOODS WITH SOME NEW VEGETABLES.

Pick-up Sticks

Serves 2

5cm/2in piece of leek

25g/1oz green beans

1 strip red (bell) pepper

1 celery stick

25g/1oz beansprouts

1 small carrot, about 50g/2oz

5ml/1 tsp oil

15ml/1 tbsp tomato ketchup

5ml/1 tsp soy sauce

pinch ground ginger

grilled (broiled) sausages, to serve

1 Rinse the leek, beans, pepper, celery and beansprouts. Peel the carrot. Halve any large beans and beansprouts. Cut the remaining vegetables into thin strips.

2 Heat the oil in a frying pan, add all the vegetables except the beansprouts and fry for 3 minutes, stirring all the time.

3 Add the beansprouts, ketchup, soy sauce, ginger and 10ml/2 tsp water. Cook for a further 2 minutes, stirring until the vegetables are hot.

4 Spoon on to serving plates and leave to cool slightly. Serve with grilled sausages.

TIP
Don't overcook the vegetables. They should be quite crisp, and firm enough for your child to pick up.

Spinach Pancakes with Ham and Cheese

Serves 2–3

50g/2oz fresh spinach, leaves only

50g/2oz plain (all-purpose) flour

1 egg yolk

300ml/½ pint/1¼ cups milk

15ml/1 tbsp oil

For the Filling

15ml/1 tbsp margarine

15ml/1 tbsp plain (all-purpose) flour

25g/1oz/¼ cup grated Red Leicester
or mild cheese

40g/1½oz thinly sliced ham, chopped

40g/1½oz button (white) mushrooms,
thinly sliced

1 Wash the spinach leaves well in cold water and then place in a frying pan, set over a medium heat. Cover and cook gently for 2–3 minutes, until the spinach has just wilted, stirring occasionally. Drain off any excess liquid and cool.

2 Put the flour, egg yolk and a little salt and pepper, if liked, into a bowl. Whisk in half of the milk to make a smooth batter. Finely chop the spinach and stir into the batter.

3 Melt the margarine in a pan, stir in the flour and then gradually stir in the remaining milk and bring to the boil, stirring continuously until smooth. Add the cheese, ham and mushrooms and stir to mix. Heat, cover and keep warm.

4 Heat a little oil in a frying pan, pour off excess, then add 30ml/ 2 tbsp pancake batter, tilting the pan so that the batter covers the base. Cook for a few minutes until browned, then flip over and cook the other side until golden. Slide the pancake on to a plate and keep warm.

5 Continue making pancakes until all the batter is used up.

6 Fold the pancakes into quarters, then spoon a little of the ham mixture into each one. Arrange the pancakes on plates and serve with tomato wedges and new potatoes.

TIP

If offering spinach to your child for the first time, make sure that the filling includes foods that you know are liked. Omit or add ingredients as necessary.

Cauliflower and Broccoli with Cheese

Serves 2

1 egg

75g/3oz cauliflower

75g/3oz broccoli

15g/½oz/1 tbsp margarine

15ml/1 tbsp plain (all-purpose) flour

150ml/¼ pint/⅔ cup milk

40g/1½oz/⅓ cup grated Red
   Leicester or mild cheese

½ tomato

salt and pepper (optional)

1 Put the egg in a small pan of cold water, bring to the boil and cook for about 10 minutes until the egg is hard-boiled.

2 Meanwhile, cut the cauliflower and broccoli into florets and thinly slice the broccoli stalks. Cook in a pan of boiling water for about 8 minutes, until just tender.

3 Drain the vegetables and dry the pan. Melt the margarine, stir in the flour, then gradually mix in the milk and bring to the boil, stirring until thickened and smooth.

TIP

Making a face or fun pattern can be just enough to tempt a fussy eater to try something new.

4 Stir two-thirds of the cheese into the sauce together with a little seasoning, if liked. Reserve two of the broccoli florets and stir the remaining vegetables into the sauce.

5 Divide the mixture between two heat-resistant shallow dishes and sprinkle with the remaining cheese.

6 Place under a hot grill (broiler) until golden brown and bubbling.

7 Make a face on each dish with broccoli florets for a nose, a halved tomato for a mouth and peeled and sliced hard-boiled egg for eyes. Cool slightly before serving.

Potato Boats

Serves 2

2 small baking potatoes

5cm/2in piece leek

25g/1oz button (white) mushrooms

10ml/2 tsp oil

25g/1oz/2 tbsp frozen corn

15ml/1 tbsp milk

knob (pat) of butter

½ small courgette (zucchini), grated

1 carrot, about 50g/2oz, grated

2 slices processed cheese

1 slice ham

salt and pepper (optional)

1 Preheat the oven to 200°C/ 400°F/Gas 6. Prick the potatoes with a fork and bake for 1 hour, until soft. Alternatively, prick well and then microwave on a sheet of kitchen paper on High (full power) for 7–8 minutes.

2 Halve the leek lengthways, wash thoroughly to remove any grit and then slice thinly. Rinse the mushrooms, pat dry and thinly slice.

3 Heat 5ml/1 tsp oil in a frying pan and gently fry the leek, mushrooms and corn for about 3 minutes, until softened, stirring frequently. Turn into a bowl and keep warm.

4 When the potatoes are cooked, cut in half and scoop the centres into the bowl with the leek and mushroom mixture. Add the milk, butter and a little salt and pepper if liked, and stir to mix. Pile the mixture back into the potato shells.

5 Reheat the remaining 5ml/1 tsp of oil and fry the grated courgette and carrot for 2 minutes, until softened. Spoon on to two small plates and spread with a fork to cover the bases of the plates.

6 Arrange two potato halves on each plate. For sails, cut the cheese and ham into triangles and secure to potatoes with cocktail sticks. Cool slightly before serving.

Fat Cats

Serves 2

oil, for greasing

200g/7oz frozen puff pastry, defrosted

a little flour, for dusting

beaten egg, to glaze

50g/2oz broccoli

25g/1oz/2 tbsp frozen mixed vegetables

15ml/1 tbsp butter or margarine

15ml/1 tbsp plain (all-purpose) flour

100ml/3½fl oz/½ cup milk

30ml/2 tbsp grated Cheddar or mild cheese

a little mustard and cress (fine curled cress), to garnish

1 Preheat the oven to 220°C/ 425°F/Gas 7 and lightly brush a baking sheet with a little oil. Roll out the pastry thinly on a surface lightly dusted with a little flour.

2 Using a shaped cookie cutter, stamp out four 13cm/5in cat shapes. Place two cats on the baking sheet and brush with egg.

3 Cut a large hole in the centres of the two remaining cats and place the shapes on top of the other two cats.

VARIATION
Ring the changes by making this recipe using different shaped cookie cutters for the pastry shapes. Get your child to choose his favourite.

4 Brush the tops with egg and cook for 10 minutes, until the pastry is well risen and golden.

5 Meanwhile chop the broccoli and cook in a small pan of boiling water with the frozen vegetables for 5 minutes. Drain.

6 Dry the pan and melt the butter or margarine. Stir in the flour and then gradually add the milk. Bring to the boil, stirring all the time until thickened and smooth.

7 Reserve two peas, two pieces of carrot, and two pieces of red bell pepper. Stir the remaining vegetables into the sauce with the grated cheese.

8 Enlarge the cavity in the centre of each pastry cat by scooping out a little of the pastry. Spoon in the vegetable mixture and arrange on two serving plates. Garnish with halved peas for eyes, halved carrot strips for whiskers and red pepper noses. Add mustard and cress. Cool slightly before serving.

Potato, Carrot and Courgette Rösti

Serves 2–4

1 small potato, about 115g/4oz

½ carrot, about 25g/1oz

½ courgette (zucchini), about 25g/1oz

10ml/2 tsp vegetable oil

sausages and baked beans, to serve

1 Grate the potato, carrot and courgette into a bowl and mix together thoroughly.

2 Place several sheets of kitchen paper on a surface and put the vegetables on top. Cover with more kitchen paper and press down to soak up all the excess liquid.

3 Heat the oil in a frying pan and spoon the vegetables into the pan to form eight rounds. Flatten slightly with a fork and fry four of the rounds for 5 minutes, turning once until the potatoes are thoroughly cooked and the rösti is golden brown on both sides.

4 Lift out of the pan and cook the remaining mixture. Cool slightly and serve with grilled sausages and baked beans.

Veggie Burgers

Serves 2–4

1 large or 2 small potatoes, about 225g/8oz

1 carrot, about 50g/2oz

25g/1oz broccoli

25g/1oz Brussels sprouts

1 egg yolk

15ml/1 tbsp plain (all-purpose) flour

15ml/1 tbsp freshly grated Parmesan cheese

15ml/1 tbsp oil

salt and pepper (optional)

canned spaghetti hoops, strips of ham, wedges of cucumber, and tomato ketchup, to serve

1 Cut the potato and carrot into chunks and cook in boiling water for 15 minutes, until tender.

2 Meanwhile, cut the broccoli into small florets, chop the stem finely and thinly slice the Brussels sprouts. Rinse under cold water then add to the potatoes and carrots for the last 5 minutes of cooking.

3 Drain the vegetables thoroughly and then mash together. Add the egg yolk, and a little salt and pepper, if liked, then mix well.

4 Divide into four and shape into burgers with floured hands. Coat in flour and Parmesan cheese.

5 Heat the oil in a frying pan, add the burgers and fry for 5 minutes, turning once until golden brown. Cool slightly, then serve with canned spaghetti hoops, strips of ham, a few cucumber wedges and a little tomato ketchup. Add a face with peas, carrot and cucumber.

TIP

To make a spider, add cooked green bean legs, a red (bell) pepper mouth and yellow pepper eyes.

Vegetable Lasagne

Serves 2–3

¼ small onion
50g/2oz carrot
50g/2oz courgette (zucchini)
50g/2oz aubergine (eggplant)
25g/1oz button (white) mushrooms
10ml/2 tsp oil
1 small garlic clove, crushed
225g/8oz can chopped tomatoes
pinch of mixed herbs
15ml/1 tbsp butter or margarine
15ml/1 tbsp plain (all-purpose) flour
150ml/¼ pint/⅔ cup milk
60ml/4 tbsp grated mild cheese
3 sheets pre-cooked lasagne
salt and pepper
mixed salad, to serve

1 Finely chop the onion and carrot, and finely dice the courgette and aubergine. Wipe and thinly slice the mushrooms.

2 Heat the oil and fry the vegetables for 3 minutes until softened. Add the garlic, tomatoes and herbs, then bring to the boil, cover and simmer for 5 minutes.

3 Melt the butter or margarine in a pan, stir in the flour. Add the milk and bring to the boil, stirring, until thickened. Stir in half of the grated cheese and a little salt and pepper.

4 Preheat the oven to 180°C/ 350°F/Gas 4. Spoon one-third of the vegetable mixture into the base of an ovenproof dish, then add a little sauce. Add a slice of lasagne, then cover with half of the remaining vegetable mixture and half the remaining sauce.

5 Add a second sheet of pasta and top with the remaining vegetable mixture. Add a third sheet of lasagne and top with the remaining cheese sauce. Sprinkle with the remaining cheese.

6 Cook for 50–60 minutes, checking after 30 minutes and covering loosely with foil if the topping is browning too quickly. Spoon on to serving plates and leave the lasagne to cool slightly. Serve with a little mixed salad.

Aubergine Bolognese

Serves 2

50g/2oz aubergine (eggplant)

1 strip red (bell) pepper

1 strip yellow (bell) pepper

5cm/2in piece of leek

1 carrot, about 50g/2oz

10ml/2 tsp oil

1 small garlic clove, crushed

25g/1oz/2 tbsp frozen corn

25g/1oz/2 tbsp red lentils

225g/8oz can chopped tomatoes

250ml/8fl oz/1 cup vegetable stock

pinch of dried herbs

50g/2oz dried pasta shapes

knob (pat) of butter or margarine

30ml/2 tbsp grated cheese (optional)

salt and pepper

1 Rinse the aubergine, peppers and leek, peel the carrot and then finely dice all the vegetables.

2 Heat the oil in a medium-size pan, add the diced vegetables and gently fry for 3 minutes, stirring frequently, until slightly softened.

TIP
Sprinkle the diced aubergine with salt, leave to drain in a colander for 30 minutes, then rinse. This removes any bitter taste.

3 Add the garlic, corn, lentils, tomatoes, stock, herbs and a little salt and pepper.

4 Bring to the boil, cover and simmer for about 30 minutes, stirring occasionally and adding a little extra stock if necessary.

5 In the last 10 minutes of cooking, bring a pan of water to the boil and add the pasta. Ccok for 10 minutes, until tender.

6 Drain, toss in a little butter or margarine. Spoon on to plates and top with the aubergine bolognese. Sprinkle with cheese.

QUICK MEALS

IF YOU'VE HAD A BUSY DAY, RUSTLE UP THESE QUICK AND TASTY TODDLERS' MEALS — THEY ALL COOK IN 10 MINUTES OR LESS, AND THERE IS A WIDE VARIETY OF RECIPES TO CHOOSE FROM. REMEMBER THE IMPORTANCE OF FUN PRESENTATION, TO TEMPT YOUR TODDLER TO TRY NEW FOODS.

Speedy Chicken Pie

Serves 2

1 celery stick

25g/1oz/2 tbsp frozen corn, defrosted

30ml/2 tbsp mayonnaise

2.5ml/½ tsp ground coriander

75g/3oz cold cooked chicken

½ small packet plain crisps (US potato chips)

15ml/1 tbsp grated Red Leicester or mild cheese

salt and pepper (optional)

peas and broccoli, to serve

2 Spoon into a shallow ovenproof dish and level the surface.

3 Roughly crush the crisps and sprinkle over the chicken. Top with the grated cheese and cook for 10 minutes, until hot and bubbly.

4 Cool slightly, then serve the pie with peas and broccoli.

1 Preheat the oven to 220°C/425°F/ Gas 7. Rinse the celery, slice thinly and place in a bowl with the corn, mayonnaise, ground coriander and a little salt and pepper, if liked. Dice the chicken, add to the bowl and mix well.

VARIATION
Mexican Chicken Pie
Replace the ground coriander with ground cumin and replace the crisps with about 30ml/2 tbsp crumbled plain tortilla chips.

Skinny Dippers

Serves 2

150g/5oz boneless, skinless chicken breast

25g/1oz/¼ cup grated Cheddar or mild cheese

50g/2oz/1 cup fresh breadcrumbs

15g/½oz/1 tbsp butter or margarine

115g/4oz frozen oven chips (french fries)

½ small carrot, cut into thin strips

½ small courgette (zucchini), cut into thin strips

45ml/3 tbsp tomato ketchup

1 Rinse the chicken under cold water and pat dry with kitchen paper. Cut into thin strips.

2 Mix the grated cheese and breadcrumbs on a plate. Melt the butter or margarine in a small pan or in a dish in the microwave on High (full power) for 20 seconds, then toss the chicken strips in the butter or margarine and roll in the breadcrumb mixture.

3 Arrange the chicken and chips on a foiled-lined baking sheet. Preheat the grill (broiler) and bring a pan of water to the boil.

4 Grill the chicken for 6–8 minutes and the chips 8–10 minutes, until both are well browned, turning once. When the chicken is ready, keep warm in a shallow dish while the chips finish cooking.

5 Cook the vegetables for 5 minutes in the pan of boiling water, until tender.

6 Spoon the ketchup into two ramekins or egg cups and place in the centre of two serving plates. Drain the vegetables and divide the vegetables, chicken and chips between the two plates. Allow to cool slightly before dipping into ketchup.

TIP

Keep a supply of fresh breadcrumbs in a sealed plastic bag in the freezer. There is no need to defrost, just take out as much as you need and use from frozen.

Sweet and Sour Chicken

Serves 2

50g/2oz/¼ cup long grain white rice

1 carrot, about 50g/2oz

1 courgette (zucchini), about 50g/2oz

2 skinless chicken thighs

10ml/2 tsp oil

25g/1oz/2 tbsp frozen peas

5ml/1 tsp cornflour (cornstarch)

5ml/1 tsp soy sauce

10ml/2 tsp tomato ketchup

60ml/4 tbsp orange juice

1 egg, beaten

1 Cook the rice in boiling water for 8–10 minutes, until tender.

2 Meanwhile, peel the carrot, trim the courgette and cut both into thin strips. Bone the chicken and cut into small chunks.

3 Heat 5ml/1 tsp of the oil in a frying pan, add the carrot, courgette, chicken and peas, and fry for 5 minutes, stirring occasionally.

4 Blend the cornflour with the soy sauce and then stir into the pan together with the ketchup and orange juice. Cook gently, stirring all the time, until the sauce is glossy and has thickened.

TIP

Make the meal into an occasion and serve the food in Chinese bowls with Chinese spoons – chopsticks may be a little too tricky to manage. All children love the idea of eating in a restaurant with a parent to wait on them.

5 Drain the rice thoroughly. Add the remaining oil to the rice together with the beaten egg and cook over a gentle heat, stirring until the egg has scrambled.

6 Spoon the rice and sweet and sour chicken on to serving plates and cool slightly before serving.

Ham and Tomato Scramble

Serves 2

2 slices ham

1 tomato

1 small strip yellow (bell) pepper

2 eggs

15ml/1 tbsp milk

2 slices bread

a little butter

salt

1 Finely chop the ham. Halve the tomato, scoop out and discard the seeds, then chop into small dice. Finely chop the strip of pepper.

2 Beat the eggs and milk together and season with a little salt. Toast the bread lightly.

3 Heat a small knob (pat) of butter in a pan, add the eggs, ham, tomato and pepper and cook gently, stirring all the time until cooked to taste. Cool slightly.

4 Butter the toast and cut into shapes with small fancy-shaped cookie cutters. Arrange on plates with the ham and tomato scramble.

TIP
If you don't have any special cutters, then cut the toast into tiny triangles and squares with a knife.

Ham Salad Clown

Serves 2

2 slices ham

1 cherry tomato

2 slices apple

1 slice cheese

2 currants (raisins)

2 slices hard-boiled egg

a little mustard and cress (fine curled cress)

2 long slices carrot

TIP
Have fun varying the ingredients for the clown. Use cheese slices, radishes, peaches, lettuce and red (bell) pepper to change the appearance and features.

1 Cut two large rounds from the slices of ham using a cookie cutter or the top of a glass or other container as a guide. Arrange on two plates and add a halved tomato for a nose and a slice of apple for the mouth, trimming if needed.

2 With a knife, cut out small triangles or stars of cheese for eyes, place on the ham and add halved currants (raisins) for eye balls.

3 Halve the egg slices and add to the face for ears. Snip the mustard and cress for hair and use snipped pieces of carrot for a ruff.

Spanish Omelette

Serves 2

2 thin slices ham

1 strip red (bell) pepper

15ml/1 tbsp frozen peas

50g/2oz frozen oven chips (french fries)

5ml/1 tsp oil

1 egg

salt and pepper

tomato wedges, to serve

1 Chop the ham and pepper. Mix the pepper and peas. Slice the oven chips.

2 Heat the oil in a non-stick frying pan, and fry the chips for 5 minutes, stirring, until lightly browned. Add the pepper and peas and cook, stirring, for a further 2 minutes. Stir in the chopped ham.

3 Beat together the egg, 10ml/2 tsp water and a little salt and pepper, and pour into the pan, tilting it so that the egg mixture covers the base evenly.

4 Cook over a medium-low heat for 2–3 minutes, until the base of the omelette is set and browned. Loosen the edges and invert the pan on to a plate to turn out the omelette. Then slide the omelette back into the pan and cook the second side for a few more minutes, until golden.

5 Cut the omelette into wedges, arrange on two plates and cool slightly. Serve with tomato wedges.

Pasta with Ham Sauce

Serves 2

50g/2oz dried pasta shapes

50g/2oz/½ cup frozen mixed
  vegetables

30ml/2 tbsp margarine

30ml/2 tbsp plain (all-purpose) flour

150ml/¼ pint/⅔ cup milk

50g/2oz/½ cup grated Red Leicester
  or mild cheese

2 slices ham, chopped

salt and pepper

3 Stir two-thirds of the grated
  cheese into the sauce and add the
drained pasta and vegetables, the
ham and a little salt and pepper.

4 Spoon into two shallow dishes
  and sprinkle with the remaining
cheese. Cool slightly if necessary.

TIP

This recipe works equally well if
you use a 100g/3½oz can tuna,
drained, in place of the ham. You
could serve the ham with rice, if
you prefer.

1 Cook the pasta in a pan of boiling
  water for 5 minutes. Add vegetables
and cook for 5 more minutes until
pasta is tender. Drain.

2 Melt the margarine in a
  medium-size pan and stir in the
flour. Gradually add the milk and
bring to the boil, stirring, until the
sauce is thick and smooth.

Quickie Kebabs

Serves 2–3

1 tomato
3 slices ham
½ small yellow (bell) pepper
6 button (white) mushrooms
6 cocktail sausages
10ml/2 tsp tomato ketchup
10ml/2 tsp oil
canned spaghetti, to serve

1 Preheat the grill (broiler). Cut the tomato into six wedges and cut each slice of ham into two strips. Roll up each strip. Cut the pepper into six chunks, discarding any seeds. Wipe the mushrooms.

2 Make six kebabs by threading a tomato wedge, a ham roll, a piece of pepper, a mushroom, and a sausage on to six cocktail sticks (toothpicks).

TIP
Use two rashers (strips) of rindless bacon, if preferred. Halve and roll up, and use in place of the ham.

3 Line a grill pan with foil and arrange the kebabs on top. Blend the ketchup and oil, and brush over the kebabs. Grill for 10 minutes, turning once and brushing with the juices until the vegetables are browned and the sausages are thoroughly cooked.

4 Cool slightly, then arrange on plates with canned spaghetti.

Sausage Wrappers

Serves 2

4 slices ham
10ml/2 tsp tomato relish or barbecue sauce
4 sausages
baked beans and grilled potato shapes, to serve

1 Spread one side of each slice of ham with relish or sauce.

2 Cut each piece of ham into three thin strips and wrap each sausage in three strips, securing them in place with cocktail sticks (toothpicks).

3 Grill (broil) for 10 minutes, turning several times until the ham is browned and crisp.

4 Cool slightly then remove the cocktail sticks and serve the sausage wrappers with baked beans and grilled potato shapes.

TIP
Use four pieces of rindless streaky (fatty) bacon instead of ham, if preferred.

Corned Beef Hash

Serves 2

1 potato, about 175g/6oz

10ml/2 tsp oil

50g/2oz green cabbage

115g/4oz corned beef

pinch of turmeric

15ml/1 tbsp tomato ketchup

hard-boiled egg slices, to garnish

1 Dice the potato and cook in a pan of boiling water for 3–4 minutes, until softened. Drain.

2 Heat the oil in a medium-size frying pan, add the diced potato and fry for 3 minutes, until golden.

3 Meanwhile, chop the cabbage and dice the corned beef.

4 Add the cabbage and turmeric to the pan with the potatoes and cook for 2 minutes. Stir in the corned beef and cook for 2 minutes.

5 Stir in the ketchup and spoon on to two plates. Cool slightly before serving. Garnish with the hard-boiled egg slices.

TIP

The hash can be garnished with tomato wedges, if liked.

Cannibal Necklaces

Serves 2

45ml/3 tbsp stuffing mix

60ml/4 tbsp boiling water

115g/4oz lean minced (ground) beef

5ml/1 tsp oil

½ carrot

1 strip red (bell) pepper

1 strip green (bell) pepper

a little tomato ketchup

1 Put the stuffing mix in a bowl and pour over the boiling water. Set aside for 5 minutes to soak.

2 Stir the meat into the stuffing mix and shape into 10 small balls with floured hands.

3 Preheat the grill (broiler). Arrange the meat balls on a piece of foil on top of the grill pan and brush lightly with a little oil. Grill (broil) for 7–8 minutes, until well browned, turning once during cooking.

4 Meanwhile, thinly slice the carrot and cut the pepper into chunks, discarding the core and seeds.

5 Arrange the meat balls around the bottom edge of two serving plates. Leave spaces in between.

TIP
If you're feeling adventurous, liven up simple meals by piping the child's initials on to the edge of the plate, the appropriate number for their age or even a short word like "hello".

6 Place carrot and pieces of red and green pepper between each meat ball and complete with a line and bow of ketchup for necklace strings, straight from the bottle, or pipe the ketchup if preferred.

Beef Burgers

Serves 2

1/4 small onion

25g/1oz button (white) mushrooms

115g/4oz lean minced (ground) beef

115g/4oz frozen oven chips (french fries)

2 burger buns

10ml/2 tsp tomato ketchup

1 tomato

salt and pepper (optional)

1 Finely chop the onion, wipe and chop the mushrooms. Place the meat in a mixing bowl, add the onion and mushrooms and a little salt and pepper, if liked, and mix together thoroughly. Alternatively blend the mixture in a processor.

2 With floured hands shape two 7.5cm/3in burgers or press the mixture into a plastic burger press or upturned pastry cutter.

3 Preheat the grill (broiler). Tear off two large pieces of foil. Fold up the edges and place on a grill pan. Put the burgers on one piece and the chips on the other.

4 Cook the burgers and chips for 10 minutes, turning the food once. Remove from the grill rack and keep warm. Split the burger buns in half and toast on one side only.

5 Spread the bases of the buns with ketchup, slice the tomato and place on the buns. Top each with a burger and the second bun half. Cut in half and arrange on serving plates with the chips. Cool slightly if necessary before serving.

Four Fast Fishes

Serves 2

115g/4oz hoki or cod fillet
½ egg, beaten
60ml/4 tbsp fresh breadcrumbs
10ml/2 tsp sesame seeds
10ml/2 tsp oil
15ml/1 tbsp frozen peas
4 frozen corn kernels
1 carrot
canned spaghetti rings, to serve

1 Cut away and discard any skin from the fish and rinse. Pat dry and cut into four pieces.

2 Put the egg in a saucer and place the breadcrumbs and sesame seeds on a plate. Dip pieces of fish in egg and then in breadcrumb mixture to coat the fish.

3 Heat the oil in a frying pan, add the fish and fry for 4–5 minutes, turning once, until the fish pieces are golden brown and cooked.

4 Meanwhile cook the peas and corn in a pan of boiling water for 5 minutes. Cut the carrot into long thin slices and then cut out fin and tail shapes and tiny triangles for mouths.

5 Arrange the pieces of fish on two plates with the carrot decorations, corn for eyes and peas for bubbles. Serve with warmed canned spaghetti rings.

TIP

You can freeze the uncooked breaded portions to provide a quick meal at a later date when you are pushed for time. Freeze them on a tray and then wrap them well to prevent the odour tainting other food in the freezer.

Tuna Risotto

Serves 2

5ml/1 tsp oil

¼ onion, finely chopped

50g/2oz long grain white rice

50g/2oz frozen mixed vegetables

1 small garlic clove, crushed

10ml/2 tsp tomato ketchup

100g/3½oz can tuna fish in water

salt and pepper (optional)

1 Heat the oil in a small pan and fry the chopped onion for about 3 minutes, until softened.

2 Add the rice, mixed vegetables, garlic, tomato ketchup and 250ml/8fl oz/1 cup water and a little salt and pepper, if liked.

TIP
If liked use cold leftover cooked chicken, lamb or beef in place of the tuna.

3 Bring to the boil and simmer uncovered for 10 minutes. Drain the tuna and add to the rice mixture, stirring to mix. Cook for 3–4 minutes, stirring occasionally, until the water has been absorbed by the rice and the rice is tender.

4 Spoon on to plates and cool slightly before serving.

Fish Finger Log Cabins

Serves 2

4 frozen fish fingers (breaded fish sticks)

25g/1oz green cabbage

8 mangetouts (snow peas)

2 frozen peas

1 strip green (bell) pepper

1 strip red (bell) pepper

1 Grill (broil) the fish fingers for 10 minutes, turning once until golden. Meanwhile, finely shred the cabbage and cook in boiling water for 3 minutes. Add the mangetouts and peas and cook for a further 2 minutes. Drain well.

2 Arrange two fish fingers side by side on each plate. Trim the mangetouts and use them to make a roof, slightly overlapping the edges of the fish fingers.

VARIATION
Sausage Log Cabin
Use four grilled (broiled) cocktail chipolata sausages for each cabin. Make the roof from green beans and use shredded spinach for the grass.

3 Cut four windows from the green pepper and two doors from the red pepper and add to the log cabins, using peas as door handles. Arrange the shredded cabbage to look like grass.

TOAST TOPPERS

ALL CHILDREN, EVEN THE FUSSIEST OF EATERS, LOVE BREAD AND TOAST, AND THERE IS NO QUICKER CONVENIENCE FOOD. RING THE CHANGES WITH THESE SUPER-SPEEDY SNACKS THAT WILL MAKE MEAL-TIMES FUN.

Shape Sorters

Serves 2

4 slices bread

butter or margarine, for spreading

30ml/2 tbsp smooth peanut butter

50g/2oz/½ cup grated Cheddar or mild cheese

4 cherry tomatoes

3 slices cucumber

VARIATION
Pizza Shape Sorters
Spread the shapes with tomato ketchup. Chop a tomato finely, and sprinkle over the shapes, then add some grated mild cheese. Grill (broil) until bubbly and golden.

1 Toast the bread lightly on both sides and remove crusts. Stamp out shapes using square, star, triangle and round cutters.

2 Spread the shapes with butter or margarine and then peanut butter. Place the shapes on a baking sheet and sprinkle with cheese.

3 Grill (broil) until the cheese is bubbly. Cool slightly, arrange on a plate and serve with tomato wedges and quartered cucumber slices.

Happy Families

Serves 2

3 slices bread

butter or margarine, for spreading

3 slices processed cheese

2 slices ham

a little mustard and cress (fine curled cress)

1 strip red (bell) pepper

½ carrot

small pieces of cucumber

1 Stamp out shapes of men and women from the bread, using small cutters. Spread with a little butter or margarine.

2 Stamp out cheese dresses using the woman cutter and trimming off the head. Press on to three of the bodies. Cut out cheese jumpers and ham trousers and braces. Add to the male shapes.

3 Snip off the leaves from mustard and cress and use for eyes. Cut tiny red pepper mouths and make necklaces and bow ties from the carrot and cucumber, using flower cutters. Arrange on plates.

French Toast Butterflies

Serves 2

4 small broccoli florets
8 peas
1 small carrot
1 slice Red Leicester or mild cheese
2 slices ham
2 slices bread
1 egg
10ml/2 tsp milk
5ml/1 tsp vegetable oil
a little tomato ketchup

1 Cook the broccoli florets and the peas in a pan of boiling water for 5 minutes. Drain well.

2 For each butterfly, cut four thin slices of carrot and cut into flower shapes with a petits four cutter. Cut out four small squares from the cheese.

3 Cut four thin strips from the rest of the carrot for antennae. Roll up each piece of ham and arrange in the middle of two serving plates, to make the two butterfly bodies.

4 Cut butterfly wings from the bread, using a small knife.

TIP

Vary the ingredients for the butterfly decorations. Make a body from a grilled sausage if preferred.

5 Beat together the egg and milk and dip the bread in to coat both sides thoroughly. Heat the oil in a medium-size frying pan and fry the bread until golden on both sides.

6 Assemble the butterfly, using the French toast for the wings and decorating with the carrot, cheese, broccoli and peas. Use a blob of ketchup for the head.

Tuna Flowers

Serves 2–3

6 thin slices bread
25g/1oz butter, plus extra if necessary
10ml/2 tsp plain (all-purpose) flour
75ml/5 tbsp milk
60ml/4 tbsp grated Red Leicester or mild cheese
100g/3½oz can tuna fish, drained
50g/2oz/4 tbsp frozen mixed vegetables, defrosted
½ carrot
6 slices cucumber, halved
a little mustard and cress (fine curled cress)
salt and pepper (optional)

1 Preheat the oven to 200°C/400°F/Gas 6. Cut out six flower shapes from the bread, using a 9cm/3½in scalloped cookie cutter. Flatten each piece slightly with a rolling pin.

2 Melt the butter in a pan or microwave. Brush a little over one side of each piece of bread and then press the bread, buttered side downwards, into sections of a patty tin (muffin pan). Brush the second side of the bread with a little more butter.

3 Bake in the oven for about 10–12 minutes, until crisp and golden around the edges.

4 Stir the flour into the remaining butter (you should have about 10ml/2 tsp left). Gradually stir in the milk and bring to the boil, stirring until the sauce is thick and smooth.

5 Stir in 30ml/3 tbsp of the cheese, the tuna, the mixed vegetables and a little salt and pepper, if liked.

6 Heat through and then spoon into the baked bread cups and sprinkle with remaining cheese.

7 Arrange the tuna cups on serving plates. Cut the carrot into thin strips for flower stems and add to the plate, with halved cucumber slices for leaves and mustard and cress for grass.

Noughts and Crosses

Serves 2

8 green beans

¼ red (bell) pepper

6 slices snack dried sausage

2 slices bread

butter or margarine, for spreading

115g/4oz Cheddar or mild cheese

TIP

To vary the topping, use thin strips of carrot or ham for the grid, sliced sausage, frankfurter or carrot for the noughts (zeros), carrot, green (bell) pepper or cucumber for the crosses.

1 Trim the beans, thinly slice the pepper, discarding any seeds, and thinly slice the sausage.

2 Cook the beans in boiling water for 5 minutes. Toast the bread lightly on both sides and spread with butter or margarine. Thinly slice the cheese and place on the toast.

3 Drain the beans and arrange four on each piece of toast to form a grid. Add crosses made from pepper strips and noughts from pieces of the sausage.

4 Grill (broil) the toasts until the cheese is bubbly. Arrange on plates and cool slightly before serving.

Cheese Strips on Toast

Serves 2

2 slices bread

butter or margarine, for spreading

50g/2oz Cheddar or mild yellow cheese

50g/2oz red Leicester or mild red cheese

2 cherry tomatoes, to serve

1 Toast the bread lightly on both sides, then spread each slice with butter or margarine.

TIP

If your child likes ketchup or peanut butter, add a thin scraping underneath the cheese slices for a surprise flavour.

2 Thinly slice the cheese and then cut into strips about 2.5cm/1in wide. Arrange alternate coloured cheese strips over the toast and grill (broil) the toasts until bubbly.

3 Cool slightly, then cut into squares, arrange on plates and serve with cherry tomato wedges.

Speedy Sausage Rolls

Makes 18

8 slices multigrain white bread

225g/8oz cocktail sausages

40g/1½oz/3 tbsp butter or
  margarine

carrot and cucumber sticks, to serve

1 Preheat the oven to 190°C/
  375°F/Gas 5. Trim the crusts off
the bread and cut into slices a little
smaller than the sausages.

2 Wrap each piece of bread around
  a sausage and secure with a
halved cocktail stick (toothpick). Place
the sausage rolls on a baking sheet.

3 Melt the butter or margarine in a
  small pan or in the microwave and
brush over the prepared sausage rolls.

TIP
Spread a little tomato relish or
ketchup, or a little mild mustard
over the bread before wrapping it
around the sausages, to give a
sharper flavour. If the bread is
thickly cut, flatten it slightly with a
rolling pin, before wrapping around
the sausages.

4 Bake in the oven for 15 minutes,
  until browned. Cool slightly
and remove the cocktail sticks.
Arrange on a plate and serve with
carrot and cucumber sticks.

Pizza Clock

Serves 3–4

20cm/8in ready-made pizza base

45ml/3 tbsp tomato ketchup or pizza sauce

2 tomatoes

75g/3oz/¾ cup grated mild cheese

pinch of dried marjoram

1 green (bell) pepper

1 large carrot

1 thick slice ham

1 Preheat oven to 220°C/425°F/ Gas 7. Place the pizza base on a baking sheet and spread with ketchup or pizza sauce. Chop the tomatoes and scatter over the pizza with the cheese and marjoram.

2 Place directly on an oven shelf and bake for 12 minutes, until the cheese is bubbly. (Place a baking tray on the shelf below the pizza to catch any drips of cheese.)

3 Meanwhile halve the pepper, cut away the core and seeds and stamp out the numbers 3, 6, 9 and 12 with small number cutters. Peel and thinly cut the carrot lengthways and stamp out the numbers 1, 2, 4, 5, 7, 8, 10 and 11. Arrange on the pizza to form a clock face.

4 Cut out a carrot circle. Cut two clock hands, each about 7.5cm/ 3in long from the ham. Arrange on the pizza with the circle of carrot.

5 Place the pizza clock on to a serving plate and arrange the numbers around the edge. Cool the pizza clock slightly before cutting into wedges and serving.

TIP

If preferred, make a smaller version of this using half a toasted muffin. Top as above and grill (broil) until the cheese melts. Add ham hands and small pieces of carrot to mark the numbers.

Spotted Sandwiches

Serves 2

1 hard-boiled egg

30ml/2 tbsp mayonnaise

2 slices white bread

2 slices brown bread

a little mustard and cress (fine curled cress)

½ small carrot

1 Peel and finely chop the egg, place in a small bowl and blend well with the mayonnaise.

2 Stamp out giraffe shapes from the brown and white bread, using an animal cookie cutter.

3 Cut tiny rounds from each shape, using the end of a metal piping tube, and then replace the rounds with opposite-coloured bread circles.

4 Spread the egg and mayonnaise over half of the shapes and top with the remaining shapes. Arrange on plates with snipped mustard and cress for grass and shaped carrot slices for flowers.

Sandwich Snails

Serves 2

1 strip red (bell) pepper

small piece cucumber

15ml/1 tbsp frozen corn, defrosted

25g/1oz/¼ cup grated Cheddar or mild cheese

15ml/1 tbsp mayonnaise

1 slice bread

2 cooked sausages

a little shredded lettuce

1 Cut away any seeds from the pepper and cut out four small squares for the snails' eyes. Cut four strips of cucumber for their antennae. Finely chop the remaining pepper and cucumber and mix with the corn, cheese and mayonnaise. Place in a bowl.

2 Trim the crusts off the bread, cut in half and overlap two short edges together to make a long strip. Flatten slightly with a rolling pin so that the bread bonds together.

VARIATION
For pasta snails, use large shell pasta instead of the bread, and stuff with the cheese mixture.

3 Spread the bread with the cheese mixture and roll up tightly. Squeeze together, then cut in half crossways to make two rounds.

4 Arrange each slice, cut side uppermost, on two serving plates. Arrange the sausages as bodies, and use the cucumber strips for antennae and the red pepper squares for the eyes. Arrange the shredded lettuce as grass.

EASY DESSERTS

WITH A YOUNG FAMILY TO FEED, DESSERTS NEED TO BE QUICK, LIGHT AND TASTE GOOD WITHOUT THE KIDS REALIZING THAT THEY'RE HEALTHY TOO! REMEMBER TO KEEP SUGAR TO A MINIMUM.

Fruit Fondue

Serves 2

150g/5oz tub ready-to-serve low-fat custard

25g/1oz milk chocclate

1 eating apple

1 banana

1 satsuma or clementine

a few strawberries or seedless grapes

1 Pour the custard into a pan, add the chocolate and heat, stirring all the time until the chocolate has melted. Cool slightly.

2 Quarter the apple, core and cut into bitesize pieces, slice the banana and break the satsuma or clementine into segments. Hull the strawberries and wash the grapes.

3 Arrange the fruit on two small plates, pour the custard into two small dishes and place on the plates. The fruit can be dipped into the custard, using either a fork or fingers.

TIP

Add the chocolate to a tub of custard and microwave on Full Power (100%) for 1½ minutes, or until the chocolate has melted. Stir and spoon into dishes. Cool slightly.

Strawberry Ice Cream

Makes 900ml/1½ pints/3¾ cups

300ml/½pint/1¼ cups double (heavy) cream

425g/15oz can custard

450g/1lb strawberries

teddy bear wafers, to decorate

strawberries, to decorate

1 Whip the cream until softly peaking, then fold in the custard.

2 Hull the strawberries and then rinse and pat dry. Process to make a smooth purée, then press through a sieve (strainer) into the cream and custard. Fold together.

3 Pour the mixture into a plastic tub and freeze the ice cream for 6-7 hours, until half frozen.

4 Beat the ice cream with a fork or process in a food blender until smooth, then return the tub to the freezer and freeze until solid.

5 Remove the ice cream from the freezer 10 minutes before serving so that it can soften slightly. Scoop into serving bowls and decorate each with teddy bear wafers and extra fruit, such as strawberries.

VARIATIONS
Strawberry Ripple Ice Cream
Purée and sieve (strain) an extra 250g/9oz strawberries and sweeten with 30ml/2 tbsp icing (confectioners') sugar. Swirl this into the half-frozen ice cream at Step 4 and then freeze until solid.

Apricot and Chocolate Chip Ice Cream
Whisk 300ml/½ pint/1¼ cups double (heavy) cream, and fold in 425g/15oz can custard. Drain and purée the contents of a 425g/15oz can apricot slices in natural juice and stir into the cream with the finely grated rind of 1 orange. Pour into a plastic tub, freeze until mushy and then beat well. Stir in 100g/3½oz packet chocolate dots and freeze again until solid. Scoop into serving dishes and decorate the ice cream with orange segments and wafers, if liked.

Raspberry Sorbet

Makes: 900ml/1½ pints/3¾ cups

10ml/2 tsp powdered gelatine

600ml/1 pint/2½ cups water

225g/8oz/1¼ cups caster (superfine) sugar

675g/1½lb raspberries, hulled

grated rind and juice of ½ lemon

1 Put 30ml/2 tbsp water in a cup, sprinkle the gelatine over and set aside for a few minutes to soak.

2 Place the water and sugar in a pan and heat, stirring occasionally, until the sugar has completely dissolved.

3 Bring to the boil and boil rapidly for 3 minutes. Remove from the heat, add the gelatine mixture to the syrup and stir until completely dissolved. Leave to cool.

4 Liquidize or process the raspberries to a smooth purée, then press through a sieve (strainer) into the syrup. Stir in the lemon rind and juice.

5 Pour into a plastic tub and freeze for 6–7 hours, or until the mixture is half frozen.

6 Beat the sorbet with a fork or transfer to a food processor and process until smooth. Return to the freezer and freeze until solid.

7 Remove the sorbet from the freezer 10 minutes before serving to soften slightly, then scoop into dishes with a melon baller or small teaspoon.

VARIATION
Summer Fruit Sorbet
Follow the recipe up to Step 3. Put a 500g/1¼lb pack of frozen summer fruits into a second pan. Add 60ml/ 4 tbsp water, cover and cook for 5 minutes until soft, then purée and sieve (strain), add to the syrup and continue as above.

Yogurt Lollies

Makes 6

150g/5oz tub strawberry yogurt

150ml/¼ pint/⅔ cup milk

10ml/2 tsp strawberry milkshake
powder

1 Mix the yogurt, milk and
milkshake powder together.

2 Pour the mixture into six small
lolly (popsicle) plastic moulds. Add
the handles and freeze overnight.

3 Dip the moulds into hot water,
count to 15, then flex handles and
remove. Serve at once.

TIP

Store lollies (popsicles) for up to a
week in the freezer. Make sure
they are tightly covered, as they
can pick up other flavours.

Jolly Jellies

Serves 4

150g/5oz packet strawberry jelly
 (flavoured gelatine)

2 ripe plums

175g/6oz fromage frais or Greek
 (US strained plain) yogurt

4 dolly mixtures (round candies)

10ml/2 tsp sugar or chocolate strands

1 Cut the jelly into pieces. Place in
a bowl and pour over 150ml/
¼ pint/⅔ cup boiling water. Stir
until dissolved, then set aside to cool.

2 Halve the plums, cut away the
stones (pits) and reserve four thin
slices. Chop the remaining fruit and
divide among four small dishes.

TIP

If the fussy eater doesn't like
different textures, finely chop or
purée the plums before adding to
the jelly (flavoured gelatine) so the
child doesn't know it's not just jelly!

3 Stir the fromage frais or yogurt
into the jelly and pour into the
dishes. Chill in the refrigerator
until set.

4 Decorate with sliced plums for
mouths, halved dolly mixtures
for the eyes and sugar or chocolate
sugar strands for hair.

Pancakes

Serves 2–3

50g/2oz/⅓ cup plain (all-purpose) flour

1 egg

150ml/¼ pint/⅔ cup milk

15ml/1 tbsp vegetable oil

For the filling

1 banana

1 orange

2–3 scoops ice cream

1 Sift the flour into a bowl, add the egg and gradually whisk in the milk to form a smooth batter. Whisk in 5ml/1 tsp of the oil.

2 To make the filling, slice the banana thinly or in chunks. Cut the peel away from the orange with a serrated knife, then cut the orange into segments.

3 Heat a little of the remaining oil in a medium-size non-stick pan, pour off any excess oil and add 30ml/2 tbsp of the batter. Tilt the pan to evenly coat it and cook for a couple of minutes, until the pancake is set and the underside is golden.

4 Loosen the edges with a knife, then toss the pancake or turn with a knife. Brown the other side and then slide out on to a plate. Fold in four and keep warm.

5 Cook the rest of the batter in the same way until you have made 6 pancakes. Place two on each plate.

6 Spoon a little fruit into each pancake and arrange on serving plates. Top with the remaining fruit and a scoop of ice cream, and pour over a little maple syrup. Serve at once.

Traffic Light Sundaes

Serves 6

½ packet lime jelly (flavoured gelatine)

½ packet orange jelly

½ packet strawberry jelly

2 kiwi fruits

275g/10oz can mandarin oranges

6 scoops vanilla ice cream, to serve

12 strawberries to decorate

4 Add a little kiwi fruit and continue making layers using the orange jelly and mandarins and topping with the strawberry jelly.

5 Add half the strawberries, top with a scoop of ice cream and decorate with the remaining strawberries. Serve immediately.

1 Make up each jelly in a separate bowl with boiling water according to the instructions on the packet. Cool, then transfer to the refrigerator and allow to set.

2 Peel and slice the kiwi fruits, hull and rinse the strawberries and cut in half. Drain the mandarins.

3 Chop all of the jellies and divide the lime jelly equally among six sundae glasses.

TIP

This is a great recipe for a party – simple but ever popular. For smaller numbers of children, halve the recipe to make three. For tiny children, make up half-size sundaes in plastic cups.

Cheat's Trifle

Serves 2

2 slices Swiss roll (jelly roll)

20ml/4 tsp orange juice

1 mandarin orange

50g/2oz strawberries

150g/5oz tub ready-to-serve custard

10ml/2 tsp Greek (US strained plain) yogurt

2 sugar flowers, to decorate

TIP
Use 150ml/¼ pint/⅔ cup leftover custard if you have it or make custard with custard powder and 150ml/¼ pint/⅔ cup milk.

1 Put a slice of Swiss roll in the base of two ramekin dishes and spoon the orange juice over the top. Peel the mandarin orange and divide the segments between the dishes.

2 Hull, rinse and chop the strawberries. Place in dishes.

3 Spoon the custard over the strawberries, top with yogurt and decorate with sugar flowers.

Baked Bananas

Serves 2

2 medium bananas

2 small scoops ice cream

1 Preheat the oven to 180°C/ 350°F/Gas 4. Separate the unpeeled bananas and put on a baking sheet. Cook for 10 minutes, until the skins have blackened and the bananas feel quite soft.

2 Hold the banana in a dish towel, make a slit along the length of the banana and peel off the skin. Peel the second banana.

3 Slice and arrange each as a ring on a plate. Place a scoop of ice cream in the centre of each plate.

TIP
For an adult version, slit the banana and spoon in a teaspoon or two of coffee cream liqueur, eat out of the skin with a teaspoon.

Quick Cakes and Bakes the Kids can Make

Cooking is fun, and the earlier you learn, the more fun it is. Even the faddiest eater can be an enthusiastic cook, and helping to decide what to cook for a meal can make a child more willing to sit down with the family and hand round their home–made goodies. Learning to weigh out ingredients, and to mix, spread and spoon out, all helps with co-ordination and encourages a basic interest in and love of food.

Getting ready
- Find a large apron or cover the child's clothes with an old adult-size shirt with the sleeves cut down.
- Always wash the child's hands before you start to cook.

- Choose a sturdy chair for your child to stand on next to the work surface or table. Alternatively, put a large cloth on the floor, set scales, bowls, ingredients etc out, and prepare food sitting down.

- Make it clear to your child that only the adult opens the oven door and touches pans on the stove.
- Keep knives and scissors out of the way; provide blunt, round-ended scissors if required.

Orange and Apple Rockies

Makes 24

oil, for greasing

115g/4oz/½ cup margarine

225g/8oz/2 cups self-raising (self-rising) flour

1 large eating apple

50g/2oz ready-to-eat dried apricots

50g/2oz sultanas (golden raisins)

grated rind of 1 small orange

75g/3oz/⅓ cup demerara (raw) sugar

1 egg

15ml/1 tbsp milk

apple slices, to serve

1 Preheat the oven to 190°C/375°F/ Gas 5 and brush two baking sheets with a little oil. Rub the margarine into the flour with your fingertips until the mixture resembles fine breadcrumbs.

2 Peel, core and finely chop the apple, chop the apricots and stir into the flour mixture with the sultanas and orange rind. Reserve 30ml/2 tbsp of the sugar and stir the rest into the mixture.

3 Beat the egg and milk, add to the flour mixture and mix until just beginning to bind together.

4 Drop spoonfuls, well spaced apart, on to the baking sheet. Sprinkle with the reserved sugar and bake in the oven for 12–15 minutes. Transfer to a serving plate and serve warm or cold with apple slices.

TIP
Freeze any left-over rockies in a plastic bag for up to three months.

Date Crunch

Makes 24 pieces

225g/8oz packet digestive biscuits (graham crackers)

75g/3oz stoned (pitted) dates

75g/3oz/⅓ cup butter

30ml/2 tbsp golden (light corn) syrup

75g/3oz sultanas (golden raisins)

150g/5oz milk or dark (bittersweet) chocolate

1 Line an 18cm/7in shallow baking tin (pan) with foil. Put the biscuits in a plastic bag and crush roughly with a rolling pin. Finely chop the dates.

2 Gently heat the butter and syrup in a small pan until the butter has melted.

TIP

For an alternative topping, drizzle 75g/3oz melted white and 75g/3oz melted dark (bittersweet) chocolate over the biscuit, to make random squiggly lines. Chill until set.

3 Stir in the crushed biscuits, the dates and sultanas and mix well. Spoon into the tin, press flat with the back of a spoon and chill for 1 hour.

4 Break the chocolate into a bowl, melt over hot water, and then spoon over the biscuit mixture, spreading evenly with a palette knife. Chill until set.

5 Lift the foil out of the tin and peel away. Cut the biscuit into 24 pieces and arrange on a plate.

Chocolate Dominoes

Makes 16

oil, for greasing

175g/6oz/¾ cup soft margarine

175g/6oz/⅞ cup caster (superfine) sugar

150g/5oz/⅔ cup self-raising
(self-rising) flour

25g/1oz cocoa powder (unsweetened)

3 eggs

For the Topping

175g/6oz/¾ cup butter, softened

25g/1oz cocoa powder (unsweetened)

300g/11oz/3 cups icing
(confectioners') sugar

a few liquorice strips and 115g/4oz
packet M & M's, for decoration

1 Preheat the oven to 180°C/350°F/
Gas 4. Brush an 18 × 28cm/7 × 11in
baking tin (pan) with a little oil and
line with baking parchment.

2 Put all the cake ingredients in a
bowl and beat until smooth.

3 Spoon into the tin and level the
surface with a palette knife.

4 Bake in the oven for 30 minutes,
or until the cake springs back
when pressed with the fingertips.

5 Cool in the tin for 5 minutes, then
loosen the edges with a knife and
turn out on to a wire rack. Peel off
the paper and allow the cake to cool.

6 Turn the cake on to a chopping
board and cut into 16 bars.

7 To make the topping, place the
butter in a bowl, sift in the cocoa
and icing sugar and beat until smooth.
Spread the topping evenly over the
cakes with a palette knife.

8 Add a strip of liquorice to each
cake, decorate with M & M's for
domino dots and arrange the cakes on
a serving plate.

VARIATION
Traffic Light Cakes
Makes 16
To make Traffic Light Cakes omit the
cocoa and add an extra 25g/1oz/3 tbsp
flour. Omit the cocoa from the icing
and add an extra 25g/1oz/3 tbsp icing
(confectioners') sugar and flavour with
2.5ml/½ tsp vanilla essence (extract).
Spread over the cakes and decorate
with eight halved red, yellow and
green glacé (candied) cherries to look
like traffic lights.

Marshmallow Krispie Cakes

Makes 45

oil, for greasing

250g/9oz bag toffees

50g/2oz/4 tbsp butter

45ml/3 tbsp milk

115g/4oz marshmallows

175g/6oz Rice Krispies

1 Lightly brush a 20 × 33cm/8 × 13in roasting pan with a little oil. Put the toffees, butter and milk in a pan and heat gently, stirring until the toffees have melted.

2 Add the marshmallows and Rice Krispies and stir until well mixed and the marshmallows have melted.

3 Spoon into the pan, level the surface and leave to set. Cut into squares, put into paper cases and serve.

Mini-muffins

Makes 24

200g/7oz/1½ cups plain (all-purpose) flour

10ml/2 tsp baking powder

50g/2oz/¼ cup soft light brown sugar

150ml/¼ pint/⅔ cup milk

1 egg, beaten

50g/2oz/4 tbsp butter or margarine, melted

50g/2oz glacé (candied) cherries

50g/2oz ready-to-eat dried apricots

2.5ml/½ tsp vanilla essence (extract)

2 Place the flour, baking powder and sugar in a bowl and add the milk, egg and melted butter or margarine. Stir thoroughly until the mixture is smooth.

1 Preheat the oven to 220°C/ 425°F/Gas 7 and place 24 petits fours cases in two mini patty tins (muffin pans).

3 Chop the cherries and apricots and stir into the muffin mixture with the vanilla essence.

4 Spoon the muffin mixture into the paper cases so they are about three-quarters full.

5 Cook for 10–12 minutes, until well risen and browned. If you have just one tin cook in two batches.

TIP
For older children, spoon the mixture into 12 medium-size muffin cases. Muffins are best served warm from the oven. If they aren't eaten immediately, they can be frozen for up to three months.

VARIATIONS
Chocolate Chip Muffins
Substitute 25g/1oz unsweetened cocoa powder for 25g/1oz/2 tbsp flour. Omit the cherries, apricots and vanilla and substitute 50g/2oz white and 50g/2oz plain (semisweet) chocolate dots.

Orange and Banana Muffins
Substitute 2 small mashed bananas for 60ml/2fl oz/¼ cup milk. Omit the cherries, apricot and vanilla, and add 15ml/1 tbsp grated orange rind.

Cup Cake Faces

Makes 12

115g/4oz/⅔ cup margarine
115g/4oz/⅔ cup caster (superfine) sugar
115g/4oz/1 cup self-raising (self-rising) flour
2 eggs
For the Topping
50g/2oz/¼ cup butter
115g/4oz/1 cup icing (confectioners') sugar
pink food colouring
115g/4oz packet M & M's
2 red liquorice bootlaces
12 dolly mixtures
75g/3oz plain (semisweet) chocolate

1 Preheat the oven to 180°C/350°F/ Gas 4. Place 12 paper cake cases in the sections of a patty tin (muffin pan). Put all the cake ingredients into a bowl and beat until smooth.

2 Divide the cake mixture among the cases and cook for 12–15 minutes, until well risen and the cakes spring back when pressed with a fingertip. Leave to cool.

3 Meanwhile, make the topping: beat the butter in a bowl, sift in the icing sugar and beat the mixture until smooth. Stir in a little pink food colouring.

4 Spread the icing over the cakes. Add M & M eyes, short pieces of liquorice for mouths and a dolly mixture nose.

5 Break the chocolate into pieces, melt in a bowl over a pan of gently simmering water and then spoon into a baking parchment piping (pastry) bag. Snip off the tip and pipe hair, eye balls, glasses and moustaches on to the cakes.

6 Carefully arrange in a single layer on a serving plate and allow the icing to set before serving.

VARIATION
Alphabet Cakes
Make up a half quantity of cake mixture as above and spoon into 24 mini muffin or petits fours cases. Put into sections of a patty tin (muffin pan) or petits fours tin (pan), or arrange on a baking sheet close together, and cook for 8–10 minutes, then cool. Blend 225g/8oz/2 cups sifted icing (confectioners') sugar with 30ml/2tbsp water until smooth. Add a little water if necessary, to make a thick spoonable icing. Spoon 30ml/2 tbsp into a piping (pastry) bag fitted with a small nozzle. Spoon half the remaining icing into a separate bowl and colour pink. Colour the remaining icing blue. Spoon the icing over the cakes, smooth the surface and pipe on letters of the alphabet. Leave to set.

Gingerbread People

Makes 24

oil, for greasing

225g/8oz/2 cups plain (all-purpose) flour

5ml/1 tsp ground ginger

1.5ml/¼ tsp ground cinnamon

7.5ml/1½ tsp bicarbonate of soda (baking soda)

50g/2oz/4 tbsp margarine

115g/4oz/⅔ cup soft light brown sugar

45ml/3 tbsp golden (light corn) syrup

30ml/2 tbsp milk

75g/3oz dark (bittersweet) chocolate

2 packets M & M's

1 Brush two baking sheets with a little oil. Sift the flour, spices and bicarbonate of soda into a bowl.

2 Place the margarine, sugar and syrup in a pan and heat until the margarine has melted.

3 Remove from heat and stir in the flour mixture and milk. Mix to a firm dough, chill for 30 minutes.

TIP

Chocolate decorations soften biscuits (cookies), so eat on the day or decorate as many biscuits as you will eat and store the rest in an air-tight container for up to four days.

4 Preheat the oven to 160°C/ 325°F/Gas 3. Knead the dough lightly and roll out on a floured surface. Cut out gingerbread men and women with 9cm/3½in cutters. Place on the baking sheets, re roll the trimmings, stamp out nine gingerbread people and continue until all the dough is used.

5 Cook for 10 minutes, until golden, and then set aside to cool and harden a little on the baking sheets. Loosen while still warm.

6 Break the chocolate into a bowl and melt over hot water, then spoon a little chocolate over the gingerbread men for trousers. Place on the baking sheets to set.

7 Spoon the remaining chocolate into a piping (pastry) bag fitted with a small nozzle and pipe faces on the gingerbread people and some swirls for petticoats on the women. Pipe two dots on all the people for buttons and stick on M & M's. Leave to set before serving.

Bread Animals

Makes 15

oil, for greasing

2 × 280g/10oz packets white bread mix

a few currants (raisins)

½ small red (bell) pepper

1 small carrot

1 egg

1 Brush two large baking sheets with a little oil. Put the bread mixes in a large bowl and make up as directed on the packet, with warm water.

2 Knead on a lightly floured surface for 5 minutes, until the dough is smooth and elastic. Return the dough to the bowl, cover with oiled clear film (plastic wrap) and leave in a warm place for ¾–1 hour, until it has doubled in size.

3 Preheat the oven to 220°C/425°F/Gas 7. Knead the dough again for 5 minutes and then divide into five pieces.

4 To make snakes, take one piece of dough, cut into three and shape each into a 15cm/6in snake, making a slit in one end for the mouth. Twist the snakes on the baking sheet. Insert two currants for eyes. Cut out a thin strip of pepper, cutting a triangle at one end for the forked tongue.

5 For hedgehogs, take another piece of dough and cut into three. Shape each into an oval about 6cm/2½in long. Place on the baking sheet and add currant eyes and a red pepper nose. Snip the dough with scissors to make the prickly spines.

6 For the mice, take a third piece of dough and cut into four pieces. Shape three pieces into ovals, each about 6cm/2½in long and place on the baking sheet. Shape tiny rounds of dough for ears and wiggly tails from the fourth piece of dough. Press on to the mice bodies and use the currants for eyes.

7 Cut small strips of carrot and use for whiskers.

TIP

Give a portion of the prepared dough to your children, with some chopped dried fruits, and allow them to create their very own bread animals.

8 For the crocodiles, cut another piece of dough into three. Take a small piece off each and reserve. Shape the large pieces into 10cm/4in long sausages. Make slits for the mouths and wedge open with crumpled foil. Add currant eyes. Shape the spare dough into feet and press into position. Make criss-cross cuts on the backs.

9 For rabbits, take the final piece of dough and cut into three. Take a small piece off each for tails. Roll the remaining pieces of dough into thick sausages 18cm/7in long. Loop the dough and twist twice to form the body and head of rabbit. Use the rest for tails.

10 Cover the shapes with oiled clear film and leave in a warm place for 10–15 minutes. Brush with beaten egg and cook for 10–12 minutes, until golden.

11 Serve warm or cold, split and filled with ham or cheese.

Cheese Shapes

Makes 15

oil, for greasing

350g/12oz/3 cups self-raising (self-rising) flour

pinch of salt

115g/4oz/½ cup margarine

115g/4oz Cheddar or mild cheese

2 eggs, beaten

60ml/4 tbsp milk

10ml/2 tsp sesame seeds

10ml/2 tsp poppy seeds

1 Preheat the oven to 220°C/ 425°F/Gas 7.

2 Place the flour and salt in a bowl, add the margarine and rub in with your fingertips, or use an electric mixer, until the mixture resembles fine breadcrumbs.

3 Grate the cheese, reserve 30ml/ 2 tbsp and stir the rest into the flour. Add three-quarters of the beaten eggs and milk to the flour and mix to a soft dough.

4 Knead the dough lightly and roll out thickly on a surface that has been dusted with flour.

5 Stamp out numbers with 7cm/3in cutters and arrange well spaced apart on two baking sheets. Re-roll trimmings and stamp out more shapes to use up the pastry.

6 Brush the tops of the numbers with the reserved egg. Sprinkle five of the numbers with sesame seeds, five with poppy seeds and the remainder with grated cheese.

7 Cook for 12–15 minutes, until well risen and browned. Cool slightly, then arrange the shapes on a plate and serve warm.

Marmite and Cheese Whirls

Makes 16

oil, for greasing

250g/9oz frozen puff pastry,
  defrosted

flour, for dusting

2.5ml/½ tsp Marmite

1 egg, beaten

50g/2oz Red Leicester, Cheddar or
  mild cheese, grated

carrot and cucumber sticks, to serve

1 Preheat the oven to 220°C/
425°F/Gas 7 and brush a large
baking sheet with a little oil.

2 Roll out the pastry on a floured
surface to a large rectangle,
about 35 × 25cm/14 × 10in.

3 Spread the pastry with Marmite,
leaving a 1 cm/½in border.
Brush the edges of the pastry with
egg and sprinkle the cheese to cover
the Marmite.

TIP

Omit the Marmite and use peanut
butter if preferred. If the shapes
become a little squashed when
sliced, reform into rounds by
opening out the layers with the end
of a knife.

4 Roll the pastry up quite tightly
like a Swiss roll (jelly roll), starting
from a longer edge. Brush the outside
of the pastry with beaten egg.

5 Cut the roll into thick slices and
place on the baking sheet.

6 Cook for 12–15 minutes until the
pastry is well risen and golden.
Arrange on a serving plate and serve
warm or cold with carrot and
cucumber sticks.

FAMILY MEALS

Eating together as a family takes on a new dimension as your family grows and there's a baby, fussy toddler and parents to feed together. Rather than attempting to prepare three different meals or to make one very simple meal you know the children will like, opt instead to cook three meals from one basic set of ingredients: a simple baby dinner, an eye-catching meal for even the fussiest of toddlers and a spicy dinner for the grown-ups.

The recipes are aimed at a baby aged nine months and over, a toddler or small child aged eighteen months to four years, and two adults.

Eating Together

Family meal-times should be a pleasure, but they can all too often turn into a battleground. Whatever family rules you have about table manners, it's important that the family knows about them and that you are consistent. What matters to some families may not be important to you. If you want your children to stay at the table until everyone has finished, make sure everyone understands this. Some parents may feel it's more relaxing if the children leave the table once they have finished, leaving the adults to eat the rest of their meal in relative peace. Whatever you decide, stick to it, and don't be browbeaten by well-meaning grandparents or friends. Try to eat together as a family at least once a day, even if you don't all

Left: *Part of the fun of eating together is sharing the preparation, too. Children love helping in the kitchen, and this involves them in the meal from the very start.*

Below: *A relaxed but polite atmosphere will enhance enjoyment and consequently encourage good eating habits.*

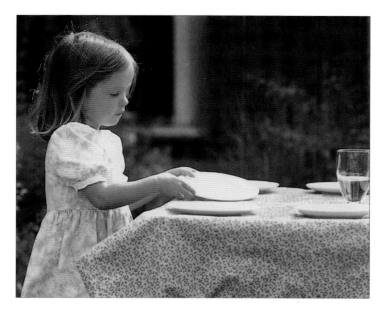

Similarly, beware of tiny hands reaching out from the high-chair to grab a mug of hot coffee or snatch a sharp knife.

Offer a variety of foods at each meal, some foods you know your toddler and baby will like and foods that you like too, so that everyone is happy. Offer very tiny portions of foods that are new or ones that your child is not very keen on, and encourage your child to have at least one mouthful.

Encourage the baby to feed herself with easy-to-pick-up finger foods. This gives the adults a chance to eat their food, too. Don't worry about the mess until you get to the end of the meal.

For added protection when your toddler is eating at the table, use a wipe-clean place mat and cover the seat of the dining chair with a towel or dish towel. Better still, buy a thin padded seat cover that is removable and machine-washable but will tie on to the seat securely.

Children cannot bear to eat foods that are too hot, not just because they may burn their mouth, but because of the frustration. Not being able to eat when the food is there and

eat the same food, so that your toddler can learn how to behave by watching the rest of the family. Explain to other members of the family that you are all setting an example for the baby – a great way to make everyone pull their socks up, whatever their age.

It is never too early to encourage children to help: laying (setting) the table can become quite a game, especially if dolly or teddy has a place set too. Passing plates, bread and salt and pepper can be perilous to begin with but with a little practice becomes second nature.

Transform a dull Monday meal-time into a special occasion with a few flowers or candles (well out of reach of very tiny children) and pretty table mats and paper napkins for added decoration.

Try to avoid using a tablecloth with very young children, as they can pull the cloth and everything with it on to the floor and themselves, with appalling consequences if there's a hot teapot or hot casserole dish.

Above: Laying the table is another task that children delight in, and another way to make them feel part of the family meal-time.

Below: Even if the child is too young to have exactly the same food, sharing the table is important.

they are hungry can lead to great outbursts of temper. Many children actually prefer their food to be just lukewarm. Cool broccoli quickly by rinsing with a little cold water. Spoon hot casseroles on to a large plate so they cool quickly, and always test the temperature of foods before serving to a child.

TABLE MANNERS

Toddlers can be incredibly messy, but try not to be too fussy and just wipe sticky hands and faces at the end of the meal. Enjoyment is the key. If your child is eating her meal with enthusiasm rather than style, then that is the most important part at the beginning – table manners will come as your child becomes more experienced and adept with a knife and fork.

Be understanding and flexible, as small children have a lot to learn when they begin to join in at family meals. An active toddler has to learn how to sit still – quite an art in itself – how to hold a knife and fork and how to drink from a cup,

Below and below right: *Never forget that food and eating are meant to be fun – don't discipline the child just for the sake of it, and don't impose adult rules too quickly.*

and somehow watch what everyone else is doing and join in too.

The baby has to adapt to sitting up at the table in his high-chair and waiting for an adult to offer him a spoonful of food. Not surprisingly, there can be a few tantrums and accidents, not to mention a mess. Try not to worry. Offer a few finger foods after a bowl of minced food so that the baby can feed himself, giving you a chance to finish your own meal and tidy up.

Above: *Good manners and sharing provide the perfect atmosphere for good eating.*

Left: Unusual and varied environments, and the different types of food that go with them, provide huge additional pleasure, and will also help to familiarize your child with situations he will encounter later.

TIPS

● Offer cubes of cheese at the end of a meal to help counteract the potentially harmful effects of any sugary foods eaten.

● Try to encourage children to eat more fruit. Cutting it into small pieces and arranging it on a plate can prove very inviting.

● Encourage children of all ages to drink full-fat (whole) milk, either cold, warm or flavoured, as it is a valuable source of the fat-soluble vitamins A and D and the important mineral calcium, vital for healthy bones and teeth.

● If you reheat baby food in the microwave, make sure you stir it thoroughly and leave it to stand for a couple of minutes so any hot spots can even out. Always check the temperature before serving.

● Always make sure a baby is well strapped into a high-chair and never leave children unattended while eating, in case of accidents.

● Children love the novelty of eating somewhere different. If it's a nice day, why not have a picnic in the local park. If eating outside, make food up separately.

● Snacks can play a vitally important part in a young child's diet, as their growth rate is so high it can be difficult to provide sufficient calories and protein at meal-times alone.

● Make sure you coordinate main meals and snacks so that you serve different foods and so that the snacks won't take the edge off the child's appetite for the main meal of the day.

● Try to limit sweets (candies) or cakes and fatty crisps (potato chips).

● Offer slices of fresh fruit, a few raisins or dried apricots, squares of cheese, a fruit yogurt or milky drink, Marmite or smooth peanut butter on toast.

● Make food fun and allow your child to choose where she eats her snack, e.g. in the camp in the garden or at the swings.

MEATY MAIN MEALS

TRYING TO PLEASE THE WHOLE FAMILY ALL OF THE TIME CAN BE A BIT OF A TALL ORDER, ESPECIALLY WHEN TRYING TO COOK TASTY MEALS ON A BUDGET. TRY THESE DELICIOUS NEW WAYS WITH QUICK-TO-COOK MINCE AND CHOPS, PLUS A SPEEDY STIR-FRY, OR SLOW-COOK BEEF BOURGUIGNON WITH CREAMED POTATOES, OSSO BUCCO PORK WITH RICE OR LAMB HOTPOT.

Mediterranean Lamb

3 lamb chump chops

350g/12oz courgettes (zucchini)

½ yellow (bell) pepper

½ red (bell) pepper

3 tomatoes

1 garlic clove, crushed

15ml/1 tbsp clear honey

few sprigs of fresh rosemary, plus extra to garnish

15ml/1 tbsp olive oil

200g/7oz can baked beans

salt and freshly ground black pepper

crusty bread, to serve

1 Rinse the chops under cold water, pat dry, trim off fat and place in the base of a grill (broiler) pan. Trim and slice the courgettes, cut away the core and seeds from the peppers and then rinse and cut into chunky pieces. Rinse and cut the tomatoes into quarters and arrange the vegetables around the lamb.

2 Season two of the chops for the adults with garlic, honey, rosemary and salt and pepper, and drizzle oil over the vegetables.

3 Cook under a hot grill for 12–14 minutes, turning once, until the lamb is well browned and cooked through and the vegetables are browned.

4 Warm the baked beans in a small pan. Drain and transfer the unseasoned chop to a chopping board and cut away the bone and fat. Thinly slice half the meat for the toddler and arrange on a plate with a few of the vegetables and 30–45ml/ 2–3 tbsp of the baked beans.

5 Chop or process the remaining lamb with four slices of courgette, two small pieces of pepper, two peeled tomato quarters and 15–30ml/1–2 tbsp of baked beans, adding a little boiled water if too dry. Spoon into a dish for the baby and test the temperature of the children's food before serving.

6 For the adult's portions, discard the cooked rosemary. Spoon the pan juices over the chops and garnish with fresh rosemary. Serve with crusty bread.

TIP
Lamb varies in price throughout the year. Depending on the season and price you may prefer to use lamb cutlets or loin chops. Allow two chops per adult and reduce the cooking time slightly, as these chops are smaller. Do not give honey to young children.

Lamb Hotpot

350g/12oz lamb fillet

1 onion

1 carrot

175g/6oz swede (rutabaga)

15ml/1 tbsp sunflower oil

30ml/2 tbsp plain (all-purpose) flour

450ml/¾ pint/1⅞ cups lamb stock

15ml/1 tbsp fresh sage or 1.5ml/
  ¼ tsp dried

½ dessert apple

275g/10oz potatoes

15g/½oz/1 tbsp butter

225g/8oz Brussels sprouts

salt and freshly ground black pepper

1 Preheat the oven to 180°C/
350°F/Gas 4. Rinse the lamb
under cold water, pat dry, trim away
any fat and then slice thinly. Peel and
chop the onion, carrot and swede.

2 Heat the oil in a large frying pan
and fry the lamb, turning until
browned on both sides. Lift the lamb
out of the pan, draining off any
excess oil, and transfer one-third to a
small 600ml/1 pint/2½ cup casserole
dish for the children and the rest to a
1.2 litre/2 pint/5 cup casserole dish
for the adults.

3 Add the vegetables to the pan
and fry for 5 minutes, stirring
until lightly browned.

4 Stir in the flour, then add the
stock and sage. Bring to the
boil, stirring, then divide between
the two casserole dishes.

5 Core, peel and chop the apple and
add both to the larger casserole
dish with a little seasoning.

6 Thinly slice the potatoes and
arrange overlapping slices over
both casserole dishes. Dot with
butter and season the larger dish.

7 Cover and cook in the oven for
1¼ hours. For a brown topping,
remove the lid and grill (broil) for a
few minutes at the end of cooking,
until browned. Cook the Brussels
sprouts in boiling water for 8–10
minutes, until tender, and drain.

8 Chop or process half the hotpot
from the small casserole, with a
few sprouts for the baby, adding
extra gravy if needed, until the
desired consistency is reached.
Spoon into a baby dish.

9 Spoon the remaining child's
hotpot on to a plate, add a few
sprouts and cut up any large pieces.
Test the temperature of the
children's food before serving.

10 Spoon the hotpot for the
adults on to serving plates
and serve with Brussels sprouts.

TIP
Traditionally neck (cross rib) or
scrag end of lamb would have
been used for making a hotpot.
This cut does require very long
slow cooking and can be fatty with
lots of bones so not ideal for
children. Fillet of lamb is very lean,
with very little waste and makes a
tasty and healthier alternative.

Beef Korma

350g/12oz lean minced (ground) beef

1 onion, chopped

1 carrot, chopped

1 garlic clove, crushed

400g/14oz can tomatoes

pinch of dried mixed herbs

25g/1oz pasta shapes

50g/2oz creamed coconut or
120ml/4fl oz/½ cup coconut milk

50g/2oz button (white) mushrooms

50g/2oz fresh spinach leaves

15ml/1 tbsp hot curry paste

salt and freshly ground black pepper

boiled rice, warm naan bread and a
little grated Cheddar cheese, to serve

1 Dry fry the meat and onion in a
medium-size pan, stirring until the
beef has browned.

2 Add the carrot, garlic, tomatoes
and herbs, bring to the boil,
stirring, and then cover and simmer
for about 30 minutes, stirring
occasionally.

3 Cook the pasta in a small pan of
boiling water for 10 minutes, until
tender. Drain.

4 Meanwhile place the coconut or
coconut milk in a small bowl, add
120ml/4fl oz/½ cup of boiling water
and stir until dissolved. Wipe and slice
mushrooms, and wash and drain
spinach, discarding any large stalks.

5 Transfer one-third of the meat
mixture to another pan. Stir the
coconut mixture, curry paste and
salt and pepper into the remaining
meat mixture and cook for about
5 minutes, stirring.

6 Mash or process one-third of the
pasta and reserved meat mixture to
the desired consistency for the baby
and spoon into a small dish.

7 Spoon the remaining pasta and
reserved meat mixture into a small
bowl for the older child.

8 Stir the mushrooms and spinach
into the curried beef and cook for
3–4 minutes, until the spinach has just
wilted. Spoon on to warmed
serving plates for the adults and
serve with boiled rice and warmed
naan bread. Sprinkle the toddler's
portion with a little grated cheese. Test
the temperature of the children's food
before serving.

TIPS

Weigh spinach after it has been
picked over and the stalks have
been removed or, buy ready-
prepared spinach. If you can't get
creamed coconut, use 120ml/4fl
oz/½ cup coconut milk instead, or
soak 25g/1oz/1 cup desiccated
(dry unsweetened shredded)
coconut in 150ml/¼ pint/⅔ cup
boiling water for 30 minutes, then
strain and use the liquid.

Bobotie with Baked Potatoes and Broccoli

3 medium baking potatoes

1 onion, chopped

350g/12oz lean minced (ground) beef

1 garlic clove, crushed

10ml/2 tsp mild curry paste

10ml/2 tsp wine vinegar

90ml/6 tbsp fresh breadcrumbs

15ml/1 tbsp tomato purée (paste)

25g/1oz sultanas (golden raisins)

15ml/1 tbsp mango chutney

1 medium banana, sliced

2 eggs

20ml/4 tsp turmeric

120ml/4fl oz/½ cup skimmed milk

4 small bay leaves

225g/8oz broccoli, cut into florets

30ml/2 tbsp fromage frais or Greek
  (US strained plain) yogurt

200g/7oz can baked beans

salt and freshly ground black pepper

1 Preheat the oven to 180°C/
350°F/Gas 4. Scrub the potatoes,
insert a skewer into each and bake
for 1½ hours, until tender.

2 Place the chopped onion and
225g/8oz of the beef in a pan and
dry fry, until browned all over, stirring
frequently.

3 Add the garlic and curry paste,
stir well and cook for 1 minute,
then remove from the heat and stir in
the vinegar, 60ml/4 tbsp of the
breadcrumbs, the tomato purée,
sultanas and a little salt and pepper.

TIP
Serve any leftover adult portions
cold with salad.

4 Chop up any large pieces of
mango chutney and stir into the
meat mixture with the banana slices.
Spoon into a 900ml/1½ pint/3¾ cup
ovenproof dish and press into an
even layer with the back of a spoon.

5 Place the dish on a baking sheet,
cover loosely with foil and cook
for 20 minutes.

6 Meanwhile, mix the remaining
beef with the remaining
breadcrumbs, then beat the eggs
together and stir 15ml/1 tbsp into
the meat. Make eight small
meatballs about the size of a grape
for the baby. Form the remaining
beef into a 7.5cm/3in burger, using an
upturned cookie cutter as a mould.

7 Blend the turmeric, milk and a
little salt and pepper with the
remaining eggs. Remove the cover
from the bobotie, and lay the bay
leaves over the meat.

8 Pour the egg mixture over.
Return to the oven for a further
30 minutes, until well risen and set.

9 When the adults' portion is
ready, heat the grill (broiler) and
cook the burger and meatballs until
browned, turning once. The burger
will take 8–10 minutes, while the
meatballs will take about 5 minutes.

10 Cook the broccoli in boiling
water until tender and drain.

11 Cut the bobotie for the adults
into wedges and serve with
baked potatoes topped with fromage
frais or Greek yogurt and broccoli.

12 Serve the toddler's burger
with half a potato, warmed
baked beans and a few broccoli
florets. Serve the baby's meatballs
with chunky pieces of peeled potato
and broccoli. Spoon a few baked
beans into a small dish for the baby.
Test the temperature of the food
before serving to the children.

Moussaka

1 onion, chopped

350g/12oz minced (ground) lamb

400g/14oz can tomatoes

1 bay leaf

1 medium aubergine (eggplant), sliced

2 medium potatoes

1 medium courgette (zucchini), sliced

30ml/2 tbsp olive oil

2.5ml/½ tsp grated nutmeg

2.5ml/½ tsp ground cinnamon

2 garlic cloves, crushed

salt and freshly ground black pepper

For the Sauce

30ml/2 tbsp margarine

30ml/2 tbsp plain (all-purpose) flour

200ml/7fl oz/1 cup milk

pinch of grated nutmeg

15ml/1 tbsp freshly grated Parmesan cheese

20ml/4 tsp fresh breadcrumbs

1 Dry fry the onion and lamb in a pan until browned, stirring. Add the tomatoes and bay leaf, bring to the boil, stirring, then cover and simmer for 30 minutes.

2 Place the aubergine slices in a single layer on a baking sheet, sprinkle with a little salt and set aside for 20 minutes. Preheat oven to 200°C/400°F/Gas 6.

3 Slice the potatoes thinly and cook in boiling water for 3 minutes. Add the courgette and cook for 2 minutes, until tender.

4 Remove most of the slices with a slotted spoon and place in a colander, leaving just enough for the baby portion. Cook these for 2–3 minutes more until soft, then drain. Rinse the vegetables and drain well.

5 Rinse the salt off the aubergine and pat dry. Heat the oil in a frying pan and fry the aubergines until browned on both sides. Drain.

6 Spoon 45ml/3 tbsp of the meat mixture into a bowl with the baby vegetables and chop or purée to the desired consistency.

7 Spoon 60ml/4 tbsp of the meat mixture into an ovenproof dish for the older child. Arrange four slices of potato, a slice of aubergine and three slices of courgette on top.

8 Stir the spices, garlic and seasoning into the remaining lamb mixture, and cook for 1 minute and then spoon into a 1.2 litre/ 2 pint/5 cup shallow ovenproof dish discarding the bay leaf.

9 Arrange the remaining potatoes overlapping on top of the lamb, and then add the aubergine slices, tucking the courgette slices in between the aubergines in a random pattern.

10 To make the sauce, melt the margarine in a small pan, stir in the flour, then gradually add the milk and bring to the boil, stirring until thickened and smooth. Add a pinch of nutmeg and a little salt and pepper.

11 Pour a little of the sauce over the toddler's portion, then pour the rest over the adults' portion. Sprinkle the larger dish with Parmesan cheese and 15ml/3 tsp breadcrumbs, sprinkling the remaining breadcrumbs over the toddler's portion.

12 Cook the moussakas in the oven. The larger dish will take 45 minutes, while the toddler's portion will take about 25 minutes.

13 Reheat the baby portion, and test the temperature of the children's food before serving.

Chilli con Carne

3 medium baking potatoes

1 onion, chopped

450g/1lb lean minced (ground) beef

1 carrot, chopped

½ red (bell) pepper, cored, seeded and diced

400g/14oz can tomatoes

10ml/2 tsp tomato purée (paste)

150ml/¼ pint/⅔ cup beef stock

3 small bay leaves

30ml/2 tbsp olive oil

115g/4oz button (white) mushrooms, sliced

2 garlic cloves, crushed

10ml/2 tsp mild chilli powder

2.5ml/½ tsp ground cumin

5ml/1 tsp ground coriander

200g/7oz can red kidney beans, drained

40g/1½oz frozen mixed vegetables

15ml/1 tbsp milk

knob (pat) of butter or margarine

60ml/4 tbsp fromage frais or Greek (US strained plain) yogurt

15ml/1 tbsp chopped fresh coriander (cilantro) leaves

salt and freshly ground black pepper

green salad, to serve

1 Preheat the oven to 180°C/ 350°F/Gas 4. Scrub and prick the potatoes and cook in the oven for 1½ hours. Dry fry the onion and beef in a pan until browned. Add the carrot and red pepper and cook for 2 minutes.

2 Add the tomatoes, tomato purée and stock and bring to the boil. Transfer one quarter of the mixture to a 600ml/1 pint/2½ cup casserole dish, add 1 of the bay leaves, cover with a lid and set aside.

3 Spoon the remaining meat mixture into a 1.2 litre/2 pint/ 5 cup casserole. Heat 15ml/1 tbsp of the oil in the same pan and fry the mushrooms and garlic for 3 minutes.

4 Stir in the spices and seasoning, cook for 1 minute, then add the drained red kidney beans and the remaining bay leaves and stir into the meat mixture. Cover and cook both dishes in the oven for 1 hour.

5 When the potatoes are cooked, cut into halves or quarters and scoop out the potato, leaving a thin layer of potato on the skin.

6 Brush the potato skins with the remaining oil and grill (broil) for 10 minutes, until browned.

7 Boil the frozen mixed vegetables for 5 minutes and mash the potato centres with milk and a knob of butter or margarine.

8 Spoon the meat from the smaller casserole into an ovenproof ramekin dish for the toddler and the rest into a bowl for the baby. Top both with some of the mashed potato.

9 Drain the vegetables, arrange two pea eyes, carrot pieces for the mouth and mixed vegetables for hair on the toddler's dish.

10 Spoon the remaining vegetables into a baby bowl and chop or process to the desired consistency. Test the temperature of the children's food before serving.

11 Spoon the adults' chilli on to warmed serving plates, add the potato skins and top with fromage frais or Greek yogurt and chopped coriander. Serve with a green salad.

Beef Bourguignon with Creamed Potatoes

450g/1lb stewing beef

15ml/1 tbsp vegetable oil

1 onion, chopped

30ml/2 tbsp plain (all-purpose) flour

300ml/½ pint/1¼ cups beef stock

15ml/1 tbsp tomato purée (paste)

small bunch of fresh herbs or 1.5ml/
¼ tsp dried

2 garlic cloves, crushed

90ml/6 tbsp red wine

75g/3oz shallots

75g/3oz button (white) mushrooms

25g/1oz/2 tbsp butter

450g/1lb potatoes

175g/6oz green cabbage

30–60ml/2–4 tbsp milk

salt and freshly ground black pepper

a few fresh herbs, to garnish

1 Preheat the oven to 160°C/
325°F/Gas 3. Trim away any fat
from the beef and cut into cubes.

2 Heat the oil in a frying pan, add
half of the beef and fry until
browned. Transfer to a plate and fry
the remaining beef and the chopped
onion until browned.

3 Return the first batch of beef to
the pan with any meat juices, stir
in the flour and then add the stock
and tomato purée. Bring to the boil,
stirring, until thickened.

4 Spoon one-third of the beef
mixture into a small 600ml/
½ pint/1¼ cup casserole dish for
the children, making sure that the
meat is well covered with stock.
Add a few fresh herbs or half a dried
bay leaf. Set the casserole aside.

5 Add the remaining herbs, garlic,
wine and seasoning to the beef
in the frying pan and bring to the
boil. Transfer the beef to a 1.2 litre/
2 pint/5 cup casserole dish. Cover
both dishes and cook in the oven
for about 2 hours, or until the meat is
very tender.

6 Meanwhile, halve the shallots if
they are large, wipe and slice
the mushrooms, cover and put to
one side.

7 Half an hour before the end of
cooking, fry the shallots in a
little butter until browned, then add
the mushrooms and fry for 2–3
minutes. Stir into the larger casserole
and cook for the remaining time.

8 Cut the potatoes into chunky
pieces and cook in a pan of
boiling, salted water for 20 minutes.
Shred the cabbage, discarding the
hard core, rinse and steam above the
potatoes for the last 5 minutes.

9 Drain the potatoes and mash
with 30ml/2 tbsp of the milk and
the remaining butter.

10 Chop or process one-third of
the child's casserole with a
spoonful of cabbage, adding extra
milk if necessary. Spoon into a dish
for the baby, with a little potato.

11 Spoon the remaining child's
casserole on to a plate for the
toddler. Remove any bay leaf and
cut up any large pieces of beef. Add
potato and cabbage.

12 Garnish the adults' casserole
with fresh herbs and serve
with potatoes and cabbage. Test the
temperature of the children's food.

Osso Bucco Pork with Rice

3 pork spare rib chops, about 500g/
1¼lb

15ml/1 tbsp olive oil

1 onion, chopped

1 large carrot, chopped

2 celery sticks, thinly sliced

2 garlic cloves, crushed

400g/14oz can tomatoes

few sprigs fresh thyme or 1.5ml/
¼ tsp dried

grated rind and juice of ½ lemon

150g/5oz/⅔ cup long grain rice

pinch of turmeric

115g/4oz green beans

knob (pat) of butter

20ml/4 tbsp freshly grated Parmesan
cheese

salt and freshly ground black pepper

1 or 2 sprigs parsley

1 Preheat the oven to 180°C/
350°F/Gas 4. Rinse the chops
under cold water and pat dry.

2 Heat the oil in a large frying pan,
add the pork, brown on both
sides and transfer to a casserole dish.

3 Add the onion, carrot and celery
to the frying pan and fry for
3 minutes, until lightly browned.

4 Add half the garlic, the
tomatoes, thyme and lemon
juice and bring to the boil, stirring.
Pour the mixture over the pork,
cover and cook in the oven for 1½
hours, or until tender.

5 Half fill two small pans with water
and bring to the boil. Add
115g/4oz/½ cup rice to one with a
pinch of turmeric and salt, add the
remaining rice to the second pan.
Return to the boil, and simmer.

6 Trim the beans and steam above
the larger pan of rice for 8
minutes, or until the rice is tender.

7 Drain both pans of rice, return
the yellow rice to the pan and
add the butter, Parmesan cheese and a
little pepper. Mix together well and
keep warm.

8 Dice one chop, discarding any
bone if necessary. Spoon a little
of the white rice on to a plate for the
toddler and add half of the diced
chop. Add a few vegetables and a
spoonful of the sauce. Process the
other half of chop, some vegetables,
rice and sauce to the desired
consistency and turn into a small
bowl for the baby.

9 Spoon the yellow rice on to the
adults' plates and add a pork
chop to each. Season the sauce to
taste and then spoon the sauce and
vegetables over the meat, discarding
the thyme sprigs if used. Finely chop
the parsley and sprinkle over the
pork with the lemon rind and the
remaining crushed garlic.

10 Serve the adults' and
toddler's portions with green
beans. Test the temperature of the
children's food before serving.

Pork Stir-fry

250g/9oz pork fillet (tenderloin)
1 courgette (zucchini)
1 carrot
½ green (bell) pepper
½ red (bell) pepper
½ yellow (bell) pepper
200g/7oz packet fresh beansprouts
20ml/4 tsp vegetable oil
25g/1 oz cashew nuts
150ml/¼ pint/⅔ cup chicken stock
30ml/2 tbsp tomato ketchup
10ml/2 tsp cornflour (cornstarch), blended with 15ml/1 tbsp cold water
1 garlic clove, crushed
10ml/2 tsp soy sauce
20ml/4 tsp yellow bean paste or hoisin sauce

1 Rinse the pork under cold water, cut away any fat and thinly slice. Halve the courgette lengthways, then thinly slice the carrot, and cut the peppers into strips, discarding the core and the seeds. Place the beansprouts in a sieve (strainer) and rinse well.

2 Heat 15ml/3 tsp of the oil in a wok or large frying pan, add the cashews and fry for 2 minutes, until browned. Drain and reserve.

3 Add the sliced pork and stir-fry for 5 minutes, until browned all over and cooked through. Drain and keep warm.

4 Add the remaining oil and stir-fry the courgette and carrot for 2 minutes. Add the peppers and fry for a further 2 minutes.

5 Stir in the beansprouts, stock, ketchup and the cornflour mixture, bring to the boil, stirring until the sauce has thickened.

6 Transfer 1 large spoonful of the vegetables to a bowl and 2–3 large spoonfuls to a plate for the children and set aside. Add the garlic and soy sauce to the pan and cook for 1 minute.

7 Chop or process four slices of pork with the baby's reserved vegetables to the desired consistency and turn into a baby bowl. Arrange six slices of pork on the toddler's plate with the reserved vegetables. Spoon the vegetables in the wok on to two adult serving plates.

8 Return the remaining pork to the wok with the nuts and yellow bean paste or hoisin sauce and cook for 1 minute. Spoon on to the adults' plates and serve immediately. Test the temperature of the children's food before serving.

Sausage Casserole

450g/1lb large sausages

15ml/1 tbsp vegetable oil

1 onion, chopped

225g/8oz carrots, chopped

400g/14oz can mixed beans in water, drained

15ml/1 tbsp plain (all-purpose) flour

450ml/¾ pint/1⅞ cup beef stock

15ml/1 tbsp Worcestershire sauce

15ml/3 tsp tomato purée (paste)

15ml/3 tsp soft brown sugar

10ml/2 tsp Dijon mustard

1 bay leaf

1 dried chilli, chopped

3 medium baking potatoes

salt and freshly ground black pepper

butter and sprigs of fresh parsley, to serve

1 Preheat the oven to 180°C/ 350°F/Gas 4. Prick and separate the sausages.

2 Heat the oil in a frying pan, add the sausages and cook over a high heat until evenly browned but not cooked through. Drain and transfer to a plate.

3 Add the chopped onion and carrots to the pan and fry until lightly browned. Add the drained beans and flour, stir well and then spoon one-third of the mixture into a small casserole. Stir in 150ml/ ¼ pint/⅔ cup stock, 5ml/1 tsp tomato purée and 5ml/1 tsp sugar.

4 Add the Worcestershire sauce, remaining beef stock, tomato purée and sugar to the pan, together with the mustard, bay leaf and chopped chilli. Season and bring to the boil, then pour the mixture into a large casserole.

5 Add two sausages to the small casserole and the rest to the larger dish. Cover both and cook in the oven for 1½ hours.

6 Scrub and prick the potatoes and cook on a shelf above the casserole for 1½ hours, until tender.

7 Spoon two-thirds of the child's casserole on to a plate for the toddler. Slice the sausages and give her two-thirds. Halve one of the baked potatoes, add a knob (pat) of butter and place on the toddler's plate.

8 Scoop the potato from the other half and mash or process with the remaining child's beans to the desired consistency for the baby. Spoon into a dish and serve the remaining sausage slices as finger food.

9 Spoon the adults' casserole on to plates, halve the other potatoes, add butter and garnish with parsley. Test the temperature of the children's food.

PERFECT POULTRY

WHATEVER THE AGE OF THE DINER, CHICKEN AND TURKEY ARE ALWAYS POPULAR. AVAILABLE IN A RANGE OF CUTS AND PRICES, THERE'S SOMETHING TO SUIT ALL BUDGETS AND TASTES, FROM A TASTY SALAD TO PAN-FRIED TURKEY WITH CORIANDER, TANDOORI-STYLE CHICKEN OR CHICKEN WRAPPERS WITH PESTO, HAM AND CHEESE.

Chicken and Thyme Casserole

6 chicken thighs

15ml/1 tbsp olive oil

1 onion, chopped

30ml/2 tbsp plain (all-purpose) flour

300ml/½ pint/1¼ cups chicken stock

few sprigs fresh thyme or 1.5 ml/ ¼ tsp dried

To Serve

350g/12oz new potatoes

1 large carrot

115g/4oz/¾ cup frozen peas

5ml/1 tsp Dijon mustard

grated rind and juice of ½ orange

60ml/4 tbsp fromage frais or natural (plain) yogurt

salt and freshly ground black pepper

fresh thyme or parsley, to garnish

1 Preheat the oven to 180°C/ 350°F/Gas 4. Rinse the chicken under cold water and pat dry.

2 Heat the oil in a large frying pan, add the chicken and brown on both sides, then transfer to a casserole.

3 Add the onion and fry, stirring until lightly browned. Stir in the flour, then add the stock and thyme and bring to the boil, stirring.

4 Pour over the chicken, cover and cook in the oven for 1 hour, or until tender.

5 Meanwhile, scrub the potatoes and cut any large ones in half. Cut the carrot into matchsticks.

6 Cook the potatoes in boiling water 15 minutes before the chicken is ready and cook the carrots and peas in a separate pan of boiling water for 5 minutes. Drain.

7 Take one chicken thigh out of the casserole, remove the skin and cut the meat away from the bone. Place in a food processor or blender with some of the vegetables and gravy and chop or process to the desired consistency. Turn into a baby bowl.

8 Take a second chicken thigh out of the casserole for the toddler, remove the skin and bone and slice if necessary. Arrange on a plate with some of the vegetables and gravy. Test the temperature of the children's food before serving.

9 Arrange two chicken thighs on warmed serving plates for the adults. Stir the mustard, orange rind and juice, fromage frais or yogurt, and seasoning into the hot sauce and then spoon over the chicken. Serve at once, with the vegetables, garnished with a sprig of thyme or parsley.

Tandoori-style Chicken

6 chicken thighs

150g/5oz natural (plain) yogurt

6.5ml/1¼ tsp paprika

5ml/1 tsp hot curry paste

5ml/1 tsp coriander seeds, roughly crushed

2.5ml/½ tsp cumin seeds, roughly crushed

2.5ml/½ tsp turmeric

pinch of dried mixed herbs

5ml/2 tsp vegetable oil

To Serve

350g/12oz new potatoes

3 celery sticks

10cm/4in piece cucumber

15ml/1 tbsp olive oil

5ml/1 tsp white wine vinegar

5ml/1 tsp mint

salt and freshly ground black pepper

few sprigs of watercress, knob (pat) of butter and cherry tomatoes, to serve

1 Cut away the skin from the chicken thighs and slash the meat two or three times with a small knife. Rinse under cold water and pat dry.

2 Place four thighs in a shallow dish, the other two on a plate. Place the yogurt, 5ml/1 tsp of the paprika, the curry paste, both seeds and almost all the turmeric into a small bowl and mix together. Spoon over the four chicken thighs.

3 Sprinkle the remaining paprika and the mixed herbs over the other chicken thighs and sprinkle the remaining pinch of turmeric over one thigh. Cover both dishes loosely with clear film (plastic wrap) and chill in the refrigerator for 2–3 hours.

4 Preheat the oven to 200°C/ 400°F/Gas 6. Arrange the chicken thighs on a roasting rack set over a small roasting pan and drizzle oil over the herbed chicken. Pour a little boiling water into the base of the pan and cook for 45–50 minutes, until the juices run clear when the chicken is pierced with a skewer.

5 Meanwhile, scrub the potatoes and halve any large ones. Cook in a pan of boiling water for 15 minutes, until tender.

6 Cut one celery stick and a small piece of cucumber into matchsticks. Chop or shred the remaining celery and cucumber.

7 Blend together the oil, vinegar, mint and seasoning in a bowl and add the chopped or shredded celery, cucumber and watercress, tossing well to coat.

8 Drain the potatoes and toss in a little butter. Divide the potatoes among the adults' plates, toddler's dish and the baby bowl. Cut the chicken off the bone for the toddler and arrange on a plate with half of the celery and cucumber sticks.

9 Cut the remaining chicken thigh into tiny pieces for the baby, discarding the bone, and allow to cool. Add to the bowl with the cooled potatoes and vegetable sticks and allow the baby to feed herself. Add a few halved tomatoes to each portion. Test the temperature of the children's food before serving.

10 For the adults, arrange the chicken thighs on warmed serving plates with the potatoes. Serve with the piquant salad.

Chicken Wrappers

3 boneless, skinless chicken breasts

5ml/1 tsp pesto

40g/1½oz thinly sliced ham

50g/2oz Cheddar or mild cheese

350g/12oz new potatoes

175g/6oz green beans

15g/½oz/1 tbsp butter

10ml/2 tsp olive oil

1 tomato

6 stoned (pitted) black olives

10ml/2 tsp plain (all-purpose) flour

150ml/¼ pint/⅔ cup chicken stock

15ml/1 tbsp crème fraîche or sour
    cream (optional)

1 Rinse the chicken under cold water and pat dry. Put one chicken breast between two pieces of clear film (plastic wrap) and bat out with a rolling pin. Repeat with the other two chicken breasts.

TIP
Depending on the age of the baby, you may prefer to omit the sauce and serve the meal as finger food, cutting it into more manageable pieces first.

2 Spread pesto over two of the chicken breasts and divide the ham among all three. Cut the cheese into three thick slices, then add one to each piece of chicken. Roll up so that the cheese is completely enclosed, then secure with string.

3 Scrub the potatoes, halve any large ones and cook in a pan of boiling water for 15 minutes, until tender. Trim the beans and cook in a separate pan of boiling water for 10 minutes.

4 Meanwhile, heat the butter and oil in a large frying pan, add the chicken and cook for about 10 minutes, turning several times, until well browned and cooked through.

5 Lift the chicken out of the pan, keeping the pieces spread with pesto warm, and leaving the other one to cool slightly.

6 Cut the tomato into wedges and halve the olives. Stir in the flour and cook for 1 minute. Gradually stir in the stock and bring to the boil, stirring until thickened. Add the tomato and olives.

7 Snip the string off the chicken and slice the children's chicken breast thinly. Arrange four chicken slices on a child's plate with a couple of spoonfuls of sauce and a few potatoes and green beans. (Don't offer olives unless the child is a very adventurous eater.)

8 Chop or process the remaining cut chicken with 30ml/2 tbsp of the sauce, one or two potatoes and three green beans to the desired consistency. Test the temperature of the children's food before serving.

9 Arrange the remaining chicken on plates. Add the crème fraîche or sour cream to the pan, if using, and heat gently. Spoon over the chicken and serve with vegetables.

Pan-fried Turkey with Coriander

3 turkey breast steaks

1 onion

1 red (bell) pepper, cored and seeded

15ml/1 tbsp vegetable oil

5ml/1 tsp plain (all-purpose) flour

150ml/¼ pint/⅔ cup chicken stock

30ml/2 tbsp frozen corn

150g/5oz/⅔ cup long grain white rice

1 garlic clove

1 dried chilli

50g/2oz creamed coconut or
   200ml/7fl oz/1 cup coconut cream

30ml/2 tbsp chopped fresh coriander
   (cilantro)

fresh coriander sprigs, to garnish

fresh lime wedges, to serve

1 Rinse the turkey steaks under cold water, and pat dry. Chop one of the steaks, finely chop one quarter of the onion and dice one quarter of the red pepper. Heat 5ml/ 1 tsp of the oil in a small frying pan and fry the diced turkey and chopped onion until lightly browned all over.

2 Stir in the flour, add the stock, corn and chopped pepper, then bring to the boil, cover and simmer for 10 minutes.

3 Cook the long grain rice in boiling water for 8–10 minutes, or until just tender. Drain.

4 Meanwhile, process or finely chop the remaining pieces of onion and red pepper with the garlic and chilli, including the seeds if you like hot food.

5 Put the coconut into a bowl, pour on 200 ml/7fl oz/1 cup boiling water and stir until it has completely dissolved.

6 Heat the remaining oil in a large frying pan. Brown the turkey breasts on one side, turn over and add the pepper paste. Fry for 5 minutes, until the second side of the turkey has also browned.

7 Pour the coconut milk over the turkey and cook for 2–3 minutes, stirring until the sauce has thickened slightly. Sprinkle with the chopped fresh coriander.

8 Chop or process one-third of the children's portion with 30ml/ 2 tbsp of the rice until the desired consistency is reached. Spoon into a baby bowl.

9 Spoon the child's portion on to a child's plate and serve with a little rice. Test the temperature of the children's food before serving.

10 Spoon the rest of the rice on to warmed serving plates for the adults, and add the turkey and sauce. Garnish with coriander sprigs and serve with lime wedges.

Chicken Salad

3 chicken breasts, boned and skinned

½ onion, chopped

1 carrot, chopped

150ml/¼ pint/⅔ cup chicken stock

few fresh herbs or a pinch of dried mixed herbs

30ml/2 tbsp butter or margarine

15ml/1 tbsp plain (all-purpose) flour

30ml/2 tbsp frozen corn, defrosted

3 slices bread

2 celery sticks

1 green eating apple

1 red eating apple

mixed green salad leaves, to serve

For the Dressing

45ml/3 tbsp natural (plain) yogurt

45ml/3 tbsp mayonnaise

5ml/1 tsp ground coriander

salt and freshly ground black pepper

1 Rinse the chicken breasts under cold water and place in a pan with the chopped onion and carrot, stock and herbs. Cover and cook for 15 minutes, or until the chicken is cooked through.

2 Cut one chicken breast into small dice, cutting the other two into larger pieces.

3 Strain the stock into a jug (cup), finely chop the carrot and remove and discard the onion and herbs.

4 Preheat the oven to 190°C/ 375°F/Gas 5. Melt 15ml/1 tbsp of the butter or margarine in a small pan, stir in the flour. Gradually stir in the strained stock and bring to the boil, stirring continuously, until the sauce is thick and smooth. Add the finely diced chicken, carrot and corn.

5 Cut the bread into three 7.5cm/ 3in squares, cutting the trimmings into tiny shapes, using cutters. Spread both sides of the squares and one side of the tiny bread shapes with the remaining butter or margarine. Press the squares into sections of a patty tin (muffin pan).

6 Bake the small shapes in the oven for 5 minutes and the squares for 10 minutes, until crisp and golden brown all over.

7 Rinse and thinly slice the celery, and quarter, core and chop half of each of the apples.

8 To make the salad dressing, blend the yogurt, mayonnaise, ground coriander and salt and pepper in a bowl. Add the thickly diced chicken and the celery, pepper and apples, and mix together.

9 Tear the salad leaves into pieces and arrange on the adults' serving plates. Spoon the chicken salad over the salad leaves.

10 Chop or process half of the child's chicken mixture to the desired consistency for the baby and spoon into a dish with the tiny bread shapes. Reheat the remaining mixture if necessary, spoon into the bread cases and arrange on a plate for the toddler. Slice the two apple halves, cutting the peel away from a few slices and add to the children's dishes. Check the temperature before serving to the children.

FISH DINNERS

Q UICK TO MAKE FOR EVERYDAY MEALS OR A SPECIAL OCCASION — HERE ARE SOME FISH RECIPES
FOR ANY DAY OF THE WEEK. CHOOSE FROM FRESH, FROZEN OR CANNED FISH FOR ADDED
CONVENIENCE. ENCOURAGE THE CHILDREN TO TRY HOME-MADE FISH CAKES, WITH A TASTY SAUCE FOR
THE ADULTS, EYE-CATCHING FISH VOL-AU-VENTS OR COLOURFUL SALMON AND COD KEBABS.

Paella

400g/14oz cod fillet
115g/4oz fish cocktail or a mixture of prawns (shrimp), mussels and squid
15ml/1 tbsp olive oil
1 onion, chopped
1 garlic clove, crushed
150g/5oz/⅔ cup long grain white rice
pinch of saffron or turmeric
few sprigs of fresh thyme or a pinch of dried thyme
225g/8oz can tomatoes
½ red (bell) pepper, cored, seeded and chopped
½ green (bell) pepper, cored, seeded and chopped
50g/2oz frozen peas
30ml/2 tbsp fresh chopped parsley
salt and freshly ground black pepper

1 Remove any skin from the cod
and place the fish cocktail in a
sieve (strainer) and rinse well with
cold water.

2 Heat the oil in a frying pan, add
the onion and fry until lightly
browned, stirring occasionally. Add
the garlic and 115g/4oz/½ cup of the
rice and cook for 1 minute.

3 Add the saffron or turmeric,
thyme, 2 of the canned
tomatoes, 350ml/12fl oz/1½ cups
water, and salt and pepper. Bring to
the boil and cook for 5 minutes.

4 Put the remaining rice and
canned tomatoes in a small pan
with 90ml/3fl oz/⅓ cup water.
Cover the pan and cook for about
5 minutes.

5 Add 15ml/1 tbsp of the mixed
peppers and 15ml/1 tbsp of the
frozen peas to the small pan, adding
all the remaining vegetables to the
large pan. Place 115g/4oz of the fish
in a metal sieve (strainer), cutting in
half if necessary. Place above a small
pan of boiling water, cover and steam
for 5 minutes. Add the remaining fish
to the paella in the large pan, cover
the pan and cook for 5 minutes.

6 Add the fish cocktail to the
paella, cover the pan and cook
for a further 3 minutes.

7 Stir the chopped parsley into the
paella and spoon on to two
warmed serving plates for the adults.
Spoon half of the tomato rice
mixture and half the fish on to a plate
for the child and process the
remaining fish and rice to the desired
consistency for the baby. Spoon into a
dish and check both children's meals
for bones. Test the temperature of
the children's food before serving.

Fish Cakes

450g/1lb potatoes, cut into pieces

450g/1lb cod fillet

75g/3oz prepared spinach leaves

75ml/5 tbsp full-fat (whole) milk

25g/1oz/2 tbsp butter

1 egg

50g/2oz/1 cup fresh breadcrumbs

25g/1oz drained sun-dried tomatoes

25g/1oz drained stuffed olives

115g/4oz Greek (US strained plain)
  yogurt

3 tomatoes, cut into wedges

½ small onion, thinly sliced

15ml/1 tbsp frozen peas, cooked

vegetable oil, for frying

salt and pepper

lemon and tomato wedges, sliced
  onion and green salad, to serve

1 Half fill a large pan or steamer base with water, add the potatoes and bring to the boil. Place the cod in a steamer top or in a colander above the pan. Cover and cook for 8–10 minutes, or until the fish flakes easily when pressed.

2 Take the fish out of the steamer and place on a plate. Add the spinach to the steamer, cook for 3 minutes, until just wilted, and transfer to a dish. Test the potatoes, cook for 1–2 minutes more if necessary, then drain and mash with 30ml/2 tbsp of the milk and the butter.

3 Peel away the skin from the fish, and break into small flakes, carefully removing any bones. Chop the spinach and add to the potato with the fish.

4 For the baby, spoon 45ml/3 tbsp of the mixture into a bowl and mash with another 30ml/2 tbsp of milk. Add a little salt and pepper, if liked, to the remaining fish mixture.

5 For the older child, shape three tablespoons of mixture into three small rounds with floured hands. For the adults, shape the remaining mixture into four cakes.

TIP
Make sure you remove all bones from the fish.

6 Beat the egg and the remaining milk on a plate. Place the breadcrumbs on a second plate and dip both the toddler and the adult fish cakes first into the egg and then into the crumb mixture.

7 Chop the sun-dried tomatoes and stuffed olives and stir into the yogurt with a little salt and pepper. Spoon into a small dish.

8 Heat some oil in a frying pan and fry the small cakes for 2–3 minutes on each side until browned. Drain well and arrange on a child's plate. Add tomato wedges for tails and peas for eyes.

9 Fry the adult fish cakes, in more oil if necessary, for 3–4 minutes on each side, until browned and heated through. Drain and serve with the dip, lemon and tomato wedges, thinly sliced onion and a green salad. Reheat the baby portion if necessary, but test the temperature of the children's food before serving.

Fish Vol-au-Vents

250g/9oz puff pastry, thawed if frozen

a little flour

beaten egg, to glaze

350g/12oz cod fillet

200ml/7fl oz/⅓ cup milk

½ leek

30ml/2 tbsp margarine

30ml/2 tbsp plain (all-purpose) flour

50g/2oz fresh prawns (shrimp)

salt and pepper

broccoli, young carrots and mangetouts (snow peas), to serve

1 Preheat the oven to 220°C/ 425°F/Gas 7. Roll out the pastry on a lightly floured surface to make a rectangle 23 × 15cm/9 × 6in. Cut into three 7cm/3in wide strips.

2 Cut two fish shapes from one strip. Knock up edges with a knife and cut an oval shape just in from the edge and almost through to the bottom of the pastry. Place the fish shape on a wet baking tray.

TIP
You may find it easier to cut a fish shape out of paper and then use this as a template on the pastry.

3 Neaten the edges of the remaining pastry strips, then cut smaller rectangles 1cm/½in in from the edge of both and remove.

4 Roll out the smaller rectangles to the same size as the pastry frames. Brush the edges with a little egg and place the frames on top.

5 Transfer to the baking sheet. Knock up the edges of both rectangles with a small knife and flute between finger and thumb. Repeat the whole process with the third strip of pastry.

6 Stamp out tiny fish shapes from the pastry trimmings, re-rolling if necessary, and place on the baking sheet. Brush the top of the vol-au-vents with beaten egg and cook for 10 minutes. Remove the small fish and cook the larger vol-au-vents for a further 5 minutes, until they are well risen and golden brown.

7 Meanwhile make the filling. Cut the fish in two and put in a pan with the milk. Halve the leek lengthways, wash thoroughly, then slice and add to the pan.

8 Cover and simmer for 6–8 minutes, or until the fish flakes easily when pressed with a knife. Lift out of the pan, peel away the skin and then break into pieces, removing and discarding any bones.

9 Strain the milk, reserving the leeks. Melt the margarine, stir in the flour and then gradually add in the milk and bring to the boil, stirring until thick and smooth.

10 Stir the fish into the sauce. Scoop out the centres of the fish-shaped vol-au-vents and fill with a little mixture. Spoon 30ml/2 tbsp of fish mixture into a baby bowl.

11 Add a prawn to each fish-shaped vol-au-vent and stir the rest into the pan with the leeks and a little seasoning. Heat gently and spoon into the two large pastry cases (pie shells). Transfer to plates and serve with steamed vegetables.

12 Chop the baby portion with some vegetables, and serve this with some tiny pastry fishes, if wished, in a small bowl. Check the temperature of the children's food before serving.

Salmon and Cod Kebabs

200g/7oz salmon steak
275g/10oz cod fillet
15ml/3 tsp lemon juice
10ml/2 tsp olive oil
2.5ml/½ tsp Dijon mustard
350g/12oz new potatoes
200g/7oz frozen peas
50g/2oz/4 tbsp butter
15–30ml/1–2 tbsp milk
3 tomatoes, chopped, seeds discarded
¼ round (butterhead) lettuce, finely shredded
salt and freshly ground black pepper
For the Mustard Sauce
1 sprig fresh dill
20ml/4 tsp mayonnaise
5ml/1 tsp Dijon mustard
5ml/1 tsp lemon juice
2.5ml/½ tsp soft dark brown sugar

1 Rinse the fish under cold water and pat dry. Cut the salmon steak in half, cutting around the central bone. Cut away the skin and then cut into chunky cubes, making sure you remove any bones. Remove the skin from the cod and cut into similar sized pieces.

2 Cut a few pieces of fish into smaller pieces and thread on to five cocktail sticks (toothpicks). Thread the remaining fish pieces on to long wooden skewers.

3 Mix together the lemon juice, oil, Dijon mustard and a little salt and pepper to taste in a small bowl and set aside.

4 Finely chop the dill and place in a bowl with the other sauce ingredients and mix. Set aside.

5 Scrub the potatoes, halve any large ones and then cook in lightly salted water for 15 minutes, or until tender. Place the peas and half of the butter in a frying pan, cover and cook very gently for 5 minutes.

6 Preheat the grill (broiler), place the kebabs on a baking sheet and brush the larger kebabs with the lemon, oil and mustard mixture. Grill (broil) for 5 minutes, until the fish is cooked, turning once.

7 Remove the fish from two cocktail sticks and mix in a small bowl with a few new potatoes and 15ml/1 tbsp of the peas. Chop or process with a little milk until the desired consistency is reached, then transfer to a baby bowl.

8 Arrange the toddler's kebabs on a small serving plate with a few potatoes, 30ml/2 tbsp peas and a small amount of chopped tomato. Remove the cocktail sticks from the kebabs before serving.

9 Add the tomatoes to the remaining peas and cook for 2 minutes, then stir in the shredded lettuce and cook for 1 minute. Spoon on to serving plates for the adults, add the kebabs and potatoes, and serve.

CAUTION

For younger toddlers, it would be safer to remove the cocktail sticks before serving.

Tuna Florentine

50g/2oz pasta shapes

175g/6oz fresh spinach leaves

50g/2oz frozen mixed vegetables

200g/7oz can tuna in brine

2 eggs

buttered toast and grilled (broiled)
tomatoes, to serve

For the Sauce

25g/1oz/2 tbsp margarine

45ml/3 tbsp plain (all-purpose) flour

300ml/½ pint/1¼ cups milk

50g/2 oz/½ cup grated Cheddar or
mild cheese

1 Cook the pasta in boiling water
for 10 minutes. Meanwhile, tear
off any spinach stalks, wash the
leaves in plenty of cold water and
place in a steamer or colander.

2 Stir the frozen vegetables into
the pasta as it is cooking, and
then place the spinach in the steamer
over the top. Cover and cook for the
last 3 minutes, or until the spinach
has just wilted.

TIP
Frozen vegetables are usually
more nutritious than fresh
vegetables, as they are frozen at
their peak of perfection – they're
a great time-saver too.

3 Drain the pasta and vegetables
through a sieve (strainer). Chop
one quarter of the spinach and add to
the pasta and vegetables, dividing the
remainder between two shallow
300ml/½ pint/1¼ cup ovenproof
dishes for the adults.

4 Drain the tuna and divide among
the dishes and sieve (strain).

5 Refill the pasta pan with water,
bring to the boil, then break the
eggs into the water and gently
simmer until the egg whites are set.
Remove the eggs with a slotted
spoon, trim the whites and shake off
all the water. Arrange the eggs on
top of the tuna for the adults.

6 To make the sauce, melt the
margarine in a small pan, stir in
the flour, then gradually add the milk
and bring to the boil, stirring until
thick and smooth.

7 Stir the cheese into the sauce,
reserving a little for the topping.
Spoon the sauce over the adults'
portions until the eggs are covered.
Stir the children's pasta, vegetables
and tuna into the remaining sauce
and mix together.

8 Spoon the pasta on to a plate for
the toddler and chop or process
the remainder for the baby, adding a
little extra milk, if necessary, to make
the desired consistency. Spoon into a
dish. Test the temperature of the
children's food before serving.

9 Preheat the grill (broiler),
sprinkle the adults' portions with
the reserved cheese and grill for
4–5 minutes, until browned. Serve
with buttered toast and grilled
(broiled) tomatoes.

VEGETABLE FEASTS

MORE AND MORE OF US ARE OPTING TO EAT LESS MEAT FOR EITHER HEALTH OR BUDGETARY REASONS. EATING LESS MEAT DOESN'T MEAN LOSING OUT ON FLAVOUR – FAR FROM IT! CHOOSE FROM MEALS SUCH AS PENNE WITH TOMATO SAUCE, CHEESE AND VEGETABLE CRUMBLE OR SLOW-COOKED, SPICED VEGETABLE TAGINE.

Cheese on Toast

2 thick slices bread

2 thin slices bread

butter or margarine, for spreading

5ml/1 tsp Marmite (optional)

2 thin slices ham

1 garlic clove, halved

15ml/1 tbsp olive oil

200g/7oz Cheddar or mild cheese

1 tomato

6 stoned (pitted) black olives

15ml/1 tbsp chopped fresh basil

a few red onion slices

cucumber sticks and green salad, to serve (optional)

1 Toast all the bread and spread the thin slices with butter or margarine. Spread one slice with Marmite, if using, and top this with ham.

2 Drizzle the oil over the thick slices of toast, then rub with the cut surface of the garlic.

3 Thinly slice the cheese and place over all of the pieces of toast.

4 Slice the tomato and halve the olives. Arrange on the thick toast for the adults, season with pepper and add basil and onion.

5 Grill until the cheese is bubbly. Cut the plain cheese on toast into tiny squares, discarding crusts. Arrange on a small plate for the baby and allow to cool. Cut the Marmite and/or ham-topped toast into triangles and arrange on a plate. Add cucumber sticks to the toddler's portion and test the temperature before serving.

6 Slice the adults' toast and arrange on plates, with a green salad if liked, and serve.

Penne with Tomato Sauce

150g/5oz penne or small pasta quills

1 onion

2 celery sticks

1 red (bell) pepper

15ml/1 tbsp olive oil

1 garlic clove, crushed

400g/14oz can tomatoes

2.5ml/½ tsp caster (superfine) sugar

8 stoned (pitted) black olives

10ml/2 tsp pesto

1.5ml/¼ tsp dried chilli seeds (optional)

50g/2oz/½ cup grated Cheddar or mild cheese

salt and freshly ground black pepper

10ml/2 tsp freshly grated Parmesan cheese, to serve

green salad, to serve (optional)

1 Cook the pasta in salted boiling water for about 10–12 minutes, until just tender.

2 Meanwhile, chop the onion and the celery. Cut the pepper in half, then scoop out the core and seeds and dice the pepper finely.

3 Heat the oil in a second pan, add the vegetables and garlic and fry for 5 minutes, stirring until lightly browned.

4 Add the tomatoes and sugar and cook for 5 minutes, stirring occasionally, until the tomatoes are broken up and pulpy.

5 Drain the pasta, return to the pan and stir in the tomato sauce.

6 Spoon 45–60ml/3–4 tbsp of the mixture into a bowl or processor and chop or process to the desired consistency for the baby. Spoon 75–90ml/5–6 tbsp of the mixture into a bowl for the toddler.

7 Quarter the olives and stir into the remaining pasta with the pesto, chilli seeds if using, and a little salt and pepper. Spoon into dishes.

8 Sprinkle the grated cheese over all the dishes, and serve the adults' portions with the Parmesan cheese, and a green salad if wished. Test the temperature of the children's food before serving.

Courgette Gougère

50g/2oz/4 tbsp butter

65g/2½oz plain (all-purpose) flour

2 eggs

2.5ml/½ tsp Dijon mustard

115g/4oz Cheddar or mild cheese

salt and pepper

For the Filling

15ml/1 tbsp olive oil

350g/12oz courgettes (zucchini), sliced

1 small onion, chopped

115g/4oz button (white) mushrooms, sliced

225g/8oz tomatoes, skinned and chopped

1 garlic clove, crushed

20ml/4 tsp chopped fresh basil

1 Preheat the oven to 220°C/425°F/ Gas 7 and grease a large baking sheet. Place the butter in a medium pan with 150ml/¼ pint/⅔ cup water. Heat gently until the butter has melted, then bring to the boil.

2 Remove the pan from the heat and quickly add the flour, stir well, then return to the heat and cook for 1–2 minutes, stirring constantly until the mixture forms a smooth ball. Leave to cool for 10 minutes.

3 Beat the eggs, mustard and a little salt and pepper together. Cut 25g/1oz of the cheese into small cubes and grate the rest.

4 Add 50g/2oz of the grated cheese to the dough and then gradually beat in the eggs to make a smooth, glossy paste.

5 Spoon the mixture into a large piping (pastry) bag fitted with a medium plain nozzle. Pipe whirls close together on the baking sheet to make an 18cm/7in circular shape.

6 Pipe the remaining mixture into small balls for the baby and into the older child's initials.

7 Sprinkle the top with the remaining grated cheese.

8 Bake for 15–18 minutes for the small shapes and 25 for the ring, until well risen and browned.

9 Heat the oil in a frying pan, add the courgettes and onion, and fry until lightly browned. Add the mushrooms, fry for a further 2 minutes and then add the tomatoes. Cover and simmer for 5 minutes, until the vegetables are cooked.

10 Spoon a little mixture into the baby's bowl or into a food processor, and chop or process to the desired consistency. Serve with a few cheese balls and a little diced cheese.

11 Spoon a little on to a plate for the toddler, add an initial and the remaining diced cheese. Test the temperature of the children's food before serving.

12 Transfer the cheese ring to a serving plate and split in half horizontally. Stir the garlic, basil and a little extra seasoning into the courgette mixture and heat through. Spoon over the bottom half of the cheese ring and add the top half. Serve the gougère immediately.

TIP

Beat the gougère mixture, cheese and eggs together in a food processor, if preferred.

Cheese Vegetable Crumble

1 onion
225g/8oz carrot
175g/6oz swede (rutabaga)
175g/6oz parsnip
15ml/1 tbsp olive oil
220g/7½oz can red kidney beans
10ml/2 tsp paprika
5ml/1 tsp ground cumin
15ml/1 tbsp plain (all-purpose) flour
300ml/½ pint/1¼ cups vegetable stock
225g/8oz broccoli, to serve
For the Topping
115g/4oz Cheddar or mild cheese
50g/2oz wholemeal (whole-wheat) flour
50g/2oz plain (all-purpose) flour
50g/2oz margarine
30ml/2 tbsp sesame seeds
25g/1oz blanched almonds
salt and freshly ground black pepper

1 Preheat the oven to 190°C/ 375°F/Gas 5. Peel and roughly chop the onion. Then peel and cut the carrot, swede and parsnip into small cubes. Heat the oil in a large pan and fry the vegetables for 5 minutes, stirring until lightly browned.

2 Drain the kidney beans and add to the pan with the spices and flour. Stir well, add the stock, then cover and simmer for 10 minutes.

3 Meanwhile, make the topping. Cut a few squares of cheese for the baby and grate the rest. Put the two flours in a bowl, add the margarine and rub in with your fingertips until the mixture resembles fine breadcrumbs. Stir in the grated cheese and sesame seeds.

4 Spoon a little of the vegetable mixture into a 300ml/½ pint/ 1¼ cup ovenproof dish for the toddler. Spoon the remaining mixture into a 900ml/1½ pint/ 3¾ cup ovenproof pie dish for the adults, leaving a little vegetable mixture in the pan for the baby. Season the adults' portion with a little salt and pepper.

VARIATION
Lentil and Herb Crumble
Substitute canned lentils for the red kidney beans. Instead of the paprika and cumin, use 30ml/2 tbsp chopped, fresh mixed herbs. Add more fibre and nuttiness by replacing the plain (all-purpose) flour with rolled oats.

5 Spoon 45ml/3 tbsp of crumble over the older child's portion. Roughly chop the almonds, add to the remaining crumble with a little salt and pepper and spoon over the large dish. Bake in the oven for 20 minutes for the small dish, and 30 minutes for the large dish, until golden brown on top.

6 Add 90ml/3fl oz/⅓ cup water to the baby's portion, cover and cook for 10 minutes, stirring occasionally, until the vegetables are very tender. Mash or process to the desired consistency and spoon into a bowl.

7 Cut the broccoli into florets and cook for 5 minutes, or until tender; drain. Spoon the toddler's portion out of the dish and on to a small plate. Serve the broccoli to all members of the family, allowing the baby to pick up and eat the broccoli and cubed cheese as finger food. Check the temperature before serving to the children.

Note: Never give whole nuts to children under five, as they may choke.

Vegetable Tagine

1 onion

225g/8oz carrots

225g/8oz swede (rutabaga)

75g/3oz prunes

20ml/4 tsp olive oil

425g/15oz can chickpeas

2.5ml/½ tsp turmeric

10ml/2 tsp plain (all-purpose) flour, plus extra for dusting

2 garlic cloves, finely chopped

450ml/¾ pint/1⅞ cups chicken stock

15ml/1 tbsp tomato purée (paste)

2cm/¾in piece fresh root ginger

2.5ml/½ tsp ground cinnamon

3 cloves

115g/4oz couscous

8 green beans

2 frozen peas

piece of tomato

knob (pat) of butter or margarine

salt and freshly ground black pepper

fresh coriander (cilantro), to garnish

1 Peel and chop the onion, and peel and dice the carrots and swede. Cut the prunes into chunky pieces, discarding the stones (pits).

2 Heat 15ml/3 tsp of the olive oil in a large pan, add the onion and fry until lightly browned. Stir in the carrots and swede and fry for 3 minutes, stirring.

3 Drain the chickpeas and stir into the pan with the turmeric, flour and garlic. Add 300ml/½ pint/1¼ cup of the stock, the tomato purée, and the prunes. Bring to the boil, cover and simmer for 20 minutes, stirring occasionally.

4 Place three heaped spoonfuls of mixture in a bowl or food processor, draining off most of the liquid. Mash or process and then form the mixture into a burger with floured hands.

5 Chop or process two heaped spoonfuls of mixture and sauce to the desired consistency for the baby and spoon into a bowl.

6 Finely chop the root ginger and stir into the remaining vegetable mixture with the cinnamon, cloves, remaining stock and seasoning.

7 Place the couscous in a sieve (strainer), rinse with boiling water and fluff up the grains with a fork. Place the sieve above the vegetables, cover and steam for 5 minutes.

8 Fry the veggie burger in the remaining oil until browned on both sides. Trim and cook the beans and peas for 5 minutes. Drain and arrange on a plate like an octopus, with a piece of tomato for a mouth and peas for eyes.

9 Stir the butter or margarine into the couscous and fluff up the grains with a fork. Spoon on to warmed serving plates for adults, add the vegetable mixture and garnish with a sprig of coriander. Check the temperature of the children's food before serving.

Stilton and Leek Tart

175g/6oz/1½ cups plain (all-purpose) flour

75g/3oz/6 tbsp butter

1 carrot

2 slices ham

10cm/4in piece of cucumber

mixed green salad leaves, to serve

For the Filling

25g/1oz/2 tbsp butter

115g/4oz trimmed leek, thinly sliced

75g/3oz Stilton (blue) cheese, diced

3 eggs

175ml/6fl oz/¾ cup milk

40g/1½oz Cheddar or mild cheese, grated

pinch of paprika

salt and pepper

1 Put the flour in a bowl with a pinch of salt. Cut the butter into pieces and rub into the flour with your fingertips until the mixture resembles fine breadcrumbs.

2 Mix to a smooth dough with 30–35ml/6–7 tsp water, knead lightly and roll out thinly on a floured surface. Use to line an 18cm/7in flan dish, trimming round the edge and reserving the trimmings.

3 Re-roll the trimmings and then cut out six 7.5cm/3in circles, using a fluted cookie cutter. Press the pastry circles into sections of a patty tin (muffin pan) and chill all of the tarts.

4 Preheat the oven to 190°C/375°F/Gas 5. For the filling, melt the butter in a small frying pan and fry the leek for 4–5 minutes, until soft but not brown, stirring frequently. Turn into a bowl, stir in the diced Stilton, and then spread over the base of the large tart.

5 Beat the eggs and milk together in a small bowl and season with salt and pepper.

6 Divide the grated Cheddar among the small tartlet shells and pour some of the egg mixture over. Pour the remaining egg mixture over the leek and Stilton tart and sprinkle with paprika.

7 Cook the small tartlets for 15 minutes and the large tart for 30–35 minutes, until well risen and browned. Leave to cool.

8 Peel and coarsely grate the carrot. Cut the ham into triangles for "sails". Cut the ham trimmings into small strips for the baby. Cut the cucumber into matchsticks.

9 Place a spoonful of carrot, some cucumber, a small tart and some ham trimmings in the baby dish. Spread the remaining carrot on to a plate for the older child, place the tarts on top and secure the ham "sails" with cocktail sticks (toothpicks). Serve any remaining tarts the next day. Cut the large tart into wedges and serve with a mixed leaf salad.

JUST DESSERTS

No one can resist a dessert, although looking after a young family may mean it's more of a weekend treat than an everyday occurrence. Spoil the family with a selection of these tasty hot and cold treats, from fruity Eve's Pudding and Plum Crumble to Chocolate and Orange Trifle or Strawberry Pavlova – all guaranteed to get them clamouring for seconds.

Bread and Butter Pudding

3 dried apricots

45ml/3 tbsp sultanas (golden raisins)

30ml/2 tbsp sherry

7 slices white bread, crusts removed

25g/1oz/½ tbsp butter, softened

30ml/2 tbsp caster (superfine) sugar

pinch of ground cinnamon

4 eggs

300ml/½ pint/1¼ cups milk

few drops of vanilla essence (extract)

pouring cream, to serve

2 Preheat the oven to 190°C/ 375°F/Gas 5. Spread the bread with butter and cut one slice into very small triangles. Layer in a 150ml/¼ pint/⅔ cup pie dish with plain apricots and sultanas and 5ml/ 1 tsp of the sugar.

4 Beat the eggs, milk and vanilla together and pour into the ramekin and two pie dishes.

1 Chop two dried apricots and place in a small bowl with 30ml/ 2 tbsp of the sultanas and the sherry. Set aside for about 2 hours. Chop the remaining apricot and mix with the remaining sultanas.

3 Cut the remaining bread into larger triangles and layer in a 900ml/1½ pint/3¾ cup pie dish with the sherried fruits and all but 5ml/ 1 tsp of the remaining sugar, sprinkling the top with cinnamon. Put the last 5ml/1 tsp sugar in a small ramekin dish.

5 Stand the ramekin dish in a large ovenproof dish and half fill with hot water. Cook the small pie dish and the ramekin for 25–30 minutes, until the custard has just set, and the larger pudding for 35 minutes, until the bread has browned. Serve the adult portions with cream, if liked.

Eve's Pudding

500g/1¼lb cooking apples

50g/2oz/¼ cup caster (superfine) sugar

50g/2oz frozen or canned
  blackberries

For the Topping

50g/2oz/4 tbsp butter or margarine

50g/2oz/¼ cup caster (superfine) sugar

50g/2oz/⅓ cup self-raising
  (self-rising) flour

1 egg

½ lemon, rind only

15ml/1 tbsp lemon juice

icing (confectioners') sugar, for
  dusting

custard, to serve

1 Preheat the oven to 180°C/350°F/
Gas 4. Peel and slice the cooking
apples, discarding the core, and then
place in a pan with the caster sugar
and 15ml/1 tbsp water. Cover and
cook gently for 5 minutes, until
the apple slices are almost tender
but still whole.

2 Half fill a 150ml/¼ pint/⅔ cup
ovenproof ramekin with apple
for the toddler and mash 30ml/2 tbsp
of apple for the baby in a small bowl.

3 Put the remaining apple slices
into a 600ml/1 pint/2½ cup
ovenproof dish. Sprinkle the
blackberries over the apple slices.

4 To make the topping, place the
butter or margarine, sugar, flour
and egg in a bowl and beat until
smooth. Spoon a little of the
pudding mixture over the toddler's
ramekin so that the mixture is
almost to the top of the dish.

5 Half fill three petits fours cases
with the pudding mixture.

6 Grate the lemon rind and stir
with the juice into the remaining
mixture. Spoon over the large dish,
levelling the surface.

7 Put the small cakes, toddler and
adult dishes on a baking sheet and
bake in the oven for 8–10 minutes for
the small cakes, 20 minutes for the
ramekin and 30 minutes for the larger
dish, until they are well risen and
golden brown.

8 Dust the toddler's and adults'
portions with icing sugar and
leave to cool slightly before serving
with the custard. Warm the baby's
portion if liked, and test the
temperature before serving, with the
cakes taken out of their paper cases.

TIP
If you can't get blackberries, then
use raspberries instead. There's no
need to defrost before using, as
they will soon thaw when added
to the hot apple.

Orange and Strawberry Shortcakes

75g/3oz/6 tbsp plain (all-purpose) flour

50g/2oz/4 tbsp butter

25g/1oz/2 tbsp caster (superfine) sugar

grated rind of ½ orange

extra sugar, for sprinkling

For the Filling

175g/6oz Greek (US strained plain) yogurt

15ml/1 tbsp icing (confectioners') sugar

250g/9oz strawberries

5ml/1 tsp Cointreau (optional)

2 sprigs of fresh mint, to decorate

1 Preheat the oven to 180°C/350°F/ Gas 4. Place the flour in a bowl, cut the butter into pieces, and rub into the flour with your fingertips until the mixture resembles fine breadcrumbs.

2 Stir in the sugar and orange rind and mix to a dough.

3 Knead the dough lightly, then roll out on a floured surface to 5mm/¼in thickness. Stamp out four 9cm/3½in flower shapes or fluted rounds with a cookie cutter, and 12 small car, train or other fun shapes with novelty cutters, re-rolling the dough as necessary.

4 Place the shapes on a baking sheet, prick with a fork and sprinkle with a little extra sugar. Bake in the oven for 10–12 minutes, until pale golden, then leave to cool on the baking sheet.

5 For the filling, blend the yogurt with the sugar and wash and hull the strawberries. Pat dry. Reserve eight of the strawberries and process or liquidize the rest. Press through a sieve (strainer) and discard the seeds.

6 For the adults, put 45ml/3 tbsp of the yogurt in a bowl and stir in the Cointreau, if using. Slice four strawberries and halve two, place on a plate and cover.

7 For the toddler, slice two of the strawberries and arrange in a ring on a small plate. Spoon 30ml/ 2tbsp of yogurt into the centre of the ring and serve with three of the small biscuit (cookie) shapes.

8 For the baby, stir 15ml/1 tbsp of the strawberry purée into the remaining natural yogurt and spoon into a small dish. Serve with one or two of the small biscuit shapes.

9 To complete the adults' portions, spoon purée over two plates to cover completely.

10 Spoon the reserved yogurt over two biscuits, add the sliced strawberries and top with the other two biscuits. Arrange on plates and decorate with halved strawberries and tiny sprigs of mint.

TIP
If you find shortbread difficult to roll out, then chill for 20 minutes. Knead lightly and roll out on a surface dusted with flour, dusting the rolling pin too.

Exotic Fruit Brûlée

oil, for greasing

30ml/2 tbsp demerara (raw) sugar

1 ripe mango

1 kiwi fruit

1 passion fruit

30ml/2 tbsp icing (confectioners') sugar

350g/12oz Greek (US strained plain)
  yogurt

1 Line a baking sheet with foil, then
with a pencil draw round the tops
of two 250ml/8fl oz/1 cup ramekin
dishes and one 150ml/¼ pint/⅔ cup
ramekin dish. Lightly brush with
oil. Sprinkle the sugar inside each
marked circle in an even layer.

2 Grill the sugar discs for 2–3
minutes, or until the sugar has
melted and caramelized. Leave the
discs to cool on the baking sheet.

3 Slice the mango on either side of
the central stone (pit) and then cut
six thin slices for decoration, cutting
away the skin. Cut the rest of the
mango flesh from the stone, removing
the skin, and finely chop one quarter,
dividing between the baby bowl and
small ramekin. Roughly chop the
remainder and divide between the
larger ramekins.

4 Peel the kiwi fruit, cut in half
lengthways and then slice thinly.
Reserve four half slices for
decoration and divide the remaining
fruit among the dishes, finely
chopping the fruit for the baby and
toddler. Cut the passion fruit in half
and, using a teaspoon, scoop out and
place the seeds in the adults' dishes.

5 Stir the icing sugar into the
yogurt and mix 15ml/1 tbsp into
the baby's portion. Spoon 30ml/2
tbsp yogurt over the toddler's dish
and level the surface with a spoon.

6 Spoon the remaining yogurt
into the other two ramekins,
level the surface with a spoon and
chill all of them until required.

7 When ready to serve, place the
larger ramekins on two plates
with the reserved mango and kiwi
slices arranged around the sides. Peel
the sugar discs off the foil and set on
top of the adult and toddler portions.
Serve the brulees immediately.

TIP

Traditionally, the sugar topping on a
brulee is made by sprinkling
demerara sugar over the top of the
dessert and then grilling (broiling),
or by making a caramel syrup and
then pouring it over the dessert.
Making the topping on oiled foil is
by far the easiest and most foolproof
way. Add the cooled sugar discs at
the very last minute so that they
stay crisp and you get that wonderful mix of crunchy sugar, velvety
yogurt and refreshing fruit.

Plum Crumble

450g/1lb ripe red plums

25g/1oz/2 tbsp caster (superfine) sugar

For the Topping

115g/4oz/1 cup plain (all-purpose) flour

50g/2oz/4 tbsp butter, cut into pieces

25g/1oz/2 tbsp caster (superfine) sugar

10ml/2 tsp chocolate dots

75g/3oz marzipan

30ml/2 tbsp rolled oats

30ml/2 tbsp flaked (sliced) almonds

custard, to serve

1 Preheat the oven to 190°C/ 375°F/Gas 5. Wash the plums, cut into quarters and remove the stones (pits). Place in a pan with the sugar and 30ml/2 tbsp water, cover and simmer for 10 minutes.

2 Drain and spoon six plum quarters on to a chopping board and chop finely. Spoon the plums into a small baby dish with a little juice from the pan.

3 Drain and roughly chop six more of the plum quarters and place in a 150ml/¼ pint/⅔ cup ovenproof ramekin dish with a little of the juice from the pan.

4 Spoon the remaining plums into a 750ml/1¼ pint/3⅔ cup ovenproof dish for the adults.

5 Make the topping. Place the flour in a bowl, rub in the butter and then stir in the sugar.

6 Mix 45ml/3 tbsp of the crumble mixture with the chocolate dots, then spoon over the ramekin.

7 Coarsely grate the marzipan and stir into the remaining crumble with the oats and almonds. Spoon over the adults' portion.

8 Place the toddler and adult portions on a baking sheet and cook for 20–25 minutes, until golden brown. Leave to cool slightly before serving. Warm the baby's portion if liked and check the temperature of the children's food before serving. Serve with custard.

TIP

Ovens can vary in temperature: with fan-assisted ovens you may need to cover the adults' dish with foil halfway through cooking to prevent overbrowning.

Vary the fruits: cooking apples, peaches and pears also work well. If the plums are very sharp, you may need to add a little extra sugar.

Chocolate and Orange Trifle

½ chocolate Swiss roll (jelly roll)

3 clementines or satsumas

20ml/4 tsp sherry

50g/2oz dark (bittersweet) chocolate

300ml/½ pint/1¼ cups ready-made custard

90ml/6 tbsp double (heavy) cream

chocolate buttons or M & M's

1 Slice the Swiss roll, halve one slice and put on a plate for the baby. Put a second slice into a ramekin dish for the older child and arrange the remaining slices in two dessert bowls for the adults.

2 Peel one clementine, separate into segments and put a few on the baby plate. Chop the rest and add to the ramekin.

3 Peel the remaining clementines, roughly chop and add to the adults' bowls, sprinkling a little sherry over each.

4 Break the chocolate into pieces and melt in a bowl over a pan of hot water. Stir the melted chocolate into the custard.

5 Spoon 30ml/2 tbsp of the custard into a small bowl for the baby and arrange on the plate with the Swiss roll and fruit. Spoon a little more custard into the ramekin and then add the rest to the adult dishes, smoothing the surface.

6 Whip the cream until it just holds its shape. Add a spoonful to the ramekin dish and two or three spoonfuls each to the adults' dishes, decorating each dish with sweets (candies). Chill until required.

TIPS
Chocolate may be melted in the microwave in a microwave-safe bowl for 2 minutes on Full Power (100%), stirring thoroughly halfway through cooking.

Some shops sell ready-made chocolate custard. Buy this if it's available and you're short of time.

Vary the fruits depending on what is in season. Sliced strawberries and orange, or sliced banana and fresh or canned cherries also work well.

Apple Strudel

450g/1lb cooking apples

50g/2oz dried apricots

45ml/3 tbsp sultanas (golden raisins)

30ml/2 tbsp soft light brown sugar

30ml/2 tbsp ground almonds

5ml/1 tsp ground cinnamon

25g/1oz/2 tbsp butter

150g/5oz/3 sheets filo pastry, defrosted if frozen

icing (confectioners') sugar, to dust

pouring (half-and-half) cream, to serve

1 Preheat the oven to 200°C/ 400°F/Gas 6. Peel, core and chop the apples and place 150g/5oz in a pan. Chop three apricots and add to the pan with 15ml/1 tbsp sultanas, 15ml/1 tbsp sugar and 15ml/1 tbsp water. Cover and simmer for 5 minutes.

2 Chop the remaining apricots and place in a bowl with the remaining apples, sultanas, sugar, ground almonds and cinnamon. Mix together well.

3 Melt the butter in a small pan, or microwave in a microwave-proof bowl for 30 seconds on Full Power (100%).

4 Carefully open out the pastry. Place one sheet on the work surface, brush with butter, then cover with a second sheet of pastry and brush with more butter.

5 Spoon the uncooked apple mixture in a thick band along the centre of the pastry.

6 Fold the two short sides up and over the filling and brush with butter. Fold the long sides up and over the filling, opening out the pastry and folding the pastry for an attractive finish. Place on a baking sheet and brush with a little butter.

7 Brush a little of the butter over half of the third pastry sheet, then fold the unbrushed half over the top to make a square. Brush again and cut into three equal strips.

8 Put a spoonful of apple at the base of each strip, then fold the bottom right-hand corner up and over the filling, to the left side of the strip, to make a triangle.

9 Continue folding the pastry to make a triangular pasty. Repeat with the other strips.

10 Transfer to a baking sheet and brush with the remaining butter. Bake for 10 minutes, and the adults' strudel for 15 minutes, until golden and crisp. Dust with icing sugar and cool slightly.

11 Spoon the remaining cooked apple mixture into a baby dish. Mash the fruit if necessary. Transfer the toddler's portion to a plate. Slice the strudel thickly and serve with cream.

TIP
Filo pastry is usually sold frozen in 275g/10oz packets or larger. Defrost the whole pack, take out as much pastry as you need, then re-wrap the rest and return to the freezer.

Strawberry Pavlova

2 egg whites

115g/4oz caster (superfine) sugar

2.5ml/½ tsp cornflour (cornstarch)

2.5ml/½ tsp wine vinegar

For the Topping

150ml/¼ pint/⅔ cup double (heavy) cream

250g/9oz strawberries

2 chocolate dots

green jelly sweet (candy) or little pieces of angelica

1 Preheat the oven to 150°C/300°F/ Gas 2 and line a baking sheet with baking parchment.

2 Whisk the egg whites until stiff and then gradually whisk in the sugar, 5ml/1 tsp at a time. Continue whisking until smooth and glossy.

3 Blend the cornflour and vinegar and fold into the egg whites.

4 Spoon the mixture into a large piping (pastry) bag fitted with a medium-size plain nozzle. Pipe six small dots for the baby and a snail for the older child with a shell about 6cm/2½in in diameter.

5 Pipe the remaining mixture into two 10cm/4in swirly circles and cook in the oven for 20–25 minutes, or until firm. Lift the meringues off the paper and leave to cool.

TIP

For perfect meringues, whisk the egg whites in a dry grease-free bowl. Remove any trace of yolk with a piece of shell and whisk until the peaks are stiff but still moist-looking. Add sugar gradually and continue whisking until very thick. Meringues may be made 1–2 days in advance. Cover with baking parchment and decorate just before serving.

6 Whip the cream until softly peaking and spoon over the two large meringues and the snail, reserving about 15ml/1 tbsp for the baby.

7 Rinse, hull and slice the strawberries and arrange a few in rings over the snail. Place the snail on a plate and add chocolate eyes and a slice from a green jelly sweet, or a little angelica, for the mouth.

8 Add some strawberries to the adult meringues, then chop or mash a few extra slices and stir them into the reserved cream for the baby. Spoon into a small dish and serve with tiny meringues.

Poached Pears

3 ripe pears

450ml/¾ pint/1⅞ cup apple juice

5ml/1 tsp powdered gelatine

few drops of green food colouring

½ small orange, rind only

½ small lemon, rind only

10ml/2 tsp chopped glacé (candied) ginger

5ml/1 tsp clear honey

5ml/1 tsp cornflour (cornstarch)

1 red liquorice bootlace

2 small currants (raisins)

1 large raisin

½ glacé (candied) cherry

1 Peel the pears, leaving the stalks in place. Cut a small circle out of the base of two pears and tunnel out the cores with a small knife.

2 Halve the remaining pear, discard the stalk, scoop out the core and then put them all in a pan with the apple juice. Bring to the boil, cover and simmer for 5 minutes, turning the pears once.

3 Lift out the pear halves and reserve, cooking the whole pears for a further 5 minutes, or until tender. Remove with a slotted spoon and place on a serving dish, reserving the cooking liquor. Finely chop one pear half and put into a small dish for the baby. Reserve the other half pear for the toddler.

4 Pour half of the reserved apple juice into a bowl, place over a pan of simmering water, add the gelatine and stir until completely dissolved. Transfer to a measuring jug (cup) and pour half over the chopped pear and chill.

5 Stir a little green colouring into the remaining gelatine mixture, pour into a shallow dish or a plate with a rim for the toddler, and chill.

6 Cut away the rind from the orange and lemon, and cut into thin strips. Add to the remaining apple juice with the ginger and honey, and simmer over a gentle heat for 5 minutes, until the rinds are soft.

7 Blend the cornflour with a little water to make a smooth paste, stir into the pan, then bring the mixture to the boil and cook, stirring until thickened. Pour over the whole pears and leave to cool.

8 Place the toddler's pear, cut side down, on the green jelly (gelatine). To make a mouse, add a piece of red liquorice for a tail and two pieces for whiskers. Make two small cuts for eyes and tuck a currant into each slit. Add a large raisin for the nose. Halve the cherry and use for ears. Serve slightly chilled, with cream for the adults, if liked.

Peach Frangipane Tart

175g/6oz/1½ cups plain (all-purpose) flour

75g/3oz/6 tbsp butter

For the Filling

50g/2oz/4 tbsp butter

50g/2oz/¼ cup caster (superfine) sugar

1 egg

few drops of almond essence (extract)

50g/2oz/⅔ cup ground almonds

30ml/2 tbsp apricot jam

15ml/1 tbsp chopped glacéed (candied) peel

400g/14oz can peach slices

15ml/1 tbsp flaked (sliced) almonds

15ml/1 tbsp fromage frais or natural (plain) yogurt

icing (confectioners') sugar, for dusting

crème fraîche or natural (plain) yogurt, to serve

1 Place the flour in a bowl, cut the butter into small pieces and rub into the flour with your fingertips until the mixture resembles fine breadcrumbs.

2 Stir in 30–35ml/6–7 tsp water and mix to a smooth dough. Knead lightly on a floured surface and roll out thinly.

3 Lift the pastry over a rolling pin and use to line an 18cm/7in flan dish, pressing down against the sides of the dish. Trim the top.

4 Re-roll the trimmings and cut out twelve 5cm/2in circles with a fluted cookie cutter, pressing into sections of a patty tin (muffin pan). Chill the pastry for 15 minutes.

5 Preheat the oven to 190°C/375°F/Gas 5. Line the large flan dish with baking parchment and fill with baking beans. Cook for 10 minutes, then remove the baking beans and paper and cook the shell for a further 5 minutes.

6 Meanwhile, make the filling: cream together the butter and sugar in a bowl until light and fluffy. Beat the eggs and almond essence together, then gradually beat into the creamed sugar. Stir in the ground almonds and set aside.

7 Divide the jam among the small and large tarts, spread it into a thin layer in the large tart and sprinkle with glacéed peel. Spoon all of the almond mixture over the top and level the surface.

8 Drain the peaches and set aside three slices for the baby. Cut three slices into chunky pieces and divide among six of the small tarts, leaving six with just jam.

9 Arrange the remaining peaches over the top of the large tart and sprinkle with flaked almonds.

10 Cook the small tarts for 10 minutes and the large tart for 25 minutes, until the filling is set and browned. Dust the large tart with icing sugar and leave to cool slightly.

11 Purée the reserved peaches for the baby in a processor or liquidizer. Mix with fromage frais or yogurt and spoon into a small dish. Serve with two plain jam tarts.

12 Arrange a few fruity jam tarts on a plate for the toddler. Cut the large tart into wedges and serve with crème fraîche or natural yogurt for the adults. Test the temperature of the children's tarts before serving.

Honey and Summer Fruit Mousse

10ml/2 tsp powdered gelatine

500g/1¼lb bag frozen summer
  fruits, defrosted

20ml/4 tsp caster (superfine) sugar

500g/1¼lb tub fromage frais or
  Greek (US strained plain) yogurt

150ml/¼ pint/⅔ cup whipping
  cream

25ml/5 tsp clear honey

1 Put 30ml/2 tbsp cold water in a
cup and sprinkle the gelatine
over, making sure that all grains of
gelatine have been absorbed. Soak for
5 minutes, then heat in a pan of
simmering water until the gelatine
dissolves and the liquid is clear.
Cool slightly.

2 For the baby, process or liquidize
50g/2oz of fruit to a purée and
stir in 5ml/1 tsp sugar. Mix 45ml/3
tbsp fromage frais or yogurt with
5ml/1 tsp sugar in a separate bowl.

3 Put alternate spoonfuls of
fromage frais or yogurt and
purée into a small dish for the baby.
Swirl the mixtures together with a
teaspoon. Chill until required.

4 For the toddler, process 50g/2oz
fruit with 5ml/1 tsp sugar. Mix
60ml/4 tbsp fromage frais or yogurt
with 5ml/1 tsp sugar, then stir in
10ml/2 tsp fruit purée.

5 Stir 5ml/1 tsp gelatine into the
fruit purée and 5ml/1 tsp into
the fromage frais or yogurt mixture.
Spoon the fruit mixture into the base
of a clear plastic beaker or glass and
chill until set.

6 For the adults, whip the cream
until softly peaking. Fold in the
remaining fromage frais or yogurt
and honey and add the remaining
gelatine. Pour into two 250ml/8fl oz/
1 cup moulds. Chill until set.

7 Spoon the remaining fromage
frais or yogurt mixture over the set
fruit layer in the serving glass for the
toddler and chill until set.

8 To serve, dip one of the dishes
for the adults in hot water, count
to 15, then loosen the edges with
your fingertips, invert on to a large
plate and, holding mould and plate
together, jerk to release the mousse
and remove the mould. Repeat with
the other mould. Spoon the remaining
fruits and some juice around the
desserts and serve.

TIP

If you have a small novelty
mould, you may prefer to set the
toddler's portion in this rather than
a glass or plastic container.

  Make sure the gelatine isn't too
hot before adding to fromage frais
or yogurt or it may curdle.

NUTRITIONAL INFORMATION

The nutritional analysis below is for the whole recipe

p276 Vegetable Purées Energy 75Kcal/310kJ; Protein 2.6g; Carbohydrate 10.6g, of which sugars 10.1g; Fat 2.6g, of which saturates 1.6g; Cholesterol 8mg; Calcium 96mg; Fibre 2.4g; Sodium 51mg.

p277 Fruit Purées Energy 33Kcal/142kJ; Protein 0.7g; Carbohydrate 6.6g, of which sugars 6.6g; Fat 0.7g, of which saturates 0.4g; Cholesterol 2mg; Calcium 20mg; Fibre 1.1g; Sodium 8mg.

p282 Autumn Harvest Energy 420Kcal/1760kJ; Protein 15.4g; Carbohydrate 61.2g, of which sugars 35.7g; Fat 14g, of which saturates 8g; Cholesterol 42mg; Calcium 498mg; Fibre 11.4g; Sodium 199mg.

p283 Mixed Vegetable Platter Energy 412Kcal/1727kJ; Protein 19.3g; Carbohydrate 55.3g, of which sugars 28.5g; Fat 13.7g, of which saturates 8g; Cholesterol 42mg; Calcium 482mg; Fibre 8.6g; Sodium 190mg.

p284 Carrot, Lentil and Coriander Purée Energy 602Kcal/2531kJ; Protein 26.9g; Carbohydrate 97.5g, of which sugars 42.9g; Fat 13.9g, of which saturates 8.2g; Cholesterol 42mg; Calcium 478mg; Fibre 12.6g; Sodium 254mg.

p285 Red Pepper Risotto Energy 419Kcal/1744kJ; Protein 16g Carbohydrate 60g, of which sugars 19.8g; Fat 12.6g, of which saturates 7.7g; Cholesterol 42mg; Calcium 409mg; Fibre 2.4g; Sodium 163mg.

p286 Parsnip and Broccoli Mix Energy 380Kcal/1590kJ; Protein 19g; Carbohydrate 43.7g, of which sugars 28g; Fat 15.2g, of which saturates 8.2g; Cholesterol 42mg; Calcium 511mg; Fibre 13.3g; Sodium 161mg.

p287 Turkey Stew with Carrots and Corn Energy 415Kcal/1756kJ; Protein 46.5g; Carbohydrate 49.2g, of which sugars 17.3g; Fat 4.9g, of which saturates 1.9g; Cholesterol 89mg; Calcium 96mg; Fibre 6.6g; Sodium 180mg.

p288 Chicken and Parsnip Purée Energy 544Kcal/2287kJ; Protein 43.8g; Carbohydrate 57.3g, of which sugars 33.5g; Fat 16.8g, of which saturates 8.6g; Cholesterol 123mg;

Calcium 503mg; Fibre 16.1g; Sodium 233mg.

p289 Cock-a-Leekie Casserole Energy 523Kcal/2204kJ; Protein 43g; Carbohydrate 59.2g, of which sugars 18.2g; Fat 14g, of which saturates 8.2g; Cholesterol 123mg; Calcium 388mg; Fibre 3.9g; Sodium 229mg.

p290 Trout and Courgette Savoury Energy 561Kcal/2352kJ; Protein 41.6g; Carbohydrate 59.8g, of which sugars 18.9g; Fat 18.5g, of which saturates 8.6g; Cholesterol 119mg; Calcium 409mg; Fibre 4.3g; Sodium 214mg.

p291 Fisherman's Pie Energy 556Kcal/2338kJ; Protein 34.8g; Carbohydrate 76.2g, of which sugars 19g; Fat 14.2g, of which saturates 8.1g; Cholesterol 83mg; Calcium 389mg; Fibre 5.1g; Sodium 222mg.

p292 Apple Ambrosia Energy 308Kcal/1285kJ; Protein 11.8g; Carbohydrate 38.8g, of which sugars 19.5g; Fat 12.1g, of which saturates 7.5g; Cholesterol 42mg; Calcium 362mg; Fibre 1.1g; Sodium 130mg.

p293 Fruit Salad Purée Energy 142Kcal/604kJ; Protein 2.8g; Carbohydrate 33.8g, of which sugars 33.8g; Fat 0.4g, of which saturates 0g; Cholesterol 0mg; Calcium 35mg; Fibre 6.6g; Sodium 8mg.

p296 Sheperd's Pie Energy 487Kcal/2045kJ; Protein 29.4g; Carbohydrate 50.1g, of which sugars 15.2g; Fat 20.1g, of which saturates 8.4g; Cholesterol 69mg; Calcium 54mg; Fibre 5.3g; Sodium 379mg.

p297 Braised Beef and Carrots Energy 466Kcal/1959kJ; Protein 43.2g; Carbohydrate 50.7g, of which sugars 22.3g; Fat 11.3g, of which saturates 4.6g; Cholesterol 110mg; Calcium 91mg; Fibre 8g; Sodium 189mg.

p298 Lamb Hotpot Energy 365Kcal/1533kJ; Protein 26.8g; Carbohydrate 34.8g, of which sugars 16.7g; Fat 14.2g, of which saturates 6.3g; Cholesterol 87mg; Calcium 118mg; Fibre 7.2g; Sodium 159mg.

p299 Lamb and Lentil Savoury Energy 332Kcal/1397kJ; Protein 29.7g; Carbohydrate 24.4g, of which sugars 10.6g; Fat 13.6g, of which saturates 6g; Cholesterol 87mg; Calcium 97mg; Fibre 3.9g; Sodium 388mg.

p300 Country Pork and Runner Beans Energy 279Kcal/1174kJ; Protein 28.7g; Carbohydrate 30g, of which sugars 11.7g; Fat 5.7g, of which saturates 1.9g; Cholesterol 73mg; Calcium 71mg; Fibre 5.6g; Sodium 122mg.

p301 Pork and Apple Savoury Energy 410Kcal/1730kJ; Protein 42.5g; Carbohydrate 44.3g, of which sugars 16.9g; Fat 8.2g, of which saturates 2.6g; Cholesterol 110mg; Calcium 132mg; Fibre 6.4g; Sodium 170mg.

p302 Nursery Kedgeree Energy 625Kcal/2604kJ; Protein 39.2g; Carbohydrate 58.5g, of which sugars 16.3g; Fat 25.9g, of which saturates 12.1g; Cholesterol 494mg; Calcium 483mg; Fibre 1.2g; Sodium 223mg.

p303 Mediterranean Vegetables Energy 284Kcal/1202kJ; Protein 12.7g; Carbohydrate 54.5g, of which sugars 25.3g; Fat 3.1g, of which saturates 0.7g; Cholesterol 0mg; Calcium 89mg; Fibre 8.3g; Sodium 362mg.

p304 Pasta with Sauce Energy 608Kcal/2537kJ; Protein 30.8g; Carbohydrate 49.2g, of which sugars 27.6g; Fat 32g, of which saturates 20g; Cholesterol 98mg; Calcium 840mg; Fibre 6.4g; Sodium 545mg.

p305 Apple and Orange Fool Energy 219Kcal/924kJ; Protein 5.5g; Carbohydrate 37.6g, of which sugars 23.8g; Fat 6.1g, of which saturates 3.8g; Cholesterol 21mg; Calcium 188mg; Fibre 2.1g; Sodium 117mg.

p306 Orchard Fruit Dessert Energy 352Kcal/1492kJ; Protein 6.9g; Carbohydrate 71g, of which sugars 57.2g; Fat 6.3g, of which saturates 3.8g; Cholesterol 21mg; Calcium 233mg; Fibre 6.9g; Sodium 122mg.

p307 Peach Melba Dessert Energy 153Kcal/650kJ; Protein 7g; Carbohydrate 30.8g, of which sugars 30.8g; Fat 1.3g, of which saturates 0.6g; Cholesterol 2mg; Calcium 238mg; Fibre 1.7g; Sodium 98mg.

p316 Lamb Couscous Energy 631Kcal/2643kJ; Protein 40.6g; Carbohydrate 67g, of which sugars 39.3g; Fat 24.1g, of which saturates 9.6g; Cholesterol 133mg; Calcium 160mg; Fibre 6.6g; Sodium 227mg.

p317 Paprika Pork Energy 533Kcal/2248kJ; Protein 50.1g; Carbohydrate 60.2g, of which sugars

17.8g; Fat 11.9g, of which saturates 3.2g; Cholesterol 110mg; Calcium 127mg; Fibre 10.7g; Sodium 659mg.

p318 Chicken and Celery Supper Energy 331Kcal/1387kJ; Protein 39.5g; Carbohydrate 24.6g, of which sugars 22.1g; Fat 8.9g, of which saturates 2g; Cholesterol 184mg; Calcium 118mg; Fibre 7.3g; Sodium 285mg.

p319 Cauliflower and Broccoli with Cheese Energy 750Kcal/3127kJ; Protein 45.9g; Carbohydrate 50.2g, of which sugars 22.9g; Fat 39.9g, of which saturates 24.7g; Cholesterol 115mg; Calcium 1054mg; Fibre 9.4g; Sodium 720mg.

p320 Tagliatelle and Cheese with Broccoli and Ham Energy 668Kcal/2797kJ; Protein 42.9g; Carbohydrate 53.2g, of which sugars 17.4g; Fat 31.6g, of which saturates 19.3g; Cholesterol 120mg; Calcium 804mg; Fibre 4.4g; Sodium 1101mg.

p321 Baby Dhal Energy 305Kcal/1291kJ; Protein 18.1g; Carbohydrate 56.9g, of which sugars 16.6g; Fat 2g, of which saturates 0.4g; Cholesterol 0mg; Calcium 116mg; Fibre 8.8g; Sodium 59mg.

p322 Fish and Cheese Pie Energy 620Kcal/2595kJ; Protein 42.9g; Carbohydrate 49.2g, of which sugars 15.4g; Fat 27.9g, of which saturates 17.5g; Cholesterol 125mg; Calcium 701mg; Fibre 3.9g; Sodium 551mg.

p323 Fish Creole Energy 283Kcal/1185kJ; Protein 21.1g; Carbohydrate 46.4g, of which sugars 8.3g; Fat 1.2g, of which saturates 0.1g; Cholesterol 41mg; Calcium 43mg; Fibre 1.4g; Sodium 249mg.

p324 Chocolate Pots Energy 98Kcal/405kJ; Protein 5.8g; Carbohydrate 5.6g, of which sugars 5.5g; Fat 5.9g, of which saturates 2.8g; Cholesterol 106mg; Calcium 105mg; Fibre 0.1g; Sodium 77mg.

p325 Vanilla Custards Energy 94Kcal/392kJ; Protein 5.6g; Carbohydrate 5.5g, of which sugars 5.5g; Fat 5.7g, of which saturates 2.7g; Cholesterol 106mg; Calcium 104mg; Fibre 0g; Sodium 68mg.

p326 Marmite Bread Sticks Energy 15Kcal/63kJ; Protein 0.5g; Carbohydrate 2.4g, of which sugars 0.1g; Fat 0.4g, of which saturates 0.1g; Cholesterol 6mg; Calcium 4mg; Fibre 0.1g; Sodium 23mg.

p327 Bread Fingers with Egg Energy 14Kcal/58kJ; Protein 0.7g; Carbohydrate 1.8g, of which sugars 0.2g; Fat 0.5g, of which saturates 0.1g; Cholesterol 12mg; Calcium 8mg; Fibre 0.1g; Sodium 23mg.

p328 Cheese Straws Energy 41Kcal/172kJ; Protein 1.2g; Carbohydrate 3.3g, of which sugars 0.1g; Fat 2.6g, of which saturates 1.6g; Cholesterol 11mg; Calcium 27mg; Fibre 0.1g; Sodium 32mg.

p330 Mini Cup Cakes Energy 31Kcal/130kJ; Protein 0.4g; Carbohydrate 3.5g, of which sugars 2.1g; Fat 1.8g, of which saturates 0.1g; Cholesterol 7mg; Calcium 9mg; Fibre 0.1g; Sodium 25mg.

p331 Shortbread Shapes Energy 28Kcal/117kJ; Protein 0.3g; Carbohydrate 3.2g, of which sugars 0.9g; Fat 1.7g, of which saturates 1g; Cholesterol 4mg; Calcium 4mg; Fibre 0.1g; Sodium 12mg.

p340 Sticky Chicken Energy 109Kcal/458kJ; Protein 14.7g; Carbohydrate 1.2g, of which sugars 1.1g; Fat 5.1g, of which saturates 1.4g; Cholesterol 77mg; Calcium 9mg; Fibre 0g; Sodium 222mg.

p342 Coriander Chicken Casserole Energy 157Kcal/658kJ; Protein 21.8g; Carbohydrate 7.6g, of which sugars 4.8g; Fat 4.6g, of which saturates 1g; Cholesterol 105mg; Calcium 38mg; Fibre 1.6g; Sodium 101mg.

p342 Chicken and Cheese Parcels Energy 252Kcal/1050kJ; Protein 27.6g; Carbohydrate 0.2g, of which sugars 0.2g; Fat 15.1g, of which saturates 6.5g; Cholesterol 87mg; Calcium 190mg; Fibre 0g; Sodium 436mg.

p344 Peppered Beef Casserole Energy 229Kcal/958kJ; Protein 18g; Carbohydrate 26.5g, of which sugars 8.2g; Fat 6.3g, of which saturates 2.3g; Cholesterol 33mg; Calcium 43mg; Fibre 3.3g; Sodium 251mg.

p345 Lamb Stew Energy 152Kcal/635kJ; Protein 12.3g; Carbohydrate 7.5g, of which sugars 5g; Fat 8.4g, of which saturates 3.3g; Cholesterol 44mg; Calcium 29mg; Fibre 2.2g; Sodium 59mg.

p346 Mexican Beef Energy 171Kcal/715kJ; Protein 9.5g; Carbohydrate 11.8g, of which sugars 2.9g; Fat 9.8g, of which saturates 3.9g; Cholesterol 23mg; Calcium 83mg; Fibre 1.7g; Sodium 275mg.

p346 Lamb and Celery Casserole Energy 142Kcal/596kJ; Protein 12.6g; Carbohydrate 8.4g, of which sugars 3.8g; Fat 6.8g, of which saturates 3.1g; Cholesterol 44mg; Calcium 33mg; Fibre 1.5g; Sodium 67mg.

p348 Shepherd's Pie Energy 388Kcal/1617kJ; Protein 21.7g; Carbohydrate 28.7g, of which sugars 11.9g; Fat 21.5g, of which saturates 10.3g; Cholesterol 69mg; Calcium 69mg; Fibre 4.5g; Sodium 382mg.

p349 Tuna Fish Cakes Energy 263Kcal/1104kJ; Protein 16.6g; Carbohydrate 19.4g, of which sugars 4.9g; Fat 13.9g, of which saturates 1.7g; Cholesterol 81mg; Calcium 80mg; Fibre 3.3g; Sodium 183mg.

p350 Fish and Cheese Pies Energy 300Kcal/1258kJ; Protein 19.3g; Carbohydrate 25.5g, of which sugars 6.5g; Fat 13.9g, of which saturates 7.8g; Cholesterol 59mg; Calcium 228mg; Fibre 1.6g; Sodium 246mg.

p351 Surprise Fish Parcels Energy 89Kcal/376kJ; Protein 17.9g; Carbohydrate 2.5g, of which sugars 2.4g; Fat 0.9g, of which saturates 0.2g; Cholesterol 32mg; Calcium 36mg; Fibre 1g; Sodium 670mg.

p352 Cowboy Sausages and Beans Energy 225Kcal/944kJ; Protein 9.8g; Carbohydrate 22.7g, of which sugars 8.4g; Fat 11.4g, of which saturates 4.1g; Cholesterol 15mg; Calcium 89mg; Fibre 5.4g; Sodium 702mg.

p352 Mini Toad-in-the-Hole Energy 282Kcal/1183kJ; Protein 11.5g; Carbohydrate 28.3g, of which sugars 2.9g; Fat 14.6g, of which saturates 4.8g; Cholesterol 119mg; Calcium 131mg; Fibre 1.3g; Sodium 372mg.

p354 Pork Hotpot Energy 230Kcal/967kJ; Protein 21.4g; Carbohydrate 24.7g, of which sugars 7.4g; Fat 5.7g, of which saturates 1.6g; Cholesterol 55mg; Calcium 32mg; Fibre 2.5g; Sodium 134mg.

p355 Pork and Lentil Casserole Energy 369Kcal/1531kJ; Protein 17.7g; Carbohydrate 12.8g, of which sugars 5.2g; Fat 27.8g, of which saturates 9.9g; Cholesterol 63mg; Calcium 31mg; Fibre 2.1g;

Sodium 65mg.

p356 Sticky Ribs and Apple Slaw Energy 454Kcal/1896kJ; Protein 23g; Carbohydrate 25.2g, of which sugars 16.4g; Fat 29.8g, of which saturates 8g; Cholesterol 86mg; Calcium 44mg; Fibre 2.1g; Sodium 357mg.

p357 Mini Cheese and Ham Tarts Energy 100Kcal/419kJ; Protein 3.2g; Carbohydrate 9.6g, of which sugars 1.3g; Fat 5.6g, of which saturates 3.1g; Cholesterol 21mg; Calcium 59mg; Fibre 0.4g; Sodium 101mg.

p358 Pick-up Sticks Energy 54Kcal/223kJ; Protein 1.7g; Carbohydrate 7.7g, of which sugars 6.9g; Fat 2g, of which saturates 0.3g; Cholesterol 0mg; Calcium 29mg; Fibre 2.3g; Sodium 318mg.

p360 Spinach Pancakes with Ham and Cheese Energy 265Kcal/1111kJ; Protein 11.7g; Carbohydrate 22g, of which sugars 5.5g; Fat 15g, of which saturates 5g; Cholesterol 89mg; Calcium 250mg; Fibre 1.2g; Sodium 325mg.

p361 Cauliflower and Broccoli with Cheese Energy 264Kcal/1101kJ; Protein 14.6g; Carbohydrate 11.9g, of which sugars 5.9g; Fat 17.6g, of which saturates 6.1g; Cholesterol 119mg; Calcium 293mg; Fibre 2.1g; Sodium 281mg.

p362 Potato Boats Energy 257Kcal/1073kJ; Protein 10.9g; Carbohydrate 24.7g, of which sugars 7.4g; Fat 13.4g, of which saturates 6.4g; Cholesterol 39mg; Calcium 165mg; Fibre 2.9g; Sodium 573mg.

p363 Fat Cats Energy 553Kcal/2308kJ; Protein 13.5g; Carbohydrate 46.6g, of which sugars 4.7g; Fat 36.8g, of which saturates 3.9g; Cholesterol 18mg; Calcium 258mg; Fibre 0.9g; Sodium 514mg.

p364 Potato, Carrot and Courgette Rosti Energy 37Kcal/155kJ; Protein 0.7g; Carbohydrate 5.2g, of which sugars 1g; Fat 1.6g, of which saturates 0.2g; Cholesterol 0mg; Calcium 5mg; Fibre 0.5g; Sodium 5mg.

p364 Veggie Burgers Energy 118Kcal/495kJ; Protein 4.1g; Carbohydrate 13.3g, of which sugars 2g; Fat 5.8g, of which saturates 1.7g; Cholesterol 54mg; Calcium 68mg; Fibre 1.4g; Sodium 54mg.

p366 Vegetable Lasagne Energy

296Kcal/1243kJ; Protein 11.7g; Carbohydrate 30.7g, of which sugars 8.6g; Fat 14.5g, of which saturates 8g; Cholesterol 33mg; Calcium 243mg; Fibre 2.9g; Sodium 210mg.

p367 Aubergine Bolognaise Energy 184Kcal/781kJ; Protein 8.2g; Carbohydrate 36.6g, of which saturates 9.6g; Fat 1.5g, of which saturates 0.4g; Cholesterol 0mg; Calcium 39mg; Fibre 4.9g; Sodium 58mg.

p368 Speedy Chicken Pie Energy 244Kcal/1015kJ; Protein 14.9g; Carbohydrate 7.5g, of which sugars 1.6g; Fat 17.2g, of which saturates 4.6g; Cholesterol 54mg; Calcium 68mg; Fibre 0.7g; Sodium 241mg.

p370 Skinny Dippers Energy 444Kcal/1870kJ; Protein 33.4g; Carbohydrate 45.9g, of which sugars 10g; Fat 15.1g, of which saturates 8.2g; Cholesterol 99mg; Calcium 160mg; Fibre 3g; Sodium 771mg.

p371 Sweet and Sour Chicken Energy 338Kcal/1409kJ; Protein 19.3g; Carbohydrate 29g, of which sugars 6.5g; Fat 16.3g, of which saturates 4.1g; Cholesterol 170mg; Calcium 53mg; Fibre 0.9g; Sodium 351mg.

p372 Ham and Tomato Scramble Energy 192Kcal/808kJ; Protein 15.7g; Carbohydrate 16.7g, of which sugars 4g; Fat 7.6g, of which saturates 2.1g; Cholesterol 211mg; Calcium 74mg; Fibre 1.2g; Sodium 638mg.

p372 Ham Salad Clown Energy 94Kcal/391kJ; Protein 8.5g; Carbohydrate 2.2g, of which sugars 2.2g; Fat 5.5g, of which saturates 3.2g; Cholesterol 46mg; Calcium 99mg; Fibre 0.2g; Sodium 398mg.

p374 Spanish Omelette Energy 130Kcal/546kJ; Protein 9.3g; Carbohydrate 9.9g, of which sugars 1.8g; Fat 6.4g, of which saturates 1.7g; Cholesterol 110mg; Calcium 22mg; Fibre 1.2g; Sodium 349mg.

p375 Pasta with Ham Sauce
Energy 434Kcal/1814kJ; Protein 20g;
Carbohydrate 37g, of which sugars
5.6g; Fat 23.6g, of which saturates
6.7g; Cholesterol 43mg; Calcium
310mg; Fibre 2.4g; Sodium 635mg.

p376 Quickie Kebabs Energy
59Kcal/248kJ; Protein 5.2g;
Carbohydrate 3g, of which sugars
2.9g; Fat 3g, of which saturates
0.6g; Cholesterol 15mg; Calcium
6mg; Fibre 0.6g; Sodium 353mg.

p376 Sausage Wrappers Energy
272Kcal/1136kJ; Protein 20 4g;
Carbohydrate 7.8g, of which sugars
2.8g; Fat 18g, of which saturates
5.7g; Cholesterol 137mg; Calcium
24mg; Fibre 0.8g; Sodium 1342mg.

p378 Corned Beef Hash Energy
222Kcal/931kJ; Protein 16.9g;
Carbohydrate 18.1g, of which sugars
5g; Fat 9.6g, of which saturates
3.7g; Cholesterol 48mg; Calcium
34mg; Fibre 1.5g; Sodium 628mg.

p379 Cannibal Necklaces Energy
240Kcal/1003kJ; Protein 14.1g;
Carbohydrate 19.5g, of which sugars
5.2g; Fat 12.2g, of which saturates
4.8g; Cholesterol 36mg; Calcium
231mg; Fibre 2.3g; Sodium 383mg.

p380 Beef Burgers Energy
305Kcal/1282kJ; Protein 16.3g;
Carbohydrate 34.1g, of which sugars 4g; Fat 12.5g, of which saturates
5.1g; Cholesterol 35mg; Calcium
53mg; Fibre 2.5g; Sodium 222mg.

p381 Four Fast Fishes Energy
268Kcal/1124kJ; Protein 16.4g;
Carbohydrate 27.1g, of which sugars
3.8g; Fat 11.2g, of which saturates
1.6g; Cholesterol 48mg; Calcium
99mg; Fibre 2.3g; Sodium 306mg.

p382 Tuna Risotto Energy
190Kcal/798kJ; Protein 15.8g;
Carbohydrate 26.6g, of which sugars
3.7g; Fat 2.4g, of which saturates
0.4g; Cholesterol 26mg; Calcium
22mg; Fibre 1.7g; Sodium 243mg.

p382 Fish Finger Log Cabins
Energy 99Kcal/414kJ; Protein 6.4g;
Carbohydrate 9.3g, of which sugars
2.3g; Fat 4.3g, of which saturates
1.3g; Cholesterol 15mg; Calcium
81mg; Fibre 1.1g; Sodium 172mg.

p384 Shape Sorters Energy
300Kcal/1250kJ; Protein 12.2g;
Carbohydrate 16.2g, of which sugars
2.6g; Fat 20.6g, of which saturates
7.4g; Cholesterol 24mg; Calcium
223mg; Fibre 1.5g; Sodium 416mg.

p384 Happy Families Energy
251Kcal/1051kJ; Protein 13.4g;
Carbohydrate 22.2g, of which sugars
4.6g; Fat 12.7g, of which saturates
4.6g; Cholesterol 40mg; Calcium
229mg; Fibre 1.1g; Sodium 942mg.

p386 French Toast Butterflies
Energy 243Kcal/1018kJ; Protein 17.2g;
Carbohydrate 17g, of which sugars
3.9g; Fat 12g, of which saturates
5.2g; Cholesterol 127mg; Calcium
216mg; Fibre 2.4g; Sodium 615mg.

p387 Tuna Flowers Energy
384Kcal/1607kJ; Protein 17.4g;
Carbohydrate 31.8g, of which sugars
4.3g; Fat 21.3g, of which saturates
11.6g; Cholesterol 63mg; Calcium
251mg; Fibre 2g; Sodium 600mg.

p388 Noughts and Crosses Energy
379Kcal/1578kJ; Protein 20.5g;
Carbohydrate 15.4g, of which sugars
2.6g; Fat 25.4g, of which saturates
14.7g; Cholesterol 68mg; Calcium
462mg; Fibre 1.1g; Sodium 827mg.

p388 Cheese Strips on Toast
Energy 273Kcal/1137kJ; Protein 15g;
Carbohydrate 13.5g, of which sugars
0.9g; Fat 16.9g, of which saturates
10.9g; Cholesterol 49mg; Calcium
400mg; Fibre 0.5g; Sodium 503mg.

p390 Speedy Sausage Rolls
Energy 91Kcal/378kJ; Protein 2.3g;
Carbohydrate 7.1g, of which sugars
0.5g; Fat 6.1g, of which saturates
2.7g; Cholesterol 11mg; Calcium
19mg; Fibre 0.2g; Sodium 171mg.

p391 Pizza Clock Energy
204Kcal/856kJ; Protein 10g;
Carbohydrate 23.2g, of which sugars
9.3g; Fat 8.1g, of which saturates
4.3g; Cholesterol 25mg; Calcium
173mg; Fibre 2.2g; Sodium 547mg.

p392 Spotted Sandwiches Energy
275Kcal/1151kJ; Protein 8.1g;
Carbohydrate 28.2g, of which sugars
3.8g; Fat 15.3g, of which saturates
2.7g; Cholesterol 106mg; Calcium
107mg; Fibre 2.1g; Sodium 382mg.

p392 Sandwich Snails Energy
188Kcal/783kJ; Protein 6.6g;
Carbohydrate 11.6g, of which sugars
2.9g; Fat 12.9g, of which saturates
4.6g; Cholesterol 24mg; Calcium
124mg; Fibre 0.8g; Sodium 345mg.

p394 Fruit Fondue Energy
197Kcal/833kJ; Protein 3.8g;
Carbohydrate 33.7g, of which sugars
30.2g; Fat 5.4g, of which saturates
2.4g; Cholesterol 4mg; Calcium
107mg; Fibre 1.5g; Sodium 44mg.

p396 Strawberry Ice Cream Energy
2026Kcal/8391kJ; Protein 19.9g;
Carbohydrate 101.4g, of which sugars
86.5g; Fat 169.2g, of which saturates
100.2g; Cholesterol 420mg; Calcium
606mg; Fibre 5.4g; Sodium 267mg.

p397 Raspberry Sorbet Energy
1055Kcal/4518kJ; Protein 10.6g;
Carbohydrate 266.2g, of which sugars
266.2g; Fat 2g, of which saturates
0.7g; Cholesterol 0mg; Calcium
288mg; Fibre 16.9g; Sodium 34mg.

p398 Yogurt Lollies Energy
41Kcal/172kJ; Protein 1.9g;
Carbohydrate 7.3g, of which sugars
7.3g; Fat 0.6g, of which saturates
0.4g; Cholesterol 2mg; Calcium
68mg; Fibre 0g; Sodium 27mg.

p398 Jolly Jellies Energy 195Kcal/
824kJ; Protein 4.9g; Carbohydrate
39.2g, of which sugars 38.9g;
Fat 3.2g, of which saturates 2g;
Cholesterol 9mg; Calcium 55mg;
Fibre 0.3g; Sodium 26mg.

p400 Pancakes Energy 285Kcal/
1194kJ; Protein 8.1g; Carbohydrate
33.3g, of which sugars 19.9g; Fat
14.2g, of which saturates 6.1g;
Cholesterol 66mg; Calcium 163mg;
Fibre 1.5g; Sodium 78mg.

p401 Traffic Light Sundaes
Energy 224Kcal/940kJ; Protein 4.3g;
Carbohydrate 36.7g, of which sugars
36.6g; Fat 7.7g, of which saturates
4.5g; Cholesterol 0mg; Calcium
73mg; Fibre 0.5g; Sodium 41mg.

p402 Cheat's Trifle Energy
175Kcal/741kJ; Protein 4.7g;
Carbohydrate 32.5g, of which sugars
26.2g; Fat 3.1g, of which saturates
0.3g; Cholesterol 2mg; Calcium
115mg; Fibre 0.9g; Sodium 73mg.

p402 Baked Bananas Energy
184Kcal/770kJ; Protein 2.9g;
Carbohydrate 27g, of which sugars
25.1g; Fat 7.8g, of which saturates
4.6g; Cholesterol 0mg; Calcium
55mg; Fibre 0.9g; Sodium 31mg.

p404 Orange and Apple Rockies
Energy 87Kcal/366kJ; Protein 1.3g;
Carbohydrate 11.6g, of which sugars
4.5g; Fat 4.3g, of which saturates
0.9g; Cholesterol 8mg; Calcium
19mg; Fibre 0.5g; Sodium 42mg.

p406 Date Crunch Energy
120Kcal/503kJ; Protein 1.3g;
Carbohydrate 15.3g, of which sugars
10.1g; Fat 6.4g, of which saturates
3.6g; Cholesterol 12mg; Calcium
27mg; Fibre 0.4g; Sodium 85mg.

p407 Chocolate Dominoes Energy
335Kcal/1400kJ; Protein 2.9g;
Carbohydrate 38.8g, of which sugars
31.3g; Fat 19.8g, of which saturates
6.4g; Cholesterol 59mg; Calcium
41mg; Fibre 0.7g; Sodium 199mg.

p408 Marshmallow Krispie Cakes
Energy 56Kcal/235kJ; Protein 0.7g;
Carbohydrate 9g, of which sugars
4.4g; Fat 2.2g, of which saturates
1.1g; Cholesterol 3mg; Calcium
39mg; Fibre 0g; Sodium 28mg.

p408 Mini-muffins Energy
67Kcal/281kJ; Protein 1.4g;
Carbohydrate 11.1g, of which sugars
4.8g; Fat 2.2g, of which saturates
1.2g; Cholesterol 13mg; Calcium
25mg; Fibre 0.4g; Sodium 19mg.

p410 Cup Cake Faces Energy
328Kcal/1374kJ; Protein 3.2g;
Carbohydrate 42.5g, of which sugars
33.1g; Fat 17.3g, of which saturates
5.4g; Cholesterol 43mg; Calcium
53mg; Fibre 0.6g; Sodium 127mg.

p411 Gingerbread People Energy
94Kcal/395kJ; Protein 1.2g;
Carbohydrate 16.5g, of which sugars
9.3g; Fat 3g, of which saturates 0.7g;
Cholesterol 0mg; Calcium 19mg;
Fibre 0.4g; Sodium 23mg.

p412 Bread Animals Energy
147Kcal/624kJ; Protein 4.7g;
Carbohydrate 28.5g, of which sugars
1.8g; Fat 2.4g, of which saturates
0.4g; Cholesterol 13mg; Calcium
55mg; Fibre 1.4g; Sodium 139mg.

p414 Cheese Shapes Energy
184Kcal/769kJ; Protein 5.2g;
Carbohydrate 18.2g, of which sugars
0.4g; Fat 10.4g, of which saturates
2g; Cholesterol 33mg; Calcium
100mg; Fibre 0.8g; Sodium 127mg.

p415 Marmite and Cheese Whirls
Energy 76Kcal/318kJ; Protein 2.1g;
Carbohydrate 5.8g, of which sugars
0.2g; Fat 5.2g, of which saturates
0.8g; Cholesterol 15mg; Calcium
34mg; Fibre 0g; Sodium 82mg.

p422 Mediterranean Lamb Energy
1547Kcal/6457kJ; Protein 103.4g;
Carbohydrate 63.3g, of which sugars
43g; Fat 99.8g, of which saturates
42.2g; Cholesterol 333mg; Calcium
281mg; Fibre 16.5g; Sodium 951mg.

p424 Lamb Hotpot Energy
1217Kcal/5100kJ; Protein 85.2g;
Carbohydrate 90.6g, of which sugars
34.3g; Fat 59.6g, of which saturates
27.4g; Cholesterol 298mg; Calcium
256mg; Fibre 19.5g; Sodium 484mg.

p426 Beef Korma Energy 1034Kcal/4318kJ; Protein 78.6g; Carbohydrate 48.5g, of which sugars 28.9g; Fat 59.7g, of which saturates 25.2g; Cholesterol 210mg; Calcium 222mg; Fibre 9g; Sodium 542mg.

p428 Bobotie with Baked Potatoes and Broccoli Energy 2005Kcal/8426kJ; Protein 126.5g; Carbohydrate 213.8g, of which sugars 70.5g; Fat 77.7g, of which saturates 30.4g; Cholesterol 598mg; Calcium 593mg; Fibre 30.8g; Sodium 1611mg.

p430 Moussaka Energy 1805Kcal/7551kJ; Protein 98.9g; Carbohydrate 121.8g, of which sugars 37.6g; Fat 106.1g, of which saturates 46.8g; Cholesterol 360mg; Calcium 684mg; Fibre 15g; Sodium 903mg.

p432 Chilli con Carne Energy 2113Kcal/8830kJ; Protein 125.5g; Carbohydrate 155.4g, of which sugars 46.9g; Fat 114g, of which saturates 44.6g; Cholesterol 297mg; Calcium 387mg; Fibre 29.1g; Sodium 1374mg.

p434 Beef Bourguignon with Creamed Potatoes Energy 1690Kcal/7073kJ; Protein 121.4g; Carbohydrate 118.8g, of which sugars 26.2g; Fat 77.2g, of which saturates 32.7g; Cholesterol 318mg; Calcium 303mg; Fibre 12.3g; Sodium 584mg.

p436 Osso Bucco Pork with Rice Energy 2089Kcal/8726kJ; Protein 187.1g; Carbohydrate 149g, of which sugars 26.4g; Fat 82.3g, of which saturates 30.5g; Cholesterol 591mg; Calcium 449mg; Fibre 10.4g; Sodium 797mg.

p438 Pork Stir-Fry Energy 807Kcal/3377kJ; Protein 73.5g; Carbohydrate 58.8g, of which sugars 40.8g; Fat 32.2g, of which saturates 9g; Cholesterol 158mg; Calcium 163mg; Fibre 12.3g; Sodium 1458mg.

p440 Sausage Casserole Energy 2486Kcal/10416kJ; Protein 85.3g; Carbohydrate 272.4g, of which sugars 68.3g; Fat 124.7g, of which saturates 47.6g; Cholesterol 180mg; Calcium 641mg; Fibre 40.2g; Sodium 5366mg.

p442 Chicken and Thyme Casserole Energy 1320Kcal/5552kJ; Protein 147.1g; Carbohydrate 107.9g, of which sugars 20.9g; Fat 36.2g, of which saturates 10.5g; Cholesterol 635mg; Calcium 235mg;

Fibre 13.1g; Sodium 629mg.

p444 Tandoori-style Chicken Energy 1209Kcal/5080kJ; Protein 116.5g; Carbohydrate 68.6g, of which sugars 16.8g; Fat 54.1g, of which saturates 13g; Cholesterol 522mg; Calcium 401mg; Fibre 4.5g; Sodium 377mg.

p446 Chicken Wrappers Energy 1472Kcal/6187kJ; Protein 175g; Carbohydrate 72.7g, of which sugars 11.7g; Fat 54.3g, of which saturates 24.2g; Cholesterol 527mg; Calcium 512mg; Fibre 8.8g; Sodium 1451mg.

p448 Pan-fried Turkey with Coriander Energy 1568Kcal/6566kJ; Protein 122.9g; Carbohydrate 151g, of which sugars 20.5g; Fat 52.5g, of which saturates 33g; Cholesterol 222mg; Calcium 92mg; Fibre 4.2g; Sodium 375mg.

p450 Chicken Salad Energy 1058Kcal/4461kJ; Protein 119.4g; Carbohydrate 76.6g, of which sugars 22.4g; Fat 32.7g, of which saturates 17.6g; Cholesterol 379mg; Calcium 224mg; Fibre 7.3g; Sodium 995mg.

p452 Paella Energy 1212Kcal/5080kJ; Protein 112.9g; Carbohydrate 149.1g, of which sugars 22.9g; Fat 17.9g, of which saturates 2.6g; Cholesterol 408mg; Calcium 271mg; Fibre 9.7g; Sodium 498mg.

p454 Fish Cakes Energy 1349Kcal/5672kJ; Protein 110.3g; Carbohydrate 137.4g, of which sugars 30.6g; Fat 43.2g, of which saturates 21.9g; Cholesterol 287mg; Calcium 595mg; Fibre 13.2g; Sodium 2315mg.

p456 Fishy Vol-au-Vents Energy 1690Kcal/7071kJ; Protein 98.5g; Carbohydrate 128.3g, of which sugars 15.5g; Fat 93g, of which saturates 18.3g; Cholesterol 334mg; Calcium 527mg; Fibre 3.1g; Sodium 1351mg.

p458 Salmon and Cod Kebabs Energy 1636Kcal/6823kJ; Protein 114g; Carbohydrate 94.6g, of which sugars 24.7g; Fat 91.6g, of which saturates 34.7g; Cholesterol 349mg; Calcium 195mg; Fibre 16.4g; Sodium 724mg.

p460 Tuna Florentine Energy 2325Kcal/9709kJ; Protein 164.5g; Carbohydrate 95.1g, of which sugars 20.8g; Fat 139.5g, of which saturates 72.3g; Cholesterol 791mg; Calcium 3035mg; Fibre 8.9g; Sodium 3526mg.

p462 Cheese on Toast Energy 1456Kcal/6064kJ; Protein 72g;

Carbohydrate 56.1g, of which sugars 3.7g; Fat 102.1g, of which saturates 56.8g; Cholesterol 266mg; Calcium 1644mg; Fibre 3.1g; Sodium 4100mg.

p464 Penne with Tomato Sauce Energy 1027Kcal/4327kJ; Protein 38.8g; Carbohydrate 144.3g, of which sugars 36.2g; Fat 35.4g, of which saturates 15.5g; Cholesterol 58mg; Calcium 565mg; Fibre 12.7g; Sodium 519mg.

p466 Courgette Gougère Energy 1456Kcal/6051kJ; Protein 58.8g; Carbohydrate 69.4g, of which sugars 17.9g; Fat 104.4g, of which saturates 56.5g; Cholesterol 599mg; Calcium 1132mg; Fibre 9.5g; Sodium 1308mg.

p468 Cheese Vegetable Crumble Energy 2051Kcal/8546kJ; Protein 79.8g; Carbohydrate 146.4g, of which sugars 53g; Fat 128.7g, of which saturates 31.5g; Cholesterol 112mg; Calcium 1678mg; Fibre 46.4g; Sodium 2221mg.

p470 Vegetable Tagine Energy 1141Kcal/4800kJ; Protein 44.4g; Carbohydrate 190.4g, of which sugars 61.5g; Fat 27.5g, of which saturates 3.3g; Cholesterol 0mg; Calcium 444mg; Fibre 33.7g; Sodium 1071mg.

p472 Stilton and Leek Tart Energy 2221Kcal/9261kJ; Protein 81.2g; Carbohydrate 154.7g, of which sugars 20.1g; Fat 145.1g, of which saturates 85.6g; Cholesterol 933mg; Calcium 1148mg; Fibre 9.8g; Sodium 2398mg.

p474 Bread and Butter Pudding Energy 1528Kcal/6452kJ; Protein 57.5g; Carbohydrate 214.2g, of which sugars 126g; Fat 52.3g, of which saturates 22.4g; Cholesterol 832mg; Calcium 821mg; Fibre 11.3g; Sodium 1573mg.

p476 Eve's Pudding Energy 1198Kcal/5049kJ; Protein 13.7g; Carbohydrate 190.7g, of which sugars 152.6g; Fat 47.9g, of which saturates 27.7g; Cholesterol 297mg; Calcium 201mg; Fibre 11.1g; Sodium 392mg.

p478 Orange and Strawberry Shortcakes Energy 1054Kcal/4407kJ; Protein 20.7g; Carbohydrate 118.9g, of which sugars 61.7g; Fat 60.2g, of which saturates 35.3g; Cholesterol 107mg; Calcium 438mg; Fibre 5.1g; Sodium 447mg.

p480 Exotic Fruit Brûlée Energy 700Kcal/2940kJ; Protein 24.7g; Carbohydrate 82.4g, of which sugars

81.8g; Fat 36.4g, of which saturates 18.4g; Cholesterol 0mg; Calcium 584mg; Fibre 5.5g; Sodium 259mg.

p482 Plum Crumble Energy 1644Kcal/6930kJ; Protein 28g; Carbohydrate 256.1g, of which sugars 145.8g; Fat 63.7g, of which saturates 23.2g; Cholesterol 85mg; Calcium 391mg; Fibre 16.4g; Sodium 287mg.

p484 Chocolate and Orange Trifle Energy 1385Kcal/5790kJ; Protein 16.7g; Carbohydrate 139.1g, of which sugars 115.9g; Fat 80.5g, of which saturates 43.7g; Cholesterol 197mg; Calcium 441mg; Fibre 3.5g; Sodium 418mg.

p486 Apple Strudel Energy 1189Kcal/5023kJ; Protein 20.6g; Carbohydrate 200.8g, of which sugars 123.8g; Fat 39.5g, of which saturates 14.6g; Cholesterol 53mg; Calcium 316mg; Fibre 16.6g; Sodium 185mg.

p488 Strawberry Pavlova Energy 1288Kcal/5375kJ; Protein 10.7g; Carbohydrate 137.7g, of which sugars 137.7g; Fat 80.8g, of which saturates 50.1g; Cholesterol 206mg; Calcium 178mg; Fibre 2.8g; Sodium 177mg

p490 Poached Pears Energy 374Kcal/1597kJ; Protein 1.8g; Carbohydrate 95.7g, of which sugars 95.7g; Fat 0.9g, of which saturates 0g; Cholesterol 0mg; Calcium 81mg; Fibre 9.9g; Sodium 23mg.

p492 Peach Frangipane Tart Energy 2481Kcal/10368kJ; Protein 40.9g; Carbohydrate 262.6g, of which sugars 127.4g; Fat 148.2g, of which saturates 70.7g; Cholesterol 458mg; Calcium 534mg; Fibre 14.2g; Sodium 954mg.

p494 Honey and Summer Fruit Mousse Energy 1350Kcal/5603kJ; Protein 37.6g; Carbohydrate 76.9g, of which sugars 75.4g; Fat 101g, of which saturates 65.5g; Cholesterol 201mg; Calcium 728mg; Fibre 5.5g; Sodium 249mg.

GLOSSARY OF PREGNANCY TERMS

ABORTION
The spontaneous or induced delivery of the fetus before the 28th week.

ABRUPTIO PLACENTAE
Part of the placenta peels away from the wall of the uterus in late pregnancy and often results in bleeding.

ALPHA-FETOPROTEIN (AFP)
A protein produced by the fetus which enters the mother's bloodstream. A very high level can indicate neural tube defects of the fetus such as Down's syndrome or spina bifida, but it can also mean that the woman is carrying more than one child.

AMNIOCENTESIS
A small amount of amniotic fluid is taken from the uterus through a needle inserted through the woman's abdomen and tested for chromosomal disorders such as Down's syndrome.

AMNIOTIC FLUID
The fluid surrounding the fetus in the uterus.

AMNIOTIC SAC
The bag of membranes which is filled with amniotic fluid in which the fetus floats during pregnancy.

ANAEMIA
A condition where the level of red corpuscles in the blood is abnormally low, which is treated with iron supplements.

ANALGESICS
Painkilling drugs which do not cause unconsciousness. Those most commonly used during labour are Entonox (a mixture of nitrous oxide and oxygen, known as "gas and air"), pethidine and meptid.

ANTE-NATAL
Before birth.

APGAR SCORE
A simple test to assess the baby's condition after birth.

BEARING DOWN
The pushing movement made by the uterus during the second stage of labour.

BIRTH CANAL
See Vagina.

BLASTOCYST
The early stage of the developing embryo when it becomes a cluster of cells.

BRAXTON HICKS CONTRACTIONS
Contractions of the uterus which occur throughout pregnancy, but may not be felt until the last month or so. They feel like a painless, but sometimes uncomfortable, hardening across the stomach.

BREECH PRESENTATION
The position of a baby when he is bottom down rather than head down in the uterus.

CAESARIAN SECTION
Delivery of the baby through a cut in the abdomen and uterine walls.

CERVIX
The neck of the uterus or womb which is sealed with a plug of mucus during pregnancy. During labour, muscular contractions open up the cervix until it is about 10cm/4in wide so that the baby can pass through it into the vagina.

CHLOASMA
Slight discoloration of the skin, usually on the face, which occurs during pregnancy and disappears within weeks of the birth.

CHORIONIC VILLUS SAMPLING
A screening test for genetic handicap which can be done as early as 11 weeks. Cells are taken from the tissue that surrounds the fetus and are then analysed.

COLOSTRUM
A fluid that the breasts produce during pregnancy and immediately after the birth. It is full of nutrients and contains antibodies which will protect the baby from some infections.

CONCEPTION
The fertilization of the egg by the sperm and its implantation in the wall of the uterus.

CONGENITAL ABNORMALITIES
An abnormality or deformity that exists from birth. It is caused by a damaged gene or the effect of some diseases during pregnancy.

CONTRACTIONS
Regular tightening of the muscles of the uterus as they work to dilate the cervix and push the baby down the birth canal.

CROWNING
The moment when the crown of the baby's head appears in the vagina.

DILATION
The gradual opening of the cervix during labour.

DOPPLER
A method of using ultrasound vibrations to listen to the fetal heart.

ECTOPIC PREGNANCY
A pregnancy which develops outside the uterus, usually in the Fallopian tube.

EDD
Estimated date of delivery.

ELECTIVE INDUCTION
Induction done for convenience rather than for medical reasons.

ELECTRONIC FETAL MONITORING
The continuous monitoring of the fetal heart.

EMBRYO
The developing organism in pregnancy from

about the 10th day after fertilization until the 12th week of pregnancy when it becomes known as a fetus.

ENGAGED
The baby's head is engaged when it drops down deep in the pelvic cavity so that the widest part is through the mother's pelvic brim. Another term for this is "lightening". Most babies are born head first and will have engaged before labour begins.

ENGORGEMENT
The breasts become congested with milk if long periods are left between feeds which results in painful engorgement.

ENTONOX
Gas and oxygen, a short-term analgesic, which can be inhaled during labour.

EPIDURAL
An anaesthetic which is injected into the fluid surrounding the spinal cord at the base of the spine to relieve pain but leave the mother fully conscious.

EPISIOTOMY
A small cut made in the perineum to enlarge the vagina if there is a risk of tearing when the baby's head is about to be born.

FALLOPIAN TUBES
Two narrow tubes about 10cm/4in long which lead from the ovaries to the uterus.

FETUS
The developing baby from the end of the embryonic stage at about the 12th week of pregnancy, until the date of delivery.

FH
Fetal heart.

FMF
Fetal movement felt.

FOLIC ACID
A form of vitamin B which is important for the healthy development of the embryo. A daily supplement of 0.4mg should be taken before becoming pregnant and then until the 12th week of pregnancy.

FONTANELLES
The soft spots between the unjoined sections of the skull of the baby.

FORCEPS
An instrument sometimes used to assist the baby out of the birth canal.

FOREMILK
The first breast milk the baby gets when he begins to suck which satisfies his thirst before the hind milk comes through.

FUNDUS
The top of the uterus.

GAS AND AIR
See Entonox.

GENETIC COUNSELLING
Advice on the detection and risk of recurrence of inherited disorders.

GESTATION
The length of time between conception and delivery (usually around 40 weeks).

GP UNIT
A special unit, usually in a hospital, where a pregnant woman gives birth under the care of her GP and midwife.

HAEMOGLOBIN (HB)
The pigment that gives blood its red colour and contains iron and stores oxygen.

HAEMORRHAGE
Excessive bleeding.

HAEMORRHOIDS (PILES)
A form of varicose veins around the anus.

HINDMILK
The calorie-rich breast milk that follows the foremilk during feed.

HORMONE
A chemical produced by the body to stimulate organs within the body, particularly those to do with growth and reproduction.

HUMAN CHORIONIC GONADOTROPHIN (HCG)
A hormone produced early in pregnancy by the developing placenta. Its presence in the urine is used to confirm pregnancy.

IMPLANTATION
The embedding of the fertilized egg in the wall of the uterus.

INCOMPETENT CERVIX
A weakened cervix that is unable to hold the fetus in the uterus for the full nine months. Sometimes a cause of late miscarriage or premature birth.

INDUCTION
The process of artificially starting off labour.

INTRAVENOUS DRIP
The infusion of fluids directly into the bloodstream through a fine tube into a vein.

JAUNDICE
Neonatal jaundice often occurs in newborn babies because of the inability of the liver to successfully break down an excess of red blood cells.

LABOUR
The process of childbirth.

LANUGO
A very fine covering of hair which appears all over the fetus during late pregnancy.

LIE
The position of the fetus in the uterus.

LIGHTENING
See Engaged.

LINEA NIGRA
A line of dark pigmentation which appears down the centre of the abdomen on some women during pregnancy.

LOCHIA
Post-natal vaginal discharge.

MECONIUM
The green matter passed from the baby's bowels during the first days after birth. Meconium in the amniotic fluid before delivery is usually a sign of fetal distress.

MISCARRIAGE
The loss of a baby before 24 weeks gestation.

MONITOR
Machine or instrument to measure the baby's heartbeat and breathing.

MOULDING
The shaping of the bones of the baby's skull as it passes through the birth canal.

MUCUS
A sticky secretion.

NAD
A medical term often used on medical records meaning "nothing abnormal detected".

NEURAL TUBE DEFECT
Development defect of the brain and/or spinal cord.

OBSTETRICIAN
Medical specialist in pregnancy and childbirth.

OEDEMA
Swelling caused by fluid retention.

OVARY
Female organ responsible for production of sex hormones and eggs (ova).

OVULATION
The production of a ripe egg by the ovary, usually on a monthly basis.

PALPATION
Manual examination of the uterus through the wall of the abdomen.

PELVIC FLOOR
The muscles which support the bladder and the uterus.

PERINATAL
Period from before delivery until seven days after the birth.

PERINEUM
The area between the opening of the vagina and the anus.

PETHIDINE
A drug given during labour for pain relief and relaxation.

PLACENTA
Also known as "afterbirth", this is the fetus's life-support system which is attached to one side of the wall of the uterus and to the baby by means of the umbilical cord. All the fetus's nourishment passes from the mother through the placenta while the fetus's waste products pass out through it.

PREMATURE OR PRETERM
A baby born before the 37th week.

PRESENTATION
The position of the fetus in the uterus before and during the delivery.

PRIMIGRAVIDA
A woman who is having her first baby.

PROSTAGLANDIN
A hormone which stimulates the onset of labour contractions.

QUICKENING
The first movements of the fetus in the uterus.

ROOTING
The baby's instinctive searching for the mother's nipple.

RUBELLA (GERMAN MEASLES)
A virus which can be dangerous if caught during the first three months of pregnancy.

SCAN
A way of screening the fetus in the uterus by bouncing high-frequency sound waves off it which build up a picture.

SHARED CARE
Ante-natal care shared between a GP and a hospital consultant.

SHOW
A vaginal discharge of blood-stained mucus that occurs before or during labour.

STILLBIRTH
The delivery of a baby who has already died in the uterus after 28 weeks of pregnancy.

STRETCH MARKS
Silvery lines that may appear where the skin has been stretched during pregnancy.

TERM
The end of pregnancy - around 40 weeks from the date of conception.

TERMINATION
An artificially induced abortion before the end of 28th week of pregnancy.

TOXOPLASMOSIS
A parasitic disease spread by cat faeces that can cause blindness in a baby.

TRIMESTER
Pregnancy is divided into three trimesters, each making up one third of pregnancy.

UMBILICAL CORD
The cord connecting the fetus to the placenta.

UTERUS (WOMB)
The hollow muscular organ in which the fertile egg becomes embedded.

VACUUM EXTRACTOR (VENTOUSE)
An instrument sometimes used to pull the baby out of the vagina.

VAGINA
The birth canal through which the baby makes its way from the uterus.

USEFUL ADDRESSES

There is no need to feel alone during pregnancy or in the months after the birth.
The organizations mentioned below are happy to offer help and support to anyone who contacts them.
Remember to enclose an SAE when writing to them.

ANTE-NATAL AND BIRTH

Active Birth Centre
25 Bickerton Road, London N19 5JT
Tel: 020 7281 6760
www.activebirthcentre.com

Association for Improvements in the Maternity Services (AIMS)
Tel: 0870 765 1433
www.aims.org.uk

Baby Lifeline
Empathy Enterprise Building, Bramston Crescent, Tile Hill, Coventry CV4 9SW
Tel: 024 7642 2135
www.babylifeline.org.uk

Tommy's
Nicholas House, 3 Laurence Pountney Hill, London EC4R 0BB
Tel: 08707 707070
www.tommys.org

Birthchoice UK
www.birthchoiceuk.com

National Childbirth Trust (NCT)
Alexandra House, Oldham Terrace, Acton, London W3 6NH
Tel: 0870 444 8707
www.nct.org.uk

Stillbirth and Neonatal Death Society (SANDS)
28 Portland Place, London W1B 1LY
Helpline: 020 7436 5881
www.uk-sands.org

Wellbeing
27 Sussex Place, London NW1 4SP
Tel: 020 7772 6400
www.wellbeing.org.uk

Foundation for the Study of Infant Death (SIDS)
Artillery House, 11-19 Artillery Row, London SW1P 1RT
Helpline: 020 7233 2090
www.sids.org.uk

The Miscarriage Association
c/o Clayton Hospital, Northgate, Wakefield, West Yorks WF1 3JS
Tel: 01924 200799
www.miscarriageassociation.org.uk

Independent Midwives Association
PO Box 539, Abingdon, Oxon OX14 9DF
Tel: 0845 460 0105
www.independentmidwives.org.uk

FAMILY LINKS

Gingerbread
Helpline: 0800 0185026
www.gingerbread.org.uk

Parentline Plus
520 Highgate Studios, 53-79 Highgate Road, London NW5 1TL
Helpline: 0808 800 2222
www.parentlineplus.org.uk

National Childminding Association
Royal Court, 81 Tweedy Road, Bromley, Kent BR1 1TG
Helpline: 0845 8800 0448
www.ncma.org.uk

National Council for One Parent Families
255 Kentish Town Road, London NW5 2LX
Tel: 0800 0185026
www.oneparentfamilies.org.uk

Families Need Fathers
134 Curtain Road, London EC2A 3AR
Helpline: 08707 607 496
www.fnf.org.uk

SPECIAL NEEDS

The Birth Defects Foundation
BDF Centre, Hemlock Business Park, Hemlock Way, Cannock WS11 7GF
BDF Nurse Helpline: 0870 0707020
www.bdfnewlife.co.uk

Galactosaemia Support Group
31 Cotysmore Road,
Sutton Coldfield B75 6BJ
Tel: 0121 378 5143
www.galactosaemia.org

Down's Syndrome Association
Langdon Down Centre, 2a Langdon Park, Teddington TW11 9PS
Tel: 0845 230 0372
www.downs-syndrome.org.uk

Cerebral Palsy Helpline
PO Box 833, Milton Keynes, Bucks MK12 5NY
Helpline: 0808 800 3333
www.scope.org.uk

ASBAH (Association for Spina Bifida and Hydrocephalus)
ASBAH House, 42 Park Road, Peterborough PE1 2UQ
Helpline: 0845 450 7755
www.asbah.org

Climb (The National Information Centre for Metabolic Diseases)
Climb Building, 176 Nantwich Road, Crewe CW2 6BG
Tel: 0845 652 3181
www.climb.org.uk

Cystic Fibrosis Research Trust
11 London Road, Bromley, BR1 1BY
Tel: 020 8464 7211
www.cftrust.org.uk

Diabetes UK
Macleod House, 10 Parkway,
London NW1 7AA
Tel: 020 7424 1000
www.diabetes.org.uk

Epilepsy Action
New Anstey House, Gateway Drive,
Yeadon, Leeds LS19 7XY
Helpline: 0808 800 5050
www.epilepsy.org.uk

Mencap (Royal Society for Mentally
Handicapped Children and Adults)
123 Golden Lane,
London EC1Y 0RT
Tel: 020 7454 0454
www.mencap.org.uk

Asthma UK
Summit House, 70 Wilson Street,
London EC2A 2DB
Helpline: 0845 701 0203
www.asthma.org.uk

National Eczema Society
Hill House, Highgate Hill,
London N19 5NA
Helpline: 0870 241 3604
www.eczema.org

**Royal National Institute for the
Blind (RNIB)**
105 Judd Street, London WC1H 9NE
Helpline: 0845 766 9999
www.rnib.org.uk

National Autistic Society
393 City Road, London EC1V 1NG
Tel: 020 7833 2299
www.nas.org.uk

Meningitis Trust
Fern House, Bath Road, Stroud,
Glos GL5 3TJ
Helpline: 0800 028 1828
www.meningitis-trust.org

SENSE (National Deaf-Blind
& Rubella Association)
11–13 Clifton Terrace,
London N4 3SR
Tel: 0845 127 0060
www.sense.org.uk

Sickle Cell Society
54 Station Road, Harlesden,
London NW10 4UA
Tel: 020 8961 7795
www.sicklecellsociety.org

FAMILY WELFARE

TAMBA (Twins & Multiple Births
Association)
2 The Willows, Gardner Road,
Guildford, Surrey GU1 4PG
Helpline: 0870 770 3305
www.tamba.org.uk

Association for Post-natal Illness
145 Dawes Road, Fulham,
London SW6 7EB
Helpline: 020 7386 0868
www.apni.org

BLISS (Baby Life Support Systems)
2nd & 3rd Floors,
9 Holyrood Street, London Bridge,
London SE1 2EL
Helpline: 0500 618140
www.bliss.org.uk

CRY-SIS
BM Cry-sis,
London WC1N 3XX
Helpline: 08451 228 669
www.cry-sis.org.uk

La Leche League
PO Box 29, West Bridgford,
Nottingham NG2 7NP
Helpline: 0845 456 1855
www.laleche.org.uk

Pre-school Learning Alliance
The Fitzpatrick Building,
188 York Way, London N7 9AD
Tel: 020 7697 2500
www.pre-school.org.uk

**Association of Breastfeeding
Mothers**
PO Box 207, Bridgwater,
Somerset TA6 7YT
Tel: 08444 122949
www.abm.me.uk

Action for Sick Children
36 Jacksons Edge Road, Disley,
Stockport SK12 2JL
Tel: 0800 074 4519
www.actionforsickchildren.org

Contact-a-family
209-211 City Road,
London EC1V 1JN
Helpline: 0808 808 3555
www.cafamily.org.uk

Cruse (Bereavement care)
PO Box 800, Richmond,
Surrey TW9 1RG
Helpline: 0844 477 9400
www.crusebereavementcare.org.uk

Family Planning Association
50 Featherstone Street
London EC1Y 8QU
Helpline: 0845 122 8690
www.fpa.org.uk

Family Welfare Association
501-505 Kingsland Road,
London E8 4AU
Tel: 020 7254 6251
www.fwa.org.uk

**National Society for the
Prevention of Cruelty to
Children (NSPCC)**
Weston House,
42 Curtain Road,
London EC2A 3NH
Freephone: 0808 800 5000
www.nspcc.org.uk

**The Baby Products Association
(BPA)**
2 Carrera House, Merlin Court,
Gatehouse Close, Aylesbury,
Bucks HP19 8DP
Tel: 0845 456 9570
www.b-p-a.org

INDEX

ACKNOWLEDGEMENTS

Picture acknowledgements: Alamy Images 17, 18, 20, 23, 24, 33b, 36, 38, 49b, 60, 63 r, 65 t and b, 69 t, 73 t and b, 74, 75 t and b, 76, 77 t, 85 t and b, 145 tr, 265 t; Bubbles 78; /Jacquie Farrow 68, 262 br, 336 br; /Julie Fisher 11; /Nikki Gibbs 16 b, 80, 421 t; /Paul Howard 75 t; /Julia Martin 21 b, 85 (all 3); /S Price 325; /F Rombout 271 t; /Lois Joy Thurston 29 b, 47 t and r, 52, 64, 81, 289, 319 tr, 420 b, 421 t; /Ian West 77 b, 336 t, 341 t; /J. Woodcock 29 t, 78; /Richard Yard 69; Greg Evans 330; Sally and Richard Greenhill 312 t; Lupe Cunha 18, 19, 26, 27 b, 33 t, 39 t, 52, 53 t, 61 bl and t, 61 r, 82, 83 r and tr, 86, 87, 262 bl, 272, 273t, 288-289, 306, 314, 323, 420 t; Lyons Waddell 309 t; PR Communications 54 (box); Reflections/Jennie Woodcock 313 b, 316 tr, 326-327, 329, 337 cr, 347, 376, 421 b, 422 bl, 422 br; Science Photo Library/BSIP Bajande 89 b; /Mark Clarke 61 t, 72, 79 r, 88 t and b, 89 t and b; /Custom Medical Stock 61 t, 89 t; /Simon Fraser 47, 73 b; /Will & Deri McIntyre 25 b; /Joseph Mettis 72; /Petit Format/Nestle 16 t; /Chris Priest 39; /Richard G Rawlins 15 tl, 25 b, 35, 36; /Pascale Roche/Petit Format 88 t and b; /James Stevenson 20 br, 35 b, 47 bl; /Ron Sutherland 79 r; /Sheila Terry 21 t, 65, 83 bl; Carin Simon 80 r; Timothy Woodcock 262 t, 423

(Key: b – bottom, bl – bottom left, br – bottom right, r – right, t – top, tl – top left, tr – top right)

The publishers have tried to credit all agencies and photographers whose pictures appear in this book and apologize for any omissions.

ACKNOWLEDGEMENTS

The author and publisher would like to thank the many individuals who helped in the creation of the "Pregnancy and Babycare" sections of this book. In particular thanks are due to Bobbie Brown, Elsa Jacobi, Pauline Richardson, Mary Lambert and Jane Barret. Many thanks also go to everyone who modelled for special photography: Yvonne Adams and Martin; Ruth Auber and Bethany; Jo Bates and Lois; Amanda Bennet-Jones; Kim, Neil and Andrew Brown; Christine Clarke; Jacqueline Clarke and Cassia; Jocelyn Cusack and Beth; Sam Dyas and Colt; Patricia Gannon and Matthew; Nici Giles and Fergus; Yiota Gillis and Cameron; Sandra Hadfield and Annie; Louise Henriques and Joshua; Lynette Jones and Hugh and Rhys; Karen, Mark, Megan and Robert Lambert; Claire Lehain and Harriet; Lavinia Mainds and Polly; Pippa Milton and Oliver; Philippa Madden and Inca; Jackie Norbury; Jess Presland; Katey Steiner; Saatchi Spracklen and Niamh; Sophie Trotter and Archie; Josephine Whitfield and Lily May; Lucinda Whitrow and Hector.

Thanks also to companies that loaned items and photographs: Blooming Marvellous Ltd, *www.bloomingmarvellous.co.uk* (p. 40-1); Boots Children's Wear and Toys; Fisher-Price; Littlewoods Home Shopping; Maclaren Ltd; Mamas & Papas, *www.mamasandpapas.com* (p, 53, 54–5); and Mattel UK Ltd.

The author and publisher would also like to thank all those involved in the creation of the "Cooking for Babies & Toddlers" section of this book. In particular thanks are due to the Department of Health for reading and approving the section on food for babies; the National Dairy Council Nutrition Service; the Health Education Authority; Dr Nigel Dickie from Heinz Baby Foods; The British Diabetic Association; The Health Visitors Association; Broadstone Communications for their invaluable help in supplying the Kenwood equipment for recipe testing and photography; hand-painted china plates, bowls and mugs from Cosmo Place Studio, 11 Cosmo Place, London WC1N 3AP, tel 0207 278 3374; Tupperware for plain-coloured plastic bowls, plates, feeder beakers and cups; Cole and Mason for non-breakable children's ware; Royal Doulton for Bunnykins china; Spode for blue and white Edwardian Childhood china.